Maida Heatter's Book of Great Chocolate Desserts

Books by Maida Heatter

Maida Heatter's Book of Great Desserts

Maida Heatter's Book of Great Cookies

Maida Heatter's Book of Great Chocolate Desserts

Maida Heatter's New Book of Great Desserts

Maida Heatter's Book of Great American Desserts

Maida Heatter's Greatest Dessert Book Ever

Maida Heatter's Brand-New Book of Great Cookies

Maida Heatter's BOOK OF GREAT CHOCOLATE DESSERTS

MAIDA HEATTER

Drawings by Toni Evins

**Andrews McMeel
Publishing**

Kansas City

06 07 08 09 10 RR4 10 9 8 7 6 5 4 3 2

ISBN-13: 978-0-7407-5816-4
ISBN-10: 0-7407-5816-0

Library of Congress Cataloging-in-Publication Data:
Heatter, Maida.
    Maida Heatter's book of great chocolate desserts / Maida Heatter ; drawings by Toni Evins.
        p. cm.
    ISBN 0-7407-5816-0
        1. Cookery (Chocolate) 2. Desserts. I. Title: Book of great chocolate desserts. II. Title.

TX767.C5H43 2006
641.6'374—dc22

                                                                                            2005055556

Attention: Schools and Businesses
Andrews McMeel books are available at quantity discounts with bulk purchase for educational, business, or sales promotional use. For information, please write to: Special Sales Department, Andrews McMeel Publishing, LLC, 4520 Main Street, Kansas City, Missouri 64111.

To Craig Claiborne with my sincerest respect and admiration

I would like to thank Nancy Nicholas, who

edited all my books. She is a special person who

made it all a pleasure.

Contents

Introduction

After my dessert book and cookie book were published, people who love chocolate soon realized that I was a member of the club. Actually, I am the Chairperson of the Board of the Chocolate Lovers Association of the World. (I started as a Brownie and worked my way up.) Chocolate-lovers could not wait to corner me or my husband (also a member in good standing) and confess to their chocolate addictions, chocolate splurges, chocolate dreams, fantasies, and uncontrollable cravings and hunger for the stuff.

I understand it all. I have had all the same feelings. And I do, I do—I do love it!

I come from a long line of chocolate-lovers. And I have spent a good part of my life cooking with chocolate. We understand each other, chocolate and I. My husband says that I can hear chocolate.

People always ask what my favorite dessert is. My answer is "anything chocolate." But it is like the line of a song from *Finian's Rainbow*, a Broadway play many years ago, "When I'm not near the girl I love, I love the girl I'm near." So my favorite dessert is whatever is chocolate and is near: mousse, Brownies, pots de crème, Bavarian. Today I made French Chocolate Ice Cream, so today that is my favorite dessert. I would like to be near it forever.

Chocolate is a magnet to many of us. Word of a special chocolate cake at a certain restaurant draws people for hundreds of miles. People send from around the world when they hear of a chocolate dessert they can buy by mail. They rush to put dollars in envelopes to send for a chocolate mousse recipe they know nothing about. When a Swiss chocolatier opened a tiny little hole in the wall of a shop in New York City, I immediately heard about it from friends in California, Chicago, Maine, and

neighbors in Miami Beach. It appears to me that when a magazine wants to increase its circulation, they simply have to use a cover photograph of a mouth-watering, three-layer chocolate cake.

Some people (especially me) will stop at nothing to track down the recipe for a dessert they have tasted or heard about. Many, many years ago I bought a certain chocolate cake from a New York patisserie and fell madly in love with it. I simply had to have the recipe, but I could not get it. I tried to duplicate it at least thirty or forty times with no luck. Since I thought that the particular brand of chocolate used in the cake might have been a clue to its unusual flavor, I hung around on the street in front of the shop for many days hoping to see a chocolate delivery truck. I had the cake sent to all the good cooks and pastry chefs I knew around the country to see if they could help me analyze it. I wrote to all the publications that seem to be able to get recipes when no one else can. I even asked my husband to flirt with the lady who baked the cake to try to get the recipe.

I told him, "Do anything necessary—just don't come home without it." When the lady realized his motive she immediately threw him out of her shop. P.S.—I still do not have the recipe but haven't given up; I keep trying.

The one question I am asked most often is "What do you do with all the desserts you make while writing a cookbook?" Frankly, we eat an awful lot of them. And we have friends and neighbors, and delivery men, garbage men, gardeners, mailmen, and the butcher, the baker, and the candlestick maker who hope I will never finish writing this chocolate book.

But recently when a new recipe for Brownies resulted in a dry, tasteless thing, I did not want to pass them on to anyone. We live on Biscayne Bay, where the sky is usually alive with seagulls. For many years we have fed them stale bread and crackers. I didn't know what else to do with the Brownie boo-boo. I decided to try it on the gulls. I have never seen them so excited—they were frantic; they have never come as close, nor grabbed the food as hungrily; they fought with each other over every crumb. Then they sat out in the bay for hours waiting for more.

Now I not only have a new and appreciative audience, but a hitherto unknown fact about chocolate: Seagulls love it!

In a way, chocolate is like wine—or coffee. It is difficult to say which is the best. A connoisseur will be familiar with them all and will know the subtle differences. Everyone does not agree; it is a matter of taste. Just because they look like chocolate don't expect them all to be alike, any more than wines or coffees are alike.

When this book was originally published in 1980, there were only a few different brands of chocolate available. Now—wow—there are so many I can't name them all. If a recipe calls for a certain type, for instance unsweetened or semisweet, etc., please feel free to use any brand you like or any brand available. Taste as many as you can. Cook with as many as you can. See which you like best. Sometimes I prefer certain chocolates for certain recipes because I have made them before and I know the flavor I want. And at times I use different chocolates just to experiment, or simply because that is all that is available at the moment.

Since the price of all chocolate has soared sky-high, it is a truly extravagant luxury. In my years of experimenting with it I have thrown out potfuls and panfuls and bowlfuls. But I don't want you to have any failures. I am always dumbfounded when someone tells me about a recipe that did not turn out right, and then they casually add "but that might be because I used fewer eggs and baked it in a larger pan at a lower temperature and I used salad oil instead of butter." *Please follow the directions carefully.*

When I wrote my other books I left out many chocolate recipes that I loved because I thought that not everyone felt the way I did about it. But now, no holds barred; this is it—a chocolate binge.

Maida Heatter

Miami Beach, Florida

X

Author's Note

This book was originally published in 1980. It was my third book, and I have written several others since then—seven all together. They are all dessert books and are all loaded with chocolate recipes, because I love chocolate.

There is one recipe, from Maida Heatter's *Brand-New Book of Great Cookies* (Random House, 1995), that many people have told me is their number-one favorite. It is for Chocolate Chip and Almond Biscotti. I would like to share the recipe with you.

I wish you all HAPPY CHOCOLATE.
M. H.

Chocolate Chip and Almond Biscotti

ABOUT 40 BISCOTTI

Irresistible. Awesome. With a huge, tremendous (there can't be too much of a good thing) amount of chocolate chips. Chocolate chips never had it so good.

6 ounces (1¼ cups) whole blanched
   (skinned) almonds
2 cups sifted unbleached flour
½ teaspoon baking soda
½ teaspoon baking powder
⅛ teaspoon salt
1 cup minus 2 tablespoons granulated sugar
12 ounces (2 cups) semisweet chocolate
   morsels
2 eggs graded "large"
1 teaspoon vanilla extract
2 tablespoons whiskey or brandy

First toast the almonds in a single layer in a shallow pan in a 350-degree oven for 12 to 15 minutes, shaking the pan a few times, until the almonds are lightly colored and have a delicious smell of toasted almonds when you open the oven door. Set aside to cool.

Adjust two racks to divide the oven into thirds and preheat the oven to 375 degrees. If possible, use cookie sheets with two or three flat edges; otherwise use any sheets upside down. Line the sheets with baking parchment or aluminum foil, shiny side up, and set aside.

Sift together into a large bowl (preferably one with flared rather than straight sides) the flour, baking soda, baking powder, and salt. Add the sugar and stir to mix.

Place about ½ cup of these dry ingredients in the bowl of a food processor fitted with the metal chopping blade. Add about ½ cup of the toasted almonds and process for about half a minute until the nuts are fine and powdery.

Add the processed mixture to the sifted ingredients in the large bowl. Add the remaining toasted almonds and the chocolate morsels and stir to mix.

In a small bowl beat the eggs with the vanilla and whiskey or brandy just to mix.

Add the egg mixture to the dry ingredients and stir until the dry ingredients are moistened (I stir with a large rubber spatula). Be patient.

Place a length of baking parchment or wax paper on the counter next to the sink. Turn the dough out onto the parchment or wax paper. Wet your hands with cold water—do not dry them—and press the dough into a round mound.

With a long, heavy, sharp knife cut the dough into equal quarters.

Continue to wet your hands as you form each piece of dough into a strip about 9 inches long, 2½ inches wide, and a generous 1 inch high (you will press the dough into shape, more than roll it). The ends of the strips should be rounded rather than squared.

Place two strips crosswise on each of the lined sheets.

Bake for 25 minutes, reversing the sheets top to bottom and front to back once during baking.

Remove the sheets from the oven and slide the parchment or foil off the sheets. With a wide metal spatula transfer the baked strips to a large cutting board and let them cool for 20 minutes.

Reduce the oven temperature to 275 degrees.

With a serrated French bread knife, carefully cut on a sharp angle into slices about 1 inch wide. This is tricky; cut slowly with a sawing motion.

Place the slices, cut side down, on the two unlined sheets.

Bake the two sheets, turning the slices upside down and reversing the sheets top to bottom and front to back once during baking. Bake for about 25 minutes (depending on the thickness of the biscotti) until thoroughly dry.

Turn the oven heat off, open the oven door, and let the biscotti cool in the oven.

When cool, store in an airtight container.

Maida Heatter's Book of Great Chocolate Desserts

The Chocolate Tree

I often dreamed about picking chocolate from a chocolate tree and eating my fill. I have never seen a chocolate tree but I have learned that if I did, I could not pick and eat the fruit. It's a long story from the picking to the eating.

The tree is called a cocoa (*cacao*) tree, or *Theobroma cacao*, "the food of the gods." It is a wide-branching tropical evergreen that grows in many parts of the world but always within 20 degrees of the equator. Most of the cocoa tree plantations are in Africa, South and Central America, and in parts of Asia. (This is not the same tree from which cocaine is obtained; that is called cocae or coca, and is a bush, not a tree. And coco palm is the name of the tree that grows coconuts.)

These trees grow either wild or under cultivation. In controlled conditions they get their start in nurseries, where seeds from high-yielding specimens are planted and babied for the first few months of their lives, or from grafted branch cuttings from a mother tree.

When they are transferred to plantations they are planted under the shade of a larger tree of another variety (often a banana tree or a rubber tree). They begin to bear fruit when they are from three to five years old.

First, large, glossy, foot-long leaves appear; they are red when young and dark green when mature. One of the most unusual facts about the cocoa tree is that the blossoms, and then the fruit, do not sprout on the branches but directly on the main trunk or on heavy branches near the trunk. The blossoms are tiny white or pink five-petaled flowers that grow in clusters. The fruit, or pods, also grow right out of the trunk; they are shaped like elongated melons, tapered at both ends. They measure six to fourteen inches in length and two to five inches in diameter. When they first appear they are green or maroon, then they ripen to a bright golden or scarlet color. They are five-ribbed, and have a hard, woody texture.

The trees would normally grow to about forty feet in height (wild cocoa trees might be sixty feet high or more), but on the plantations they are pruned to about fifteen or twenty feet to make the harvesting easier. As a rule the plantation trees bear fruit for thirty or forty years and then they are removed and replaced by seedlings, but there are reports of some trees still bearing fruit at the ripe old age of one hundred.

Harvesting the fruit is difficult, as the trees are too fragile for workmen to climb them. A long-handled, mitten-shaped steel knife called a *goulette* is used to reach the high pods. Native women and children follow the pickers, *tumbadores*, to gather the fallen pods in baskets which they carry on their heads.

The pods are then broken open with one or two well-placed blows from a machete. A good breaker will open five hundred pods in an hour. Inside each pod are twenty-five to fifty almond-shaped seeds (or beans) that are white, cream-colored, or lavender, imbedded in a white or pink pulpy and stringy mass that holds the seeds together. Each seed is about one inch in diameter. Now the women and children come back to scoop out the seeds and the pulp.

When the seeds are exposed to the air they quickly change color through oxidation and turn different shades of purple. The pulp ferments away within two or three days. Then the seeds are placed in baskets or boxes for a period of fermentation to remove the raw, bitter taste and to develop essential oils. The fermentation period might take from two to ten days, during which time the color of the seeds turns to dark brown.

The fermenting is followed by a drying process. The seeds are either spread out in the sun, or in some countries they are dried indoors by hot air pipes. During this period, which might take several days or weeks, they must be turned frequently to dry evenly.

The seeds from an average pod weigh scarcely two ounces after they are dried; it takes about four hundred dry seeds to make a pound. The average tree will yield one to two pounds of cured seeds per year.

Finally, the dried seeds are ready for packing and shipping. Then the manufacturer takes over. Since chocolate seeds from various countries and from different plantations and different trees do not all taste alike, the chocolate manufacturer will probably blend several different types, as many coffee producers do. And manufacturing methods differ from one factory to another. Timing, temperatures, proportions of ingredients, and processing are all extremely closely guarded secrets.

Once in the factory, each step is carefully controlled under the most sanitary conditions. First the seeds are fumigated and stored in a clean, cool, airy location where they cannot absorb any odors. Next they are sieved and cleaned by a machine that removes any dried pulp, pieces of pod, etc., that may have remained. Then they are weighed and blended according to size. Next they are roasted in large rotary cylinders at a temperature of 250 to 350 degrees for thirty minutes to two hours, depending on the seeds and the manufacturer's formula. At this stage, for the first time, they begin to develop a "chocolate" flavor and aroma.

After roasting and cooling, the seeds are shelled, leaving the meat, which is called "nibs." The nibs contain an average of 50% to 54% cocoa butter, which is a natural vegetable fat. The next step is to crush the seeds between large grinding stones or heavy steel disks. This process, called conching, generates enough heat to liquefy the cocoa butter, most of which is removed, leaving a thick, dark paste which is called the chocolate "liquor." When this liquor is poured into molds and solidified, it is unsweetened chocolate. If still more of the cocoa butter is removed and the remaining "liquor" is solidified and then ground to a powder, it is cocoa powder.

If sugar and more cocoa butter are added to the chocolate liquor, it becomes sweetened chocolate (99% of the time the sugar will be sucrose, which is the same thing as granulated sugar and may be made from either cane or beet sugar). If milk is also added, it becomes milk chocolate (the milk is always dried milk).

Basically there are two types of "real" chocolate generally available: unsweetened and sweetened. There is very little choice or variety in the first category. But the second includes a wide variety, ranging from very sweet to very bittersweet. Plus milk chocolate, which is quite different and should not be substituted when a recipe calls for sweet or semisweet chocolate.

If a recipe calls for unsweetened chocolate, the answer is obvious.

BUT—if a recipe calls for sweet or semisweet, you have an endless choice. (They all began as unsweetened chocolate and had sugar added to them in varying degrees. They also vary according to their processing, amounts of cocoa butter, and other additional ingredients.) I speak from experience when I say that aside from a difference in flavor you can use any of these. It will not affect the texture or consistency. I have substituted 1-ounce squares for morsels, and 3-ounce bars for three 1-ounce squares, and bittersweet for semisweet, and extra-bittersweet for German's Sweet, and vice versa ad infinitum.

All "real" chocolate begins with chocolate liquor and cocoa butter. In "not real" chocolate they use cocoa in place of chocolate liquor—and some vegetable fat other than cocoa butter. The vegetable fat other than cocoa butter (cocoa butter is a vegetable fat) is one of two types: it is either palm kernel oil or coconut oil—or it is cottonseed or soya oil. Even though they are "natural" ingredients, it is called "imitation" chocolate.

Commercially, "imitation" chocolates are

called "compound" or "confectioners chocolate." For the retail trade the F.D.A. says they have to be labeled "chocolate flavored." (However, there are some completely artificial or synthetic chocolates that contain no ingredients derived from cocoa beans. Read the label to find out.)

Commercial Coating Chocolate (also called "dipping chocolate" or "couverture") may be "real" chocolate or compound ("imitation"), just as with other chocolates. Some of the "real" commercial chocolates are delicious for cooking or eating, and some of the compound chocolates are absolutely wonderful for making chocolate decorations because they are softer, more flexible, less brittle, and they set up faster.

I have used many different Commercial Coating chocolates that are the compound type (they do not have to be tempered). They are not generally available at retail, although there are some specialty kitchen shops that cut up the 10-pound bars and sell the chocolate by the pound. And there are some wholesale bakery supply stores that will sell a single 10-pound bar. Here are the names of three that I have good luck with: Nestlés Ice Cap, Wilbur's #37 Darkcote Confectionery Coating, and Semper Swedish Coating (made in Sweden but sold in the U.S.).

A good source for buying a variety of Commercial Coating chocolates by mail (they will also supply instructions for using them—and they have a catalog) is Maid of Scandinavia, 3244 Raleigh Avenue, Minneapolis, Minnesota 53416. They call their compound chocolate "summer coating." They have Nestlés Ice Cap, Mercken's, which comes in wafers, and Ambrosia.

I use compound chocolates for making chocolate curls with a swivel-bladed vegetable peeler; Chocolate Cigarettes, which are long, thin chocolate curls for decoration (see page 267); and, most especially, for Mushroom Meringues (see page 278). Or for dipping all kinds of things—try pretzels, saltines, or matzohs, etc.

Commercial Coating Chocolate, both "real" chocolate and compound, is used for making candy and in bakeries for cooking. The compound chocolate is often simply melted and used as an icing for cookies—frequently just the ends of finger-shaped cookies or half the diameters of round cookies are dipped into the chocolate. "Real" chocolate, when it is used in bakeries or by candy makers, usually for dipping candy centers into, is "tempered" before it is used. Tempering is a precise and complicated process involving melting the chocolate over water at a certain temperature until it reaches a certain temperature and then cooling it to still another temperature over water of yet another temperature. Without any drafts. (I think all of this belongs more in a laboratory than in a home kitchen.)

If "real" chocolate is not tempered it will discolor when it hardens. Compound chocolate can be melted and used with no extraordinary precautions and it won't discolor.

Chocolate should be stored where it is cool and dry and the temperature is about 68 to 78 degrees. When the temperature is cold, as in the refrigerator, chocolate will "sweat" when it is brought into room temperature. When the temperature is too warm, chocolate can develop a "bloom" (a paler-colored exterior). This is simply caused by a slight percentage of the cocoa butter that has separated and risen to the surface. It is O.K., the chocolate is not spoiled; use it.

Premelted (or No-Melt) chocolate, according to the F.D.A., is not real chocolate; it is a combination of powdered cocoa and hydrogenated vegetable oil. It has a less pronounced chocolate flavor.

White chocolate, according to the F.D.A., is not really chocolate because it does not contain chocolate liquor. It is pure cocoa butter with sugar, milk, and flavoring—although some brands have additional ingredients. The label from Tobler Narcisse lists "sugar, cocoa butter, milk powder, lecithin, and vanillin." Lindt Blancor lists "sugar, cocoa butter, whole milk, skimmed milk and whey powder, almonds, lecithin, and vanillin." And Toblerone Blanc lists "sugar, cocoa butter, almonds, honey, egg white, lecithin, and vanillin."

They all taste like *very* sweet, *very* mild milk chocolate.

Incidentally, according to the dictionary, vanillin, which is used in both dark and white chocolates, may be either natural or synthetic. And, according to the F.D.A., it's all right with them for manufacturers to use either, but the synthetic must be labeled "artificial."

Dutch-process cocoa is not a brand name; it is so called because it was created in Holland by a Dutchman named Coenraad van Houten, who discovered the process of adding alkali very sparingly to cocoa to neutralize the acidity, make it less bitter, and deepen the color. The label will say either Dutch Process or "processed with alkali." It may be domestic or imported. I usually use Droste.

Chocolate is a quick-energy food that contains protein, carbohydrate, and fat. And the following vitamins and minerals: calcium, phosphorus, iron, sodium, potassium, and vitamin A. Plus thiamine, riboflavin, and niacin, which are B vitamins.

Ingredients

SUGARS

All sugars should be measured in the graded measuring cups that are made for measuring dry ingredients.

Brown Sugars

Did you know that most brown sugars are made of white granulated sugar to which a dark syrup has been added? Dark brown sugar has a mild molasses, and light brown has a milder, lighter syrup (which may also be a molasses). Dark brown has a slightly stronger flavor, but they may be used interchangeably.

Brown sugar is moist; if it dries out it will harden. It should be stored airtight at room temperature. If it has small lumps in it they should be strained out; with your fingertips press the sugar through a large strainer set over a large bowl. The Savannah Sugar Refinery is now printing the following directions on their boxes of brown sugar: "If your brown sugar has been left open and becomes hard, place a dampened (not wet) paper towel inside the resealable poly bag and close the package tightly for 12 hours or more. A slice of apple can be used in place of the dampened paper towel."

Confectioners Sugar

Confectioners sugar and powdered sugar are exactly the same. They are both granulated sugar that has been pulverized very fine and has had about 3% cornstarch added to keep it in a powdery condition. Of these, 4-x is the least fine and 10-x is the finest. Confectioners sugar should be strained, but you can do several pounds at a time if you wish (it does not have to be done immediately before using as flour does). Store it airtight.

If directions say to sprinkle with confectioners sugar, place the sugar in a small strainer and shake it over the top of the cake or cookies.

Vanilla Sugar

This is a flavored confectioners sugar frequently used to sprinkle over cakes or cookies. It adds a nice mild flavor and delicious aroma. To make it, fill a covered jar (about 1-quart size) with confectioners sugar. Split a few vanilla beans the long way and bury them in the sugar. Cover tightly and let stand for at least a few days before using. As the sugar is used it may be replaced; the vanilla beans will continue to flavor the sugar for a month or two.

When you make vanilla sugar don't bother to strain the sugar beforehand. The vanilla beans give off a certain amount of moisture which the sugar absorbs, causing the sugar to become lumpy and making it necessary to strain it just before using.

Confectioners Sugar Designs

Many cakes with plain, smooth icing (or no icing) may be decorated with confectioners sugar. I have tried the popular method of covering a cake with a fancy paper doily, sprinkling with sugar, and then removing the doily, thereby leaving an intricate white design. But I like simpler designs and I would rather make my own. Plain white stripes on a dark cake are more to my taste.

If you are going to make a sugar design and if you have iced the cake and have first lined the edges of the plate with four strips of wax paper (see page 18), leave them there to catch excess sugar. Wait until the icing has set and is not wet or sticky before you sugar the top.

To make plain white stripes, cut strips of wax paper about ½ inch wide and long enough to extend slightly over the edges of the top of the cake for easy removal. Place them parallel about ½ inch apart over the top of the cake. Strain the sugar generously and evenly through a fine strainer held over the cake. Then carefully remove the paper strips by lifting both ends at the same time; do not let the sugar that is on the strips fall back onto the cake or it will mess up the design. Then pull out the strips of paper from under the edges of the cake.

Here's another design for a round cake. Cut six or eight strips about ¼ or ⅓ inch wide, each one slightly longer than the diameter of the cake. Place one across the top, right across the middle, then another one crossing it at a right angle, again right in the middle to make a cross. Then place two or three across each quarter, dividing the quarters equally (the strips will cross each other in the center and will form a sunburst or fan-like pattern). Remember which one you put on last because you will want to remove that one first. Sprinkle the cake with sugar, and then carefully remove the strips in the reverse order you put them down so that the sugar doesn't spill. The cake will have a white top with dark lines radiating from the center.

If the cake was not iced, and therefore the plate was not lined with four strips of wax paper, use a pastry brush to dust excess sugar off the plate.

Crystal Sugar

Crystal sugar, also called pearl sugar, or *hagelzucker* in German, is commonly used to sprinkle over European cookies and pastries before baking. It is coarser than granulated sugar.

FLOUR

With only one or two exceptions these recipes call for sifted flour. This means that even if the package is labeled "pre-sifted" you should sift it before measuring. If not, since flour packs down while standing 1 cup unsifted flour is liable to be a few spoonfuls more than 1 cup of just-sifted flour.

If you have one, use a triple sifter (three layers of wire mesh); otherwise sift the flour twice. Sift it onto a piece of wax paper. Make sure that there is no flour left in the sifter, then transfer the sifter to another piece of wax paper. Use a metal measuring cup and lightly spoon the sifted flour into the cup or lift it on a dough scraper and transfer it to the cup—not shake the cup or pack or press the flour down—and scrape excess off the top with a dough scraper, a metal spatula, or any flat-sided implement. Place the flour in the sifter, add any ingredients to be sifted together with it, and sift onto the second piece of wax paper. Again, make sure there is nothing left in the sifter.

It is not necessary ever to wash a flour sifter (I never do), just shake it out firmly and store it in a plastic bag.

If you don't have a sifter, flour can be sifted through a fine-meshed strainer.

Some of these recipes call for all-purpose flour, and some for cake flour. Although all-purpose has a higher gluten content than cake flour, for general cake- and cookie-baking they may be substituted one for the other if necessary: 1 cup of sifted all-purpose flour equals 1 cup plus 2 tablespoons of sifted cake flour—or, in reverse, 1 cup of sifted cake flour equals 1 cup less 2 tablespoons of sifted all-purpose.

In any recipe calling for all purpose flour you may use either bleached or unbleached.

Both the recipes that call for all-purpose flour and those that call for cake flour mean flour only—not the kind that has baking powder and salt already added to it.

EGGS

Size

The size of eggs can be very important in certain recipes (in others it might not make any difference). In cakes without flour, or with very little, if the whites are too large there might be more air beaten in than the other ingredients can support and the cake might fall. On the other hand, in certain gelatin desserts, or in some mousses, if the whites are too small there might not be enough air for the dessert to be as light as it should.

In each recipe where it is necessary, I have indicated the size or choice of sizes that should be used.

To Open Eggs

If directions call for adding whole eggs one at a time, they may all be opened ahead of time into one container and then poured into the other ingredients, approximately one at a time. Do not open eggs directly into the other ingredients—you would not know if a piece of shell had been included.

To Separate Eggs

Eggs separate more safely—there is less chance of the yolk breaking—when they are cold. Therefore, if a recipe calls for separated eggs it is usually the first step I do when organizing the ingredients so that they are cold from the refrigerator.

The safest way to separate eggs is as follows: Place three small cups or bowls in front of you (or use shallow glasses; they generally have a sharper edge and crack the shell more cleanly). One is for the whites and one for the yolks. The third one might not be needed, but if you should break the yolk when opening an egg, just drop the whole thing in the third bowl and save it for some other use.

Tap the side of the egg firmly (but not too hard or you might break the yolk) on the edge of the bowl or glass to crack the shell, with luck, in a rather straight even line. Then, holding the egg in both hands, separate the halves of the shell, letting some of the white run out into the bowl or glass. Hold the eggs so that the halves each make a cup. Pour the yolk back and forth from one half of the shell to the other, letting all of the white run out. Drop the yolk into the second bowl or glass.

Many professional cooks simply open the egg into the palm of one hand with their fingers slightly separated over a bowl. They let the white run through their open fingers and then slide the yolk into the second bowl.

As each egg is separated the white should be transferred to another container (that is, in addition to the three—it could be another bowl or glass or it might be the mixing bowl you will beat them in), because if you place all of the whites in one container there is a chance that the last egg white might have some yolk in it, which could spoil all of the whites. Generally, a tiny bit of yolk or shell can be removed from egg whites with an empty half shell. Or try a piece of paper towel dipped in cold water.

To Beat Egg Whites

Many of the recipes in this book depend on properly beaten egg whites. After you have learned how, it becomes second nature.

First, the bowl and beaters must be absolutely clean. A little bit of fat (egg yolks are fat) will prevent the whites from incorporating air as they should and from rising properly.

Second, do not overheat or the whites will become dry and you will not be able to fold them into other ingredients without losing the air you have beaten in.

Third, do not beat them ahead of time. They must be folded in immediately after they are beaten. And if it is a cake that you are making, it must then be placed in the oven right away.

You can use an electric mixer, a rotary egg beater, or a wire whisk.

If you use an electric mixer or a rotary beater, be careful not to use a bowl that is too large or the whites will be too shallow to get the full benefit of the beater's action. If the bowl does not revolve by itself (as they do in electric mixers on a stand), move the mixer or beater around the bowl to beat all the whites evenly. If you use a mixer on a stand, use a rubber spatula frequently to push the whites from the sides of the bowl into the center.

If you use a wire whisk, it should be a large, thin-wired balloon type, at least 4 inches wide at the top. The bowl should be very large to give you plenty of room for making large, circular motions with the whisk. An unlined copper bowl is the best, or you may use glass, china, or stainless steel —but do not beat egg whites in aluminum, which might discolor the whites, or plastic, which is frequently porous and might be greasy from some other use. A copper bowl should be treated each time before using as follows: Put 1 or 2 teaspoons of salt in the bowl and rub thoroughly with half a lemon, squeezing a bit of the juice and mixing it with the salt. Then rinse it with hot water (no soap) and dry. After using a copper bowl, wash it as you would any other, but be sure to treat it before beating egg whites again.

When I beat whites with an electric mixer, if they do not have sugar added to them (sugar makes them more creamy and slightly lessens the chance of overbeating), I always—and I recommend this to everyone—finish the beating with a wire whisk. There is less chance of overbeating and the whisk seems to give the whites a slightly creamy consistency. At this stage you can use a smaller whisk than the one mentioned above—use any one that seems to fit the bowl the whites are in.

People always ask me if I bring egg whites to room temperature before using them. If I do it is a rare occasion. They are usually cold when I use them.

To Freeze Egg Whites or Yolks

Many of these recipes call for yolks and no whites, and a few call for only whites. If you have just a few extra of either left over and do not want to save them for something else, add them to scrambled eggs.

Leftover egg whites may be kept covered in the refrigerator for a few days, or they may be frozen. I freeze them individually (or occasionally 2 or 4 together) in ovenproof glass custard cups. When they are frozen, hold one cup upside down under running hot water until the frozen white can be removed. Wrap each frozen white individually in plastic wrap and return to the freezer. To use, remove the number you want, unwrap and place them in a cup or bowl, and let stand at room temperature to thaw. Or place them in a slightly warm oven, or place the cup or bowl in a larger bowl of warm water.

To freeze yolks, stir them lightly just to mix, and for every yolk stir in ⅓ teaspoon of granulated sugar or ½ teaspoon of honey. Freeze them in a covered jar, labeling so you will know how many and how much sugar or honey, and can then make adjustments in the recipe for the sweetening when you use them. When thawed, stir to mix well—they will not look exactly the same as before they were frozen (not as smooth) but will work in recipes.

NUTS

Nuts (walnuts and pecans more than almonds) can turn rancid rather quickly. Always store all nuts airtight in the freezer or refrigerator. In the refrigerator nuts store satisfactorily for 9 months; in the freezer at zero degrees for 2 years. Bring them to room temperature before using; smell them and taste them before you use them (preferably, as soon as you buy them)—you will know quickly if they are rancid. If you even suspect that they might be, do not use them; they would ruin a recipe.

To Blanch Almonds

(Blanched almonds are skinned almonds.)
Cover them with boiling water—the skin will loosen almost immediately. Spoon out a few nuts at

a time. One by one, hold them under cold running water and squeeze the nut between your thumb and forefinger. The nut will pop out and the skin will remain between your fingers. Place the peeled almonds on a towel to dry, then spread them in a single layer in a shallow baking pan and bake in a 200-degree oven for half an hour or so until they are completely dry. Do not let them brown.

If the almonds are to be split, sliced, or slivered, they should remain in the hot water longer so that they soften. Let them stand in the water until the water cools enough for you to touch it. Then, one at a time, remove the skin and immediately, while the nut is still soft, place it on a cutting board and cut with a small, sharp paring knife. Bake to dry as above. Sliced almonds are those that have been cut into very thin slices; slivered almonds are the fatter, oblong, "julienne"-shaped pieces. Don't expect what you do at home to be as even as the bought ones.

To Blanch Hazelnuts

Spread the hazelnuts on a baking sheet and bake at 350 degrees for about 15 minutes or until the skins parch and begin to flake off. Then, working with a few at a time, place them on a large, coarse towel (I use a large terry-cloth bath towel). Fold part of the towel over to enclose them. Rub firmly against the towel, or hold that part of the towel between both hands and rub back and forth. The handling and the texture of the towel will cause most of the skins to flake off. Pick out the nuts and discard the skins. Don't worry about the few little pieces of skin that may remain.

This is not as quick and easy as it sounds.

Pistachio Nuts

A light sprinkling of chopped green pistachio nuts is an elegant and classy touch. But don't overdo it; less is better than more. Fine pastries in swanky patisseries might have only about a teaspoonful of them in the very center of a 9-inch cake, sprinkled on the chocolate icing or whipped cream topping.

Buy shelled, unsalted green pistachios. They are hard to find, but they keep for a long, long time in the freezer. Try wholesale nut dealers or specialty nut shops. In New York they are available (by mail, too) from Paprikas Weiss, 1572 Second Avenue, New York, New York 10028.

Chop them coarsely on a board using a long, heavy knife. Don't worry about the little pieces of skin that flake off; use them with the nuts.

WHIPPING CREAM

Plain old-fashioned heavy cream is almost impossible to find nowadays unless you have your own cow. Too bad, because the new super- or ultra-pasteurized (known as UHT—ultra-high-temperature pasteurized) is not as good, at least not to my taste. The reason dairies make it is that it has a 6- to 8-week shelf life (they call it a "pull date"; the store has to pull it off their shelves if it is not sold by the date stamped on the container).

The process of making ultra-pasteurized cream involves heating the cream to 250 degrees for one second. It gives the cream a slight caramel flavor (so mild you might not notice it), and makes it more difficult to whip (it will take longer). It is advised that you chill the bowl and the beaters in the freezer for about half an hour before using. And keep the cream in the refrigerator until you are ready to whip; do not let it stand around in the kitchen—it should be as cold as possible.

It seems to me that baked custards take longer to set if they are made with ultra-pasteurized cream, and ice cream takes longer to churn.

How to Whip Cream

Since whipped cream is such an important part of many chocolate desserts, be extra careful with it—make it just right.

If you use plain old-fashioned cream (not UHT pasteurized "super" or "ultra"), it should be at least a few days old.

The best way to whip either cream is to place it in a large bowl, set the bowl in a larger bowl of ice and water, and whip with a large, thin-wired, balloon-type wire whisk.

If that seems like more than you want to fuss with, use an electric mixer or an egg beater, and chill the bowl and beaters before using them. If the bowl does not revolve, then move the beaters around the bowl to whip all the cream evenly at the same time.

When I whip cream with an electric mixer, I always (and I recommend this to everyone) finish the whipping by hand with a wire whisk; there is less chance of overwhipping. At this stage you can use a smaller whisk than the one mentioned above.

Whipped cream, which can be heavenly, is not delicious if it is whipped until it is really stiff—softer is better.

If I am making flavored whipped cream, I add the vanilla and/or sugar to the liquid cream in the bowl and beat everything together.

Equipment

THERMOMETERS

Oven Temperature

One of the *most* important and *most* overlooked requirements for good results in baking (chocolate or otherwise) is correct oven temperature. The wrong temperature can cause a cake to fall, to burn, to be underdone, to refuse to rise; it can ruin a soufflé; it can turn wonderfully crisp cookies into pale, limp, soggy messes, or burned, bitter messes; and it is the cause of almost any other baking disaster that you might have experienced or heard about.

No matter how new, or how good, your oven is, *please* double check the temperature every time you bake. Use a small oven thermometer from a hardware store. Buy the mercury kind—it is best. Light your oven at least 20 minutes ahead of time, and place the thermometer in the middle of the oven. Give the oven plenty of time to heat and cycle and reheat before you read the thermometer; read it (and all thermometers) at eye level. If it does not register the heat you want, adjust the thermostat up or down until the mercury thermometer registers the correct heat—no matter what the oven setting says.

Other Thermometers

A friend told me she did not know that her refrigerator was too warm until she served a large chocolate icebox cake at a dinner party and found that the middle of it was thin and runny instead of firm as it should have been. And once I didn't know that my freezer was misbehaving until the very last minute, when a photographer was here to take pictures of chocolate desserts; I had waited until he was ready to shoot before I took the chocolate curls out of the freezer and found they had flattened and were no longer curls.

Keep a freezer thermometer in your freezer, and a refrigerator thermometer in your refrigerator—and look at them often.

And for many of these recipes you will need a candy-making thermometer. With a candy-making thermometer in a saucepan, bend down and read it at eye level in order to get a correct reading.

A NUT GRINDER

Many of these recipes call for ground nuts. They should be fine, dry (not oily), and powdery, or about the consistency of cornmeal.

You can use a food processor, a blender, or a nut grinder. If you use a nut grinder I recommend the nut grinder that screws onto the side of a table. The nuts go into the top and come out through the side when the handle is turned. They are available in some specialty kitchen equipment shops and in Hungarian-type food stores. In New York they are available (by mail, too) from Paprikas Weiss, 1572 Second Avenue, New York, N.Y. 10028.

DOUBLE BOILERS

Since it is essential to melt chocolate slowly it is generally best to do it in a double boiler, and many of these recipes specify a double boiler. You can buy them in hardware stores or kitchen shops; I like the plain hardware store Revere Ware. If necessary, you can create your own by placing a heat-proof bowl over a saucepan (a pot) of shallow hot water. The bowl should be wide enough at the top so its rim rests on the rim of the sauce pan, keeping the bowl suspended over the water.

ELECTRIC MIXERS

I use an electric mixer on a stand that comes with two different-size bowls and a pair of beaters (rather than one). Mine is a Sunbeam, and I am so dependent on it and so accustomed to it, that when I go to major cities far from home to do cooking demonstrations, I bring my own.

I think it is important, or at least extremely helpful, for many dessert recipes to use a mixer that:
a.   is on a stand;
b.   comes with both a small and a large bowl; and
c.   has space to scrape around the bowl with a rubber spatula while the mixer is going.

And I especially recommend that you buy an extra set of bowls and beaters—they are generally available wherever mixers are sold.

Incidentally, although I also have a hand-held mixer, I could live without it. (But if I didn't have any other I am sure I would learn to love it.) If you are using a hand-held mixer (or even an egg beater in some cases), when I say "small bowl of electric mixer," that means one with a 7-cup capacity, and "large bowl of electric mixer" means a 16-cup capacity.

ROLLING PINS

If you have many occasions to use a rolling pin, you really should have different sizes and different shapes. Often, a very long, thick, and heavy one will be best. For some mixtures you will want a smaller, lighter one. Most generally, I use the French style, which is extra long, narrow, and tapered at both ends. And occasionally it is best to start the rolling with a large, heavy pin and finish it with a French-style pin.

However, in the absence of any rolling pin at all, other things will do the same job: Try a straight-sided bottle, tall jar, or drinking glass.

BUNDT PAN

Bundt pan is a trade name for a one-piece tube pan that has a specific fancy design. There are many other similar pans with different designs; in each case the name of the pan is descriptive of the design. Turk's head, turban, and kugelhopf are the most common. When a recipe calls for a Bundt pan, any of these other pans may be substituted.

PASTRY BAGS

The best pastry bags are those made of canvas and coated on only one side with plastic. Use them with the plastic coating inside. The small opening generally has to be cut a bit larger to allow the metal tubes to fit. It is easier to work with a bag that is too large rather than one that is too small. They may be washed in hot soapy water; just hang them up to dry.

When filling a pastry bag, unless there is someone else to hold it for you, it is generally easiest if you support the bag by placing it in a tall and wide glass or jar.

A CAKE-DECORATING TURNTABLE

If you ice many cakes, this is a most important piece of equipment. Not that you can't ice a cake without it, but it will not look the same. You will love the smooth, professional-looking results, and the ease of using a turntable.

It has a flat surface that spins around when you turn it; it works on the same principle as a lazy Susan. (Although a lazy Susan can be used in place of a turntable, it usually doesn't turn as easily.)

I put the cake on a cake plate and then put the plate on the turntable.

First put the icing on freely just to cover the cake. Then hold a long, narrow metal spatula in your right hand, with the blade at about a 30-degree angle against the side or the top of the cake. With your left hand slowly rotate the turntable. Hold your right hand still as the cake turns and in a few seconds you will have a smooth, sleek, professional-looking cake. And it is fun. And exciting.

I also use it for trimming and then fluting the edge of pie crust.

Turntables are available at specialty kitchen equipment shops and at wholesale bakery or restaurant suppliers. They range in price from moderate on up. The thing to look for is one that turns easily. There is no reason why a turntable, if it is not abused, should not last a lifetime or two.

SMALL, NARROW METAL SPATULA

Many of my recipes call for this tool for smoothing icing around the sides of a cake. Mine is 8 inches long; it has a 4-inch blade and a 4-inch wooden handle. The blade is ⅝ inch wide and has a rounded tip. Although it can bend, it is more firm than flexible. Metal spatulas are generally available in specialty kitchen supply stores.

Techniques

ABOUT MELTING CHOCOLATE

There is no reason for anyone ever to have trouble melting chocolate. It is not difficult or tricky. There are two simple things to know about it.

1. When you melt chocolate with no other ingredients, the container you melt it in and the tool you stir it with must be absolutely dry. The merest drop of moisture will cause the chocolate to "tighten" or become stiff and lumpy. (More liquid, or approximately 1 tablespoon to 1 ounce of chocolate, is all right. It is the almost invisible drop that causes trouble.) If the chocolate should "tighten," you can salvage it by stirring in homogenized vegetable shortening, such as Crisco or Spry (not butter—that has water in it), 1 teaspoon for each ounce of chocolate. (If necessary, add a bit more shortening and stir until smooth; then forget that you added it—it should not affect the recipe.)

2. Chocolate should melt slowly, never over high heat—it burns easily. It may be melted in the top of a double boiler over hot water on moderate or low heat. The water in the bottom of the double boiler should not boil hard. Or it may be melted in a heavy saucepan over the lowest possible heat. Or in a slow oven. Or, to melt just 1 or 2 ounces, it may be put in a small heatproof custard cup and placed in a pan of shallow hot water over low heat. Milk chocolate should be melted even more slowly than other chocolates.

To save time chocolate may be chopped coarsely before it is melted.

I always cover the pot until the chocolate is partially melted (not long enough for steam to condense inside the cover and drop onto the chocolate—some people place a folded paper napkin or towel under the cover to absorb any steam and avoid the chance that it may drip into the chocolate), then I remove the cover and stir until the chocolate is completely melted. To be sure the chocolate doesn't overcook, remove it from the heat a bit before it is completely melted.

Unsweetened chocolate will run (liquefy) as it melts; sweet, semi-sweet, and milk chocolates hold their shape (although they are melted), and must be stirred.

Some semisweet chocolates might not melt as smoothly as unsweetened. If the chocolate is not smooth, stir it briskly with a rubber spatula, pressing against any lumps until it becomes smooth.

Various chocolates have different consistencies when they are melted. Unsweetened chocolate is the thinnest, and milk chocolate is the thickest.

When you melt chocolate in or with milk (or when you mix melted chocolate and milk), if the mixture is not smooth—if the chocolate remains in little flecks—beat it with an electric mixer, wire whisk, or an egg beater until smooth.

ABOUT MEASURING

Meticulously precise measurements are essential for good results in baking.

Glass or plastic measuring cups with the measurements marked on the side and the 1-cup line below the top are only for measuring liquids. Do not use them for flour or sugar. With the cup at eye level, fill carefully to exactly the line indicated.

Measuring cups that come in graded sets of four (¼ cup, ⅓ cup, ½ cup, and 1 cup) are for measuring flour, sugar, and other dry ingredients—and for thick sour cream. Fill the cup to overflowing and then scrape off the excess with a dough scraper, a metal spatula, or the flat side of a large knife.

Standard measuring spoons must be used for correct measurements. They come in sets of four: ¼ teaspoon, ½ teaspoon, 1 teaspoon, and 1 tablespoon. For dry ingredients, fill the spoon to overflowing and then scrape off the excess with a small metal spatula or the flat side of a knife.

TO ADD DRY INGREDIENTS ALTERNATELY WITH LIQUID

Begin and end with dry. The procedure is generally to add about one-third of the dry, half of the liquid, a second third of the dry, the rest of the liquid, and then the rest of the dry.

Use the lowest speed on an electric mixer for this (or it may be done in a bowl using a wooden spatula, or your bare hand). After each addition mix only until smooth. If your mixer is the type that allows you to use a rubber spatula while it is in motion, help the mixing along by scraping the sides of the bowl with the spatula. If the mixer does not allow room, or if it is a hand-held mixer, stop it frequently and scrape the bowl with the spatula; do not beat any more than necessary.

ABOUT FOLDING INGREDIENTS TOGETHER

Many of these recipes call for folding beaten egg whites and/or whipped cream into another mixture. The whites and/or cream have air beaten into them, and folding (rather than mixing) is done in order to retain the air.

This is an important step and should be done with care. The knack of doing it well comes with practice and concentration. Remember that you want to incorporate the mixtures without losing any air. That means handle as little as possible.

It is important not to beat the whites or whip the cream until they are actually stiff; if you do you will have to stir and mix rather than just fold, thereby losing the air.

Do not let beaten egg whites stand around or they will become dry. Do not fold whipped cream into a warm mixture or the heat will deflate the cream. Generally it is best to fold the lighter mixture into the heavier one and to actually stir a bit of the lighter mixture into the heavier (to lighten it a bit) before you start to fold. Then, as a rule, it is best not to add all of the remaining light mixture at once; do the folding in a few additions.

Although many professional chefs use their bare hands for folding in, most home cooks are more comfortable using a rubber spatula. (Rubber is better than plastic because it is more flexible. Spatulas come in three sizes. The smallest is called a bottle scraper. For most folding, the medium size is the one to use. But for folding large amounts in a large bowl, the largest rubber spatula can be very helpful. The one I mean might measure about 13 to 16 inches from the end of the blade to the end of the handle; the blade will be about 2¾ inches wide and about 4½ inches long. That large size is difficult to locate; try specialty kitchen equipment shops or wholesale restaurant suppliers.)

Folding in is best done in a bowl with a rounded bottom. Following the recipe, place part (occasionally all) of the light mixture on top of the heavier mixture. Hold the rubber spatula, rounded side toward the bottom and over the middle of the bowl, and cut through to the bottom of the bowl. Bring the spatula toward you against the bottom, then up the side and out, over the top, turning the blade as you do this so it is upside down when it comes out over the top. After each fold, rotate the bowl slightly in order to incorporate as much of the ingredients as possible. Return the spatula to its original position, then cut through the middle of the mixture again. Continue only until both mixtures are combined.

Occasionally a bit of beaten egg white will rise to the top. If it is just one or two small pieces, instead of folding more, simply smooth over the top gently with the spatula.

If the base mixture has gelatin in it, it should be chilled until it starts to thicken. The perfect situation for folding is to have the gelatin mixture, the whipped cream, and the egg whites all the same consistency.

ABOUT PREPARING PANS AND COOKIE SHEETS

In many recipes, after buttering the pan I dust it with bread crumbs, because in many recipes, but not all, there is less chance of sticking if you use crumbs rather than flour. (I have had my share of "sticking" problems. After following a recipe carefully, and using wonderful ingredients, it feels rotten to invert the pan and see half of the cake still in the pan and the rest on the cake rack.) The crumbs should be fine and dry. They may be homemade (see below) but I always have bought ones on hand also. If you buy them be sure to get the ones marked "plain" or "unseasoned," not "seasoned." Some brands are O.K. to use just as they are, some are a bit too coarse; they may be ground a little finer in a food processor or a blender. You can grind a whole boxful at a time.

To prepare a tube pan: When directions call for buttering the pan and then coating it with flour or crumbs, the only way to get the flour or crumbs on the tube itself is by lifting the flour or crumbs with your fingers and sprinkling it/them around the tube with your fingers.

Many of these cookie recipes call for lining the sheet with aluminum foil. That is not specified in order to keep your cookie sheets clean (although it will, and if you do a lot of cooking you will be delighted with not having to wash and dry the sheets). Mainly, it is so the cookies will not stick; also, it is quick and efficient, saves time, and in many cases results in cookies that hold their shape better than they would on buttered sheets. And if you have the right kind of cookie sheet, which means that the sheet has three flat sides and a raised edge on only one side (somehow manufacturers seem to have stopped making that kind, and all I can say is that I don't think they ever bake cookies themselves or they would know better), you can line up many pieces of foil, place all of the cookies on the foil, and then just slide the sheet under the foil when you are ready. And slide the foil off when they are baked. However, whichever way you do it, if a recipe calls for foil between the cookies and the sheet, do it—or the cookies might stick.

The foil may be wiped clean with a paper towel and reused.

HOMEMADE DRY BREAD CRUMBS

Remove and discard the crusts from plain sliced white bread. Place the slices in a single layer on cookie sheets in a 225-degree oven and bake until the bread is completely dry and crisp. Break up the slices coarsely and grind them in a food processor or a blender until the crumbs are rather fine, but not as fine as powder.

In all of these recipes, butter and flour or bread crumbs used to prepare the pans before baking are in addition to those called for in the ingredients.

ABOUT WRAPPING COOKIES

Unless I am baking cookies to serve right away, I wrap them in clear cellophane. It gives them an attractive and professional look, keeps them fresh, easy to handle, easy to pack for the freezer or a lunch box or picnic, and makes it quick and easy to slip a few of them into a little bag, basket, or box as a gift.

But clear cellophane is hard to find. It is available from wholesale paper companies, the kind that sell paper napkins, etc., to restaurants. In my experience they are agreeable about selling a single roll of cellophane to individuals. It usually comes in rolls of different widths, and sometimes in packages of precut squares. It you buy a roll, it is easier to handle one that is not too wide. And it is easier to cut with a knife than with scissors.

If you cannot get cellophane, wax paper is better than plastic wrap (which is too hard to handle and takes too long).

Cut off a long piece, fold it in half, cut through the fold with a long, sharp knife, fold again and cut again, and continue to fold and cut until you have the right size pieces. If the size is close but a bit too large, do not cut the papers individually (it takes too long). Instead, place the whole pile in front of you and fold one side of the entire pile to the size you want. Place your left hand firmly on the pile, holding the folded sides down and at the same time holding the pile so that the papers do not slip out of place. With your right hand cut through the fold with a knife. (If the pile is very large, cut about a dozen or two at a time.)

Bar cookies should be wrapped individually. Small drop cookies or thin rolled cookies may be wrapped two to a package, placed with their bottoms together.

Wrap one cookie as a sample to be sure that the papers are the right size.

Spread out as many pieces of paper as you have room for (or as many as you have cookies for).

1. Place a cookie in the center of each paper.
2. Bring the two long sides together up over the top.
3. Fold over twice so that the second fold brings the paper tight against the cookie.
4. Now, instead of just tucking the ends underneath, fold in the corners of each end, making a triangular point.
5. Then fold the triangle down under the cookie.

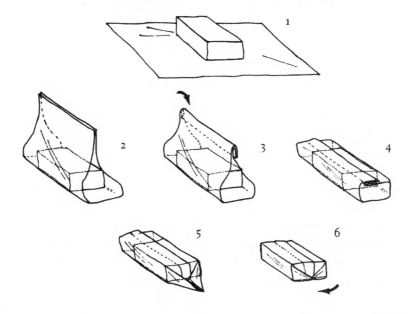

HOW TO PREPARE THE SERVING PLATE BEFORE YOU ICE THE CAKE

This is done to keep any icing off the plate. It will result in a clean, neat, professional-looking finished product.

Begin by tearing off a 10-inch piece of wax paper. Fold it crossways into four equal strips (fold it in half and then in half again), then cut through the folds with a sharp knife, making four 10 x 3-inch strips.

Lay the strips in a square pattern around the rim of the plate, put the cake on the plate over the paper, and check to be sure that the papers touch the cake all around.

After the cake is iced (before the icing hardens) remove the papers by gently pulling each one out toward a narrow end.

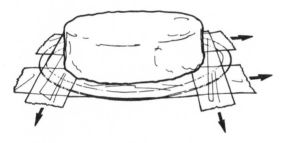

ABOUT DECORATING CAKES

Cake decorating can be just as much a creative art as painting or sculpting. But to me the pure untouched simplicity of a smooth, shiny chocolate glaze, or a topping of barely firm whipped cream, is perfection and adding anything to it would often be unnecessary and would detract from an already perfect work of art. The same goes for a plain un-iced pound cake or loaf cake. Of course there are times when I like to wield a pastry bag and don't ever want to quit. But please don't feel that every cake needs

decoration; simplicity is often decoration enough. Anything else might be gilding the lily.

ABOUT FREEZING CAKES

I don't think that any baked dessert tastes as good after freezing as when it is fresh (except cheesecake—I can't tell the difference in that). However, if it is frozen for a short time (a few days or weeks) the difference might be infinitesimal. I have indicated in many of my recipes that the dessert can be frozen. If it is a big help to you to prepare it ahead, do it. But if you have your choice, fresh is best.

If you want to ice a cake first and then freeze it, freeze until the icing is firm before it is wrapped and be sure to wrap it airtight with thin plastic wrap and then, if you wish, rewrap in aluminum foil or in a freezer bag.

Years ago I watched a chef at my husband's restaurant as he packaged something in a plastic bag for the freezer. He put the food in, placed the bag on the counter, gathered the top together as close to the food as possible, then he put his mouth to the opening and sucked out the air, which did such a complete job that the bag clung to the food all around—there was no air left in it. Then, without letting in any air, he twisted the top closed, folded the top over on itself, and wound a "twist-em" around it. I have done it that way ever since. Remember that the reason for using the bag is to keep the air out.

Everything should be thawed completely before unwrapping. (Foods sweat while thawing. If they are thawed wrapped the moisture will form on the outside of the wrapping; if they are thawed unwrapped the moisture will form on the food itself—that could spoil the looks of a beautiful chocolate glaze.) However, if you have a cake in the freezer and you want some right away, unwrap it, cut it, and serve it. Many of the chocolate cakes made without or almost without flour are delicious frozen. Just don't let the rest of the cake stand around uncovered—rewrap it immediately.

Label packages—if not, you might wind up with a freezer full of UFO's (Unidentified Frozen Objects).

ABOUT FREEZING COOKIES

Most cookies freeze quite well (but, like cakes, for a limited time). It is always extremely handy (I think it is a luxury) to have cookies in the freezer for unexpected company; they usually thaw quickly, and many can be served frozen directly from the freezer.

The same rule about thawing cakes applies to cookies—thaw before unwrapping.

Any cakes and cookies that may be frozen may be thawed and refrozen—even several times. I do it often. I would rather refreeze it immediately than let it stand around and get stale.

A FINAL WORD

I once put a cake in the oven and then realized that I had forgotten to use the baking powder that the recipe called for. I learned the hard way that it is necessary to organize all the ingredients listed in a recipe—line them up in the order they are called for—before you actually start mixing.

CAKES

Cakes Without or Almost Without Flour

I have always been attracted to recipes for cakes made with no flour or with very little. And consequently I believe I have turned out more than my share of cakes that sank to new lows. I don't have a scientific or analytic mind, but it didn't take long for me to realize that egg yolks beaten with sugar, and egg whites beaten (with or without sugar) to a high foam, will not stay up after baking no matter how carefully the two are folded together. They will sink. Even with the addition of some ground nuts or bread crumbs (either of which takes the place of flour and tends to hold the mixture up), the cake will still sink. There are exceptions, the exceptions being recipes where the proportion of air beaten into the eggs is not too much for the other ingredients to support. In other words, the cake will not sink if there is enough of something that takes the place of flour.

But by the same token, those cakes that sank when they cooled tasted divine. They had a light-moist, or heavy-moist but delicious, quality.

I've come to know beforehand which recipes will sink. Forewarned is forearmed and I am prepared. But I never make one of those recipes without thinking of a new cook/baker who might pick that for her first baking experience. I don't blame her if she says "never again."

My only advice is simple. When this type cake does sink, it sinks more in the center than on the rim. There are two solutions. One is to cover it all with whipped cream and the other is to cut the top to make it level and serve it upside down.

Several of these cakes are perfectly plain looking with a smooth, dark icing and nothing else. Beautiful.

However, here are some optional additions for any cakes that fit that description.

Fresh raspberries or strawberries or Chocolate-Covered Strawberries (see page 252) may be placed on the cake plate all around the cake. And/or a beautiful small fresh red rose may be inserted in the top center of the cake. Cut the stem short and place it directly into the cake. (Naturally, you would keep the flower in water until the last minute, then insert it.)

Of course you can use any other kind of flower, even a small bouquet of mixed tiny flowers. But there is something especially gorgeous about a deep red rose against dark chocolate.

Craig Claiborne's Rum Chocolate Dessert

8 TO 10 PORTIONS

Many years ago when Craig printed this recipe in The New York Times, *he wrote the following introduction for it: "Food cravings encompass everything from such mundane fare as peanuts, pickles and watermelon to the more sophisticated delights of oysters, caviar and champagne. Of all the foods on earth, however, it may be true that a craving for chocolate is the most universal. This rich, whipped-cream-topped chocolate pudding goes a long way to explain why."*

I don't know why Craig calls this a pudding. I call it a cake. Maybe the best of all. It slices beautifully. Serve it at your finest party, or make it just for yourself. Make it during the day for that night. Or make it the day before and ice it shortly before serving. Also, it can be frozen before it is iced—if so, thaw at room temperature for several hours.

4½ tablespoons <u>un</u>sifted all-purpose flour

¾ cup granulated sugar

5 ounces semisweet chocolate

1 teaspoon dry instant coffee

2 tablespoons boiling water

6 ounces (1½ sticks) sweet butter, at room temperature

¼ cup dark rum

6 eggs (graded large), separated

¼ teaspoon salt

Adjust rack one-third up from bottom of the oven and preheat oven to 350 degrees. You will need a round cake pan 8 inches in diameter and 3 inches deep (you can use an 8 x 3-inch cheesecake pan; see The Newest Cheesecake, page 97), or a 2½-quart soufflé dish (8 x 3½ inches). Cut a round of wax paper to fit the bottom. Butter the sides of the pan or dish and one side of the paper. Place the paper, buttered side up, in the pan. Shake a bit of flour into the pan, tap it around to coat all surfaces, then invert the pan to remove excess. Set pan aside.

Sift the flour and sugar together and set aside. Place the chocolate in the top of a large double boiler over hot water on moderate heat. Dissolve the coffee in the boiling water and pour over the chocolate. Cover the pot and leave until the chocolate is melted. Remove the top of the double boiler and stir well with a wire whisk until smooth. With the whisk gradually stir in the butter, adding about a ½-inch slice at a time and whisking until smooth after each addition. Gradually whisk in the dry ingredients and then the rum.

Place the egg yolks in a large mixing bowl and stir them lightly with the whisk just to mix. Gradually add the warm chocolate mixture, stirring well to mix.

Add the salt to the egg whites and beat until they just hold a shape or are stiff but not dry. In two or three additions fold the whites into the chocolate.

Pour the mixture into the prepared pan. Smooth the top. Place the prepared pan in a larger but not deeper pan, and pour in hot water to reach about halfway up the sides of the cake pan or soufflé dish.

Bake for 1 hour and 10 minutes. Remove the smaller pan from the hot water and place on a rack to cool to room temperature (it will take 1 hour or more but it may stand overnight). The cake will shrink as it cools—don't worry. (The cooled cake will be about 1½ inches high.)

With a small, sharp knife cut around the sides to release. Cover with a flat cake plate or a serving board, centering the plate evenly over the cake. Invert the plate and the cake pan. (If it doesn't lift off easily, bang the plate and the pan gently against a table or counter top.) Remove the pan and peel off the paper lining.

I think this cake is best at room temperature. Therefore it should be covered with the whipped cream immediately before serving. But if that is too much of a hassle, put the whipped cream on ahead of time and refrigerate the cake until serving time. (It is really divine either way.)

WHIPPED CREAM

1 cup heavy cream
2 tablespoons strained confectioners sugar
½ teaspoon vanilla extract

Whip the above ingredients until they are stiff enough to hold a shape when spread over the cake. With a small metal spatula first cover the sides of the cake and then the top. The cream may be spread smoothly or swirled into peaks.

The whipped cream may be left as is or decorated with chocolate curls or with candied violets or rose petals. (The violets or rose petals should be put on at the last minute or they might discolor the cream.)

Refrigerate.

September 7th Cake

12 PORTIONS

This cake came about when I wanted something different to serve for my birthday. Two thin, light-weight, *dark layers are filled with white whipped cream and are thickly covered with a wonderful dark coffee-chocolate whipped cream. The cake has no flour; it is really a fluffy chocolate omelet that settles down like a hot soufflé when it cools. This may be made a day before or early in the day for that night, or the layers may be frozen before they are filled and iced.*

LAYERS

6 eggs (graded extra-large), separated
¾ cup granulated sugar
¼ cup plus 1 tablespoon strained unsweetened cocoa powder (preferably Dutch process)
¼ teaspoon salt

Adjust rack one-third up from bottom of the oven and preheat oven to 375 degrees. Butter two 9-inch round layer-cake pans. Line the bottoms with rounds of wax paper or baking-pan liner paper cut to fit. Butter the paper and dust the inside of the pan all over with flour, invert the pans and tap to shake out excess flour.

In the small bowl of an electric mixer beat the egg yolks at high speed for 5 minutes until they are light lemon-colored. Add about half (6 tablespoons) of the sugar (reserve the remaining half) and continue to beat at high speed for 5 minutes more until the mixture is very thick and forms a wide ribbon when the beaters are lifted.

Add the cocoa and beat on lowest speed, scraping the bowl with a rubber spatula, and beating only until the cocoa is completely mixed in. Remove from the mixer and set aside.

Add the salt to the egg whites in the large bowl of the electric mixer. With clean beaters beat at high speed until the whites increase in volume and barely hold a soft shape. Reduce the speed to moderate while gradually adding the reserved sugar. Increase the speed to high again and continue to beat until the whites hold a definite shape when the beaters are raised or when some of the mixture is lifted on a rubber spatula—they should not be stiff or dry.

In several additions, small at first (about a large spoonful), fold half of the beaten whites into the chocolate mixture. Then fold the chocolate mixture into the remaining whites. Do not handle any more than necessary.

Turn half of the mixture into each of the prepared pans. Gently smooth each layer.

Bake for 30 to 35 minutes or until the layers spring back when lightly pressed with a fingertip and begin to come away from the sides of the pans.

Remove from the oven. With a small sharp knife carefully cut around the sides of the layers to release them. Cover each layer with a rack, invert pan and rack, remove pan, peel off the paper lining, cover layer with another rack, and invert again to let the layers cool right side up.

While they are cooling the layers will sink and the sides will buckle and look uneven but don't worry. That is to be expected in this recipe. The filling and icing will cover them and they will be light, moist, and delicious.

When the layers are completely cool, prepare a flat cake plate as follows. Cut four strips of wax paper, each one about 10 x 3 inches. Place them around the outer edges of the plate.

Place one layer upside down on the plate and see that the wax paper touches all the edges of the cake.

FILLING

¾ teaspoon unflavored gelatin
1½ tablespoons cold water
1½ cups heavy cream
⅓ cup confectioners sugar
¾ teaspoon vanilla extract

Sprinkle the gelatin over the water in a small heat-proof cup. Let stand for 5 minutes. Place the cup in a small pan containing about an inch of hot water. Set over moderate heat and let stand until the gelatin dissolves, then remove from the hot water and set aside.

Reserve 2 or 3 tablespoons of the cream and place the remainder in the small bowl of an electric mixer (if the room is warm the bowl and beaters should be chilled). Add the sugar and vanilla. Beat only until the cream has increased in volume and holds a soft shape. Then quickly stir the reserved tablespoons of cream into the warm, dissolved gelatin and, with the mixer going, pour the gelatin all at once into the slightly whipped cream and continue to beat. The cream should be beaten until it is firm enough to hold a shape.

Place the whipped cream on the bottom cake layer. Carefully spread it evenly. Cover it with the other layer, placing the top layer right side up. Place in the refrigerator and prepare the icing.

ICING

8 ounces semisweet chocolate
2 ounces (½ stick) butter
1 tablespoon dry instant coffee
¼ cup boiling water
2 cups heavy cream
¾ cup confectioners sugar
1 teaspoon vanilla extract

Break up or coarsely chop the chocolate and place it in the top of a small double boiler over hot water on moderate heat. Add the butter. In a small cup dissolve the coffee in the boiling water and pour it over the chocolate. Stir with a rubber spatula until the mixture is melted and smooth. Remove it from the hot water and transfer it to a medium-size mixing bowl.

Now the chocolate must cool to room temperature. You can let it stand or, if you are very careful not to overdo it, stir it briefly over ice and water—but not long enough for the chocolate to harden. In any event, the chocolate must cool to room temperature—test it on the inside of your wrist.

When the chocolate has cooled, place the cream, sugar, and vanilla in the small bowl of the electric mixer. Beat only until the cream holds a soft shape. It is very important that you do not whip the cream until it holds a definite shape; that would be too stiff for this recipe and would not only cause the icing to be too heavy but would also give it a slightly curdled appearance. Everything about this cake should be light and airy, and the chocolate will stiffen the cream a bit more.

In two or three additions fold about half of the cream into the chocolate, and then fold the chocolate into the remaining cream.

Remove the cake from the refrigerator.

If you have a turntable for decorating cakes or a lazy Susan, place the cake plate on it.

Use as much of the icing as you need to fill in any hollows on the sides of the cake—use a spoon or a metal spatula—and then smooth the icing around the sides. If you are working on a turntable, rotate it while you hold a small metal spatula against the sides to smooth the icing.

Now the cake can be finished in one of two ways (depending on whether or not you want to use a pastry bag). You can either use all of the icing to cover the top very thickly, or you can spread it very thinly and reserve about 3 cups of the icing and decorate the top with a pastry bag and a star-shaped tube.

Place the icing on the top and spread it smoothly. Then spread the sides again to make them neat.

To decorate the top, which will be completely covered with rippled lines of icing, fit a 15-inch pastry bag with a #6 star tube and fold down a deep cuff on the outside of the bag. Place the icing in the bag. Unfold the cuff. Close the top of the bag. To form the icing lines, begin at the edge of the cake furthest from you, at the middle of the edge. Squeeze an inch or two of icing out of the tube in a line coming toward you. Continuing to squeeze and without stopping the flow of the icing, move the tube back away from you over

about half the line you have just formed, making another layer of icing on the first. Still without stopping the flow of the icing, bring the tube toward you again and make another 1- to 2- inch line, then double back over half of this distance again. Continue across the whole diameter of the cake. The finished line will be along the middle of the cake. Make another, similar line to one side of the first, touching it. I find it easier to work from the middle—one side all the way and then the other side all the way to entirely cover the top of the cake with these wavy lines.

Remove the strips of wax paper by pulling each one out toward a narrow end.

Refrigerate for at least 6 hours or overnight and serve cold. To slice this cake without squashing it, insert the point of a sharp knife in the center of the cake. Then cut with an up-and-down sawing motion.

Torta di Cioccolata

8 to 10 Portions

This comes from the Isle of Capri. I got it from Marilyn Evins, a fabulous hostess famous for her terrific parties. It is an elegant no-flour chocolate cake, very rich, dense, dark, extremely moist. It looks very plain, and is really easy to make, but it may be served at your most important parties.

Although this does not have any flour, it does not sink (it doesn't rise either)—it will be quite flat on top, 1½ inches high. This is served without any icing but with plenty of whipped cream on the side.

In Italy it is always served warm, but it may be made early in the day or the day before, or it may be frozen (remove it from the freezer at least half an hour before serving). When very fresh it is quite soft, moist, and scrumptious—after standing, or if it is cold from the freezer, it is more firm and drier but still scrumptious.

8 ounces (1⅔ cups) blanched almonds
7 ounces (7 squares) unsweetened chocolate
½ pound (2 sticks) sweet butter
1 cup plus 1 tablespoon granulated sugar
4 eggs (graded large), separated
Optional: Confectioners sugar

Adjust rack one-third up from bottom of the oven and preheat oven to 300 degrees. Butter an 8- or 8½-inch spring form that is 2 or 2½ inches high. Line the bottom with a round of baking-pan liner paper or wax paper cut to fit, and butter the paper. (It is not necessary to flour or crumb the paper or the pan.) Set the pan aside.

The almonds and the chocolate have to be ground together to a fine powder. This may be done in a food processor, a blender, or a nut grinder. If you use a processor, chop the chocolate coarsely by hand first and then place all of the nuts and the chocolate in the processor bowl fitted with the steel blade and grind until the mixture is fine. If you use a blender, chop the chocolate coarsely by hand first and then grind the nuts and chocolate together, but only part at a time. Set the ground mixture aside.

In the large bowl of an electric mixer cream the butter. Add the sugar and beat to mix. Add the egg yolks all at once and beat to mix. Then add the ground nut and chocolate mixture and beat on low speed to mix. Remove from the mixer and set aside.

In the small bowl of the electric mixer with clean beaters beat the egg whites until they hold a rather firm shape—but not until they are stiff or dry.

The chocolate mixture will be stiff. Stir about one-quarter of the beaten whites into it, then fold in the remaining whites.

Turn into the prepared pan and smooth the top. Bake for 45 minutes.

Let the cake cool in the pan until it is tepid or until it reaches room temperature.

Remove the sides of the spring form. Then cover the cake with anything flat (a board, plate, or the bottom of a loose-bottomed quiche pan or cake pan), and invert. Remove the bottom of the pan and the paper lining.

Cover the bottom of the cake with another flat cake plate or a serving board and very gently and carefully invert again, leaving the cake right side up. Let stand at room temperature.

OPTIONAL: *The top may be sprinkled with confectioners sugar.*

Serve with vanilla ice cream or cold whipped cream—have plenty of the cream, the cake needs it.

WHIPPED CREAM

1 pint (2 cups) heavy cream
¼ cup strained confectioners sugar
1 teaspoon vanilla extract

In a chilled bowl with chilled beaters, whip the above ingredients until the cream thickens and holds a soft shape, like a sauce. If the cream is whipped

ahead of time and refrigerated it will separate slightly; just stir it a bit with a wire whisk before serving.

Spoon a generous amount of the cream alongside each portion.

NOTE: *Any brandied fruit may also be served with this, ice cream or whipped cream on one side and fruit on the other.*

Hungarian Rhapsody

12 PORTIONS

This is an important cake. It is a large three-layer, light-as-a-whisper, Hungarian walnut sponge cake (made without folding in beaten egg whites), filled and covered with a silky-smooth, dark, rich, rich chocolate buttercream that is divine. It has optional chopped walnut trim and buttercream rosettes which, if you do it all, results in a terrific-looking production (get your camera ready); and it tastes heavenly.

You will need an electric mixer on a stand for the long beating. And you need four racks for cooling three layers.

    1 ounce (1 square) unsweetened chocolate
    2 teaspoons dry powdered (not granular) instant espresso or other powdered instant coffee
    5 tablespoons fine, dry bread crumbs

    8 ounces (2¼ cups) walnuts
    7 eggs (graded large, or 6 if they are extra-large or jumbo, preferably at room temperature)
    Pinch of salt
    1 cup granulated sugar
    Optional: 3½ ounces (generous 1 cup) walnuts, cut into small pieces (to be used after the cake is iced)

Adjust two racks to divide the oven into thirds and preheat oven to 350 degrees. Butter three 9-inch round layer-cake pans, line the bottoms with baking-pan liner paper or wax paper cut to fit, butter the paper, dust with flour, invert pans over paper and tap lightly to shake out excess and set aside.

The chocolate and nuts must be ground to a fine powder. This may be done in a food processor, a blender, or a nut grinder. If you use a food processor or a blender, the chocolate should first be coarsely chopped.

If you are using a processor, fit it with the steel blade and place the chopped chocolate in the bowl. Process until it is fine. Then add the dry coffee, and bread crumbs and process until fine. Now add the nuts and process, but be careful not to overdo it; walnuts are oily and if you process too long they will turn to nut butter (stop the machine before the nuts become oily).

If you are using a blender, follow the same directions but it will have to be done in several batches instead of all at once.

If you are using a nut grinder, grind the chocolate, then the nuts, and mix them together in a bowl with the coffee and bread crumbs.

Set the mixture aside.

Place the whole eggs, salt, and sugar in the large bowl of an electric mixer. Beat at high speed for 15 minutes until the mixture is very pale and forms a wide ribbon when the beaters are raised.

Now, to add the ground dry ingredients without overbeating, use the lowest speed, add the dry ingredients gradually but not too slowly, and as you do, scrape the bottom of the bowl constantly with a rubber spatula. Beat for only 2 or 3 seconds. Then remove the bowl from the mixer and use the rubber spatula to finish folding the egg mixture and the dry ingredients together. Fold only until they are incorporated.

Divide the mixture among the prepared pans—if necessary tilt the pans gently to level the batters—and place in the oven, being sure that you do not place one pan directly over another.

Bake for 30 minutes until the tops barely spring back when lightly pressed with a fingertip (but the cake is so light, do not expect it to feel firm to the touch). The layers will rise and then shrink during baking.

Remove from the oven and immediately, with a small, sharp knife, carefully cut around the sides of the pans to release the layers. Cover each pan with a rack, invert, remove pan, cover with another rack and invert again, leaving the layers right side up to cool. Do not remove wax paper linings until the cakes are cool. Then peel the papers off carefully.

While the layers are cooling, prepare the buttercream.

HUNGARIAN CHOCOLATE BUTTERCREAM

12 ounces semisweet chocolate
¼ cup plus 2 tablespoons boiling water
1 teaspoon dry instant espresso or other dry instant coffee
1 cup granulated sugar
½ pound (2 sticks) sweet butter
5 egg yolks
1 tablespoon rum or Cognac

Coarsely chop the chocolate or break it into small pieces and set aside.

Remove the top of a large double boiler. Place the boiling water and the coffee in it and stir to dissolve, then stir in the sugar. Place over direct moder-

ate heat and stir with a wooden spatula until the sugar is dissolved and the mixture comes to a boil. Wash down the sides with a pastry brush dipped in cold water to remove any undissolved sugar granules. Boil without stirring for 1 minute.

Add the chocolate and immediately place over the bottom of the double boiler partially filled with hot water on moderate heat, and stir only until the chocolate is barely melted

Remove from the hot water and set aside, stirring frequently, until the chocolate cools to tepid, or warm.

Meanwhile, in the small bowl of the electric mixer, cream the butter.

Add the egg yolks one or two at a time, scraping the bowl and beating until smooth after each addition. Beat in the rum or Cognac.

When the chocolate is tepid, add it gradually (about ½ cup at a time) to the butter and egg mixture, scraping the bowl with a spatula and beating until smooth after each addition.

Now, if the buttercream is not too soft it may be used immediately. But if the chocolate was not cool enough when it was added, the buttercream may be too soft. If so, place it (in the bowl with the beaters) in the freezer or refrigerator. Chill briefly, stirring frequently, only until thickened but not firm. Then beat again until smooth and the consistency of thick mayonnaise.

To ice the cake: Cut four strips of wax paper and place them around the outer edges of a flat cake platter. Place one layer of the cake, upside down, on the platter, checking to be sure that the papers touch the cake all around.

If you have a cake-decorating turntable or a lazy Susan, place the cake platter on it.

If you are going to decorate the cake with a pastry bag, reserve about ½ cup of the buttercream. Spread some of the remaining buttercream about ¼ inch thick over the cake. Cover with another layer upside down and more buttercream. Cover with the top layer, placing it upside down.

Spread the rest all over the sides and then the top. (It may be spread smoothly or in swirls, but if you are going to decorate the cake, spread it smoothly, using a long, narrow metal spatula.)

The optional walnuts are for coating the sides of the cake. Hold a generous amount in the palm of your right hand, hold your hand very close to the cake, and turn your palm toward the cake, pressing the nuts gently into the sides of the buttercream. Some of the nuts will fall down onto the plate. That's O.K. After you have pressed them all around the cake, use a long, narrow metal spatula to pick up the nuts that fell and, with the spatula, press them into any empty spots.

If you are going to decorate the cake with the reserved buttercream, fit a small pastry bag with a medium-size star tube (about #4), fold back a deep cuff on the outside of the bag, place the bag in an upright jar or tall glass to support it, transfer the buttercream to the bag, then unfold the cuff and close the top of the bag.

Now, press out a circle of even rosettes touching one another all around the top rim of the cake.

Remove the four wax paper strips by gently pulling each one out toward a narrow end.

Gorgeous?

This cake may be served very soon or it may stand for several hours or overnight at room temperature. But it should not be served refrigerated; if it is refrigerated the buttercream becomes too firm. The cake should be served at room temperature. (However, if the room is extremely warm and you want to refrigerate the cake, remove it from the refrigerator long enough before serving for the buttercream to soften again.)

To make this way ahead of time for freezing: Freeze it (on the cake platter) before wrapping, then wrap securely with plastic wrap. To thaw, let it stand at room temperature for about an hour before removing the wrapping. If you have decorated it with buttercream rosettes, be very careful not to scar them as you remove the wrapping. Then let the cake stand several hours longer until completely thawed.

Brauner Kirschenkuchen Brown Cherry Cake

8 TO 10 PORTIONS

Wunderbar! *This is an old German classic recipe for a typically European torte: a single layer, not too sweet, extra-moist sour cherry nut cake made without flour. Not as "schokolade" as many other cakes in this collection. Best when it is very fresh.*

1 1-pound can red sour pitted cherries packed in water (approximately 1 ¾ cups cherries, drained)

3 ounces (3 squares) unsweetened chocolate

7½ ounces (1½ cups) almonds, blanched or unblanched

⅓ cup fine, dry bread crumbs

6 ounces (1½ sticks) sweet butter

¼ teaspoon almond extract

¾ cup granulated sugar

5 eggs (graded large, extra-large, or jumbo)

Pinch of salt

Confectioners sugar (to be used before serving)

Adjust rack one-third up from bottom of the oven and preheat oven to 350 degrees. Use a 9-inch cake pan that is 2 inches deep, or a 9-inch spring form either 2 or 3 inches deep (although the finished cake is only 1½ inches high, it rises slightly during baking and then settles down). Butter the pan, line it with baking-pan liner paper or wax paper cut to fit, butter the paper, and dust all over with fine, dry bread crumbs (these are in addition to those called for in the ingredients). Invert the pan over paper and tap lightly to shake out excess crumbs. Set the prepared pan aside.

Drain the cherries in a strainer (you will not use the liquid) and then spread them out in a single layer on several thicknesses of paper towels. Let stand.

The chocolate and the almonds must be ground to a fine powder. This may be done in a food processor fitted with a steel blade or in a blender or a nut grinder. If you use a processor or a blender, the

chocolate should be coarsely chopped first. If you are using a processor, place the chocolate, almonds, and bread crumbs in the bowl all together and process until fine. In a blender or nut grinder, grind the chocolate and then the almonds and stir them together with the bread crumbs. Set aside.

Cream the butter in the large bowl of an electric mixer. Add the almond extract. Reserve 2 table-spoons of the sugar and add the rest to the butter and beat to mix well.

Separate 3 of the eggs; place the whites in the small bowl of the electric mixer and set aside.

Add the 3 yolks all together to the creamed butter mixture and beat well. Then add the 2 whole eggs, one at a time, scraping the bowl with a rubber spatula and beating well after each addition.

On low speed mix in the dry ingredients. Remove from the mixer.

Add the salt to the 3 egg whites in the small bowl of the mixer. Use clean beaters and beat until the whites hold a soft shape. Reduce the speed to moderate and gradually add the reserved 2 tablespoons of sugar. Then increase the speed to high again and beat until the whites hold a definite shape but are not stiff or dry.

Stir 1 large spoonful of the whites into the chocolate mixture, then fold in one-third of the remaining whites, and then fold in all the rest.

Turn into the prepared pan and smooth the top.

Now place the drained cherries in a single layer all over the top of the batter.

Bake for 1 hour and 5 minutes, until the top springs back when lightly pressed with a fingertip and a cake tester or toothpick inserted into the middle comes out clean and dry. (During baking the cherries will partially sink into the top, leaving a bumpy surface.)

Let stand for about half an hour.

Cut around the sides to release (the cherries on the edge might stick). Then cover with a rack and invert, remove the pan and paper lining, cover with another rack and invert again, leaving the cake right side up to cool.

Serve at room temperature.

Before serving sprinkle confectioners sugar through a fine strainer over the top of the cake.

WHIPPED CREAM

This may be served plain or with whipped cream (my husband and many friends insist it must have cream).

This amount of cream is for 8 or more people.

2 cups heavy cream
⅓ cup strained confectioners sugar
3 to 4 tablespoons kirsch, or 1 teaspoon
vanilla extract

In a chilled bowl with chilled beaters, whip the above ingredients until the cream holds a soft shape. If you whip it ahead of time, refrigerate it, and then stir briefly with a small wire whisk just before serving (it separates a bit while it stands). Serve the cream separately and place a generous amount alongside each portion.

Torte Soufflé au Chocolat

12 TO 16 PORTIONS

Le Français is an extraordinary French restaurant in Wheeling, a suburb of Chicago. We were handed enormous menus, but before we had a chance to look at them a parade of food was presented at each table— incredibly elaborate displays on magnificent yard-long silver trays of almost every item on the menu. I couldn't see the forest for the trees. It was mind-boggling— more than I could cope with. I whispered to the maitre d' that I would appreciate it if he would please save some of each of the many chocolate desserts for me, and then I left the rest of the ordering to someone else.

After dinner, on a tour of the kitchen, I asked Jean Banchet, the chef-owner of Le Français, for the recipe for this cake, which he created and which is one of the restaurant's specialties. (I have adapted it slightly.)

It is a cake, of sorts, not a soufflé (not even light). It is compact, dense, moist, dark, bittersweet—a sophisticated and elegant dessert. When you remove it from the cake pan your heart might sink, as the cake does—but just wait until you taste it. And you can camouflage it with whipped cream and make it look as fabulous as it tastes.

This is not for children, it is for grown-up bittersweet-chocolate-lovers.

Make this early in the day or the day before but do not refrigerate it.

You will need a 10-inch spring-form pan.

4 ounces (4 squares) unsweetened chocolate
6 ounces semisweet chocolate
5 ounces (1¼ sticks) sweet butter, cut into
1-inch pieces
1 cup plus 1 tablespoon granulated sugar
7 eggs (graded large or extra-large), separated
⅓ cup Grand Marnier
Pinch of salt

Adjust rack one-third up from bottom of the oven and preheat oven to 300 degrees. You will need a 10-inch spring-form pan which must be at least 2½ inches deep, but it may be deeper. Butter the pan, line the bottom with a round of baking-pan liner paper or wax paper cut to fit, butter the paper, and dust all over with flour. Invert the pan over a piece of paper and tap lightly to shake out excess. Set the prepared pan aside.

Place both chocolates and the butter in the top of a large double boiler over hot water on moderate heat. Cover until partially melted, then uncover and stir until completely melted and smooth. Remove from the hot water and set aside, uncovered, to cool slightly.

Set aside ¼ cup of the sugar, then in the small bowl of an electric mixer beat the egg yolks with the remaining ¾ cup plus 1 tablespoon sugar. Beat at high speed for about 5 minutes until very pale and thick. On low speed gradually add the Grand Marnier, scraping the bowl with a rubber spatula and beating only until mixed. Then, still on low speed, add the tepid chocolate mixture and beat, scraping the bowl, only until mixed. Transfer to a large mixing bowl and set aside.

In the large bowl of the electric mixer, add the salt to the egg whites and, with clean beaters, beat until they hold soft peaks when the beaters are raised or when the whites are lifted with a rubber spatula. Reduce the speed and gradually add the reserved ¼ cup sugar. Then increase the speed and continue to beat only until the whites hold a definite shape—they must not be dry.

If you have a very large rubber spatula, use it now. Add about 1 cup of the whites to the chocolate and fold them in. Then, without being too thorough, fold in about 1 cup more. And then add all the remaining whites and fold in carefully only until the mixtures are blended.

Turn into the prepared pan. Rotate the pan briskly back and forth a bit to level the top.

Bake for 1 hour at 300 degrees, then reduce the temperature to 250 degrees and bake for an additional 30 minutes. (The cake will start to settle down after the temperature is reduced—it is O.K.) When the 30 minutes at 250 degrees are up (or a total baking time of 1½ hours), turn off the oven but do not remove the cake. Open the oven door only about 2 inches (prop it open with a pot holder if necessary) and let the cake cool completely in the oven with the heat off.

When the cake has reached room temperature remove it from the oven. Remove the sides of the pan. Cover the cake with a rack and invert. Then remove the bottom of the pan and the paper lining. Now gently place a large, flat cake plate or serving board on the cake and carefully invert plate and cake, leaving the cake right side up on the plate. The cake will be 1½ inches high.

Now, about camouflaging the cake. It should be served at room temperature—it has a softer and more delicate quality than if it is refrigerated. But if it is covered with whipped cream it will naturally have to be refrigerated.

That leaves two alternatives.

Either wait until just before serving to spread the cream over the top and sides of the cake. Or, if you don't expect most of the cake to be eaten at the first serving, cut the cake in the kitchen and place large spoonfuls of the cream alongside each portion.

Either way, you may also sprinkle the cream with a few candied violets or rose petals or a dainty sprinkling of shaved chocolate. (At Le Français the cake is served plain with just a sprinkling of confectioners sugar on the top, but I do think it tastes better with whipped cream.)

WHIPPED CREAM

2 cups heavy cream
½ cup strained confectioners sugar
1½ teaspoons vanilla extract

In a chilled bowl with chilled beaters, whip all the ingredients until the cream is stiff enough to be spread over the cake. Or, if it is to be served on the side, whip it a bit less so it has the consistency of a sauce.

The cream may be whipped ahead of time and refrigerated. If so, it will probably separate slightly. Just stir it a bit with a wire whisk before using.

Austrian Chocolate Walnut Torte

10 TO 12 PORTIONS

This is special! It is a huge (over 4 inches high) flourless chocolate nut sponge cake that is not too sweet and is served without icing . . . the cake itself is pure drama.

    7 ounces semisweet chocolate
    8 ounces (2¼ cups) walnuts
    12 eggs (graded large), separated (see Notes)
    1 cup granulated sugar
    ¼ teaspoon salt

Adjust rack one-third up from bottom of the oven and preheat oven to 350 degrees. You will need an angel-food cake pan that measures 10 inches across the top and 4¼ inches in depth. It must not be coated with Teflon. And it must be the kind that comes in two pieces, the bottom and tube being in one piece and the sides in another piece. Do not butter the pan.

Place the chocolate in the top of a small double boiler over hot water on moderate heat. Cover until the chocolate is partially melted, then uncover and stir until completely melted.

Remove the top of the double boiler and set it aside for the chocolate to cool slightly.

The nuts must be ground. This can be done in a nut grinder, a food processor, or a blender. In a food processor or a blender you must be careful not to grind the nuts until they become oily—they must stay dry. They do not have to be very finely powdered but they must be ground, not chopped. Uneven pieces, some a little larger, are O.K. (In a blender do only one-third or one-half at a time. In a processor you can do them all together.) Set the prepared nuts aside.

In the small bowl of an electric mixer beat the egg yolks with ½ cup (reserve ½ cup) of the sugar at high speed for 2 minutes. (Do not beat until the mixture becomes very thick.) On low speed mix in the chocolate (which may be warm but not hot). Then gradually add about half the nuts (reserve the remaining nuts). Remove the bowl from the mixer and set it aside.

Place the egg whites in the large bowl of the electric mixer and add the salt. With clean beaters, beat until the whites barely hold a soft shape. Reduce the speed to moderate and gradually add the reserved ½ cup of sugar. Then, at high speed, continue to beat until the whites hold a firm shape but not until they are stiff or dry.

With a rubber spatula fold one large spoonful of the whites into the chocolate mixture. Then fold in a second large spoonful.

Now transfer the chocolate mixture to a mixing bowl that is larger than the large bowl of the electric mixer. Add about one-third of the remaining whites. If you have an extra-large rubber spatula use it now. Slightly fold the two-mixtures together; do not be too thorough. Then add the remaining nuts and egg whites and fold them all together gently and carefully.

Turn the batter into the unbuttered 10-inch tube pan, handling it lightly in order not to lose the air that has been beaten into it. Smooth the top.

Bake for 1 hour and 15 minutes. During baking the top of the cake will rise in a dome shape, but it will flatten almost level with the top of the pan when done.

Remove the pan from the oven.

Now the pan has to be inverted to "hang" until the cake is cool. Even if the pan has three little legs for this purpose they don't really raise the cake enough. Turn the pan (with the cake) upside down and fit the tube of the inverted pan over a narrow-necked bottle (a 5-ounce Lea & Perrins Worcestershire Sauce bottle is a perfect fit) or place it over an inverted metal funnel.

Now, to remove the cake from the pan: You will need a small sharp knife with a *firm* (it must be firm) blade about 6 inches long. And you must be careful. Insert the blade at the inside of the pan between the cake and the pan, inserting the blade all the way down to the bottom of the pan and *pressing the blade firmly against the pan* in order not to cut into or to crush the sides of the cake. With a short up and down motion (something like using a saw) cut all the way around the cake, remembering to keep pressing the blade against the pan constantly as you cut. Then remove the cake from the sides of the pan by pulling up on the tube and/or by placing your hands under the bottom of the pan and pushing the bottom up. And then, carefully, again pressing the blade against the pan, cut the bottom of the cake away from the pan. Now cut around the tube of the pan.

Cover the cake with a flat serving plate and invert the plate and the cake. Remove the bottom of the pan.

I serve this wonderful cake just as it is. If you want to sprinkle the top with confectioners sugar, do it, leaving the cake upside down. Or make a design with strips of wax paper, sprinkle with confectioners sugar, and then remove the strips of paper (see page 7).

To serve the cake, use a serrated bread knife in order not to squash this extremely light creation.

NOTES: *1. If you do not have the right size eggs, you can use any size. What you want is 1⅔ cups of egg whites and a scant 1 cup of egg yolks.*

2. Because removing this cake from the pan is such a ticklish job, I have been asked, "Why don't you butter the pan?" The reason is that the cake is so light and airy that it must cling to the sides of the pan or it will flop.

3. To freeze this cake, do it before removing the cake from the pan. Just wrap it all airtight in the pan. Then thaw before removing the cake from the pan.

The Orient Express Chocolate Torte

12 PORTIONS

This was served on the Orient Express during its heyday when it was renowned for luxurious food and service. It is a wonderfully not-too-sweet flourless sponge cake made with ground almonds and ground chocolate that give it a speckled tweed-like appearance and a light, dry, crunchy texture—enhanced by a smooth, rich, chocolate buttercream filling and icing. It may be frozen iced.

3 ounces (3 squares) **unsweetened chocolate**
7½ ounces (1½ cups) **unblanched almonds**
5 eggs (graded large), separated, plus 2 egg
    yolks
¾ cup granulated sugar
Pinch of salt

Adjust rack one-third up from bottom of the oven and preheat oven to 300 degrees. Butter a 9 x 3-inch spring-form pan or a one-piece 9 x 2½- or 9 x 3-inch cake pan, line the bottom with baking-pan liner paper or wax paper cut to fit, butter the paper, dust all over with fine, dry bread crumbs, invert to shake out excess, and set the pan aside.

The chocolate and almonds must be finely ground. First chop the chocolate coarsely and then grind it with the almonds in a food processor fitted with the steel blade or grind in a blender. Or this may be ground in a nut grinder. Set aside.

Place the 7 egg yolks in the small bowl of an electric mixer. Add the sugar and beat until the yolks are pale lemon-colored but not until thick.

Add the ground chocolate and then the ground almonds and beat until mixed. Transfer to a larger mixing bowl.

Add the salt to the 5 egg whites and beat (with clean beaters) until they hold a definite shape but not until they are stiff or dry.

Add the beaten whites to the chocolate mixture and fold together only until incorporated.

Turn into the prepared pan and rotate a bit briskly first in one direction, then the other, to level the batter.

Bake for about 65 minutes until the top barely springs back when lightly pressed with a fingertip.

Remove from the oven and immediately, with a small, sharp knife, cut around the sides to release. Let the cake cool in the pan for 10 to 15 minutes.

Cover with a rack and invert cake pan and rack, remove the pan, peel off the paper slowly and carefully, cover with another rack and invert again, leaving the cake right side up to cool on the rack.

The cake will be cut to make two layers. (It is a delicate and fragile cake so if you freeze it first it will be easier to cut and safer to handle).

Meanwhile, prepare the buttercream.

BUTTERCREAM

This takes a lot of beating and some chilling and more beating to dissolve the sugar and achieve its silken, smooth texture.

3 ounces (¾ stick) sweet butter
½ teaspoon vanilla extract
½ cup granulated sugar
2 eggs (graded large)
3 ounces (3 squares) unsweetened chocolate

In the small bowl of an electric mixer cream the butter with the vanilla. Add the sugar and beat for 3 to 4 minutes. Add the eggs one at a time and beat at high speed for a few minutes after each addition.

Meanwhile, place the chocolate in the top of a small double boiler over hot water on moderate heat. Cover until partially melted, then uncover and stir until completely melted.

Add the warm melted chocolate to the buttercream and beat again for several minutes.

Now, place the bowl of buttercream and the beaters in the freezer or the refrigerator until the mixture is quite firm.

When you are ready to fill and ice the cake, prepare a cake plate by placing four strips of wax paper around the outer edges.

Using a serrated bread knife cut the cake horizontally to make two even layers.

Place the bottom layer of the cake, cut side up, on the plate, checking to see that the wax paper touches the cake all around. If you have a cake-decorating turntable or a lazy Susan, place the cake plate on it.

To finish the buttercream, remove it from the freezer or refrigerator and beat again for several minutes. It should be beaten until it is soft enough to spread easily, light in color, and as smooth as honey. Don't be afraid of overbeating now.

Spread about one-third of the buttercream over the bottom layer, cover with the top layer, placing it cut side down, and spread the remaining butter-cream smoothly over the sides and top.

Remove the wax paper strips by pulling each one out toward a narrow end.

Serve at room temperature.

NOTE: *When this was served on the Orient Express, the top was covered with toasted sliced almonds and confectioners sugar and the rim was decorated elaborately with mocha buttercream. I don't think it needs any decoration but it lends itself to almost anything you might like to design for it—chocolate leaves, cones, curls, etc. Or cover the top with chocolate shavings and sprinkle with confectioners sugar. Or form a circle of whole toasted blanched almonds around the rim.*

Petit Gâteau au Chocolat

6 PORTIONS

This is special! Small, dark, rich—a precious little gem. It should be made for a special occasion for few people. It is not too much for two or three, or it may be cut into eight small wedges.

You will need a 6-inch round spring-form pan. Generally they are 3 inches deep. The cake will be only 1½ inches deep, but if the pan is deeper it doesn't hurt. (There are 6-inch spring-form pans available at specialty kitchen equipment stores or wholesale bakery supply stores.)

The cake may be made early in the day or it may be made ahead of time and frozen, even with the icing.

4 ounces (4 squares) semisweet chocolate
½ cup granulated sugar
3 ounces (¾ stick) sweet butter, at room temperature
2 tablespoons sifted all-purpose flour (yes, only 2 tablespoons)
3 eggs (graded large), separated
Pinch of salt

Adjust rack one-third up from bottom of the oven and preheat oven to 350 degrees. Butter a 6-inch spring-form pan, line the bottom with a round of baking-pan liner paper or wax paper cut to fit, butter the paper, dust the pan and paper with flour. Invert the pan over a piece of paper and tap lightly to shake out excess flour. Set the prepared pan aside.

Place the chocolate in the top of a large double boiler over hot water on moderate heat. Cover until melted. Remove the top of the double boiler from the hot water and let stand, uncovered, for 2 or 3 minutes. Reserve 2 tablespoons of the sugar. Then add to the chocolate in the following order, the butter, the remaining sugar, the flour, and then the egg yolks, stirring after each addition until incorporated.

In the small bowl of an electric mixer add the salt to the egg whites and beat until the whites hold a soft shape. Gradually add the reserved 2 tablespoons of sugar and beat only until the whites hold a definite shape.

The chocolate mixture will be stiff. First add about ½ cup of the beaten whites and stir them in. Then gradually, in about four small additions, fold in the remaining whites, handling as little as possible.

Turn into the prepared pan and smooth the top.

Bake for 35 minutes. (The cake will seem soft but it will firm as it cools.)

Let the cake stand in the pan until it cools to tepid. Gently remove the sides of the spring form.

Cover with a rack and invert, remove the bottom of the pan and the paper, cover with another rack and invert again, leaving the cake right side up. Let stand until completely cool.

The glaze has to stand for about half an hour before it is used, so prepare it now or when the cake is completely cool.

Place four strips of wax paper around the edges of a small cake plate. Place the cake on the plate, right side up (the top will be slightly domed), checking to see that the wax papers touch the cake all around. If you have a cake-decorating turntable or a lazy Susan, place the cake plate on it.

FRENCH CHOCOLATE GLAZE

This is very dark, as smooth as velvet, and as shiny as satin.

3 ounces semisweet chocolate
2 tablespoons granulated sugar
2 tablespoons water
1 ounce (2 tablespoons) sweet butter, at room temperature
Optional: unsalted green pistachio nuts, chopped (to be used on top of the glaze)

Break up or coarsely chop the chocolate and place it in the top of a small double boiler. Add the sugar and water. Place over hot water on moderate heat. Stir occasionally until the chocolate is melted and the mixture is smooth. Remove from the hot water. Add the butter and stir until smooth.

Let stand at room temperature, stirring occasionally, until the mixture starts to thicken slightly—it will probably take half an hour or a bit longer. (If the glaze is used too soon it will be so thin that too much of it will run off the sides of the cake.)

When the glaze is slightly thickened, pour it slowly over the top of the cake. If it has thickened enough, and if you pour it slowly enough, it will cover the top of the cake in a smooth layer and just

a very little bit will run down the sides. Use a small metal spatula to smooth the sides (that should be a thinner layer than the top).

Remove the wax paper strips by pulling each one out toward a narrow end.

OPTIONAL: *Sprinkle the middle of the top with about 1 teaspoon of chopped, unsalted green pistachio nuts or decorate as you wish.*

Let the cake stand for at least an hour or two for the glaze to set slightly. (To freeze the cake after it is glazed, let it stand until the glaze is set, freeze it, and then wrap it. Thaw wrapped at room temperature.)

WHIPPED CREAM

1 cup heavy cream
¼ cup strained confectioners sugar
½ teaspoon vanilla extract

In a chilled bowl with chilled beaters, whip the above ingredients until the cream holds a shape. If the cream is whipped ahead of time and refrigerated, stir it briefly with a wire whisk before using.

Place a spoonful of the whipped cream alongside each portion of cake.

Chocolate Carrot Torte

12 PORTIONS

This is an elegant single layer European-type torte with a shiny chocolate glaze. Delicious! It has a moist, rather firm, and slightly coarse texture. No one will identify the carrots but they do make the cake moist and juicy.

4 ounces semisweet chocolate (see Note)

7½ ounces (1½ cups) almonds, blanched or unblanched

3 medium-size carrots (to make 1 cup grated, pressed firmly into the cup)

5 eggs (graded large or extra-large), separated

¾ cup granulated sugar

⅓ cup fine, dry bread crumbs

Optional: finely grated rind of 1 deep-colored orange

Pinch of salt

Adjust rack one-third up from bottom of the oven and preheat oven to 350 degrees. Butter a 9 x 2½- or 3-inch spring-form pan. Line the bottom with a round of wax paper or baking-pan liner paper cut to fit. Butter the paper. Dust the inside lightly with fine, dry bread crumbs (these crumbs are in addition to those called for in the recipe); invert over paper and tap lightly to shake out excess crumbs. Set the prepared pan aside.

Place the chocolate in the top of a small double boiler over hot water on moderate heat. Cover until partially melted, then uncover and stir until completely melted and smooth. Remove the top of the double boiler and set aside, uncovered, to cool.

The nuts must be ground to a fine powder. This may be done in a food processor, a blender, or a nut grinder. Set the ground nuts aside.

There is no need to peel the carrots. Just wash them well, cut off both ends, and grate fine on a standing metal grater. Set the grated carrots aside.

Place the egg yolks and ½ cup (reserve remaining ¼ cup) of the sugar in the small bowl of an electric mixer. Beat at high speed for 2 or 3 minutes until the yolks are pale lemon-colored and creamy. On low speed add the cooled chocolate and beat only to mix well. Remove from the mixer and transfer to a large mixing bowl. Stir in the bread crumbs, carrots, ground almonds, and optional orange rind.

Then, in the small bowl of the electric mixer (the bowl and beaters must be clean), add the salt to the egg whites and beat until they hold a very soft shape. On moderate speed gradually add the reserved ¼ cup sugar. Then beat briefly on high speed only until the whites hold a shape when a bit of them is lifted with a spatula—they must not be stiff or dry.

In four or five additions, small at first, add the beaten whites to the chocolate mixture. Gently fold them in. Don't handle any more than necessary; if a few bits of white remain on the surface, smooth over them with the rubber spatula to incorporate them without any more folding in than necessary.

Turn the batter into the prepared pan. Rotate the pan briskly back and forth just to level the top of the batter.

Bake for about 1 hour and 5 or 10 minutes until a cake tester gently inserted in the middle comes out clean, and the cake barely begins to come away from the sides of the pan.

Let the cake cool completely in the pan.

When cool, cut around the sides of the cake to release it, cover with a rack, invert the cake pan and the rack, and remove the pan and the paper lining. Cover with another rack and invert again, leaving the cake right side up.

The cooled cake will be a scant 2 inches high.

The cake is extremely fragile; in order to transfer it safely to a cake plate I recommend freezing the cake on the rack until it is firm enough to handle.

Place four strips of wax paper around the edges

of a cake plate to protect the plate while icing the cake (see page 18). Place the cake right side up on the cake plate and check to see that the wax paper touches the cake all around the bottom. With a pastry brush, brush away any loose crumbs from the sides of the cake and the plate.

If you have a turntable for icing cakes or a lazy Susan, place the cake plate on it.

CHOCOLATE ICING

6 ounces semisweet chocolate (see Note)
3 tablespoons butter, at room temperature
1 egg plus 1 egg yolk

Place the chocolate in the top of a small double boiler over hot water on moderate heat. Cover until partially melted, then uncover and stir until completely melted and smooth. Transfer the melted chocolate to the small bowl of an electric mixer. Let stand for a minute or two to cool slightly. Then add the butter, egg, and egg yolk and beat at low speed only until the mixture is smooth. Do not overbeat; additional beating will lighten the color and it is best if it stays dark.

The icing should be ready to use now, but if it is too thin let it stand at room temperature for about 10 minutes to thicken very slightly.

Pour the icing onto the top of the cake. With a long, narrow metal spatula smooth the top, spreading the icing to make a little bit (not much) run down the sides. Then with a small, narrow metal spatula smooth the icing on the sides—it should be a very thin layer on the sides, only enough to coat the cake but not enough to run down onto the plate.

Let stand at room temperature for at least a few hours (or overnight if you wish) before serving.

NOTE: *Any semisweet chocolate may be used. If you use bars, break them into pieces before melting; 1-ounce squares may be melted whole.*

Viennese Chocolate Almond Torte

10 to 12 PORTIONS

This is a single-layer cake 2½ inches high, with a thin, dark chocolate glaze. It is typically Viennese—chic, classy, and simple-looking. Made without flour, it is not as fine-textured as cakes made with flour. It is light, moist, and not too sweet.

It may be made the day before serving or the cake may be made well ahead of time, frozen, and then iced the day it is served. (If you freeze the cake, give it plenty of time to thaw, wrapped, at room temperature before icing it—see Note.)

4 ounces semisweet chocolate
8 ounces (1⅔ cups) almonds (they can be blanched or unblanched, whole, sliced, or slivered)
¼ cup plus 1 tablespoon fine, dry bread crumbs
1 tablespoon baking powder
¼ pound (1 stick) sweet butter
1 cup granulated sugar
6 eggs (graded large), separated
2 tablespoons whiskey, rum, bourbon or kirsch
Pinch of salt

Adjust rack one-third up from bottom of the oven and preheat oven to 375 degrees. Butter an 8 x 3-inch spring-form pan. Line the bottom of the pan with a round of baking-pan liner paper or wax paper cut to fit, and butter the paper. Dust the inside of the pan lightly with fine, dry bread crumbs, invert over paper and tap the pan lightly to shake out excess crumbs. (The crumbs for preparing the pan are in addition to those called for in the ingredients.)

The chocolate and the almonds must be ground to a fine powder. They may easily be done all together in a food processor (if you are using 1-ounce squares of chocolate they should first be chopped coarsely—bar chocolate should be broken into pieces). Or they may be ground in a blender, doing only part at a time. Or use a nut grinder.

In a medium-size mixing bowl mix the ground chocolate and almonds with the bread crumbs and baking powder, stirring until thoroughly mixed.

In the large bowl of an electric mixer cream the butter. Add ¾ cup of the sugar (reserve ¼ cup) and beat to mix. Add the egg yolks all at once and beat well, scraping the bowl with a rubber spatula, until very smooth. Add the whiskey, rum, bourbon, or kirsch and beat well for 2 to 3 minutes until light in color. Then on low speed add the chocolate-nut mixture and beat only until incorporated. Remove from the mixer.

In the small bowl of the mixer, add the salt to the egg whites and beat with clean beaters until they hold a soft shape. Reduce the speed to medium, gradually add the reserved ¼ cup sugar, increase the speed again and beat until the mixture holds a definite shape but is not stiff or dry.

The chocolate mixture will be rather thick; stir a large spoonful of the whites into the chocolate to lighten it a bit and then, in several additions, small at first, fold in the remaining whites.

Turn the batter into the prepared pan. Level the top by rotating the pan briskly back and forth a few times.

Bake for 60 to 65 minutes until a cake tester inserted in the middle comes out thoroughly dry.

Let the cake cool in the pan on a rack for about 20 minutes. Then with a thin, sharp knife carefully cut around the sides to release. Remove the sides of the pan. Cover the cake with a rack. Carefully invert the rack and the cake (it is safest to hold your right hand directly under the middle of the cake to keep it from slipping). Remove the bottom of the pan and the paper. Cover with another rack and invert again, leaving the cake right side up. Let stand until completely cool. (If you let it stand overnight or longer, or if you freeze it, wrap it in plastic wrap after it has cooled to room temperature.)

If the top of the cake is uneven use a long thin sharp knife to level it.

To ice the cake, cut four strips of wax paper and place them around the outer edges of a flat cake plate. Place the cake upside down on the plate, adjusting the paper strips so they touch the bottom of the cake all around. With a pastry brush, brush the sides of the cake to remove any loose crumbs.

If you have a cake-decorating turntable or a lazy Susan, place the cake plate on it. (Incidentally, it is best to ice the cake about 4 to 6 hours before serving, although a bit more or less really won't matter much.)

THIN CHOCOLATE GLAZE

4 ounces semisweet chocolate
1½ teaspoons dry instant coffee
¼ cup boiling water
2 tablespoons butter, at room temperature, cut into small pieces
¼ cup sifted confectioners sugar

Break or chop the chocolate into small pieces. Place it in a small, heavy saucepan over low heat or in the top of a small double boiler over hot water on moderate heat. Dissolve the coffee in the boiling water and pour it over the chocolate. Stir until the chocolate is melted and smooth. Remove from the heat. Add the butter and stir until smooth. Then add the sugar and stir until smooth (it must be smooth)—either stir with a wire whisk or press against any lumps with a rubber spatula, but do not beat.

Let the glaze stand for about 15 or 20 minutes until it is cool and very slightly thickened. Or refrigerate or stir over ice, but be careful not to let it thicken too much.

Once this glaze is on the cake it is important not to spread it or work over it any more than necessary. It will be beautifully shiny if you don't fool with it too much; the more you work over it the more of its shine it will lose.

Pour all the glaze over the top of the cake. With a long, narrow metal spatula spread the glaze so that just a very little bit of it runs down on the sides; there should be only enough to cover the sides with a very thin layer (if you have too much of it on the sides it will run off). With the spatula smooth the sides.

In Vienna this cake simply has a small sprinkling of chopped green pistachio nuts in the middle of the glaze. Or you could use a bit of crumbled toasted sliced almonds. Or nothing.

And, although it is wonderful just as it is, it is also wonderful with whipped cream served on the side.

The cake should be at room temperature when it is served.

NOTE: *The iced cake may be frozen if you don't mind the fact that the icing will lose its shine—I don't mind. If so, let the cake stand at room temperature long enough for the icing to set. Freeze the cake first and then wrap it. Thaw it, wrapped, at room temperature.*

Chocolate Almond Sponge Torte

6 PORTIONS

This is a small and classy dessert cake which will serve 4 to 6 people. Two chocolate almond sponge layers, made without flour, are filled and covered with chocolate buttercream; the top is coated with small chocolate curls. It may be made a few hours before serving or the day before (or it may be frozen with the icing and then thawed before serving).

5 ounces (I cup) whole blanched almonds
4 eggs (graded extra-large), separated
½ cup granulated sugar
2 tablespoons strained unsweetened cocoa powder (preferably Dutch process)
1 tablespoon rum or Cognac
½ teaspoon vanilla extract
¼ teaspoon almond extract
Pinch of salt

Adjust rack to center of the oven and preheat oven to 350 degrees. Butter two 8-inch round cake pans. Line the bottoms with rounds of wax paper, butter the paper, dust the insides lightly with flour, then invert and tap gently to remove excess flour.

The almonds must be ground into a fine powder; this can be done in a food processor, a blender, or a nut grinder. But they must be fine. Set them aside.

In the small bowl of an electric mixer beat the egg yolks and the sugar at high speed for 5 minutes. Add the cocoa, rum or Cognac, and vanilla and almond extracts and beat at low speed, scraping the bowl with a rubber spatula only until mixed. On low speed add the ground almonds and beat only until mixed. Remove from the mixer.

In a clean bowl with clean beaters add the salt to the egg whites and beat only until they hold a firm shape or are stiff but not dry.

The chocolate mixture will be stiff. Stir a large spoonful of the whites into the chocolate to lighten it a bit. Then, in three additions, fold the whites into the chocolate, handling lightly and as little as possible.

Place half of the mixture in each of the prepared pans. Smooth the layers.

Bake for 20 to 25 minutes or until the tops spring back when lightly pressed with a fingertip and the cakes begin to come away from the sides of the pans.

Remove from the oven. With a small, sharp knife cut around the sides to release. Cover a pan with a rack and invert the pan and the rack. Remove the pan, peel off the paper, cover with another rack, and invert again to cool right side up. Repeat with remaining layer.

Place four strips of wax paper around the sides of a cake plate to protect the plate while icing the cake. Place one layer right side up on the plate, checking to see that the wax paper touches the cake all around.

If you have a cake-decorating turntable or a lazy Susan, place the cake plate on it.

BUTTERCREAM

1 ounce (1 square) unsweetened chocolate
1 ounce semisweet chocolate
1 egg (graded extra-large)
⅓ cup confectioners sugar
1 teaspoon dry powdered instant coffee or espresso
3 ounces (¾ stick) sweet butter, at room temperature, cut into 8 pieces
½ teaspoon vanilla extract

Place both chocolates in the top of a small double boiler over hot water on moderate heat. Cover for a minute or so and then uncover and stir until melted and smooth. Remove from the hot water and set aside, uncovered, to cool.

In the small bowl of an electric mixer, beat the egg with the sugar and coffee for 5 minutes. Add the cooled chocolate and beat only to mix. Then add the butter, one piece at a time, and beat until smooth. Add the vanilla and continue to beat briefly until the mixture holds its shape enough to be spread on the cake—it will be the consistency of whipped cream.

Spread about one-third of the buttercream over the cake layer on the plate. Cover with the top layer, placing it upside down.

With a metal spatula cover the sides of the cake and then the top with the remaining buttercream. (If you are working on a cake-decorating turntable, spread the sides and the top smoothly. If not, the buttercream may be swirled.)

DECORATION: *With additional chocolate make small shavings (see page 263). With a spoon sprinkle them generously over the top of the cake. If you wish, sprinkle confectioners sugar over the shavings.*

Remove the wax paper strips by pulling each one out toward a narrow end.

Refrigerate the cake and serve it chilled.

Countess Toulouse-Lautrec's French Chocolate Cake

10 PORTIONS

Mapie, the Countess de Toulouse-Lautrec, wrote French cookbooks, food columns, magazine articles about food, and she was the directress of a cooking school for young ladies at Maxim's restaurant in Paris. She was married to an admiral in the French navy who belonged to the same family as the artist (the artist was her father-in-law's cousin). Incidentally, like most great artists, Toulouse-Lautrec was also a gourmet and a fine cook himself. The Countess introduced this recipe to America in an article for McCall's Magazine in 1959. Since then it has continued to grow in popularity under a variety of names and adaptations. (The "one tablespoon" measures of flour and sugar are correct.)

This cake is not a cake by American standards. It is rather like a rich, moist, dense cheesecake—like unadulterated and undiluted chocolate. It is best to make it a day before serving or at least 6 to 8 hours before, or make it way ahead of time and freeze it. (Thaw before serving.)

1 pound semisweet chocolate (see Note)
5 ounces (1¼ sticks) sweet butter, at room temperature
4 eggs (graded large or extra-large), separated
1 tablespoon <u>un</u>sifted all-purpose flour
Pinch of salt
1 tablespoon granulated sugar

Adjust rack one-third up from bottom of the oven and preheat oven to 425 degrees. Separate the bottom and the sides of an 8-inch spring-form pan. (The cake will be only 1½ inches high on the sides, so the pan may be shallow or deep—either is all right. Or you could use an 8-inch layer-cake pan that has a loose bottom.) Cut a round of baking-pan liner paper or wax paper to fit the bottom of the pan, and butter it on one side. Butter the sides (not the bottom) of the pan. Put the bottom of the pan in place, close the clamp on the side, and place the buttered paper in the pan, buttered side up. Set aside.

Break up or coarsely chop the chocolate and place it in the top of a large double boiler over hot water on moderate heat. Cover until partially melted, then uncover and stir with a rubber spatula until completely melted. Remove the top of the double boiler from the hot water.

Add about one-third of the butter at a time and stir it into the chocolate with the rubber spatula. Each addition of butter should be completely melted and incorporated before the next is added. Set aside to cool slightly.

In the small bowl of an electric mixer beat the egg yolks at high speed for 5 to 7 minutes until they are pale-colored and thick. Add the tablespoon of flour and beat on low speed for only a moment to incorporate the flour.

Add the beaten yolks to the chocolate (which may still be slightly warm but should not be hot) and fold and stir gently to mix.

In a clean, small bowl, with clean beaters, beat the egg whites and the salt until the whites hold a soft shape. Add the granulated sugar and continue to beat only until the whites hold a definite shape but not until they are stiff or dry. Fold about one-half of the beaten whites into the chocolate—do not be too thorough. Then fold the chocolate into the remaining whites, handling gently and folding only until both mixtures are blended.

Turn into the prepared pan. Rotate the pan a bit, first in one direction, then the other, to level the batter.

Bake for 15 minutes. The cake will be soft and you will think it is not done. But remove it from the oven. Do not throw the cake away now. You may think that is the only thing to do, but it is O.K. (However, it might be wise not to let anyone else see it now.) It will be only about an inch high in the middle, the rim will be higher than the middle, and the top will be cracked. Don't worry—it's O.K. Baking this cake longer will not prevent it from sinking.

With a small, sharp knife, carefully cut around the side of the hot cake, but do not remove the sides of the pan. Let the cake stand in the pan until it cools to room temperature. Then refrigerate it for at least several hours or overnight. The cake must be firm when it is removed from the pan.

To remove the cake, cut around the sides again with a small, sharp knife. Remove the sides of the pan. Cover the cake with a small cookie sheet or the bottom of a quiche pan or anything flat, and invert. Then carefully insert a narrow metal spatula or a table knife between the bottom of the pan and the paper lining; move it just enough to release the bottom of the pan. Remove the bottom and peel off the paper lining. Invert a serving plate over the cake and invert the plate and the cake, leaving the cake right side up.

The Countess serves the cake just as it is. But you have several alternatives. The most obvious is to cover the top generously (excluding the rim) with whipped cream. But if you do not plan to serve it all at once and you might want to freeze the leftovers, that is not the best plan. You can cover the top generously with large, loose, free-form Chocolate Shavings (see page 263) made with a vegetable peeler and a thick piece of milk chocolate. If you do that, sprinkle confectioners sugar over the top of the shavings. Or cover the top of the cake with a generous amount of fresh raspberries or strawberries or Chocolate-Covered Strawberries (see page 252), and, if you wish, pass soft whipped cream as a sauce. Or cover the top with peeled and sliced kiwi fruit and strawberries. Or cover the cake with whipped cream, cover the cream generously with chocolate shavings, and pass brandied cherries separately to be spooned alongside each portion. Or mound about two-thirds of the cream on top of the cake. Cover the cream generously with chocolate shavings, or dot it with candied violets or rose petals. Fit a pastry bag with a star-shaped tube and use the remaining cream to form a border of rosettes around the rim of the cake. One final option: Cut the top of the firm, chilled cake, removing the raised rim and making the top smooth. Then serve the cake upside down, either just as it is or with confectioners sugar on top.

WHIPPED CREAM

2 cups heavy cream
3 tablespoons confectioners sugar
1 teaspoon vanilla extract, or 2 tablespoons
   framboise or kirsch

In a chilled bowl with chilled beaters whip the above ingredients until they reach the stiffness you want, depending on how you will use the cream.

Serve the cake cold, in small portions—this is rich!

NOTE: *Many recipes for this cake specify Baker's German's Sweet chocolate. Jean Hewitt made a version of it for* The New York Times *and she used Maillard's Eagle Sweet chocolate. Sue Britt, the home economist for the Nestlé Company, used semisweet morsels. I have used them all and they were all good.*

Sponge Roll with Bittersweet Chocolate Filling and Icing

8 TO 10 SLICES

This recipe is from a little patisserie on the French Riviera. I asked the owner if I could watch him make éclairs and he said, "Certainly, come in at four o'clock tomorrow morning." I was there and for the first few hours I watched him make bread and croissants and brioche and kugelhopf and then I watched napoleons and palmiers and then fruit tarts and petits fours and layer cakes and—this delicate, extremely light sponge roll with bittersweet filling and icing. I didn't see a single éclair but I thanked him profusely, he gave me a little bag of petits fours, we shook hands and bid each other au revoir.

This is a lovely and elegant cake roll—very French. It can be made a few hours before serving or the day before or it can be frozen (thaw it wrapped). It is quite simple to make and great fun, beautifully professional looking—festive and delicious.

SPONGE LAYER

¼ cup granulated sugar
4 eggs (graded large), separated
3 tablespoons sifted all-purpose flour
Pinch of salt
About 3 tablespoons confectioners sugar (to be used after the cake is baked)

Adjust oven rack one-third up from bottom of the oven and preheat oven to 350 degrees. Butter a 15½ x 10½ x 1-inch jelly-roll pan. Line it all, bottom and sides, with one long piece of aluminum foil and butter the foil. Set the prepared pan aside.

In the small bowl of an electric mixer add 3 tablespoons of the sugar (reserve 1 tablespoon) to the egg yolks and beat at high speed for 5 to 7 minutes until the yolks are cream-colored (the French patisserie called it white). Add the flour and beat on low speed, scraping the bowl with a rubber spatula, only until incorporated. Remove from the mixer.

If you do not have another small bowl and an extra set of beaters for the mixer, transfer the yolk mixture to a second bowl and wash and dry the first bowl and the beaters. (Or beat the whites with an egg beater or a wire whisk.)

Add the salt to the whites in the small bowl of the electric mixer and beat until they increase in volume and begin to thicken. Gradually add the reserved 1 tablespoon sugar and continue to beat only until the whites hold a definite shape when the beaters are raised or when some of the whites are lifted with a spatula—they should not be beaten until stiff and dry.

Fold one-third of the whites into the yolks, then fold in a second third, and then the final third—do not handle any more than necessary.

Turn the batter into the prepared pan and gently spread it—it should be reasonably smooth and it will stay just where you put it, it will not run—check the corners. But don't waste any time before putting it into the oven.

Bake for about 18 minutes or until the top springs back when lightly pressed with a fingertip—it will be a pale golden color—do not overbake.

When the cake is done, sprinkle the confectioners sugar through a fine strainer generously over the top. Quickly cover the cake with a piece of wax paper several inches longer than the cake pan (the confectioners sugar will keep it from sticking). Cover the paper with a cookie sheet, invert the pan and cookie sheet (holding them firmly together), remove the pan, and quickly and carefully peel off the foil. Then quickly roll the cake and the wax paper together, rolling from a narrow end—don't squash the cake but roll firmly and compactly.

Let stand until cool.

The glaze may be made while the cake is baking or while it is cooling.

BITTERSWEET CHOCOLATE GLAZE

6 ounces semisweet chocolate

1 ounce (1 square) unsweetened chocolate

3 tablespoons prepared coffee (normal strength or stronger), or water

3 tablespoons sweet butter, at room temperature (or if cold, cut into small pieces)

2 tablespoons light or dark rum or Cognac

½ to 1 cup Chocolate Shavings (See page 263. To be used after the roll is iced—the shavings must be made ahead of time and ready to use before the icing hardens.)

Confectioners sugar (to be used after the cake is finished)

Place both chocolates and the coffee in a small, heavy saucepan over low heat. Stir frequently until the chocolate is melted and the mixture is smooth. Add the butter and stir until smooth. Remove from the heat and stir in the rum or Cognac.

If the glaze was made while the cake was baking, just set the glaze aside and let stand at room temperature.

When the cake is cool and ready to be filled and iced, place some ice and water in a mixing bowl that is large enough to hold the saucepan of glaze.

Place the pan of glaze in the ice water and stir constantly until the glaze thickens slightly—it should not harden but it should be thick enough so that it does not run out of the cake when the cake is rolled. (Lift the pan from the ice water occasionally and stir well to be sure it is not thickening too much on the bottom or sides.)

When it has thickened to the consistency of a very soft mayonnaise remove it from the ice water and work quickly as it will continue to thicken now.

Remove and reserve ⅓ cup, which will be used to cover the outside of the roll. Unroll the cake, loosen it from the wax paper, spread the glaze evenly to the edge on three sides of the cake—stop it a little short of the farther narrow end—then reroll the cake firmly. With a pastry brush, brush excess sugar off the top of the cake and, with a narrow metal spatula, spread the reserved glaze over the top and sides—then quickly, before the glaze hardens, with a spoon sprinkle the chocolate shavings over the top and as much of the sides as possible.

The cake roll should still be on the wax paper on one end of the cookie sheet; transfer it to the refrigerator for about half an hour or until the glaze is firm.

Then, through a small fine-mesh strainer, sprinkle confectioners sugar generously over the top.

With a wide metal spatula (or the flat side of a cookie sheet) transfer the cake to a serving platter and let stand at room temperature. It may stand all day or overnight. It should be served at room temperature unless the room is too warm, in which case it should be refrigerated as necessary—but it is best if the chocolate is not too firm.

Cut into 1- to 1¼-inch slices.

Layer Cakes with Filling and Icing

Sachertorte

8 TO 10 PORTIONS

This is unquestionably the most internationally famous of all chocolate cakes. According to one story it was created in 1832 by a Viennese cook named Eduard Sacher at the request of his employer, Prince Metternich, Imperial Chancellor of Austria. Sometime later Sacher built a hotel, the Hotel Sacher, which soon became Vienna's most distinguished hotel and his chocolate cake became world famous.

Demel's, the leading patisserie in Vienna (perhaps in the whole world), was as famous as the Hotel Sacher for its Sachertorte, and both claimed to be the originators of the cake. It turned into a heated argument that culminated in a lawsuit that went on for seven years. (It was a very sweet suit.)

Eventually the judges handed down a decision proclaiming the cake from the Hotel Sacher as the original, or "genuine." (Incidentally, Demel's later gained legal right to use the name "original Sachertorte.") The decision was based on the fact that at Demel's it is a one-layer cake with apricot jam on the top; at the Hotel Sacher the cake is sliced into two layers and the jam is put in the middle. There were witnesses who testified that the original was sliced in two.

The cakes otherwise are very similar. I ordered them both by mail a few years ago. (It seems I sent too much money, so they each sent me two cakes—all four arrived rather quickly in individual small wooden boxes and in very good condition.)

The story is that Prince Metternich asked Eduard for a "dense, solid, masculine" cake. And that is what it is, be it Demel's or Hotel Sacher's. It is unusual by our standards; it is a plain, dry, slightly heavy, not very sweet, shallow, dark chocolate cake with a chocolate glaze. It is served with mountains of whipped cream. I like it very much; so do innumerable people who eat it in Vienna or order it to be shipped all over the world. But I want to be sure that you understand what to expect before you make it. And I can tell you that if you do make it, it will be better than what you would get if you ordered it by mail from Vienna.

I would gather from many cookbooks that Anna Sacher, Eduard's cigar-smoking granddaughter, has been playing a game she must be enjoying tremendously; everyone claims to have the original recipe from Frau Sacher herself, and yet no two are alike. This recipe makes no claims to authenticity, but it is a combination of many of the different versions I have read.

It is best to make the cake a day ahead, wrap airtight and let it stand overnight, or freeze it for a longer time, but don't ice it until the day it is to be served.

6 ounces semisweet chocolate

6 ounces (1½ sticks) sweet butter

⅓ cup granulated sugar

5 eggs (graded large), separated, plus 1 extra egg white (The extra white may be one that was left over from some other recipe, frozen, and thawed.)

¾ cup sifted all-purpose flour

Pinch of salt

3 tablespoons apricot preserves (to be used after the cake is baked)

Adjust rack one-third up from bottom of the oven and preheat oven to 350 degrees. Butter an 8-inch spring-form pan, or an 8 x 1¾- or 2-inch layer-cake pan; line the bottom with wax paper cut to fit, butter the paper, dust with flour, invert over a piece of paper, and tap lightly to shake out excess. Set aside.

Place the chocolate in the top of a small double boiler over hot water on moderate heat. Cover until partially melted, then uncover and stir until completely melted and smooth. Set aside uncovered to cool slightly.

In the large bowl of an electric mixer, cream the butter. Beat in the sugar. Add the egg yolks (all at once is O.K.) and beat well, scraping the bowl with a rubber spatula. On low speed beat in the melted chocolate. Then add the flour and beat only until mixed. Remove from the mixer.

Add the salt to the 6 egg whites in the small bowl of the electric mixer. With clean beaters, beat until the whites hold a definite shape but not until they are stiff or dry.

Stir two large spoonfuls of the whites into the chocolate to lighten it a bit. Then fold in the remaining whites in four or five additions—the first three or four additions should be small and not too thorough. Incorporate about half the whites in these small additions. The last large addition should be folded in until no whites show, but no more.

Turn the mixture into the prepared pan and rotate the pan briskly first in one direction, then the other, to level the top. (In a layer pan that is 1¾ inches deep the batter will be only ¼ inch from the top of the pan—it is O.K.)

Bake for 45 to 50 minutes. The top will feel rather firm and will spring back when lightly pressed with a fingertip; a toothpick gently inserted in the middle will come out clean and dry.

Let the cake stand in the pan for 10 minutes. Then cover it with a rack, invert, remove the pan and the paper lining, cover with another rack and invert again, leaving the cake right side up. It will be 1½ inches high.

Let stand for several hours or preferably overnight or freeze it.

When you are ready to glaze the cake, prepare a flat cake plate by placing four strips of wax paper around the outer edges.

Place the cake upside down on the plate, checking to be sure that the papers touch it all around.

If you have a cake-decorating turntable or a lazy Susan, place the cake plate on it.

Strain the apricot preserves—they should be very smooth. Place them in a small pan over moderate heat and bring them to a boil.

Pour the boiling preserves over the cake and, with a long, narrow metal spatula, spread evenly over the top.

CHOCOLATE GLAZE

This will have an incredible mirrorlike sheen which neither the Hotel Sacher's nor Demel's had, but this glaze will not dry as hard as theirs, therefore this cake cannot be mailed as theirs can.

8 ounces semisweet chocolate
¼ cup light corn syrup
3 tablespoons water
2 tablespoons butter

If you use 1-ounce squares of chocolate, chop them coarsely; if you use bars, break them up; if you use morsels, use as is. Set the chocolate aside.

Place the syrup and water in a medium-size heavy saucepan. Cut the butter into small pieces and add them to the pan. Place over moderate heat and stir occasionally until the mixture comes to a full boil. Remove from the heat, immediately add the chocolate and stir until it has melted. With a small wire whisk, beat briskly until completely smooth.

Set aside, stirring occasionally, until the glaze reaches room temperature and begins to thicken slightly.

Now, hold everything for a minute. At Demel's they decorate the top with the name "Sacher" written in script with the same glaze. At the Hotel Sacher they top each portion with a chocolate seal imprinted with "Hotel Sacher Wien." If you want to write Sacher, reserve about 2 tablespoons of the glaze; just set it aside at room temperature.

Stir the remainder and pour it carefully onto the very middle of the cake. It will spread out and run to the edges. You do not want too much of it to run down the sides (but if it does, scoop it up with a metal spatula and replace it on the top). With a long, narrow metal spatula spread the top to make a smooth layer, being careful while you are spreading that you do not force much of it down the sides. The sides should be covered with a thin coating. When the top is smooth use a small, narrow metal spatula to smooth the sides.

If the glaze is still running off the sides (if you have used it too soon or if you have spread too much from the top over the edges) do not remove the wax paper strips now. Wait until it has stopped running, smooth the sides again if necessary, and then remove the wax paper strips by pulling each one out toward a narrow end.

If you are going to write "Sacher" on the top, let the cake stand for an hour or so for the glaze to set. It will not become dry or hard but it will set enough so the lettering does not run.

Prepare a small paper cone with baking-pan liner paper or wax paper (see page 266). With scissors cut off a tiny bit of the tip to make a very small opening.

Place the reserved glaze in the paper cone, close the top by folding it down. "Sacher" is traditionally written with a slanted script in lettering large enough to reach almost from one side of the cake to the other. Practice it on paper if you wish—you can scrape it up and reuse it. Write "Sacher" and if you have a steady hand, and if you would like the lettering to show up more, go over it a second time. Obviously, if you would like to write your own name or someone else's, do it—but since it is brown on brown it will not show up very much.

WHIPPED CREAM

Sachertorte is *always* served with a generous helping of whipped cream ("*schlag*" in Vienna)—it is an important part of this dessert. If you plan to serve the whole cake to eight or ten people, use the following amounts or more; if you are serving fewer people, cut the amounts in half.

> 2 cups heavy cream
> ¼ cup strained confectioners sugar
> ½ teaspoon vanilla extract

In a chilled bowl with chilled beaters, whip the above ingredients only until the cream holds a soft shape, not stiff. (If you prepare it ahead of time, refrigerate it. It will probably separate slightly; if so, stir it a bit with a wire whisk just before serving.)

Pass it, or serve it on the side of individual portions.

St. Louis Chocolate Layer Cake

12 PORTIONS

This is a prized heirloom recipe that has been kept secret for many years. It is a two-layer devil's food cake with a wonderful fluffy white marshmallow filling and icing. (Do not freeze this cake after it has been iced.)

1¾ cups sifted all-purpose flour

2 teaspoons baking powder

⅛ teaspoon salt

2 ounces (2 squares) unsweetened
   chocolate

⅓ cup water

6 ounces (1½ sticks) butter

1½ cups granulated sugar

3 eggs (graded large), separated

¾ cup milk

Adjust rack to center of the oven and preheat oven to 375 degrees. Butter two 9-inch round layer-cake pans and dust all over with flour, invert over paper and tap to shake out excess flour. Set the prepared pans aside.

Sift together the flour, baking powder, and salt and set aside.

Place the chocolate and water in a small saucepan over low heat and stir until the chocolate is melted and the mixture is smooth. Set aside to cool slightly.

In the large bowl of an electric mixer cream the butter. Add the sugar and beat well. Add the egg yolks all at once and beat, scraping the bowl with a rubber spatula, until well mixed. Add the chocolate and beat to mix.

On low speed add the sifted dry ingredients in three additions, alternating with the milk in two additions, scraping the bowl with the spatula and beating until smooth after each addition. Remove from the mixer and set aside.

In the small bowl of the electric mixer, with clean beaters, beat the egg whites until they hold a firm shape but are not dry.

Fold the whites into the chocolate mixture.

Divide between the two pans and smooth the tops.

Bake for 25 to 30 minutes until the tops barely spring back when lightly pressed with a fingertip. (The cakes are soft and will not spring back as sharply as most cakes do. Do not overbake or the cake will be dry.)

Let the layers cool in the pans for 10 to 15 minutes. Then, with a small, sharp knife, cut around the sides to release. Cover each layer with a rack, invert, remove pan, cover with another rack and invert again, leaving the layers right side up to cool on the racks. Cool completely.

Prepare a flat cake plate or serving board by placing four strips of wax paper around the outer edges.

These layers are tender and delicate and must be completely cool and handled with care. Place one layer upside down on the cake plate, checking to be sure that the wax paper touches the cake all around.

If you have a cake-decorating turntable or a lazy Susan, place the cake plate on it.

Prepare the icing.

MARSHMALLOW ICING

This is a perfect marshmallow-like filling or icing. You will love it. It will not form a crust if it stands for even a few days. You must use a candy thermometer.

1½ cups granulated sugar

⅔ teaspoon cream of tartar (see Note)

⅔ cup water

⅛ teaspoon salt

⅔ cup egg whites (from 4 to 5 eggs; you can use
   whites that have been left over from other
   recipes, frozen, and then thawed)

1¼ teaspoons vanilla extract

Place the sugar, cream of tartar, and water in a 6-cup saucepan (preferably one that is tall and narrow—in a wide one the mixture will be too low to reach the bulb of the candy thermometer). With a wooden spatula stir over moderate heat until the sugar is dissolved and the mixture begins to boil. Cover and let boil for 3 minutes. (This keeps the steam in the pot and dissolves any sugar crystals that cling to the sides. However, if you still see any granules when you remove the cover, dip a pastry brush in cold water and use it to wipe the sides.)

Uncover and insert a candy thermometer. Raise the heat to high and let boil without stirring until the thermometer registers 242 degrees.

Shortly before the sugar syrup is done (or when the thermometer registers about 236 degrees—softball stage) add the salt to the egg whites in the large bowl of an electric mixer. Beat until the whites are stiff. (If the sugar syrup is not ready, turn the beater to the lowest speed and let beat slowly until the syrup is ready. Or you can let the whites stand, but no longer than necessary.

When the syrup is ready (242 degrees—medium-ball stage), put the mixer on high speed and gradually add the syrup to the beaten whites in a thin stream. Then beat at high speed, scraping the bowl occasionally with a rubber spatula, for about 5 minutes or until the icing is quite thick and stiff. Mix in the vanilla. If necessary beat some more. The icing may still be warm when it is used.

Spread one-third of the icing over the bottom layer about ⅓ to ½ inch thick. Cover with the top layer, placing it right side up so that both layer bottoms meet in the middle.

With a long, narrow metal spatula spread the remaining icing around the sides and on the top and spread it smoothly. Or form it into loose swirls and high peaks—these will stay just where you put them. It is the most agreeable and cooperative icing I have ever used with a pastry bag. If you like to use a pastry bag, spread the icing more thinly and reserve a generous amount for decorating. Fit the bag with a large star-shaped tube and you will have great fun with rosettes and curlicues of all kinds.

Remove the wax paper strips by pulling each one out toward a narrow end.

Let the cake stand uncovered at room temperature for several hours before serving.

NOTE: *To measure ⅔ teaspoon, measure 1 teaspoon and, with a small metal spatula or a table knife, mark it into thirds. Then cut away one-third and return it to the box.*

Black Forest Cherry Torte

12 GENEROUS PORTIONS

QUESTION: *What is better than chocolate cake and whipped cream?*
ANSWER: *Chocolate cake and whipped cream with cherries and kirsch.*

This is adapted from a famous old classic Viennese recipe. It is named in honor of the Black Forest region of Germany because that is where kirsch (cherry brandy) comes from. It is huge, dramatic, extravagant, wunderbar! Make it for a big occasion and have your camera ready. The cake (which is a chocolate nut sponge cake), cherry filling, and kirsch syrup may all be prepared ahead of time, but it should be assembled and the whipped cream should be put on the day it is served.

You will need a 10 x 3-inch round cake pan or spring-form pan. And plenty of room in the refrigerator.

2½ ounces (½ cup) almonds, blanched or
　　unblanched
½ cup sifted all-purpose flour
⅓ cup unsweetened cocoa powder (preferably
　　Dutch process)
9 eggs (graded large)
1 tablespoon water
1 cup granulated sugar
¾ cup fine, dry bread crumbs
¼ teaspoon salt

Adjust rack one-third up from bottom of the
oven and preheat oven to 350 degrees. Butter a 10 x
3-inch round cake pan or spring-form pan, dust all
over with fine, dry bread crumbs (these are in addition to those called for in the ingredients), invert
over paper and tap lightly to shake out excess, and
set the prepared pan aside.

The almonds must be finely ground; this may be
done in a food processor, a blender, or a nut grinder.
Set the ground almonds aside.

Sift together the flour and cocoa and set aside.

Separate 8 of the eggs. Place the yolks, the 1
remaining whole egg, and the tablespoon of water in
the small bowl of an electric mixer. Beat at high
speed for 4 or 5 minutes until pale lemon-colored.
Reduce the speed and gradually add ¾ cup (reserve
¼ cup) of the sugar. Increase the speed to high again
and beat for a few minutes until the mixture forms a
wide ribbon when the beaters are raised (it will be a
pale creamy color).

On lowest speed add the ground almonds and the
bread crumbs, scraping the bowl with a rubber spatula
and beating only until incorporated. During the mixing, if the mixture fills the bowl too much and it looks
as though it might run over, transfer it to the large
bowl of the mixer. Now, in order to avoid spattering,
use the rubber spatula to fold in the sifted dry ingredients a bit, then beat briefly at lowest speed only until
everything is incorporated. Remove from the mixer.

Place the 8 egg whites and the salt in the large
bowl of the electric mixer. (If you do not have two
large bowls for your electric mixer, transfer the egg
yolk mixture to any other bowl. You will need a large
one for beating the egg whites.) With clean beaters
beat at high speed until the whites barely hold a soft
shape. Reduce the speed to moderate and gradually
add the reserved ¼ cup of sugar. Then increase the
speed again and beat until the whites hold a firm
shape but are not stiff or dry.

Add two or three large spoonfuls of the whites
to the chocolate mixture and stir to lighten the
chocolate a bit. Fold in two or three more spoonfuls.
Then add all of the chocolate to the whites and fold
only until blended.

Turn the mixture into the prepared pan and
briskly rotate the pan a bit first one way, then
another, to level the top.

Bake for 45 minutes or until the top springs
back when lightly pressed with a fingertip.

Immediately cut around the sides with a firm,
sharp knife to release the cake. Cover with a rack and
invert, remove the pan, cover with another rack and
invert again, leaving the cake right side up to cool.

If possible, chill the cake in the freezer for about
an hour to make it easier to slice into two layers.

CHERRY FILLING

This may be made several days ahead if you wish.

　　2 1-pound cans red sour pitted cherries
　　　　(water-packed)
　　¾ cup plus 2 tablespoons liquid drained from
　　　　the cherries
　　½ cup granulated sugar
　　2 tablespoons cornstarch
　　Few drops red food coloring
　　¼ teaspoon almond extract
　　Optional: additional kirsch (to be used when
　　　　assembling the cake)

Drain the cherries (you will have about
3½ cups of cherries), setting aside ¾ cup plus 2

tablespoons of the liquid—you will not need the remaining liquid.

Spread out the cherries on several thicknesses of paper towels to drain thoroughly.

In a small saucepan stir the sugar and cornstarch to mix thoroughly. Gradually add ¾ cup of the liquid, reserving the remaining 2 tablespoons. Stir constantly to keep the mixture smooth.

Place over moderate heat and stir gently with a rubber spatula until the mixture comes to a low boil. Reduce the heat slightly and barely simmer, stirring gently, for 5 minutes. Remove from the heat and gently stir in the food coloring and the almond extract.

Pour into a bowl, add the drained cherries, and stir. Let cool, then cover and refrigerate.

KIRSCH SYRUP

This may be made ahead of time if you wish.

2 tablespoons liquid reserved from the
drained cherries above (or water)
2 tablespoons granulated sugar
⅓ cup kirsch

Place the cherry liquid and the sugar in a small saucepan. Stir over moderate heat until the mixture comes to a boil. Let boil for 1 minute. Remove from the heat, stir in the kirsch, and let stand to cool.

WHIPPED CREAM

4 cups heavy cream
½ cup confectioners sugar
1½ teaspoons vanilla extract
⅓ cup kirsch

Before whipping the cream, chill the large bowl and the beaters of the electric mixer. (Or the cream may be whipped with a large wire whisk, in which case place the large mixing bowl in which you are whipping the cream in a larger bowl of ice and water.)

Place all the ingredients in the chilled bowl and beat (or whisk) until the cream is firm enough to use as filling and icing—it must hold a definite shape (watch it very carefully toward the end).

To assemble the cake: Prepare a large, flat cake plate by lining the sides with four strips of aluminum foil. (For this recipe it is better to use foil than wax paper because the kirsch syrup and the whipped cream might wet the paper and wet wax paper could tear.)

With a pastry brush, brush loose crumbs off the sides of the cake. Now the cake will be cut horizontally to make two layers. Mark a few spots on the sides of the cake with toothpicks to indicate the middle. If you have a cake-decorating turntable or a lazy Susan place the cake on it— it is easier to cut this large cake evenly if you can rotate it. And it is easier to cut with a long serrated bread knife. Carefully cut through the middle, making two even layers.

Place the bottom layer cut side up on the cake plate, checking to be sure that the aluminum foil strips touch the cake all around.

Brush the bottom layer with half of the kirsch syrup.

If the cherry filling has stiffened too much, stir in very little (1 to 2 teaspoons) of the additional kirsch.

Place all of the cherry filling on the cake, moving the cherries around to make an even layer—and keeping the cherries about ½ inch away from the edges.

Spread some of the whipped cream about ⅓ to ½ inch thick over the cherries.

Cover with the second layer of cake, placing it cut side down.

Brush the top with the remaining kirsch syrup.

Cover the top and sides of the cake with the remaining whipped cream. Or reserve about 2 cups of the cream for decorating. Spread the cream smooth.

If you have used all of the cream and are not going to decorate the cake, the cream may be smoothed or it may be shaped into swirls with the back of a spoon or with a rubber spatula.

If you have reserved some cream for decorating, fit a pastry bag with a large star-shaped tube (about #7 or #8), fold down a deep cuff on the outside of the bag, place the cream in the bag, unfold the cuff and twist the top of the bag closed. Form twelve large rosettes close to the edge of the cake. And one in the middle.

Although the traditional decoration for this cake is rococo, elaborate and busy, I think that just a few small shavings of chocolate sprinkled over each rosette is enough. And possibly a glacéed red cherry over the chocolate shavings on top of each rosette.

Remove the foil strips by pulling each one out toward a narrow end.

Refrigerate for the better part of a day. It should have time to mellow (it gets better), but whipped cream is not as light and delicious if it stands overnight.

New Orleans Chocolate Layer Cake

12 TO 14 GENEROUS PORTIONS

Recently my husband and I had dinner at a seafood restaurant in New Orleans. We struck up a conversation with a delightful couple at an adjoining table and were very flattered when they suggested cake and coffee at their house. The house was fabulous—it had been in the family for many generations. Ditto the cake— which it appeared they just happened to have on hand, although it looked like something for an important occasion (that is Southern hospitality). I was told that the recipe had never been given out before; here it is.

It is a large, dramatic two-layer dark-chocolate sour-cream cake with a thick layer of a creamy chocolate pudding-like filling and whipped cream icing.

It is best to fill and ice this cake the day it is served.

CAKE

4 ounces (4 squares) unsweetened chocolate
¼ pound (1 stick) sweet butter
½ cup sour cream
1½ teaspoons baking soda
2 cups granulated sugar
½ teaspoon vanilla extract
¼ teaspoon salt
2 eggs (graded large or extra-large)
2 cups sifted all-purpose flour
1 cup boiling water

Adjust rack to center of the oven and preheat oven to 350 degrees. Butter two 9-inch round layer-cake pans and line them with baking-pan liner paper or wax paper cut to fit. Butter the paper and dust the inside of the pan with flour, invert and tap to shake out excess. Set the pans aside.

Place the chocolate and butter in a small, heavy saucepan over low heat and stir frequently until melted and smooth.

When the chocolate is almost melted stir the sour cream and baking soda together in a small bowl and set aside.

When the chocolate and butter are melted transfer to the large bowl of an electric mixer. Add the sugar, vanilla, and salt and beat just to mix. Then add the eggs one at a time, beating until mixed after each addition. Mix in the sour cream and baking soda and then, on low speed, add the flour, scraping the bowl with a rubber spatula and beating only until smooth. Now, on the lowest speed, very gradually add the boiling water, scraping the bowl and beating only until smooth.

The mixture will be thin. Pour half of it into each of the prepared pans.

Bake for 25 to 28 minutes until the tops spring back lightly when gently pressed with a fingertip.

Cool the layers in the pans for 10 minutes. Then with a small, sharp knife cut around each layer to release. Cover with a rack, invert, remove pan and paper lining, cover with another rack and invert again to cool right side up.

(These layers might stick to the racks as they cool. After they have cooled for about 10 minutes on the racks, cover each layer with another rack, invert for a moment just to release, and then replace right side up to finish cooling.)

CHOCOLATE FILLING

2 cups milk
2 ounces (2 squares) unsweetened chocolate
1 tablespoon (1 envelope) unflavored gelatin
¼ cup cold water
⅓ cup sifted all-purpose flour
1 cup less 2 tablespoons granulated sugar
2 egg yolks
½ teaspoon vanilla extract
Pinch of salt

Scald the milk in a small, uncovered, heavy saucepan over moderate heat.

Meanwhile, place the chocolate in the top of a small double boiler, cover, and place over hot water on low heat to melt. When the chocolate is melted, remove it from the hot water and set aside uncovered.

Sprinkle the gelatin over the cold water in a small custard cup and let stand.

In the top of a large double boiler, off the heat, stir together the flour and sugar.

When the milk is scalded (when it has a slightly wrinkled skin on top) gradually add it to the flour and sugar mixture, stirring well to keep the mixture smooth. Place over hot water in the bottom of the double boiler on moderate heat. Stir constantly and scrape around the bottom and sides of the pot with a rubber spatula until the mixture thickens to the consistency of a thin cream sauce. Cook, stirring, for about 5 minutes more.

Stir the yolks lightly in a mixing bowl just to mix. Very gradually add about half of the hot milk mixture, stirring constantly, and then add the yolks to the remaining milk. Stir well and place over hot water again. Cook, stirring, for 2 minutes.

Remove from the heat. Add the softened gelatin and stir to melt the gelatin, then stir in the chocolate, vanilla, and salt. (If you wish, the mixture may be strained but it is not essential.)

Place some ice and water in a large bowl and place the pan of filling into the ice water. Stir occasionally at first until cool; then stir more frequently but gently until the filling is thick enough to spread—it should be like a very thick mayonnaise—it must be stiff enough not to run when it is spread on the cake.

While the filling is chilling prepare a large, flat cake plate or serving board by placing four strips of wax paper around the outer edges.

Place one layer upside down on the plate. Check to see that it is touching the paper all around.

If you have a cake-decorating turntable or a lazy Susan place the cake plate on it.

Spread the thick filling smoothly over the cake—do not spread it beyond the edges. It will be almost 1 inch thick. Then place the other layer right side up over the filling.

Refrigerate.

WHIPPED CREAM ICING

2 cups heavy cream
1/3 cup strained confectioners sugar
Scant 1 teaspoon vanilla extract

In the small bowl of the electric mixer (the bowl and beaters should be chilled), whip the above ingredients until they are thick enough to spread. (As a safety precaution against overwhipping it is a good idea to finish the whipping with a wire whisk.)

Spread the cream over the sides and then over the top—it will be a thick layer. It may be spread smooth or into swirls and peaks.

This does not need any decoration, but it is a perfect background for anything you might want to do—a ring of Chocolate Curls (see page 264) or Chocolate Cones (see page 266) or Chocolate Leaves (see page 264) around the top looks great.

Carefully remove the wax paper strips by pulling each one out toward a narrow end.

The cake should be refrigerated for at least an hour or so before serving; whipped cream is not as light and delicious if it stands overnight.

County-Fair Chocolate Layer Cake

12 GENEROUS PORTIONS

A dark and tender two-layer cocoa cake with a luscious dark chocolate filling and icing, that stays rather soft and creamy. It is over 4 inches high and is quite easy for such an impressive and delicious cake.

COCOA CAKE LAYERS

2 cups sifted cake flour
1 teaspoon baking soda
1/2 teaspoon salt
6 tablespoons strained unsweetened cocoa
    powder (preferably Dutch process)
1/4 pound (1 stick) sweet butter
1 teaspoon vanilla extract
1 1/4 cups granulated sugar
2 eggs (graded large)
1 cup milk

Adjust rack to center of the oven and preheat oven to 350 degrees. Butter two 8-inch round layer-cake pans, dust them with flour, invert and tap lightly to shake out excess, and then set aside.

Sift together the flour, baking soda, salt, and cocoa and set aside.

In the large bowl of an electric mixer cream the butter. Add the vanilla and then the sugar and beat well. Beat in the eggs one at a time, scraping the bowl with a rubber spatula and beating well after each addition.

On low speed add the sifted dry ingredients in three additions alternating with the milk in two additions. Scrape the bowl with the spatula and beat only until smooth after each addition.

Divide the batter between the prepared pans and spread smoothly.

Bake for 35 to 40 minutes until the layers just begin to come away from the sides of the pans.

Cool the layers in the pans for 5 to 6 minutes. Then, with a small, sharp knife cut around the sides to release. Cover each layer with a rack, invert, remove the pan, cover with another rack and invert again, leaving the layers right side up to finish cooling.

Prepare a flat cake plate or serving board by placing four strips of wax paper around the outer edges of the plate. Place one cooled cake layer upside down on the plate, checking to see that the papers touch the cake all around.

If you have a cake-decorating turntable or a lazy Susan, place the cake plate on it.

CHOCOLATE ICING

5 ounces (5 squares) unsweetened chocolate
1 cup heavy cream
1¼ cups granulated sugar
¼ pound (1 stick) sweet butter
1 teaspoon vanilla extract

Chop the chocolate into small pieces—it is all right for them to be uneven—and set aside. In a heavy 2½- to 3-quart saucepan stir the cream and sugar to mix. With a wooden or rubber spatula stir over moderate heat until the mixture comes to a boil. Then reduce the heat and let simmer for exactly 6 minutes.

Remove from the heat, add the chocolate, stir until it is melted, then add the butter and stir until it is melted. Add the vanilla and stir.

Partially fill a large bowl with ice and water. Place the saucepan of icing in the bowl of ice water and stir frequently until completely cool. Then stir constantly until the mixture begins to thicken.

When the icing begins to thicken remove it from the ice water and stir/beat briskly with a rubber or wooden spatula until it becomes smooth and thick enough to spread—or about like a very heavy mayonnaise. It should take only a few seconds or maybe a minute or so of stirring/beating. If the icing remains too soft return it to the ice water briefly, then remove and stir/beat again.

When the icing is thick enough, quickly spread it about ⅓ inch thick over the cake on the plate. Cover with the second layer, placing it right side up (both flat sides meet in the middle), pour the remaining icing over the cake, and with a long, narrow metal spatula spread it over the top and sides of the cake. If you wish, form large swirls on the top, using the spatula to indent the icing from the outer rim toward the center in a rather abstract daisy shape.

Remove the wax paper strips by pulling each one toward a narrow end.

Chocolate Buttermilk Layer Cake

12 to 16 Portions

This is a very impressive three-layer cake.

It looks like a county-fair prizewinner, or a glorious finale to a family get-together, or like "happiness" to a bunch of kids. It is a fine-grained sweet chocolate cake filled and covered with chocolate whipped cream. The cake may be made early in the day for that night, or it may be frozen, but the whipped cream should be put on the day it is served (at least several hours before serving).

6 ounces (1 cup) semisweet chocolate morsels
¼ cup water or prepared coffee
2 cups sifted all-purpose flour
I teaspoon baking soda
¼ teaspoon salt
6 ounces (1½ sticks) sweet butter
1 teaspoon vanilla extract
1¾ cups granulated sugar
3 eggs (graded large or extra-large)
1 cup buttermilk

Adjust two racks to divide the oven into thirds and preheat oven to 375 degrees. Butter three 9-inch round layer-cake pans. Line the bottoms with baking pan liner paper cut to fit. Butter the paper and dust lightly with fine, dry bread crumbs; invert the pans over a piece of paper and tap them lightly to shake out excess crumbs. Set the pans aside.

Place the chocolate and water or coffee in the top of a small double boiler over hot water on moderate heat and cover until the chocolate is partially melted. Then uncover and stir until completely melted and smooth. Remove the top of the double boiler and set aside uncovered to cool.

Sift together the flour, baking soda, and salt and set aside.

In the large bowl of an electric mixer cream the butter. Add the vanilla and then the sugar and beat to mix well. Add the eggs one at a time, scraping the bowl with a rubber spatula and beating until well mixed after each addition. (The mixture might look curdled—O.K.) Add the melted chocolate and stir until smooth. On low speed gradually add the sifted dry ingredients in three additions, alternating with the buttermilk in two additions. Scrape the bowl with the spatula and beat only until smooth after each addition.

Divide the batter evenly between the prepared pans and smooth the tops.

Place one pan on one rack and two on the other rack; do not place one directly above another.

Bake for about 25 minutes or until a toothpick gently inserted in the middle of the cake comes out clean and dry—the layer or layers on the upper rack will probably bake in less time than the layer or layers on the bottom rack, and a layer near the back might bake in less time than one near the front. So test each one carefully and do not overbake.

Let the layers stand in the pans for 10 to 15 minutes. Then with a small, sharp knife carefully cut around the sides to release. (During baking the layers will have formed a slight crust on the tops and when you cut around the sides some of that crust will flake off. It's O.K., just work near the sink where you won't mind a few crumbs.) Cover each pan with a rack, invert pan and rack, remove the pan and the paper lining, cover with another rack and invert again, leaving the layers right side up. Let stand until completely cool. (These layers have a tendency to stick to the racks as they cool; after about 5 minutes cover each layer with a rack and invert only to release the bottom of the cake from the rack and then replace it right side up.)

Prepare a flat cake plate by placing four strips of wax paper around the outer edges.

Handle the layers gently—they are fragile. A safety precaution is to chill them in the freezer until they are firm before handling them.

Place one layer upside down on the plate, checking to be sure that the wax papers touch the cake all around. If you have a cake-decorating turntable or a lazy Susan, place the cake plate on it.

Prepare the following Chocolate Whipped Cream.

CHOCOLATE WHIPPED CREAM

6 ounces (1 cup) semisweet chocolate morsels
¼ cup honey
2 tablespoons water
Pinch of salt
2 cups heavy cream
Optional: 1½ teaspoons dry powdered (not granular) instant coffee or espresso

Place the chocolate, honey, water, and salt in the top of a small double boiler over hot water on moderate heat. Cover until partially melted, then uncover and stir until completely melted and very smooth. Remove the top of the double boiler and set aside uncovered to cool to room temperature. Stir occasionally while the chocolate cools, and test the temperature often by dropping a bit of the chocolate on the inside of your wrist. (It must be completely cool—if the chocolate is warm it will deflate the whipped cream.) The chocolate mixture will thicken slightly as it cools.

In the small bowl of an electric mixer or in a large mixing bowl (the bowl and beaters should be chilled if the room is warm) add the optional powdered coffee to the cream and beat or whisk until the cream holds a definite shape.

Very gradually fold some of the whipped cream into the cooled chocolate—about three large spoonfuls, one at a time. That will thin the chocolate slightly. When the chocolate is thin enough to be folded into the whipped cream, transfer both mixtures to a large bowl and fold them together only until incorporated.

Use this to spread between the layers and over the top and sides of the cake, placing all the layers upside down—the layers of filling should not be too thick, make them about ⅓ to ½ inch thick, leaving enough for a generous topping. Before placing the cream on the top and sides of the cake, brush away any loose crumbs on the plate.

The top and sides may be spread smoothly or shaped into swirls and/or peaks.

The cake is so big and beautiful that it really does not need any decoration. However, if you wish, it lends itself to any of the chocolate decorations (see pages 262 through 267). The easiest, and it is attractive, is to sprinkle shaved chocolate generously over the top of the cake.

Remove the wax paper strips by gently pulling each one out toward a narrow end.

Refrigerate for several hours or all day; the whipped cream will thicken and stiffen slightly with refrigeration.

Use a large, sharp knife to serve.

Old-Fashioned Fudge Cake

12 TO 16 PORTIONS

An old recipe for a large two-layer cake—dark-colored, light-textured, and delicate, with a thick layer of bittersweet chocolate filling and icing that stays soft and creamy. This is a delicious cake, and easy. So easy, in fact, that after I recommended the recipe to a young girl as her first experience in cake baking, she not only proudly brought me a slice, but has started making it for friends and relatives. She is eleven years old.

3 ounces (3 squares) unsweetened chocolate
1¾ cups sifted cake flour
1 teaspoon baking powder

1 teaspoon baking soda

½ teaspoon salt

¼ pound (1 stick) sweet butter

1½ cups granulated sugar

2 eggs (graded large or extra-large)

2 tablespoons plus 1½ teaspoons white vinegar (see Note)

1 cup milk

Adjust rack to center of the oven and preheat oven to 350 degrees. Butter two 9-inch round layer-cake pans, line the bottoms with baking-pan liner paper or wax paper cut to fit, butter the paper, dust with flour, then invert over a piece of paper and tap lightly to shake out excess. Set aside.

Place the chocolate in the top of a small double boiler over hot water on moderate heat. Cover until partially melted, then uncover and stir until completely melted. Remove from the hot water and set aside, uncovered, to cool slightly.

Sift together the cake flour, baking powder, baking soda, and salt and set aside.

In the large bowl of an electric mixer cream the butter. Add the sugar and beat to mix well. Add the eggs one at a time, beating until the egg is thoroughly incorporated after each addition. Mix in the vinegar. The mixture will look curdled—it is O.K. Add the melted chocolate and beat only until smooth.

On low speed add the sifted dry ingredients in three additions, alternating with the milk in two additions. Scrape the bowl with a rubber spatula and beat only until smooth after each addition.

Place half of the mixture in each prepared pan and smooth the tops.

Bake for 35 to 40 minutes until the layers begin to come away from the sides of the pans and the tops spring back when lightly pressed with a fingertip.

Remove from the oven and, with a small, sharp knife, cut around the insides of the pans to release. Then let the layers stand in the pans for 5 minutes.

Cover each layer with a rack, invert, remove the pan, peel off the paper lining, cover with another rack and invert again, leaving the layer right side up to cool.

Prepare a large, flat cake plate by lining the sides with four strips of wax paper. Place one layer upside down on the plate, checking to be sure that the papers touch the layer all around. If you have a cake-decorating turntable or a lazy Susan, place the plate on it. Prepare the icing.

WHIPPED CHOCOLATE ICING

6 ounces (6 squares) unsweetened chocolate

¼ pound (1 stick) sweet butter

2¼ cups confectioners sugar

2 eggs (graded large or extra-large)

3 tablespoons hot water

½ teaspoon vanilla extract

Place the chocolate and the butter in the top of a small double boiler over hot water on moderate heat. Cover until partially melted, then uncover and stir until completely melted.

Meanwhile, place all the remaining ingredients in the small bowl of an electric mixer. Beat briefly only to mix. Set the small bowl in a large bowl and fill the empty space left in the large bowl with ice and water, filling to about three-quarters the depth of the large bowl. (If you are using an electric mixer on a stand, use the large mixer bowl for the ice and water but adjust the stand for "small bowl.")

Add the melted chocolate and butter, and beat until the mixture thickens slightly. Remove both bowls (together) from the mixer. With a rubber spatula stir the icing over the ice and water until it thickens to the consistency of thick mayonnaise.

Spread a scant third of it about ¼ inch thick over the bottom layer of cake. Cover with the other layer, placing it right side up (both bottoms meet in the middle). Spread the sides and the top with the remaining icing. It may either be spread smoothly with a long, narrow metal spatula, or it may be formed into swirls.

Remove the strips of wax paper by gently pulling each one out toward a narrow end.

NOTE: *Although I told an eleven-year-old to do the following when measuring the vinegar, it is advisable for everyone. I do it myself. Pour it out into a small cup first, then scoop it out with the measuring spoon. If you pour a clear liquid into a measuring spoon held over the mixing bowl, it is easily possible to splash in more than you mean to.*

F.B.I. Chocolate Layer Cake

10 TO 12 PORTIONS

When J. Edgar Hoover came to dinner at my parents' home this is the cake my mother served for dessert. Mr. Hoover liked it so much he threatened an F.B.I. investigation if he didn't get the recipe. I was assigned to deliver it by hand the following morning.

It is two dark and delicious chocolate layers quite easy to make, filled and covered with whipped cream.

1¾ cups sifted all-purpose flour
1 teaspoon baking powder
½ teaspoon baking soda
¼ teaspoon salt
½ cup unsweetened cocoa powder (preferably Dutch process)
¼ pound (1 stick) sweet butter
1 teaspoon vanilla extract
1¾ cups granulated sugar
4 eggs (graded large or extra-large), separated
1¼ cups milk

My mother made this, as I do, in two 10-inch layer-cake pans. They are not generally available at hardware stores but they are at specialty kitchen equipment shops, and they do make a beautiful cake. If you do not have that size it may be made in two 9-inch pans.

If you are using 10-inch pans, adjust two racks to divide the oven into thirds: For 9-inch pans adjust one rack to the center of the oven; preheat oven to 325 degrees. Butter the pans, line the bottoms with baking-pan liner paper or wax paper cut to fit, butter the paper, dust all over with flour, invert and tap lightly to shake out excess. Set the prepared pans aside.

Sift together the flour, baking powder, baking soda, salt, and cocoa and set aside.

In the large bowl of an electric mixer cream the butter. Add the vanilla and sugar and beat to mix well. Add the egg yolks and beat to mix well. On low speed add the dry ingredients in three additions, alternating with the milk in two additions. (Use a small amount for the first dry addition.) Add the milk very gradually, scraping the bowl with a rubber spatula while adding, and beat only until each addition is incorporated. Remove from the mixer.

In a small, clean bowl with clean beaters beat the egg whites until they hold a definite shape but not until they are stiff or dry.

Add the whites to the chocolate mixture and fold together only until they are incorporated.

Pour half of the batter into each of the prepared pans and smooth the tops.

If you have used 10-inch pans, place one pan on each rack, staggering the pans so one is not directly over the other. If you have used 9-inch pans, they may both fit on the one rack in the center. (However, if your oven is small, you may have to use two racks even for 9-inch pans.)

Bake until the layers begin to come away from the sides of the pans; it will take about 45 minutes in 10-inch pans, a little longer in 9-inch pans.

As soon as the layers are removed from the oven, with a small, sharp knife cut around the sides to release. Let stand for 4 or 5 minutes, then cover each layer with a rack, invert, remove pan and paper lining, cover with another rack and invert again, leaving the layers right side up to cool.

Prepare a large, flat plate by placing four strips of wax paper around the outer edges. Place one layer upside down on the plate, checking to be sure that the papers touch it all around.

If you have a cake-decorating turntable or a lazy Susan, place the cake plate on it.

Prepare the whipped cream.

WHIPPED CREAM

2 cups heavy cream
1 teaspoon vanilla extract
¼ cup strained confectioners sugar
Optional: about 4 ounces (1 cup), or more,
   almonds, thinly sliced

In a large, chilled bowl with chilled beaters, whip the above ingredients until the cream is firm enough to hold its shape.

Spread about one-third of the cream about ½ inch thick over the layer on the plate. Carefully place the other layer right side up (the two flat sides meet in the middle) on the whipped cream. Spread the remaining cream over the sides and top of the cake; it may be spread smoothly or lifted into swirls and peaks.

This does not need any decoration but it lends itself to whatever. It is especially attractive and delicious if the cream is spread smooth and the sides are coated with toasted sliced almonds as follows.

To toast the almonds: Place about 1 cup of thinly sliced almonds in a shallow pan in a 350-degree oven and stir occasionally for 10 minutes or so until the almonds are golden brown. Cool completely.

Place a few spoonfuls of the almonds in the palm of your hand; turn your hand close to the sides of the cake, leaving the almonds on the whipped cream. Many of them will fall down onto the plate—O.K. They may be lifted with a small metal spatula or a table knife and replaced on the cream.

Or use more almonds and sprinkle them on the top, too.

Remove the four strips of wax paper by pulling each one out toward a narrow end.

Refrigerate for a few hours before serving.

NOTE: *My mother always used the almonds, and she either made the following strawberry version or served strawberries on the side. The strawberries, if they were served on the side, were sliced thick and sprinkled with just a bit of granulated sugar and kirsch. (The strawberries should be prepared about an hour or so before serving to absorb the flavors and give off a bit of their juice.)*

Strawberry Chocolate Layer Cake

This is a variation of the F.B.I. cake.

Quickly wash and then hull 1 or 2 pints of strawberries and drain them thoroughly on paper towels. Reserve the largest berries for the top of the cake. For the filling, cut some berries in halves or quarters if they are very large. Press them down into the filling; if necessary, cover with a bit more cream so they are barely covered. Place the reserved large berries, pointed ends up, in the whipped cream, either in a circle around the rim of the cake or all over the top.

Cocoa Sponge Cake

12 TO 16 PORTIONS

This recipe is not for beginners. It makes a large and impressive, dark and delicious, three-layer sponge cake (it is baked in one large pan and then sliced into layers), filled and covered with a rich and extravagant chocolate buttercream. It may be made that day or the day before, but it must be refrigerated for several hours before serving. It may be frozen before or after it is iced—if it is frozen after it is iced, it should be thawed for several hours or overnight in the refrigerator before it is unwrapped.

You will need a 10 x 3- or 10 x 3½-inch round cake pan or spring-form pan. The pan cannot be shallower than that or the cake will run over. The cake itself, before it is sliced into layers, is a generous 3 inches deep.

1 cup sifted all-purpose flour

⅔ cup strained unsweetened cocoa powder (preferably Dutch process)

8 eggs (graded large), separated, plus 4 egg whites (you will use 4 yolks for the buttercream)

2 cups granulated sugar

1 teaspoon vanilla extract

¼ teaspoon salt

1 teaspoon cream of tartar

Adjust rack one-third up from the bottom of the oven and preheat oven to 325 degrees. Butter a 10 x 3- or 10 x 3½-inch spring-form pan. Line the bottom with a round of baking-pan liner paper or wax paper cut to fit, butter the paper, and dust the inside of the pan with flour. Invert over a piece of paper and tap lightly to shake out excess flour. Set the pan aside.

Sift together the flour and the cocoa and set aside.

In the small bowl of an electric mixer beat the egg yolks with 1 cup (reserve 1 cup) of the sugar at high speed for only a minute or two. Mix in the vanilla. Transfer the mixture to the large bowl of the mixer. On low speed gradually add the sifted dry ingredients, scraping the bowl with a rubber spatula and beating only until mixed. The mixture will be very thick. Scrape the beaters and remove from the mixer. (You will need the large bowl now for the egg whites; if you do not have an extra one, transfer the chocolate mixture to any large mixing bowl.)

Place the 12 egg whites in a large, clean electric-mixer bowl. Add the salt. With clean beaters start to beat until the whites are foamy. Add the cream of tartar through a fine strainer and beat at high speed until the whites hold soft peaks. Reduce the speed slightly and gradually add the reserved 1 cup sugar. Then, on high speed again, continue to beat until the whites hold firm peaks or are stiff but not dry.

The next step will be a bit of a challenge. The chocolate mixture will probably be stiffer than any you have ever had to fold beaten whites into. So here's how. Use a wooden spatula. Add about ½ cup of the whites and stir them in. (Use a rubber spatula occasionally to scrape the heavy chocolate off the wooden spatula.) When the whites are incorporated, stir in another ½ cup of the whites. Repeat this step four or five times altogether, stirring in about 2 to 2½ cups of the whites in order to thin the chocolate gradually until it is thin enough for the rest of the whites to be folded in.

Now change to a rubber spatula and, in three or four additions, fold in the remaining whites. (The trick is to thin the chocolate gradually or you will wind up with a lumpy batter.)

Gently pour the batter into the prepared pan. Bake for 1 hour and 30 to 40 minutes until the center of the top springs back sharply when lightly pressed with a fingertip and the cake comes away from the sides of the pan.

Let the cake cool in the pan for about 20 minutes. Then cover it with a rack, invert pan and rack, remove the pan and the paper lining. (If the cake sticks, let it stand upright for about 5 minutes more and then invert again—when it is ready it will come out easily.) Cover with another rack and invert again, leaving the cake right side up. Let stand until completely cool, or overnight if you wish.

If the top of the cake is very uneven it may be cut level (if it sinks much in the middle, you *should* cut the top to make it smooth), but the cake may be iced with either side up, and the icing will hide minor irregularities. Use a long serrated bread knife and carefully cut the cake into three layers.

Place four strips of wax paper around the outer sides of a large flat cake plate. Place the bottom layer on the plate checking to see that the wax paper touches the cake all around.

If you have a cake-decorating turntable or a lazy Susan, place the cake plate on it.

Prepare the following buttercream.

CHOCOLATE BUTTERCREAM

8 ounces semisweet chocolate
1 tablespoon dry instant coffee
2 tablespoons boiling water
4 egg yolks
2 cups strained confectioners sugar
Pinch of salt
12 ounces (3 sticks) sweet butter, at room
    temperature

Break up the chocolate and place it in the top of a small double boiler over hot water on moderate heat. Cover until partially melted, then uncover and stir until smooth. Remove the top of the double boiler and set aside uncovered to cool.

Dissolve the coffee in the boiling water and set aside.

In the small bowl of an electric mixer beat the egg yolks with the sugar and the salt for 4 or 5 minutes at high speed, it will be very pale and thick. On low speed gradually add the dissolved coffee and then the chocolate, scraping the bowl with a rubber spatula and beating until smooth. Add the butter about 2 tablespoons at a time, beating until smooth after each addition. Then beat until the color lightens.

With a long, narrow metal spatula spread the buttercream about ¼ inch thick between the layers and then spread it over the sides and top. It may be spread smooth or swirled into peaks.

Or some of it may be used with a pastry bag fitted with a star-shaped tube to decorate the cake. Or the cake may be decorated, if you wish, with any of the chocolate decorations (see pages 262 through 267).

Remove the wax paper strips by slowly pulling each one out toward a narrow end.

Refrigerate for at least a few hours or overnight.

Gâteau au Chocolat

10 PORTIONS

This is a dark, bittersweet chocolate sponge cake made in two thin layers with a rich, pale chocolate buttercream filling and icing. It may be decorated to look fancy and professional—or it may be left quite plain. It may be made just a few hours before serving or it may be refrigerated overnight.

CHOCOLATE SPONGE LAYERS

½ cup sifted all-purpose flour
½ teaspoon baking powder
⅓ cup strained unsweetened cocoa powder
  (preferably Dutch process)
7 eggs (graded large)
⅓ cup strained confectioners sugar
1 teaspoon vanilla extract
Generous pinch of salt

Adjust rack to the center of the oven and preheat oven to 350 degrees. Butter two 9-inch round layer-cake pans. Line the bottoms with baking-pan liner paper or wax paper cut to fit. Butter the paper and dust the sides of the pans with flour, invert and tap lightly to shake out excess. Set the pans aside.

Sift together the flour, baking powder, and cocoa and set aside.

Separate 6 of the eggs; leave 1 whole.

In the small bowl of an electric mixer add the confectioners sugar to the egg yolks and beat just to mix, then scrape the sides with a rubber spatula to incorporate all the sugar and beat at high speed for 2 minutes—no longer. On low speed gradually add the sifted dry ingredients, scraping the bowl with the spatula and beating only until mixed. Add the vanilla and the 1 whole egg and beat only to mix. Remove from the mixer. (Scrape the mixture thoroughly off the beaters using your index finger.)

In a clean bowl (the small-size bowl of the electric mixer is large enough) with clean beaters beat the egg whites with the salt until they hold a definite shape, but they must not be stiff or dry.

One at a time, fold three large spoonfuls of the whites into the chocolate mixture. Transfer the chocolate to a larger bowl. Then fold in about one-quarter of the remaining whites. (The whites will have dried a bit while standing—whisk them briefly with a wire whisk; it will soften them and make them creamier.) Fold in the remaining whites.

Place half of the mixture in each of the prepared pans and level the tops with the spatula.

Bake for 12 to 13 minutes (that's all it takes) until a toothpick inserted in the middle comes out clean.

Cool in the pans for 2 or 3 minutes. With a small, sharp knife cut around the sides to release.

Cover each pan with a rack and invert. Quickly remove the pan and the paper lining, cover with another rack and invert again. (These should not be left standing upside down on a rack or they will stick to it.) Let stand until cool. The layers will be ¾ inch thick.

Prepare the following rum syrup and the buttercream.

RUM SYRUP

⅓ cup water
2 tablespoons granulated sugar
1½ teaspoons dry instant coffee
3 tablespoons light rum

In a small saucepan stir the water and sugar over high heat until the sugar dissolves and the mixture comes to a boil. Remove from the heat, stir in the coffee and rum, and set aside.

CHOCOLATE BUTTERCREAM

4 ounces semisweet chocolate
½ pound (2 sticks) sweet butter
½ teaspoon vanilla extract
2 tablespoons light rum
2 egg yolks

Break up the chocolate and place it in the top of a small double boiler over hot water on moderate heat. Cover until partially melted, then uncover and stir until smooth. Remove from the hot water and set aside uncovered to cool slightly.

In the small bowl of an electric mixer cream the butter. Mix in the vanilla, rum, and the melted chocolate. Then add the yolks one at a time, beating well after each addition. Now beat at high speed for a minute or two until the color lightens to a pale caramel shade and the mixture is very smooth and light.

Prepare a cake plate by placing four strips of wax paper around the outer edges. Place one cake layer upside down on the cake plate, checking to be sure that the papers touch the layer all around.

If you have a cake-decorating turntable or a lazy Susan, place the cake plate on it.

With a pastry brush, brush half of the prepared Rum Syrup over the cake on the plate (the cake will absorb it quickly).

Spread the buttercream about ¼ inch thick over the layer. Cover with the other layer right side up and brush with the remaining syrup.

If you plan to decorate the cake, reserve a scant ½ cup of the buttercream. If not, use it all. Spread the buttercream over the sides and then the top of the cake; with a small, narrow metal spatula smooth the sides and, with a long spatula, smooth the top.

OPTIONAL: *Cover the top of the cake with a scant ½ cup of small Chocolate Shavings (see page 263), sprinkling them less densely toward the edges of the cake, and leaving about ½ to ¾ inch unsprinkled around the very edge—the buttercream rosettes will not stick to shavings.*

Fit a 10-inch pastry bag with a #3 (small) star tube. Fold down a deep cuff on the outside of the bag, place the reserved buttercream in the bag, unfold the cuff, and twist the top of the bag closed.

Press out the buttercream to form a border of small rosettes touching one another around the top rim of the cake.

Remove the wax paper strips by pulling each one out toward a narrow end.

Refrigerate for at least a few hours. But do not serve directly from the refrigerator—the buttercream will be too firm. Remove from the refrigerator about an hour or so before serving. The buttercream should be close to room temperature when the cake is served.

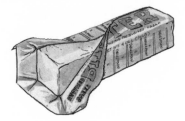

Devilish Cake

12 PORTIONS

This is a dark, two-layer sour-cream cake with a thin layer of deliciously bittersweet chocolate filling and icing. It is a very old recipe from New England where it has been made by a Maine sail-making family for generations.

> ½ cup strained unsweetened cocoa powder
>   (preferably Dutch process)
> ¾ cup boiling water
> ¼ pound (1 stick) sweet butter
> 1 teaspoon vanilla extract
> ½ teaspoon salt
> 1½ cups granulated sugar
> 2 eggs (graded large or extra-large)
> 1 teaspoon baking soda
> 1 cup sour cream
> 2 cups sifted all-purpose flour

Adjust rack to the center of the oven and preheat oven to 350 degrees. Butter two 9-inch round layer-cake pans. Dust them with flour, invert over a piece of paper and tap to shake out excess. Set pans aside.

In a small bowl mix the cocoa and boiling water until smooth. Set aside.

In the large bowl of an electric mixer cream the butter. Add the vanilla, salt, and sugar and beat to mix well. Add the eggs one at a time, beating until smooth after each addition.

In a small bowl stir the baking soda into the sour cream. On low speed add the flour to the egg mixture in three additions alternating with the sour cream in two additions, scraping the bowl with a rubber spatula and beating only until smooth after each addition. Then add the cocoa and beat only until smooth.

Pour the batter into the prepared pans. Shake the pans a bit, and rotate them slightly to level the tops.

Bake for 30 minutes until the layers barely begin to come away from the sides of the pan, or the tops barely leave an impression when lightly pressed with a fingertip. Do not overbake or the cake will be dry.

Cool in the pans for 15 minutes.

Cover each layer with a rack and invert, remove pans, cover with another rack and invert again, leaving the layers right side up on the racks to cool.

Place four strips of wax paper around the outer edges of a cake plate. Place one layer of cake upside down on the plate; check to see that the papers touch the cake all around. If you have a cake-decorating turntable or a lazy Susan. Place the plate on it.

Prepare the icing.

CHOCOLATE ICING

4 ounces (4 squares) unsweetened chocolate
2 tablespoons butter
½ cup minus 1 tablespoon milk
1 cup strained confectioners sugar
1 egg
½ teaspoon vanilla extract
Pinch of salt

Place the chocolate in the top of a large double boiler over hot water on moderate heat. Cover until the chocolate is melted. Add the butter, milk, and sugar, and stir until the butter is melted. Cook, stirring, for 3 minutes.

Beat the egg in a small bowl only to mix. Very gradually stir a few spoonfuls at a time of the hot chocolate into the egg. Stir constantly until you have added about one-third to one-half of the chocolate. Then stir the egg into the remaining hot chocolate. Add the vanilla and salt.

Transfer the mixture to the small bowl of an electric mixer. Place the small bowl in the larger mixer bowl. Fill the remaining empty space between the two bowls about halfway with ice and water. (If you are using a mixer on a stand it should be adjusted to the setting for the small bowl.)

Beat at high speed, scraping the bowl constantly with a rubber spatula, for only 1 to 2 minutes until the mixture thickens very slightly—do not let it harden.

Pour about one-third of the icing over the bottom layer and spread it smoothly—it will be a very thin layer.

Cover with the second layer of cake, placing it right side up so that both bottoms meet in the center. Pour the remaining icing over the top. Spread it over the top and sides.

Remove the wax paper strips by slowly pulling each one toward a narrow end.

Chocolate Merry-Go-Round

12 PORTIONS

This is just a delicious white sponge cake with a wonderful rich, dark chocolate buttercream, but the method of putting the two together is most unusual—it will be an eight-layer cake but the layers will go vertically instead of horizontally. Although I think that all baking is an art, this one is a little more artsy-craftsy than the usual—but not difficult.

This should be made very early in the day of the night you plan to serve it, or made the day before–it must be served very cold. It may be frozen.

You will need two 10½ x 15½ x 1-inch jelly-roll pans.

SPONGE CAKES

1 cup sifted all-purpose flour
½ teaspoon baking powder
2 tablespoons orange juice
2 tablespoons tasteless salad oil
5 eggs (graded large), separated
½ teaspoon vanilla extract
1 cup granulated sugar
⅛ teaspoon salt

Adjust two racks to divide the oven into thirds and preheat oven to 350. Butter two 10½ x 15½ x 1-inch jelly-roll pans. Line each pan with piece of wax paper to cover the bottoms and the sides. Butter the paper and set aside.

Sift together the flour and baking powder and set aside.

Measure the orange juice and the salad oil into a glass measuring cup (you should have ¼ cup) and set aside.

Place the egg yolks, vanilla, and ½ cup (reserve ½ cup) of the sugar in a small bowl of an electric mixer. Beat at high speed until the yolks are pale lemon-colored.

On low speed add half of the dry ingredients, then the liquids, and then the remaining dry ingredients, scraping the bowl with a rubber spatula and beating only until smooth after each addition.

Transfer to a larger mixing bowl.

Place the egg whites and the salt in a clean, small electric mixer bowl. With clean beaters beat at high speed until the whites hold a very soft shape. Reduce the speed to moderate and gradually add the reserved ½ cup sugar. Then increase the speed again and beat only until the whites hold a definite shape, but not until they are stiff or dry.

Fold two or three large spoonfuls of the whites into the yolks. Fold in two or three more spoonfuls. Then add all the remaining whites and fold in.

It is important for the layers to be the same thickness; measure 3 cups (which is half) of the batter into each pan. The batters must be spread as smoothly as possible; watch the corners—be careful they aren't thinner—and there should be no hollows in the middles. The layers will be very thin.

Bake for 10 minutes. Then quickly reverse the pans top to bottom and front to back to insure even baking. Bake for 3 to 5 minutes more (total baking time 13 to 15 minutes) until the tops of the cakes spring back when lightly pressed with a fingertip. They will be a pale golden color when done. They should not be overbaked.

While the cakes are baking spread out two smooth linen or cotton towels—not terry-cloth.

As soon as the layers are done, invert them onto the towels. Quickly remove the pans, peel off the paper linings (the layers will be ½ inch thick), and cover each layer loosely with a second smooth linen or cotton towel. Let stand until cool.

Meanwhile, prepare the buttercream.

CHOCOLATE BUTTERCREAM

6 ounces (6 squares) unsweetened chocolate

1 cup plus 2 tablespoons granulated sugar

3 tablespoons plus 2 teaspoons water

¾ pound (3 sticks) sweet butter

½ teaspoon vanilla extract

2 tablespoons unsweetened cocoa powder
   (preferably Dutch process)

3 eggs (graded large)

Chop the chocolate into rather fine pieces and set aside on a piece of wax paper.

Place the sugar and water in a small saucepan over moderate heat. Stir constantly with a wooden spatula until the sugar is dissolved and the mixture comes to a fast boil. Dip a pastry brush in water and wash down the sides to remove any undissolved granules of sugar.

Add the chopped chocolate and stir over heat until the chocolate is melted and the mixture is smooth.

Remove from the heat and let stand, stirring occasionally, for 5 minutes.

Meanwhile, in the large bowl of an electric mixer cream the butter. Add the vanilla and cocoa and beat well. Then add the eggs one at a time, scraping the bowl with a rubber spatula and beating after each addition until it is incorporated.

On low speed gradually add the chocolate mixture (which will still be warm), scraping the bowl with a rubber spatula and beating only until smooth, (The warm chocolate will thin the buttercream.) Remove from the mixer and set aside.

Now you will invert the cooled cakes onto a large cutting surface. Remove the top towels and then lift the remaining towels with the layers on them, invert onto the surface, and remove the towels, leaving the cakes right side up.

Partially fill a large bowl with ice and water. Place the bowl of buttercream in the bowl of ice and water and stir constantly with a rubber spatula until the mixture is as thick as mayonnaise. While it is chilling it will thicken unevenly (the coldest part will thicken sooner); when that happens remove the bowl of buttercream and stir it well with the spatula until it smooths out, then return it to the ice and continue to stir.

When the mixture is thick enough, remove and set aside 2 cups for the icing. With a long, narrow metal spatula spread half of the remaining buttercream (¾ cup) on each sponge sheet. Spread very smooth all the way to all the edges.

Now each cake will be cut into four strips the long way. It is important that the strips are all cut exactly the same width; use a ruler and toothpicks to mark both of the narrow ends of each cake into quarters.

With a long, sharp knife cut the strips.

To form the cake: Roll one of the strips (with the chocolate to the inside) into a tight spiral like a jelly roll. Place the rolled strip on the end of another strip, fitting the ends together. Continue to roll.

Place the rolled strips (which will be the middle of the cake) on a flat side so the spiral pattern is up, in the center of a large, flat cake plate. Carefully pick up another strip, place a narrow end of it against and touching the end of the rolled strips, and roll it around the cake. Continue this way with all of the remaining strips, being careful not to leave air spaces where the ends of the strips come together.

When all of the strips are rolled around in a spiral, you will have a cake 9 inches in diameter and 2½ inches high.

If you have a cake-decorating turntable or a lazy Susan, place the cake plate on it.

Briskly stir the reserved 2 cups buttercream to soften it slightly. Spread it over the top and sides of the cake, spreading it smooth with a long, narrow metal spatula.

Wipe the cake plate if any icing is on it.

Refrigerate the cake overnight, or freeze it for several hours or longer. (Freeze until the icing is firm before wrapping. Thaw for several hours or overnight in the refrigerator before unwrapping.) It must be cold when it is served or it will not slice well.

Hungarian Seven-Layer Cake

12 PORTIONS

This is a first cousin to Dobosh Torte—it is seven thin layers of a classic white sponge cake, filled and covered with a deliciously bittersweet dark chocolate buttercream.

You will need 8-inch layer-cake pans and, since you will bake seven separate layers, it will go a little faster if you have many pans. However, the layers bake quickly, so even with only a few pans this is not a tremendous chore (although it does take more patience than baking a one- or two-layer cake). This is fun, and a wonderful cake.

It may be refrigerated for a day or two, or it may be frozen.

6 eggs (graded large), separated
¾ cup granulated sugar
1 cup sifted all-purpose flour
¼ teaspoon salt

If you have only two or three 8-inch pans, and if they will fit on the same rack, adjust the rack to the lowest position in the oven. If you have more pans than will fit on one rack, adjust two racks, one to the lowest position and the other closer to the middle. Preheat oven to 350 degrees.

Cut seven circles of wax paper to fit the 8-inch pans. Butter as many pans as you have, line them with the papers and butter the papers. Set the prepared pans aside and reserve the extra circles of wax paper.

In the small bowl of an electric mixer beat the egg yolks and about half of the sugar at high speed for about 5 minutes until very pale and thick. On low speed gradually add the flour and beat, scraping the bowl with a rubber spatula and beating only until the flour is incorporated. The mixture will be very thick. Remove it from the mixer (use your index finger to scrape the beaters clean).

Add the salt to the egg whites in the large bowl of the electric mixer. With clean beaters, beat until the whites hold a soft shape. Reduce the speed to moderate, gradually add the remaining sugar, then increase the speed again and beat until the whites hold a firm shape.

Add about ½ cup of the beaten whites to the yolks and stir it in. Then stir in another ½ cup. Then, adding about ½ cup at a time, fold in all but about 2 cups of the whites. Fold the yolks into the remaining whites.

You will have about 6½ cups of batter to make seven layers, therefore each layer should use a scant 1 cup of batter. It is not necessary to measure the amount—you can approximate it. Spread the batter smooth all the way to the edges of the prepared pans—it must touch the sides of the pans all the way around, and it should be smooth.

The layers should bake about 15 minutes. If you are using more than one rack, the pans must be reversed top to bottom once during baking; each layer should spend some time on the lowest rack so that the bottom bakes well. When done, the tops will be barely colored, and the layers may show signs of beginning to come away from the pans at the edges.

Spread out a large, smooth (not terry-cloth) cotton or linen towel.

When the layers are done, cut around the sides to release and then invert the layers onto the towel. Remove the pans and peel off the papers. If the bottoms are baked dry enough the papers will peel off in one piece; if they don't, it is all right to tear the papers off, one section at a time. (The bottoms should be a little darker than the tops.) With your hands immediately turn the layers right side up—the tops of the layers are sticky and would stick to the towel. Let stand until cool.

The remaining batter may wait uncovered at room temperature, but don't waste any time getting it all baked. Wash the pans, prepare them as before, and bake the remaining layers.

Prepare a flat cake plate by lining the sides with four strips of wax paper. Place one layer right side up on the plate, checking to be sure that the papers touch the cake all around.

If you have a cake-decorating turntable or a lazy Susan, place the cake plate on it.

Prepare the filling and icing.

BITTERSWEET CHOCOLATE FILLING AND ICING

5 ounces (5 squares) unsweetened chocolate
   (see Notes)
¼ cup water
½ cup granulated sugar
I tablespoon dry instant coffee
4 egg yolks
¼ pound (1 stick) sweet butter, cut into
   ½-inch pieces and at room temperature

Place the chocolate in the top of a small double boiler over hot water on moderate heat. Cover until partially melted, then uncover and stir until completely melted.

Meanwhile, in a small saucepan, mix the water with the sugar and instant coffee. Place over moderate heat and stir until the sugar is dissolved and the mixture comes to a boil.

Also meanwhile, in the small bowl of an electric mixer, beat the egg yolks at high speed until they are pale lemon-colored.

When the sugar/coffee syrup is ready, turn the mixer speed to low and very slowly, in a thin stream, beat the syrup into the yolks. Then add the warm melted chocolate and beat only until smooth—it will be very thick.

Now, beating slowly, add the butter, one or two pieces at a time, and beat well until completely blended.

With a long, narrow metal spatula spread a very thin layer of the buttercream over the cake, spreading it smoothly all the way to the edges. The layers of filling must be thin or there will not be enough to cover the top and sides—this amount is just right if you spread it thin enough.

All the layers should be placed right side up except the top one, which should be upside down to insure a perfectly flat top.

After filling all the layers, cover the top and sides. But just before spreading the icing on the top and sides of the cake, if it is not silken smooth, and if you have a food processor, process the icing (use the metal blade) for a few seconds and like magic it will become completely smooth, Then, with a long, narrow metal spatula, spread the icing smooth.

Remove the wax paper strips by pulling each one out toward a narrow end.

Refrigerate for several hours to set the icing. The cake may be cold when it is served or at room temperature. It should be cut with a sharp, heavy knife.

NOTES: *1. For a sweeter filling and icing, substitute semisweet chocolate for all or part of the unsweetened chocolate.*

2. If you freeze this, chill it until the icing is firm before wrapping; then thaw overnight or for several hours in the refrigerator before unwrapping.

3. Before serving the top may be covered with small chocolate shavings which may, if you wish, be coated with a sprinkling of dry powdered sweetened or unsweetened cocoa.

Chocolate Cakes with Fruit

CHOCOLATE
  DATE-NUT CAKE 76

CHOCOLATE-
  NUT-PRUNE CAKE 77

SOUR CHERRY
  CHOCOLATE TORTE 78

CHOCOLATE
  APPLESAUCE CAKE 79

CHOCOLATE
  PUMPKIN CAKE 80

Chocolate Date-Nut Cake

12 Bars

This has won blue ribbons at county fairs all around the country—it is a small, plain, old-fashioned sour-cream cake without icing.

6 ounces (¾ cup) pitted dates
⅓ teaspoon baking soda (see Note)
¼ cup boiling water
1 ounce (1 square)
  unsweetened chocolate
1 ounce semisweet chocolate
¼ pound (1 stick) butter
¼ teaspoon salt
⅔ cup granulated sugar
½ teaspoon vanilla extract
1 egg
¾ cup sifted all-purpose flour
⅓ cup sour cream
½ cup walnuts, cut or broken into medium-
  size pieces

Adjust rack to center of the oven and preheat oven to 350 degrees. Prepare an 8-inch square cake pan as follows: Turn the pan upside down. Cut a 12-inch square of aluminum foil and center it over the inverted pan. Fold down the sides and the corners and then remove the foil and turn the pan right side up. Place the foil inside the pan and, in order not to tear it with your fingernails, press against it all over with a pot holder or a folded towel until it is firmly in place. With a pastry brush, brush all around the inside lightly with melted butter. Set the prepared pan aside.

Finely chop or cut the dates—they should be in very small pieces, but not pureed. Place them in a small mixing bowl, sprinkle the baking soda over the top, and add the boiling water. Mix well and set aside.

Place both chocolates in the top of a small double boiler over hot water on moderate heat. Cover and let stand until melted. Then uncover, stir until smooth, and remove the top of the double boiler. Set aside uncovered to cool slightly.

In the large bowl of an electric mixer cream the butter. Add the salt, sugar, and vanilla and beat to mix well. Beat in the egg and then the melted chocolate. On low speed add about half the flour, then the sour cream, and then the remaining flour, scraping the bowl with a rubber spatula and beating only until smooth after each addition.

Remove from the mixer and stir in the dates with their liquid and then the nuts.

Turn the batter into the prepared pan. Smooth the top.

Bake for 45 minutes until a toothpick inserted in the middle comes out clean.

Let the cake cool in the pan for 10 to 15 minutes. Then cover it with a rack, invert pan and rack, remove pan and aluminum toil, and cover the cake with another rack. Invert again, leaving the cake right side up on the rack. Let it stand until cool.

Transfer to a cutting board or a serving platter and cut into squares or bars.

NOTE: *To measure ⅓ teaspoon, fill and level a teaspoon, then, with a table knife or a small metal spatula, mark it into thirds, and cut away two-thirds.*

Chocolate-Nut-Prune Cake

16 BARS

Mildly spiced, soft, tender, moist, cakelike squares without icing—a delicious old recipe.

> About 24 large stewed prunes, sweetened or not (or use dried prunes and stew them yourself; you will need enough to make 1 cup pitted and finely chopped prunes)
> 1 ounce (1 square) unsweetened chocolate
> 1¼ cups plus 1 tablespoon sifted all-purpose flour
> 1⅓ teaspoons baking powder (see Note)
> ¼ teaspoon baking soda
> ¼ teaspoon salt
> 1 teaspoon cinnamon
> ¼ teaspoon mace or powdered cloves
> 2⅔ ounces (5⅓ tablespoons) sweet butter
> ½ teaspoon vanilla extract
> ¾ cup granulated sugar
> 2 eggs (graded large or extra-large)
> ½ cup milk
> 4 ounces (generous 1 cup) walnuts, cut or broken into medium-size pieces

Adjust rack to the center of the oven and preheat oven to 350 degrees. Butter a 9 x13-inch shallow rectangular cake pan, dust it with fine, dry bread crumbs, invert over a piece of paper, and tap lightly to shake out excess. Set the pan aside.

Drain the prunes, pit them, and chop them very fine or process them in a food processor very briefly—they should not be puréed. You need 1 cup of pulp. Set it aside.

Place the chocolate in the top of a small double boiler over hot water on low heat, or in a small custard cup in a small pan of shallow hot water over low heat. Cover until the chocolate has melted, then remove the top of the double boiler or the custard cup and set aside, uncovered, to cool.

Sift together the flour, baking powder, baking soda, salt, cinnamon, and mace or cloves. Set aside.

Cream the butter in the large bowl of an electric mixer. Beat in the vanilla and then the sugar. Add the eggs, one at a time, scraping the bowl with a rubber spatula and beating until well mixed after each addition. Beat in the chocolate. Then, on low speed, add half of the sifted dry ingredients, scraping the bowl with the spatula and beating only until smooth. Gradually add all of the milk and again beat only until smooth. Then add the remaining dry ingredients and beat only until smooth.

Remove from the mixer and stir in the prunes and then the nuts.

Turn the batter into the prepared pan and smooth the top.

Bake for 25 to 30 minutes until the top springs back when lightly pressed with a fingertip.

Cool in the pan on a rack until tepid. Cover with another rack and invert, remove the pan, cover with another rack or a cookie sheet and invert again, leaving the cake right side up until completely cool. The cake will be about 1 inch high.

Gently and carefully slide the cake onto a cutting board and, with a long, sharp knife, cut it into bars.

Because this cake is so moist it has a tendency to stick to wax paper. Place the bars on a tray and if you

plan to serve them within a few hours, do not cover. But for longer storage I find that it is best to cover them with plastic wrap.

NOTE: *To measure ⅓ teaspoon, first fill and level a 1-teaspoon measuring spoon, then cut away and remove two-thirds.*

Sour Cherry Chocolate Torte

10 PORTIONS

Chocolate and cherries is a marriage made in heaven. This is a shallow, single-layer chocolate cake without icing, with a hidden layer of sour cherries baked into the middle. It is not only an intriguing taste combination, but the cherries keep the cake marvelously moist. It is a chic, sophisticated little cake for a dinner party. Extremely quick and easy to make, it can be made a few hours before serving and can be served while it is still slightly warm, or made early in the day and served at room temperature.

1 1-pound can red sour pitted cherries packed in water

6 ounces semisweet chocolate

2½ ounces (½ cup) almonds, blanched or unblanched

6 ounces (1½ sticks) sweet butter

1 teaspoon vanilla extract

¼ teaspoon almond extract

⅔ cup granulated sugar

3 eggs (graded large or extra-large)

⅔ cup sifted all-purpose flour

Adjust rack one-third up from bottom of the oven and preheat oven to 350 degrees. Butter a 9-inch spring-form pan and dust it with fine, dry bread crumbs, invert over a piece of paper and tap to shake out extra crumbs. Set the pan aside.

Drain all the liquid off the cherries (you should have a scant 2 cups of drained cherries) and then spread them in a single layer on several thicknesses of paper towels and let stand.

Place the chocolate in the top of a small double boiler over hot water on moderate heat. Cover until partially melted, then uncover and stir until completely melted and smooth. Remove the top of the double boiler and set aside uncovered to cool slightly.

The almonds must be ground to a fine powder; do them in a food processor, a blender, or a nut grinder and set aside.

Cream the butter in the large bowl of an electric mixer. Add the vanilla and almond flavorings and then the sugar and beat well. Add the eggs one at a time, scraping the bowl with a rubber spatula and beating after each addition until thoroughly mixed. On low speed add the chocolate and beat until mixed; add the almonds and beat to mix, then the flour and beat, scraping the bowl with a rubber spatula, only until incorporated.

Place about half or slightly more of the batter in the prepared pan and spread it to make a smooth layer about ¾ inch thick.

Now, with your fingers pick up the cherries one at a time and place them, almost touching one another, in a single layer all over the chocolate mixture (they may touch the sides of the pan).

Spoon the remaining chocolate mixture over the cherries and spread it to make a thin, smooth layer.

Bake for 50 minutes. The cake will be dry and

crusty on top, and a toothpick inserted in the center will come out clean.

Cool in the pan on a rack for 15 minutes. Then remove the sides of the spring form and let the cake stand on the bottom of the pan, still on the rack, until the cake is almost completely cool. (If you want to serve it slightly warm, let it stand for about half an hour or a bit longer—just until it is firm enough to handle.)

Cover with a rack and invert. Remove the bottom of the pan. Cover with a flat cake plate or a serving board and invert again, leaving the cake right side up.

This is delicious as it is (to me it is irresistible), but I serve it with whipped cream and I have had guests comment that it *must* be served with whipped cream. The combination is perfect!

WHIPPED CREAM

1 cup heavy cream
2 tablespoons granulated or confectioners sugar
1 tablespoon kirsch (see Note)

In a small, chilled bowl with chilled beaters, whip all the ingredients only until the cream holds a soft shape. (If you whip the cream ahead of time, refrigerate it in the whipping bowl. It will probably separate slightly as it stands. Just before serving, beat it a bit with a small wire whisk until it goes together again and has the correct thickness.)

Place a large spoonful of the cream alongside each portion of the cake.

NOTE: *That small amount (1 tablespoon) of kirsch will barely be detectable but to me it is just enough. Kirsch, cherries, chocolate, and whipped cream is one of the world's greatest taste combinations. If you would like a more noticeable kirsch taste, add another table-spoon. Or, if you wish, use ½ teaspoon of vanilla extract in place of the kirsch. And if you love whipped cream, double the amounts.*

Chocolate Applesauce Cake

12 TO 14 PORTIONS

A tube cake with no icing—so lusciously moist it is almost a pudding, although it holds its shape and slices beautifully. The combination of applesauce, cin-namon, and chocolate is simply wonderful—everyone loves it. It is an unusual cake and unusually good. Although this is appropriate for any time of the year, it seems to belong especially to the Thanksgiving or Christmas holiday. It is a marvelous cake to bring to someone's house as a gift.

3 ounces (¾ cup) raisins
1½ cups sifted all-purpose flour
2 teaspoons baking soda
½ teaspoon salt
3 teaspoons cinnamon
½ teaspoon nutmeg
¼ cup plus 1 tablespoon unsweetened cocoa powder (preferably Dutch process)
6 ounces (1½ sticks) sweet butter
2 cups granulated sugar
3 eggs (graded large, extra-large, or jumbo)
16½ ounces (scant 2 cups) sweetened or unsweetened applesauce
6 ounces (1½ cups) walnuts or pecans, cut or broken into medium-size pieces
Optional: confectioners sugar (to be used after the cake has cooled)

Adjust rack one-third up from bottom of the oven and preheat oven to 350 degrees. Butter a one-piece plain tube pan that measures 10 inches across the top. (The standard depth of this size pan is 4 inches. The cake will not be that deep but it is all right to use a pan that size.) Line the bottom with baking-pan liner paper or wax paper cut to fit, butter the paper, dust the inside of the pan with fine, dry bread crumbs, and invert over a piece of paper to tap out excess. Set aside.

Cover the raisins with boiling water and let stand for about 5 minutes. Then pour into a strainer and let stand with the strainer over a cup, to allow any remaining water to run off.

Sift together the flour, baking soda, salt, cinnamon, nutmeg, and cocoa and set aside.

In the large bowl of an electric mixer cream the butter. Add the sugar and beat well. Add the eggs one at a time, beating until thoroughly incorporated after each addition. Beat at high speed for about a minute after adding the last egg.

On low speed add the sifted dry ingredients in three additions, alternating with the applesauce in two additions, scraping the bowl with a rubber spatula and beating only until thoroughly mixed after each addition. (The applesauce will make the mixture look curdled—it's all right.)

Remove from the mixer and stir in the raisins and nuts.

Turn into the prepared pan and rotate the pan a bit one way, then the other, to smooth the top.

Bake for 1 hour and 25 to 30 minutes until the cake begins to come away from the sides of the pan

and the top springs back when lightly pressed with a fingertip. (The baked cake will fill the pan only a little more than halfway—that is correct; it will be about 2½ inches high.)

Cool in the pan on a rack for about 15 minutes. Cover with a rack and invert, peel off the paper lining, and let the cake cool upside down. During cooling, cover the cake with a rack and turn it over briefly a few times just to make sure that it doesn't stick to the rack.

Serve it upside down. If you wish, it may be sprinkled with confectioners sugar pressed through a fine strainer held over the cake.

This is so rich and dense that it should be cut into small slices—two small slices for a portion.

Chocolate Pumpkin Cake

12 TO 16 PORTIONS

Moist, mildly spiced, not too sweet, very dark and chocolaty, plain (no icing), beautiful-looking (made in a fancy-shaped pan). Don't shy away from this because of pumpkin with chocolate; the pumpkin is only to keep it moist and doesn't give much taste to the cake. It is a perfect cake for the holiday season, or to wrap as a gift. A perfect cake for any time with tea or coffee. Wonderful to have on hand for any occasion. Everyone loves it. And it is easy to make and keeps well.

You will need a Bundt pan, kugelhopf, or turban pan with a 3-quart capacity.

2¾ cups sifted all-purpose flour

2 teaspoons baking powder

1 teaspoon baking soda

½ teaspoon salt

1½ teaspoons cinnamon

½ teaspoon ginger

¼ teaspoon cloves

¼ teaspoon nutmeg

¾ cup unsweetened cocoa powder (preferably Dutch process)

½ pound (2 sticks) sweet butter

1½ teaspoons vanilla extract

2 cups granulated sugar

4 eggs (graded large or extra-large)

1 pound (scant 2 cups) canned solid-pack pumpkin (not the one labeled "pumpkin pie filling")

6 ounces (1½ cups) walnuts, cut or broken into medium-size pieces

Optional: confectioners sugar (to be used after the cake is baked)

Adjust rack one-third up from the bottom of the oven and preheat oven to 325 degrees. Butter a 10-inch Bundt pan or any fancy-shaped tube pan with a 3-quart capacity. It is best to do this with very soft but not melted butter, applying it with a pastry brush. Then dust the whole pan, including the tube (see page 16), with fine, dry bread crumbs. Invert the pan over paper and tap lightly to shake out excess. Set the prepared pan aside.

Sift together the flour, baking powder, baking soda, salt, cinnamon, ginger, cloves, nutmeg, and cocoa. Set aside.

In the large bowl of an electric mixer cream the butter. Add the vanilla and sugar and beat to mix well. Add the eggs one at a time, scraping the bowl with a rubber spatula and beating after each addition until it is incorporated. On low speed add half of the sifted dry ingredients, then the pumpkin, and finally the remaining dry ingredients, scraping the bowl with the spatula and beating after each addition only until it is incorporated.

Stir in the nuts.

Turn the batter into the prepared pan. Smooth the top.

Bake for 1½ hours or until a cake tester gently inserted into the middle of the cake comes out clean and dry.

Let it stand for about 15 minutes.

Cover with a rack and carefully invert. Remove the pan and let the cake cool on the rack. Then let it stand for several hours or overnight before serving.

OPTIONAL: *Cover the top generously with confectioners sugar, sprinkling it through a fine strainer held over the cake.*

Old-Fashioned Cakes Without Icing

86-proof Chocolate Cake

12 PORTIONS

This is an especially moist and luscious dark chocolate cake generously flavored with bourbon and coffee. Sensational. It is made in a fancy pan and is served without icing. I have made this at demonstrations all around the country. It is one of my favorite cakes to teach because people can't wait to make it.

5 ounces (5 squares)
   unsweetened chocolate
2 cups sifted all-purpose flour
1 teaspoon baking soda
¼ teaspoon salt
¼ cup dry instant coffee or espresso
Boiling water
Cold water
½ cup bourbon (see Note)
½ pound (2 sticks) sweet butter
1 teaspoon vanilla extract
2 cups granulated sugar
3 eggs (graded large or extra-large)
Optional: additional bourbon
Optional: confectioners sugar

Adjust rack one-third up from bottom of the oven and preheat oven to 325 degrees. You will need a 9-inch Bundt pan (that is the smaller size; it is called a Mini-Bundt pan) or any other fancy tube pan with a 10-cup capacity. Butter the pan (even if it is a non-stick pan). Then dust the whole inside of the pan with fine, dry bread crumbs; invert over a piece of paper and tap lightly to shake out excess crumbs. Set the pan aside.

Place the chocolate in the top of a small double boiler over hot water on low heat. Cover and cook only until melted; then remove the top of the double boiler, and set it aside, uncovered, to cool slightly.

Sift together the flour, baking soda, and salt and set aside.

In a 2-cup glass measuring cup dissolve the coffee in a bit of boiling water. Add cold water to the 1½-cup line. Add the bourbon. Set aside.

Cream the butter in the large bowl of an electric mixer. Add the vanilla and sugar and beat to mix well. Add the eggs one at a time, beating until smooth after each addition. Add the chocolate and beat until smooth.

Then, on low speed, alternately add the sifted dry ingredients in three additions with the liquids in two additions, adding the liquids very gradually to avoid splashing, and scraping the bowl with a rubber spatula after each addition. Be sure to beat until smooth after each addition, especially after the last. It will be a thin mixture.

Pour into the prepared pan. Rotate the pan a bit briskly, first in one direction, then in the other, to level the top. (In a Mini-Bundt pan the batter will almost reach the top of the pan, but it is O.K.—it will not run over, and you will have a beautifully high cake.)

Bake for 1 hour and 10 or 15 minutes. Test by inserting a cake tester into the middle of the cake and bake only until the tester comes out clean and dry.

Cool in the pan for about 15 minutes. Then cover with a rack and invert. Remove the pan, sprinkle the cake with a bit of optional bourbon, and leave the cake upside down on the rack to cool.

Before serving, if you wish, sprinkle the top with confectioners sugar through a fine strainer.

This is a simple, no-icing cake, wonderful as is. Or with a spoonful of vanilla- or bourbon-flavored whipped cream.

NOTE: *Of course you can substitute rum, Cognac, or Scotch whiskey for the bourbon; or Amaretto, the suggestion of a friend of mine in Ohio.*

Black and White Cake

12 GENEROUS PORTIONS

This is a marble cake in which the black and white batters form a dramatically beautiful swirling pattern. And whereas most marble cakes have more white batter than dark, this one deliciously has more dark than white. And the dark is very dark.

2 teaspoons dry instant coffee

¼ cup boiling water

⅓ cup strained unsweetened cocoa powder (preferably Dutch process)

2½ cups sifted all-purpose flour

2 teaspoons baking powder

Finely grated rind of 1 small lemon (see Note)

2 teaspoons lemon juice (see Note)

½ pound (2 sticks) sweet butter

1 teaspoon vanilla extract

1½ cups granulated sugar

4 eggs (graded large or extra-large), separated

⅔ cup milk

½ teaspoon almond extract

Generous pinch of salt

Optional: confectioners sugar (to be used after the cake is baked)

Adjust rack one-third up from the bottom of the oven and preheat oven to 375 degrees. Use a 9-inch Bundt pan (called Mini-Bundt—10-cup capacity) or a 9 x 3½-inch tube pan. Or you can use a 10-inch Bundt pan, but the cake will not be as high. (In the 9-inch Bundt pan the cake will rise high and make a cute, fat little cake that is adorable.) Butter the pan (even if it is a non-stick pan), dust it thoroughly with fine, dry bread crumbs and invert over paper to shake out excess crumbs. Set aside.

In a small mixing bowl dissolve the coffee in the boiling water. Add the cocoa and stir until smooth; remove small lumps by stirring and pressing against the lumps with a rubber spatula. Set aside to cool slightly.

Sift the flour with the baking powder and set aside.

Mix the grated lemon rind with the lemon juice and set aside.

In the large bowl of an electric mixer cream the butter. Mix in the vanilla and 1¼ cups (reserve ¼ cup) of the sugar. Beat to mix thoroughly. Then add the yolks all at once and beat well. On low speed add the sifted dry ingredients in three additions, alternating with the milk in two additions. Scrape the bowl with a rubber spatula and beat only until each addition is incorporated.

Remove 2 cups of the batter and transfer it to a medium or large bowl. This will be the white batter. Stir in the lemon rind and juice and set aside.

To the batter remaining in the mixer bowl add the almond extract and cocoa mixture and mix until smooth. Set aside.

In the small bowl of the electric mixer, with clean beaters, add the salt to the egg whites and beat until they hold a soft peak. On moderate speed gradually add the reserved ¼ cup of sugar, then increase the speed to high and beat until the whites hold a shape—but they must not be too stiff or dry; stop beating just before they are stiff.

Stir about ½ cup of the meringue into each of the batters to lighten them a bit. Then alternately fold a generous ½ cup into each of the batters until it is all used.

You will have more chocolate batter than white. Use a tablespoon for spooning the chocolate and a teaspoon for the white. Place about five well rounded tablespoons of the chocolate batter in the bottom of the pan, leaving a small space between the spoonfuls. Then place a well-rounded teaspoonful of the white batter in each empty space. Use large spoonfuls; they will make a bolder dramatic pattern. For the second layer, place white on chocolate and vice versa. Continue until you have used all of both batters. (Do not cut through as with most marble cakes.)

Briskly rotate the pan first in one direction and then the other to level the top.

Bake for about 1 hour or until a cake tester gently inserted into the middle of the cake comes out dry. If the top of the cake becomes too dark cover it loosely with aluminum foil.

Let the cake cool in the pan for 10 to 15 minutes. Then cover it with a rack and invert the pan and the rack. Remove the pan and let the cake cool upside down. If you have baked it in a smooth tube pan cover it with another rack and invert again to let the cake cool right side up.

This does not need any icing. If you wish, sprinkle a bit of confectioners sugar over the top, shaking it through a fine strainer held over the cake.

Cut in thin slices, two or three to a serving.

NOTE: *Equivalent amounts of orange rind and orange juice may be substituted for the lemon rind and lemon juice.*

Chocolate Angel Food Cake

8 TO 12 PORTIONS

This is a light, airy, moist beauty that stands 4 inches high. It can be made with thawed egg whites which have been left over from other desserts and frozen. Angel Food may be made a day before it is to be served or early in the day to be served that night. But don't freeze Angel Food—freezing toughens it. This is quite quick and easy, but you must be careful with all the folding in.

1 cup less 2 tablespoons sifted cake flour
1½ cups sifted confectioners sugar
½ cup less 1 tablespoon unsweetened cocoa powder (preferably Dutch process)
1 tablespoon dry powdered (not granular) instant coffee or espresso
1½ cups egg whites (from 10 to 12 eggs), at room temperature (they should be removed from the refrigerator at least 1 hour ahead)
½ teaspoon salt
1½ teaspoons cream of tartar
1 cup granulated sugar

Adjust rack one-third up from the bottom of the oven and preheat oven to 375 degrees. You will need an angel-food tube pan measuring 10 inches across the top and 4 inches in depth. (The tube and the bottom of the pan are in one piece; the side rim is a separate piece. The pan should be aluminum, not Teflon.) Do not butter or line the pan.

Sift together three times the flour, confectioners sugar, cocoa, and dry powdered instant coffee. (Even if you are using a triple-sifter—three layers of wire mesh—which I think is the best kind, sift three times.) Set aside.

Place the egg whites and the salt in the large bowl of an electric mixer. Beat briefly until foamy. Place the cream of tartar in a small, fine strainer and, while beating, strain the cream of tartar onto the whites. Continue to beat at high speed until the whites hold a firm shape or are stiff but not dry; test by lifting a large portion of the beaten whites with a rubber spatula—they should mound high on the spatula without sliding off.

Now the granulated sugar and then the sifted flour mixture will be folded into the whites. It is important not to dump the dry ingredients into one spot; they should be sprinkled lightly all over the top of the whites. If you use a wider bowl you will have more surface to sprinkle over. (I use one that measures 13 inches across the top.) Or the folding may be done on a large, deep turkey platter. So, now, if you have a wider, larger bowl or a turkey platter, transfer the whites to it.

Place the granulated sugar in a strainer or a sifter, or sprinkle it on carefully with a large spoon, using about ¼ cup at a time and distributing it lightly all over the surface. After each addition, very gently fold the sugar in, using the largest size rubber spatula you can find.

After all the sugar is folded in, place the sifted flour mixture in the strainer or sifter and sift about ¼ cup of it all over the surface. Fold it in. Continue until all of the flour mixture has been folded in.

At no time should you fold in, or handle the mixture, any more than necessary.

Pour the mixture evenly into the ungreased pan. With a long, narrow metal spatula, or a table knife, cut through the mixture in widening circles to cut through any large air bubbles. Smooth the top. (The pan will be slightly more than one-half full.)

Bake for about 40 minutes or until the cake just barely springs back when lightly pressed with a fingertip.

Now the pan has to be inverted to "hang" until the cake is cool. Even if the pan has three little legs for this purpose, they don't really raise the cake enough. Place the tube of the inverted pan over a narrow-necked bottle, or an upside-down metal funnel.

Let the cake "hang" until cool—at least 1 hour.

Then turn the pan right side up. With a knife that has a firm, sharp blade about 6 inches long, cut around the outside edge of the cake, pressing the blade firmly against the pan, and then cut around the tube in the middle. Push up the bottom of the pan to remove the sides. Insert the knife between the bottom of the cake and the pan; press the blade firmly against the pan and cut all around to release the cake.

Place a cake plate over the cake and invert the plate and the cake. Lift off the bottom of the pan. Leave the cake upside down. Cover it, top and sides, with plastic wrap.

It is best to let Angel Food stand at room temperature for several hours or overnight before serving.

Angel Food may be served as is, or with confectioners sugar sprinkled through a fine strainer over the top. Or it may be completely covered with whipped cream. Or serve it with ice cream and chocolate sauce. Or serve it with fresh fruit and whipped cream (raspberries, either fresh or frozen, thawed and drained—or bananas, sliced just before serving and sprinkled with kirsch). Or try canned black bing cherries, plain or brandied, drained.

Or to make this plain cake a special occasion dessert, cover it with the following 7-Minute Icing. It is best to ice the cake early in the day for that night.

7-MINUTE ICING

½ cup egg whites (from 3 to 4 eggs; you may use whites which have been left over from other desserts and frozen, but thaw completely before using)
1½ cups granulated sugar
¼ cup plus 1 tablespoon cold water
1 teaspoon cream of tartar
⅛ teaspoon salt
1½ teaspoons vanilla extract

Place everything except the vanilla in the top of a large double boiler; it must have at least an 8- to 10-cup capacity. Place over hot water on moderate heat. Beat with an electric mixer at high speed for 4 to 5 minutes until the mixture stands in peaks when the beaters are raised. Or beat with an egg beater for about 7 minutes.

Immediately, in order to stop the cooking, transfer the mixture to the large bowl of the electric mixer. Add the vanilla and beat at high speed very briefly only until the mixture is smooth and barely firm enough to spread. Do not overbeat or the icing will become too stiff. Use immediately!

With a long, narrow metal spatula spread a very thin layer of the icing over the entire cake, including the center hole made by the tube, in order to seal any loose crumbs. Then spread the remaining icing to make a thick layer over the sides first and then the top. The icing may be spread smooth (which is easiest to do by using a long, narrow metal spatula and working on a cake-decorating turntable), or pull it up into peaks and/or stripes by using the back of a large spoon. Either way, do it quickly; if you work over the icing too much it will lose its fine shiny quality.

To serve, cut the cake gently with a serrated bread knife, using a sawing motion—do not press down on the cake or it will squash. Or cut with a special tool called a cake rake, which is meant for cutting Angel Food. Or use two long-pronged forks, back to back, to separate into portions.

Chocolate Chiffon Cake

16 GENEROUS PORTIONS

This fantastically dramatic cake is over 4 inches high, as light as a cloud, moist, and very dark. (It is made with salad oil, not butter.)

½ cup strained unsweetened cocoa powder (preferably Dutch process)
1 tablespoon dry instant coffee
¾ cup boiling water
1¾ cups sifted cake flour
1 tablespoon baking powder
½ teaspoon salt
1¾ cups granulated sugar
7 eggs (graded large), separated, plus 1 egg white (you should have 1 generous cup of whites)
½ cup tasteless salad oil (such as Mazola or Wesson oil)
1 teaspoon vanilla extract
½ teaspoon cream of tartar

Adjust rack one-third up from the bottom of the oven and preheat oven to 325 degrees. You will need a 10 x 4-inch angel-food tube pan with a loose rim, the bottom and tube being in one piece. Do not butter or line the pan.

Place the cocoa and coffee in a small mixing bowl. Add the boiling water and stir well to dissolve; stir until completely smooth and then set aside to cool to room temperature.

Sift together into a large mixing bowl (I use an 8-quart stainless steel bowl) the flour, baking powder, salt, and sugar. With a rubber spatula make a well in the middle. Pour the egg yolks, salad oil, vanilla, and cooled chocolate mixture into the well. Stir slowly and then briskly with a rather large wire whisk until the mixture is smooth.

In the large bowl of an electric mixer add the cream of tartar to the egg whites and beat until the whites hold a firm shape; they must be firm, but do not beat until stiff or dry.

Add the beaten whites all at once to the bowl with the chocolate mixture and fold together carefully only until the mixtures are blended.

Turn into the cake pan and smooth the top.

Bake for 55 minutes at 325 degrees. Then increase the heat to 350 degrees and bake for 10 to 15 minutes longer until the top springs back when lightly pressed with a fingertip.

Now the cake must cool upside down in the pan. Even though the pan has little feet to raise it from the counter top, they do not raise it high enough. To raise the pan even more, turn it upside down over an inverted funnel, or over the neck of a small bottle, and let it hang until completely cool.

Then turn the pan right side up. To cut the cake out of the pan use a knife with a sharp, *very firm* (not flexible) 6-inch blade. Insert the knife at the outer rim of the cake, cutting all the way to the bottom of the pan. Cut around the cake, pressing the blade very firmly against the pan. Now lift the pan and with your hands push up on the bottom of the pan to remove the sides. Then cut around the tube in the middle and then cut around the bottom of the cake, pressing the blade firmly against the pan to release the cake completely.

Cover it with a flat platter and invert. Remove the bottom of the pan. Again cover the inverted cake with a flat platter and turn again, leaving the cake right side up. The top will be dome-shaped and it should be cut flat. Use a long, thin, sharp knife. Cover with a serving platter, centered carefully, and invert once again, leaving the cake upside down—the way it will be served.

OPTIONAL: *This cake may be covered with the following soft, rich, and creamy icing.*

Before icing the cake, prepare a large, flat cake plate or serving board by placing four strips of wax paper around the outer edges of the plate.

Place the cake on the plate, checking carefully to see that the papers touch the cake all around. If you have a cake-decorating turntable or a lazy Susan, place the cake on it. Prepare the icing.

CHOCOLATE ICING

12 ounces semisweet chocolate (you can use morsels or any other semisweet)
6 ounces (1½ sticks) sweet butter
1 teaspoon vanilla extract
3 eggs (graded large)

If you use bars of chocolate, break them up. If you use morsels or 1-ounce squares, use them as they are. Place the chocolate in the top of a small double boiler over warm water on low heat. Cover and let stand until partially melted. Uncover and stir until completely melted and smooth. Remove the top of the double boiler and let stand, stirring occasionally, until completely cool.

In the small bowl of an electric mixer cream the butter. Add the vanilla and 1 egg. Then add about one-third of the cooled chocolate. Alternately add the remaining eggs and chocolate. Then beat at high speed for a minute or two until the icing lightens in color and is very smooth.

With a long, narrow metal spatula spread the icing on the sides of the cake and then on top. With a small, narrow metal spatula or with a table knife spread the icing around the hole in the middle of the cake. There will be a generous amount of icing and it should make a thick layer all over. It may be spread smooth or it may be formed into swirls and peaks.

Remove the wax paper strips by pulling each one out toward a narrow end of the paper.

Chocolate Gingerbread

16 Portions

This is a thick, soft, moist, spicy, old-fashioned dark chocolate cake. It is quite plain. Marvelous between meals with milk or coffee, or with whipped cream as a dessert. Or anytime with ice cream and chocolate sauce.

2½ cups sifted all-purpose flour
1½ teaspoons baking soda
1 teaspoon salt
1 teaspoon ground ginger
1 teaspoon cinnamon
1 teaspoon allspice
2 ounces (2 squares) unsweetened chocolate
½ pound (2 sticks) sweet butter, cut into small pieces
1 cup boiling water or hot prepared coffee

1 cup dark brown sugar, firmly packed
1 cup light molasses
4 eggs (graded large or extra-large)
Optional: ⅓ cup finely chopped candied or preserved ginger

Adjust rack one-third up from the bottom of the oven and preheat oven to 325 degrees. Butter a shallow 9 x 13-inch baking pan; dust it with fine, dry bread crumbs and invert it over paper to shake out excess crumbs. Set aside.

Sift together the flour, baking soda, salt, ginger, cinnamon, and all-spice, and set aside.

Place the chocolate in the top of a small double boiler over hot water on low heat. Cover until the chocolate is melted. Then remove the top of the double boiler and set it aside, uncovered, to cool slightly.

Place the butter in the large bowl of an electric mixer. Add the boiling water or hot coffee and mix until the butter is melted. Add the brown sugar and mix well. Then mix in the molasses. Add the eggs all together and beat until well mixed. Mix in the chocolate. On low speed gradually add the sifted dry ingredients and beat only until they are incorporated. Stir in the optional ginger. The mixture will be thin.

Pour it into the prepared pan and tilt the pan to level the batter.

Bake for about 50 minutes until the top of the cake springs back when it is gently pressed with a fingertip.

Cool in the pan for 15 or 20 minutes. Cover with a cookie sheet or a rack and invert. Remove the pan. Cover the cake again with a sheet or a rack and invert again leaving the cake right side up to cool.

Cut the cake into 16 large squares or 32 slices.

Loaf Cakes

ORANGE CHOCOLATE LOAF CAKE
   FROM FLORIDA   91

CHOCOLATE TEA BREAD   92

SOUR CREAM CHOCOLATE LOAF
   CAKE   92

BUENA VISTA LOAF CAKE   94

OLD-FASHIONED CHOCOLATE LOAF
   CAKE   94

Orange Chocolate Loaf Cake from Florida

ABOUT 12 SLICES

This recipe comes from a magnificent orange grove in Central Florida where the cake is a specialty of the house. When we visited there large trays of the sliced cake were served along with extra-tall glasses of ice-cold, sweet-and-tart just-squeezed orange juice.

It is a deliciously plain, moist, coal-black loaf which is flavored with orange rind and steeped in orange juice after it is baked. The cake is made with whipped cream instead of butter. The recipe may easily be doubled and baked in two pans.

1¼ cups sifted all-purpose flour
2 teaspoons baking powder
¼ teaspoon salt
½ cup unsweetened cocoa powder (preferably Dutch process)
1 cup granulated sugar
1 cup heavy cream
1 teaspoon vanilla extract
2 eggs (graded large)
Finely grated rind of 1 large, deep-colored orange

Adjust rack one-third up from the bottom of the oven and preheat oven to 350 degrees. You will need a loaf pan measuring about 8½ x 4½ x 2¾ inches, or one with about a 6-cup capacity. Butter the pan and dust it all over lightly with fine, dry bread crumbs, shake out excess crumbs, and set the pan aside.

Sift together the flour, baking powder, salt, cocoa, and sugar, and set aside.

Beat the cream and vanilla in the small bowl of an electric mixer until the cream holds a definite shape. On low speed add the eggs, one at a time, scraping the bowl with a rubber spatula and beating only until the egg is incorporated after each addition. (The eggs will thin the cream slightly.)

Transfer to the large bowl of the mixer and gradually, on low speed, add the sifted dry ingredients, scraping the bowl and beating only until smooth.

Remove from the mixer and stir in the grated rind.

That's all there is to it.

Turn the batter into the prepared pan and smooth the top. Bake for about 1 hour and 5 minutes until the top springs back when lightly pressed with a fingertip.

GLAZE

⅓ cup orange juice
3 tablespoons granulated sugar

As soon as the cake goes into the oven, mix the orange juice with the 3 tablespoons sugar and let it stand while the cake is baking.

When you remove the cake from the oven let it cool for 5 minutes. Then, a little at a time, brush the orange juice/sugar mixture all over the cake; encourage most of it to run down the sides between the cake and the pan, but thoroughly wet the top also. The cake will absorb it all.

Let the cake stand in the pan until it is completely cool. Then cover the pan loosely with a piece of wax paper. Invert the cake into the palm of your hand—easy does it—remove the pan, cover the cake with a rack, and invert again, leaving the cake right side up.

Chocolate Tea Bread

1 9-INCH LOAF

This is a plain, old-fashioned raisin-nut loaf cake. It is not as sweet as most desserts. Serve it between meals with coffee, tea, milk, or sherry. Or make a sweet sandwich with cream-cheese filling.

1¾ cups sifted all-purpose flour

1 teaspoon baking soda

½ teaspoon salt

2 ounces (½ stick) butter

½ teaspoon vanilla extract

⅔ cup granulated sugar

1 egg

1 teaspoon dry powdered (not granular) instant coffee or espresso

⅓ cup unsweetened cocoa powder (preferably Dutch process)

1 cup buttermilk

5 ounces (1 cup) raisins (see Note)

4 ounces (generous 1 cup) walnuts, cut or broken into coarse pieces

Adjust rack one-third up from the bottom of the oven and preheat oven to 350 degrees. Butter a 9 x 5 x 3-inch loaf pan (8-cup capacity) and dust it lightly with fine, dry bread crumbs; set aside.

Sift together the flour, baking soda, and salt and set aside.

In the large bowl of an electric mixer cream the butter. Add the vanilla and sugar and beat until well mixed. Beat in the egg, then, on low speed, add the espresso and the cocoa. Add the sifted dry ingredients in three additions, alternating with the buttermilk in two additions. Scrape the bowl with a rubber spatula and beat only until mixed after each addition. Stir in the raisins and nuts.

Turn the mixture into the prepared pan and smooth the top.

Bake for 1 hour to 1 hour and 15 minutes, or until a cake tester inserted in the center comes out clean and dry.

Cool the cake in the pan for about 10 minutes. Then cover it with a rack and invert the rack and the cake pan. Remove the pan and gently turn the cake right side up to cool on the rack.

The top of this loaf will crack—it is supposed to.

Refrigerate the loaf before slicing or it may crumble.

NOTE: *Dates or dried prunes, cut up, may be substituted for the raisins, or for part of them.*

Sour Cream Chocolate Loaf Cake

12 GENEROUS PORTIONS

This is a fine-grained, sweet chocolate loaf cake similar to a pound cake—with a creamy, semi-soft, fudge-like icing.

2 ounces (2 squares) unsweetened chocolate, coarsely chopped

2 teaspoons dry instant coffee

1 cup boiling water

2 cups sifted all-purpose flour

1 teaspoon baking soda

¼ teaspoon salt

¼ pound (1 stick) sweet butter

1 teaspoon vanilla extract

1¾ cups dark or light brown sugar, firmly packed

2 eggs (graded large)

½ cup sour cream

Adjust rack one-third up from the bottom of the oven and preheat oven to 325 degrees. Butter a 9 x 5 x 3-inch loaf pan (8-cup capacity). Dust it lightly with fine, dry bread crumbs; invert the pan over paper and tap to shake out excess.

Place the chocolate and instant coffee in a small mixing bowl. Add the boiling water. Stir occasionally until the chocolate is melted. Then let stand to cool to room temperature. It is all right if the chocolate settles to the bottom.

Sift together the flour, baking soda, and salt and set aside.

In the large bowl of an electric mixer cream the butter. Add the vanilla and brown sugar and beat to mix well. Add the eggs one at a time, beating after each addition until it is thoroughly incorporated. On low speed gradually add the sifted dry ingredients, scraping the bowl with a rubber spatula and beating only until smooth. Then add the sour cream and again beat only until smooth. Finally, stir the cooled chocolate and gradually, on low speed, beat it in.

The batter will be thin. Pour it into the prepared pan.

Bake for 60 to 75 minutes until a cake tester inserted all the way to the bottom of the cake comes out clean and dry.

Cool the cake in the pan for several minutes. Then cover it with a rack, invert pan and rack, remove pan, and let the cake cool upside down.

When the cake is cool prepare the following Fudge Icing.

FUDGE ICING

2 ounces (2 squares) unsweetened chocolate

2 tablespoons butter, at room temperature

½ teaspoon vanilla extract

1 cup strained confectioners sugar

1 egg (graded large)

Place the chocolate in the top of a small double boiler over hot water on low heat. Cover and let the chocolate melt.

Meanwhile, place the butter, vanilla, confectioners sugar, and the egg in the small bowl of an electric mixer and beat well until smooth. Add the warm melted chocolate and continue to beat until smooth and creamy.

Spread the icing over the top of the cake. Smooth it, or you can make deep zigzag ridges by moving a spatula or the back of a spoon through this thick, creamy icing.

Let the cake stand for an hour or so until the icing is set. (If you refrigerate this cake, the icing will become firm fudge candy.)

VARIATION: *You may stir ¼ to ½ cup of walnuts or pecans, cut into medium-fine pieces, into the icing just before it is spread on the cake.*

Buena Vista Loaf Cake

This won first prize at several county fairs in Colorado and California. It is a plain and wonderful chocolate loaf loaded with fruit, nuts, and chocolate chips—almost a fruit cake but not as sweet. It is easy to wrap and makes a marvelous gift.

2 cups sifted all-purpose flour

½ teaspoon salt

1 teaspoon baking soda

1 teaspoon cinnamon

3 tablespoons unsweetened cocoa powder
   (preferably Dutch process)

¼ pound (1 stick) sweet butter

1 teaspoon vanilla extract

1 teaspoon dry instant espresso or other
   powdered (not granular) instant coffee

1 cup granulated sugar

2 eggs (graded large or extra-large)

½ cup milk

8 ounces (1 cup, packed) dates, cut in half

3 ounces (⅔ cup) raisins

7 ounces (2 cups) walnut and/or pecan halves
   or large pieces

6 ounces (1 cup) semisweet chocolate morsels

Adjust rack one-third up from the bottom of the oven and preheat oven to 350 degrees. Butter a 9 x 5 x 3-inch loaf pan (8-cup capacity) and dust it with fine, dry bread crumbs, invert to shake out excess, and then set aside.

Sift together the flour, salt, baking soda, cinna-mon, and cocoa and set aside. In the large bowl of an electric mixer cream the butter. Add the vanilla, dry instant espresso, and sugar and beat to mix well. Beat in the eggs one at a time. On low speed add about half of the sifted dry ingredients, scraping the bowl with a rubber spatula and beating only until incorporated. Then gradually beat in the milk, and finally the remaining dry ingredients, again scraping the bowl and beating only until incorporated. Remove from the mixer.

Add the dates and stir to mix well, then stir in the raisins, nuts, and chocolate morsels.

Turn into the prepared pan and smooth the top.

Bake for about 1½ hours or until a cake tester inserted into the middle comes out clean and dry.

Let the cake stand in the pan for about 10 minutes. Then cover with a rack and invert pan and rack. Remove the pan and then carefully turn the cake right side up and let it stand until it is cool.

The crust will be very crisp and crunchy; slice with a serrated knife.

Old-Fashioned Chocolate Loaf Cake

This is a plain, fine-grained cake similar to a pound cake. It slices beautifully, keeps well if wrapped air-tight, and makes a great gift. Serve it with tea or cof-fee, with cold milk, or as a dessert with ice cream and hot fudge sauce. It is best to let it (and all pound cakes) stand overnight before slicing. This recipe calls for long, slow baking.

2 cups sifted all-purpose flour
½ teaspoon baking powder
½ teaspoon salt
2 ounces (2 squares) unsweetened chocolate
4 ounces semisweet chocolate
½ pound (2 sticks) sweet butter
2 teaspoons vanilla extract
1¼ cups granulated sugar
5 eggs (graded large or extra-large), **separated**

Adjust rack one-third up from the bottom of the oven and preheat oven to 300 degrees. You will need a bread-loaf pan with an 8-cup capacity. I have made this in many different pans. Since there is no conformity among manufacturers as to pan sizes, you will have to check the pan's contents with measuring cups of water.

Butter the pan and dust it with fine, dry bread crumbs; invert and tap the pan to shake out excess. Or line the pan with buttered foil, buttered side up (in which case the crumbs are not necessary). Set aside.

Sift together the flour, baking powder, and salt and set aside.

Place both chocolates in the top of a small double boiler over hot water on moderate heat. Stir occasionally until the chocolate is melted and smooth and then remove the top of the double boiler and set aside to cool the chocolate slightly.

In the large bowl of an electric mixer cream the butter. Add the vanilla and then 1 cup (reserve remaining ¼ cup) of the sugar and beat to mix thoroughly. Add the egg yolks all at once and beat well, scraping the bowl with a rubber spatula. Add the chocolate and beat until blended. On low speed gradually add the sifted dry ingredients and beat, scraping the bowl with the spatula, only until they are smoothly incorporated.

In the small bowl of the mixer (with clean beaters) beat the egg whites on moderately high speed until the whites hold a soft shape. Gradually add the reserved ¼ cup sugar and continue to beat until the whites hold a firm shape or are stiff but not dry.

To fold the whites into the thick chocolate mixture: If you have a large rubber spatula use that, or start the folding with a large wooden spatula and then change to a standard-size rubber spatula. Fold in one-third of the whites, then another third, and finally fold in the remainder—with the first two additions do not fold completely (a bit of white may remain), but after the last addition fold until no white remains.

Turn the mixture into the prepared pan and smooth the top.

Bake until a cake tester inserted in the center of the cake comes out clean and dry. A 14 x 4 ¼ inch pan will take about 1 hour and 40 minutes. (A long, thin pan takes less time than a short, wide one.)

While it bakes the cake will crack along the top as do most pound cakes.

Let the cake cool in the pan for about 15 minutes. Then very gently invert the cake onto a rack and remove the pan. With your hands carefully turn the cake right side up and let it stand until cool.

Wrap the cake in plastic wrap and let it stand at room temperature (preferably overnight) before serving.

Pound cake should be sliced rather thin. Use a long, thin, sharp knife and cut with a sawing motion.

Since pan sizes vary so much, I can't tell you what size cake you will have. But it will be 2¼ pounds.

NOTE: *Because of the long, slow baking, called for in recipes for old-fashioned pound cakes, these cakes develop a crumbly top crust. To soften the crust slightly, steam it. That is, cover the cake loosely with a cotton towel or napkin as soon as it is removed from the oven, and then again when it is removed from the pan.*

Cheesecakes

The Newest Cheesecake

My favorite cheesecake recipe came from Craig Claiborne. I made it every day for 10 years for restaurants my husband owned. Sometime during those years I made up a black-and-white version. And Craig made a hazelnut version. (All three are in my dessert book.) This is an exciting combination of the three cakes.

It is formed into three layers before baking, one white, one nut, and one chocolate. None of these cakes individually takes very much time to put together—but this combination one takes longer since the two bottom layers must be frozen before the next one is put on or they will run into each other.

You will need a special cheesecake pan (they are deep and do not have removable bottoms) which used to be difficult to find. But since the cheesecakes in the dessert book became so popular, the pan is now generally available at specialty kitchen equipment shops all around the country. (It may be bought at, or ordered by mail from, Bridge Kitchenware, 214 East 52nd Street, New York, New York 10022.)

This may be made early in the day for that night (it must be refrigerated at least 5 to 6 hours before serving), or it can be made a day or two before, or it may be frozen (cheesecakes freeze wonderfully) and thawed before serving.

3¾ ounces (¾ cup) blanched hazelnuts
   (filberts), or almonds, walnuts, or pecans
   (see Note)
2 pounds cream cheese, at room temperature
1 teaspoon vanilla extract
1¾ cups granulated sugar
4 eggs (graded large or extra-large)

⅛ teaspoon almond extract
2 ounces (2 squares) unsweetened chocolate
⅓ cup graham-cracker crumbs (to be used
   after cake is baked)

Use an 8-inch round one-piece cheesecake pan 3 inches deep. Butter it lightly all over the bottom, up to the rim, and around the inside of the rim or the cake will stick and will not rise evenly. Any unbuttered spot will prevent the finished cake from sliding out of the pan easily. Set the buttered pan aside.

The nuts must be finely chopped or ground. This may be done in a nut grinder, a food processor, or a blender. If there are a few uneven or larger pieces, it is all right (it is even better with some large pieces). Set the ground nuts aside.

In the large bowl of an electric mixer beat the cheese, scraping the bowl frequently with a rubber spatula until it is very smooth. Beat in the vanilla and then the sugar very well, and then add the eggs one at a time, scraping the bowl with the spatula and beating only until smooth after each addition. After adding the eggs, do not beat any more than necessary—this cheesecake should not be airy.

Remove 2 cups of the mixture and transfer it to a mixing bowl. (The remaining batter should be left at room temperature while the layers are being frozen.) Add the ground nuts and the almond extract to the 2 cups and stir to mix.

This will be the first layer. Pour it carefully into the middle of the pan. Very gently shake the pan to make the cheese mixture as smooth and level as you can. Keep the edges clean and straight.

Place the pan in the freezer for 1 hour or a bit longer until the layer is firm enough to be covered with the next layer without losing its shape.

Remove and set aside 2 more cups of the basic batter for the top layer.

Place the chocolate in the top of a small double boiler over hot water on moderate heat. Cover until melted. Then uncover and remove the top of the double boiler.

Mix the chocolate into the batter that is remaining in the mixer bowl.

Place the chocolate batter carefully by rounded teaspoonfuls all over the cold nut layer and very gently shake the pan to level the chocolate mixture—keep the edge as straight and neat as you can.

Return the cake to the freezer. The chocolate layer will need only about 15 or 20 minutes to become firm.

Adjust a rack to the lowest position in the oven and preheat the oven to 350 degrees.

When the chocolate layer is firm enough, spoon or pour the white layer carefully and evenly over it. Level the top by briskly rotating the pan a bit first in one direction and then another.

Place the cheesecake pan inside a larger pan. The larger pan must not touch the sides of the cake pan and it must not be deeper than the cake pan. Pour hot water into the larger pan to a little more than halfway up the side of the cake pan. (If the large pan is aluminum, adding about ½ teaspoon cream of tartar to the hot water will keep the pan from discoloring. You don't have to mix it—just put it in.)

Bake for 1 hour and 50 minutes. (This takes more baking than the other cheesecakes because it is partially frozen when it goes into the oven.) The top of the cake will be a rich golden brown and feel dry to the touch, but the cake will still be soft inside. (The cake will rise to or above the rim of the pan while it is baking, but it will sink below the rim as it cools.)

Lift the cake pan out of the water and place it on a rack for about 2 hours until it is completely cool. Do not chill the cake in the refrigerator or the butter will harden and the cake will stick to the pan.

Let stand until the bottom of the cake pan has reached room temperature. Then, to facilitate removing the cake from the pan, dip the pan for a few seconds into a large container of deep hot water (it can be boiling hot). Dry the pan. Place a flat plate or board over the top of the pan and invert. Remove the cake pan.

Sprinkle the bottom of the cake evenly with the graham-cracker crumbs. (If you are going to freeze the cake, place a round of wax paper on top of the crumbs so that you will be able to lift the frozen cake from the plate and wrap it in plastic wrap.) Now, very gently place another flat plate or board (it should not be too heavy) on top of the crumbs (or on top of the round of wax paper). Hold it all with one hand underneath and one hand on top, with the fingers of both hands spread out. Very carefully and quickly turn everything over so the cake is right side up (once you start to turn it over do not hesitate—it should be an even and smooth motion). Do this without pressing too hard or you will squash the cake, which is still soft.

Refrigerate for at least 5 to 6 hours or overnight. Or freeze it. (Wrap after freezing and thaw before unwrapping.)

Serve at room temperature—it is more delicate and creamy at room temperature. But some people love it very cold. I'm wild about it either way.

NOTE: *Hazelnuts usually come with brown skins which must be removed (see directions for blanching, page 10). Or, if you buy them already skinned but not toasted, toast them to bring out their flavor. (To toast, place them in a shallow baking pan in a 350-degree oven. Shake the pan occasionally until the nuts are only lightly colored.) Hazelnuts are difficult to find. I buy them unblanched at a health-food store, or blanched but not toasted from a wholesale nut dealer. If you use almonds they should be blanched (see page 10) and toasted as above.*

If you use walnuts or pecans they should not be toasted. But if they are ground in a processor or a blender you must be very careful (especially with walnuts). Stop the machine while they are still in small pieces, or they will become oily and pasty—they should remain in little pieces and should not become a nut-butter.

Mocha Velvet

11 to 14 Portions

My friend, Lora Brody, a cateress and chocolate-dessert-and-cookie expert in West Newton, Massachusetts, has had a special reputation for her cheesecakes since her original recipes for Ginger Cheesecake and Main Course Cheesecakes were printed in The New York Times. *This is Lora's recipe for a chocolate cheesecake. It is a large, beautiful, delicious refrigerator cake (the filling is not baked) with an unusually mellow and exotic flavor that comes from a combination of ricotta cheese, coffee, and chocolate.*

It is best to make this a day ahead. You will need a 10-inch spring-form pan.

CRUST

8 ounces Amaretti (see Note)
½ cup graham-cracker crumbs
¼ pound (1 stick) sweet butter, melted

Adjust rack one-third up from the bottom of the oven and preheat oven to 400 degrees. Butter the sides only (not the bottom) of a 10 x 2- or 3-inch spring-form pan.

The Amaretti must be ground into fine crumbs. Grind them in a food processor fitted with the steel blade, or in two or three batches in a blender, or place them in a strong bag and pound them with a rolling pin. You will have 2 cups of crumbs. Set aside and reserve ½ cup. Place the remaining 1½ cups in a mixing bowl. Stir in the graham-cracker crumbs and then add the melted butter and mix well.

Turn the crumb mixture into the pan. With your fingertips press some of the crumbs against the sides of the pan, but leave a rim of uncrumbed pan about 1½ inches wide around the top of the pan. The crust should be 1½ inches high. Don't worry about the top edge of the crumbs being a perfectly straight line. Press the remaining crumbs firmly against the bottom of the pan. (Try not to concentrate the crumbs too heavily where the sides and the bottom of the pan meet.)

Bake the crust for 5 minutes, then let it cool completely.

FILLING

1 tablespoon plus 1½ teaspoons
   (1½ packages) unflavored gelatin
3 tablespoons plus 1 teaspoon cold water
8 ounces semisweet chocolate
⅓ cup dry instant espresso or other dry
   instant coffee
1 cup boiling water
½ cup granulated sugar
32 ounces (2 pounds) whole-milk ricotta
   cheese
1 teaspoon vanilla extract
1 cup heavy cream

Sprinkle the gelatin over the cold water in a small cup and set aside to soften.

Break up the chocolate and place it in a heavy 2- to 3-quart saucepan.

Dissolve the espresso in the boiling water and pour it over the chocolate. Place over low heat and stir frequently until the chocolate is melted. Then stir with a wire whisk until smooth. Add the softened gelatin and the sugar and stir over low heat for a few minutes to dissolve. Remove from the heat and set aside, stirring occasionally, until cool.

In the large bowl of an electric mixer beat the ricotta cheese well. Add the vanilla and the chocolate mixture and beat until thoroughly mixed. Remove from the mixer.

Whip the cream until it holds a shape but not until it is stiff. Fold into the chocolate mixture.

Pour about half of the filling into the cooled crumb crust. Sprinkle the reserved ½ cup of ground Amaretti evenly over the filling. Cover with the remaining filling. Spread the top smooth, or form a neat design with the back of a spoon (I make parallel ridges).

Cover with aluminum foil and refrigerate overnight.

Several hours before serving, remove the sides of the pan as follows:

Insert a sharp, heavy knife between the crust and the pan. Pressing firmly against the pan cut all the way around the crust, then release and remove the sides.

The cake may be removed from the bottom of the pan if you wish. If so, it should be done now. Use a firm (not flexible) metal spatula (either a wide one or a long, narrow one). Insert it gently and carefully under the bottom crust and ease it around to release the cake completely. Use two wide metal spatulas, or a small, flat cookie sheet, or the removable bottom of a quiche pan or layer-cake pan to transfer the cake to a platter.

TOPPING

1 cup heavy cream
1 tablespoon granulated or confectioners sugar
½ teaspoon vanilla extract
About ¼ cup toasted almonds, blanched or unblanched, and thinly sliced (toast by baking in a 350-degree oven for 10 to 15 minutes until lightly browned)

In a small, chilled bowl with chilled beaters whip the cream with the sugar and vanilla until it holds a shape and is firm enough to be used with a pastry bag.

Fit a pastry bag with a star-shaped tube, place the cream in the bag, and form a decorative border with the cream around the rim of the cake. Or place it by spoonfuls around the rim.

Crumble the toasted almonds slightly and sprinkle them over the whipped cream.

Refrigerate.

NOTE: *Amaretti are extremely crisp Italian macaroons. All Amaretti are not the same—some are made with almonds—but the brand I buy, Amaretti di Saronno, Lazzaroni & Company, is made with apricot kernels and they have a special flavor. These come in an 8-ounce box (as well as larger tins), with the macaroons wrapped two together in pastel tissue papers, 20 little packages (40 1½-inch cookies).*

Amaretto-Amaretti Chocolate Cheesecake

16 OR MORE PORTIONS

This is a chocolate cheesecake flavored with Amaretto and Amaretti and almond paste, on a bottom crust of chocolate and Amaretti. It is an extravaganza par excellence, with a radically unusual and irresistible

taste. (Amaretto is an Italian almond-flavored
liqueur; the brand I use is Amaretto di Saronno.
Amaretti are crisp Italian macaroons; the brand I use
is Amaretti di Saronno, Lazzaroni & Company.
Incidentally, this liqueur and these macaroons are
both made with apricot kernels, not almonds. It is
important to use this special liqueur and these special
macaroons in order to have the special flavor of this
special cake. See Note at end of recipe for sources.)

CRUST

7 ounces (about 15 tissue-paper packages with
   2 1½-inch macaroons in each package)
   Amaretti di Saronno, Lazzaroni & Company
   (see Note)
2 tablespoons granulated sugar
1 ounce (1 square) unsweetened chocolate
2½ ounces (5 tablespoons) sweet butter

Adjust rack one-third
up from the bottom of the
oven and preheat to 350
degrees. Butter the sides
only (not the bottom) of a
9-inch spring-form pan
which may be 2½ or 3
inches deep.

The Amaretti must
be ground very fine. Place
them in a food processor
bowl fitted with the steel
blade, or in a blender. (In
a blender you may have to
do them half at a time.) Process or blend until you
have made fine crumbs. You should have 1⅓ to 1½
cups of crumbs. Place the crumbs in a mixing bowl.
Stir in the sugar.

Place the chocolate and the butter in the top of
a small double boiler over hot water on moderate
heat. Stir occasionally until melted.

Add the melted chocolate and butter to the
Amaretti crumbs and sugar and stir to mix thoroughly.

Turn the mixture into the prepared pan. With
your fingers distribute it evenly over the bottom of
the pan and then, with your fingers, press it firmly
over the bottom. It must be a very firm, compact
layer and should be on the bottom only, not the sides.

Refrigerate while you prepare the filling.

FILLING

6 ounces semisweet chocolate
7 ounces (about 15 tissue-paper packages with
   2 1½-inch macaroons in each package)
   Amaretti di Saronno, Lazzaroni & Company
   (see Note)
4 ounces almond paste (see Note)
⅓ cup Amaretto di Saronno liqueur
   (see Note)
24 ounces (3 8-ounce packages)
   cream cheese, at room temperature
½ cup granulated sugar
4 eggs (graded large or extra-large)
½ cup heavy cream

Place the chocolate in the top of a small double
boiler over hot water on moderate heat. Cover until
partially melted, then uncover and stir until completely melted. Remove the top of the double boiler
and set it aside, uncovered, to cool slightly.

Place the Amaretti in their tissue-paper wrap-
pings on a cutting board. With the broad side of a
heavy cleaver (or a hammer) hit each package hard
enough to break the macaroons coarsely but not hard
enough to tear the paper. Then unwrap the broken
macaroons and place them in a bowl and set aside.

Cut the almond paste into very small pieces and
place it in the small bowl of an electric mixer. While
beating on low speed, very gradually add the
Amaretto liqueur and beat until thoroughly mixed.
Remove from the mixer and set aside.

In the large bowl of the electric mixer (you can

use the same beaters again without washing them), beat the cream cheese until it is smooth. Add the sugar and beat until smooth again. Then add the almond paste Amaretto mixture and beat once again until thoroughly mixed. Add the melted chocolate and beat well once more. Set the mixer at low speed and add the eggs one at a time and beat only until they are incorporated after each addition. Add the heavy cream and beat only until smooth.

(This cheesecake should not be beaten until it is light and airy.) Remove the bowl from the mixer.

Add the coarsely broken macaroons and stir together gently only to mix.

Turn into the prepared pan, pouring the mixture over the bottom crust.

Rotate the pan gently, first in one direction, then the other, to level the batter. If you have used a pan that is 2½ inches deep the cheesecake mixture will come almost to the top of the pan. It is O.K.; it will not run over.

Bake for 45 minutes. It will seem soft and not done but do not bake any longer; it will become firm when it is chilled. Remove from the oven.

The top of the cake will look bumpy because of the large chunks of Amaretti; it is supposed to.

Set aside and let stand at room temperature until completely cool. Then carefully remove the sides of the pan.

Refrigerate the cake, which is still on the bottom of the pan, for 4 to 6 hours or overnight.

Now the cake can be left on the bottom of the pan (in which case it should be set on a folded napkin on a cake plate to keep it from sliding when you serve it). Or it can be removed from the bottom of the pan and transferred to a cake plate or a serving board. To remove it from the pan, carefully insert a sharp, heavy, firm knife between the cake and the pan, pressing the blade firmly against the pan in order not to cut the crust. Gently rotate the knife around the pan to release the cake. Use a flat-sided cookie sheet as a spatula (or use two wide metal spatulas), slide it (or them) under the crust, carefully lift the cake and transfer it to the cake plate. Or if you want to freeze the cake (this freezes wonderfully) transfer it to a large piece of plastic wrap and wrap airtight.

This may be served as is, or topped with a pile of Chocolate Cigarettes (see page 267) or Chocolate Shavings (see page 263).

Serve the cake refrigerated, the colder the better. Serve small portions.

NOTE: *Amaretto di Saronno liqueur is generally available at any well-stocked liquor store.*

Almond paste is available (generally in 8-ounce cans) in specialty food stores.

Amaretti di Saronno, Lazzaroni & Company, macaroons, are generally available at fine specialty food stores or good Italian markets. They can be bought at, or ordered by mail from, Manganaro Foods, 488 Ninth Avenue, New York, New York 10018. Manganaro has a catalog. Or, Williams-Sonoma, P.O. Box 3792, San Francisco, California 94119.

Chocolate-Marbleized Cheesecake

8 TO 10 PORTIONS

A silky smooth and custardlike marbleized cheesecake, rather small and elegant. It should be made very early in the day for that night (it must chill well) or the day before, or make it way ahead and freeze it.

CRUST

4 ounces chocolate wafer cookies, or any crisp chocolate or chocolate nut cookies (or you can bake your own—use Chocolate Wafers, page 129, or Old-Fashioned Chocolate Sugar Cookies, page 130)

1 ounce (2 tablespoons) sweet butter, melted

Separate the sides from the bottom of an 8 x 2½- or 3-inch spring-form pan. Butter the sides only. (If the bottom is not buttered the finished cake can be transferred easily to a cake plate.) Then replace the bottom in the pan and set aside.

The cookies must be ground to crumbs. Either break them into pieces and grind them all at once in a food processor fitted with the steel blade, or grind the pieces about half at a time in a blender, or place them in a heavy plastic bag and pound and roll them with a rolling pin until they are fine. You should have 1 cup of crumbs.

In a mixing bowl add the melted butter to the crumbs and stir well with a rubber spatula, pressing against the mixture with the spatula until the butter is evenly distributed. You will think there is not enough butter, but do not add more—the mixture should be dry and crumbly.

Pour the crumb mixture into the prepared pan. With your fingertips distribute it evenly over the bottom of the pan and then press it firmly to make a smooth, compact layer on the bottom only. Refrigerate.

CHEESE MIXTURE

6 ounces semisweet chocolate
12 ounces cream cheese, at room temperature
1 teaspoon vanilla extract
½ cup granulated sugar
2 eggs (graded large)
2 cups sour cream
Pinch of salt

Adjust rack one-third up from bottom of the oven and preheat oven to 350 degrees.

Break up the chocolate and place it in the top of a small double boiler over hot water on moderate heat. Cover until partially melted, then uncover and stir until completely melted and smooth. Remove the top of the double boiler and set aside, uncovered, to cool slightly.

In the large bowl of an electric mixer beat the cream cheese until very smooth. Add the vanilla and sugar and beat to mix. Add the eggs one at a time, scraping the bowl with a rubber spatula and beating until smooth after each addition. Then add 1½ cups (reserve remaining ½ cup) of the sour cream and the salt and beat until smooth.

Remove from the mixer and set aside 1½ cups of the mixture.

In the small bowl of the mixer (you can use the same beaters) mix the melted chocolate with the reserved ½ cup sour cream; then add the reserved 1½ cups of cheese mixture and beat until smooth.

Place the two batters, alternating colors, by spoonfuls over the chilled crust in the pan; use large rather than small spoonfuls (or pour the batters)—you will have roughly three varicolored layers.

Then use the face side (not the edge) of a small, thin, metal spatula or a table knife to marbleize the mixtures. Cut down through the batters and use the spatula or knife to swirl the batter into large spirals and/or zig-zags and form an attractive pattern. But do not overdo it or you will lose the contrast between the two batters.

Briskly rotate the pan a bit first in one direction, then the other, to level the top of the cheese mixtures.

Bake for 30 minutes. It will seem soft but it is done.

Remove to a rack and let stand to cool to room temperature.

Refrigerate for at least 5 or 6 hours or longer.

This should be cold when it is served. It will become firm when adequately chilled. When just right it should be slightly soft and custardlike in the middle.

Carefully, with a small, sharp knife cut around the sides to release, then remove the sides of the pan. Now, use a firm (not flexible) metal spatula (either a wide one or a long, narrow one). Insert the spatula gently and carefully under the crust and ease it around to release the cake completely from the bottom of the pan. With a wide spatula (or using a flat-sided cookie sheet as a spatula) carefully transfer the cake to a serving plate.

New York City Chocolate Cheesecake

10 TO 16 PORTIONS

This is a thick, dense, heavy, and rich chocolate cheesecake in a chocolate-cookie crumb crust. It is a big-party dessert. It may be made a day or two before serving, or it may be made way ahead and frozen.

CRUST

8 ounces chocolate wafers (The bought ones are sometimes called icebox wafers. Better yet, make your own Chocolate Wafers, page 129.)

3 ounces (¾ stick) sweet butter

Adjust rack one-third up from the bottom of the oven and preheat oven to 375 degrees. Separate the bottom from the sides of a 9 x 3-inch spring form pan; butter the sides only (if you butter the bottom the crust will stick to the bottom and it will be difficult to serve), and then replace the bottom in the pan and set aside.

Crumble the cookies coarsely and place them in a food processor or a blender to make fine crumbs (or place them in a plastic bag and pound and roll them with a rolling pin); you should have 2 cups of crumbs. Place them in a mixing bowl. Melt the butter and stir it into the crumbs until thoroughly mixed.

Pour about two-thirds of the mixture into the prepared pan.

To form a thin layer of crumbs on the sides of the pan, tilt the pan at about a 45-degree angle and, with your fingertips, press a layer of the crumbs against the sides. Press from the bottom up toward the top of the pan and leave a rim of uncrumbed pan ¾ of an inch deep around the top. Rotate the pan gradually as you press on the crumbs. Then turn the pan upright on its bottom, pour in the remaining crumbs and, with your fingertips, distribute them evenly around the bottom of the pan. Then press them firmly to make a compact layer.

FILLING

12 ounces semisweet chocolate (2 cups morsels or 12 squares, coarsely chopped)

24 ounces (3 8-ounce packages) cream cheese, at room temperature

1 teaspoon vanilla extract

⅛ teaspoon salt

1 cup granulated sugar

3 eggs (graded large or extra-large)

1 cup sour cream

Place the chocolate in the top of a small double boiler over hot water on low heat. Cover until partially melted, then uncover and stir until completely melted and smooth. Remove from the hot water and set aside to cool slightly.

In the large bowl of an electric mixer, cream the cream cheese until it is very smooth. Add the vanilla, salt, and sugar and beat well, scraping the sides with a rubber spatula, until very smooth. Add the chocolate and beat to mix. Add the eggs one at a time, scraping the bowl with the spatula and beating until thoroughly blended after each addition. Add the sour cream and beat until smooth.

Pour the filling into the crumb crust (it will not quite reach the top of the crumbs) and rotate the pan briskly first in one direction, then in the other, to smooth the top. (It might also be necessary to smooth the top a bit with a spatula.)

Bake for 1 hour. (It will still seem quite soft.)

Let stand on a rack until completely cool. Cover the top of the pan with aluminum foil and refrigerate overnight.

The cheesecake may be removed from the pan just before serving or days before. With a firm, sharp, heavy knife, cut around the sides of the crust, pressing the knife blade firmly against the pan as you cut. Then release and remove the sides of the pan. Now use a firm (not flexible) metal spatula (either a wide one or a long narrow one): Insert the spatula gently and carefully under the crust and ease it around to release the cake completely from the bottom of the pan. The cake will be firm and strong and easy to transfer. If you are serving it within a day or two (the cake may be refrigerated a day or two before serving), place it on a large, flat dessert platter; if you are going to freeze it, place it on a large

piece of plastic wrap and wrap airtight. Refrigerate or freeze. If you freeze the cake it should thaw completely, overnight in the refrigerator, before it is unwrapped. Serve it cold.

OPTIONAL: *This cake is so dense that I like to serve a large bowl of soft whipped cream on the side. And a bowl of brandied cherries. Or fresh strawberries, raspberries, or drained, canned bing cherries. Or peeled and sliced kiwi fruit.*

Or, if you prefer a more decorated presentation, the rim of the cake may be trimmed with whipped cream applied through a pastry bag fitted with a large star-shaped tube. Either make large rosettes touching one another, or C- or S-shaped patterns, also touching. And the border of whipped cream may be topped with chopped green pistachio nuts, Chocolate Shavings (see page 263), or with candied violets or rose petals (which should be put on just before serving—they may run into the cream if they stand).

To decorate the border, use 1 cup of cream, 2 tablespoons confectioners sugar, and a scant ½ teaspoon of vanilla extract. Whip until the cream holds a definite shape.

If you are going to serve a lot of people, serve the cream separately and use 3 cups of cream and three times the amount of sugar and vanilla. Whip only until the cream holds a soft shape. If you whip it ahead of time, refrigerate it, and then stir it with a wire whisk before serving.

This cake is very rich and should be served in small portions.

COOKIES

Chocolate Chip Cookies

Positively-the-Absolute-Best-Chocolate-Chip Cookies

ABOUT 55 3-INCH COOKIES

There's a battle raging across the country for the title of The Absolute Best Chocolate Chip Cookie. The whole country has suddenly gone chocolate-chip cookie crazy and everyone who makes them claims his is the most delicious.

It all started in 1930 when Ruth Wakefield and her husband Kenneth bought an old house on Route 18 in Whitman, Massachusetts. Originally it had been a toll house where the horses were changed on the way from Boston to New Bedford. The Wakefields thus named it Toll House and opened it as a restaurant and inn.

I have been told that there was a popular cookie at the time called Butter Drop-Do. Mrs. Wakefield decided to add some chopped chocolate to the recipe. She did not know that at that moment she was making history and creating a whole, new food industry. The story is that she thought the chocolate would melt and run throughout the cookies, and she was surprised when it stayed in chunks. Needless to say, they were delicious cookies and popular with the inn's guests. Somehow a chocolate company heard about them and made a special bar of semisweet chocolate just for those cookies; it was scored into tiny sections and sold with a special utensil for separating the sections. And then the Nestlé Company manufactured semisweet morsels expressly for the Toll House® Cookies and also printed the original recipe for the cookies on the back of each package of morsels. That's when it all started and it has been snowballing ever since.

Ruth Wakefield wrote a wonderful cookbook of all the recipes used at Toll House, Toll House Cook Book (Little, Brown and Company, Boston, 1930). Unfortunately, the book is out of print now. But I have a copy. And although the recipe that is printed on each package of Nestlé's Semi-Sweet Real Chocolate Morsels is very close to Mrs. Wakefield's original (which incidentally is called Toll House Chocolate Crunch Cookies in the book), it is not exactly the same. Here is my version of the recipe in the book, and I, too, claim that this is The Absolute Best, positively.

In a revised edition of her book, Mrs. Wakefield says about these cookies: "People never seem to tire of them and they carry well, too. During the war we shipped thousands of dozens of them to boys and girls in service all over the world."

8 ounces (2 sticks) sweet butter
1 teaspoon salt
1 teaspoon vanilla extract
¾ cup granulated sugar
¾ cup light brown sugar, firmly packed
2 eggs (graded large or extra-large)
2¼ cups <u>unsifted</u> all-purpose flour
1 teaspoon baking soda
1 teaspoon hot water
8 ounces (2 generous cups) walnuts, cut or
    broken into medium-size pieces
12 ounces (2 cups) semisweet chocolate morsels

Adjust two racks to divide the oven into thirds and preheat oven to 375 degrees. Cut aluminum foil to fit cookie sheets.

In the large bowl of an electric mixer cream the butter. Add the salt, vanilla, and both sugars and beat well. Add the eggs and beat well. On low speed add about half of the flour and, scraping the bowl with a rubber spatula, beat only until incorporated. In a small cup stir the baking soda into the hot water to dissolve it (see Note), then mix it into the dough. Add the remaining flour and beat only to mix.

Remove the bowl from the mixer and stir in the walnuts and the morsels.

Now although this dough can be, and usually is, simply dropped from a teaspoon, I think the cookies are much better if you roll the dough between your hands into balls. The cookies will have a more even shape and a more even color, and I think they taste better. Mrs. Wakefield refrigerated the dough overnight before rolling it into balls. But here's how I do it. Spread out a large piece of wax paper on the counter next to the sink. Use a rounded teaspoonful of the dough for each cookie and place the mounds any which way on the wax paper. Then wet your hands with cold water, shake off excess water but do not dry your hands. Pick up a mound of dough and roll it between your wet hands into a smooth, round shape, then press it between your hands to flatten it evenly into a round shape about ½ inch thick and place it on the foil. (If you refrigerate the dough overnight it is not necessary to wet your hands; just roll a mound of dough between your hands, flatten it, and place it on the foil. And if you do not refrigerate the dough and do not roll it between your hands but simply drop it from a teaspoon, at least flatten the mounds by pressing them with the back of the bowl (of a wet teaspoon.) Place the flattened rounds of dough 2 inches apart on the foil.

Slide a cookie sheet under the foil and bake two sheets at a time, reversing the sheets top to bottom and front to back as necessary during baking to insure even browning. Bake for about 12 minutes or a little longer until the cookies are browned all over. (If you bake only one sheet at a time, bake it on the upper rack.) They must be crisp; do not underbake. Ruth Wakefield says, "They should be brown through, and crispy, not white and hard as I have sometimes seen them." (Baking at a lower temperature for a longer time would make them white and hard.)

Let the cookies cool for a few seconds on the foil until they are firm enough to be moved. Then, with a wide metal spatula, transfer them to racks to cool.

Store airtight.

NOTE: *This method of dissolving the baking soda before adding it is the way Mrs. Wakefield did it. Toll House, which is under different ownership now, still bakes the cookies but they sift the soda with the flour; and the recipe on the Nestlé morsels also sifts the soda with the flour. I do not know which method is better. I only know these are delicious this way (dissolved).*

VARIATIONS: *Cooks have varied the above recipe in just about every way possible. Some use whole-wheat flour for all or half of the flour, or less flour to make thinner cookies, or more flour to make thicker cookies. Or more sugar. Some add 2 cups of raisins or chopped dates, or coconut, either with or in place of the nuts. Some cooks add grated orange rind or chopped candied orange peel. Or chopped candied ginger. Or pumpkin seeds and/or wheat germ. Or 1 teaspoon cinnamon. Some add about 1 cup of peanut butter to the basic recipe and use peanuts in place of walnuts. (If you use salted peanuts, shake them vigorously in a large strainer to remove as much salt as possible; then use slightly less salt in the ingredients.) And a popular cookie that I have seen in many places across the country is what appears to be the basic recipe but it probably has more flour; it is formed into extra-large cookies that are 6 to 8 inches in diameter.*

The quickest way of shaping and baking the dough is in a pan for bar cookies. Butter a 10½ x 15½ x 1-inch jelly-roll pan, spread the dough smoothly in the pan, bake in the middle of a 375-degree oven for 20 minutes. Cool in the pan. Use a small, sharp knife to cut into 35 squares and use a wide metal spatula to remove the cookies.

Dolly's Crisp Toffee Bars

32 Cookies

My friend Dolly (Mrs. Andy) Granatelli is a superb cook and hostess who says that asking her not to cook would be like asking her not to breathe. These cookies are one of her specialties, chocolate chip butter bars, extremely crisp and crunchy, chewy and buttery, quick and easy; they keep well, mail well, and everyone loves them.

½ pound (2 sticks) sweet butter

½ teaspoon salt

1 teaspoon vanilla extract

1 cup light or dark brown sugar, firmly packed

2 cups sifted all-purpose flour

4 ounces (generous 1 cup) walnuts, cut into medium-size pieces

6 ounces (1 cup) semisweet chocolate morsels

Adjust rack to the center of the oven and preheat oven to 350 degrees.

In the large bowl of an electric mixer cream the butter. Add the salt, vanilla, and sugar and beat well. On low speed gradually add the flour, scraping the bowl with a rubber spatula and beating until the mixture holds together.

Add the nuts and chocolate morsels and stir until they are evenly distributed.

The dough will be stiff. With a teaspoon or with your fingers place small mounds of the dough in an unbuttered 10½ x 15½ x 1-inch jelly-roll pan. With floured fingertips press the dough firmly to make an even layer—it will be thin.

Bake for 25 minutes, reversing the pan front to back once to insure even baking. The cake will be golden brown.

Let cool in the pan for only a minute or so. Then, with a small, sharp knife, cut into bars. Let stand in the pan until cool.

With a wide metal spatula transfer the cookies to paper towels to dry the bottoms.

Wrap them individually in clear cellophane or wax paper or store them in an airtight container.

Ralph's Cookies

32, 48, OR 64 Bars

I had often made a certain layered, nut, bar cookie. One day my husband suggested adding chocolate to the bottom layer. I tried it and it came out just fine.

These have a very thin, crisp chocolate-cookie layer on the bottom, a layer of solid chocolate in the middle, and a vanilla walnut layer on top. They are rather fragile and fancy.

Without the chocolate in the bottom layer these are the same as the nut bars made by Betsy's Place in New York City.

BOTTOM LAYER

1 ounce semisweet chocolate

1¼ cups sifted all-purpose flour

1 teaspoon baking powder

Pinch of salt

1 teaspoon granulated sugar

¼ pound (1 stick) sweet butter

1 egg yolk

2 tablespoons prepared coffee, cooled

12 ounces (2 cups) semisweet chocolate
  morsels (to be used after the layer is baked)

Adjust rack to the center of the oven and pre-heat oven to 350 degrees. Butter a 10½ x 15½ x 1-inch jelly-roll pan and set aside.

Place the chocolate in the top of a small double boiler over hot water on moderate heat and let stand, covered, until it has melted. (Or the chocolate may be melted in a heatproof custard cup set into a pan of shallow hot water over low heat.) Stir until smooth and set aside, uncovered, to cool.

Sift together the flour, baking powder, salt, and sugar.

Now the mixture may be put together in a food processor or in the traditional manner.

In a processor fitted with the steel blade: Place the sifted dry ingredients in the processor bowl. Cut the butter into pieces and add it. Process until the particles are fine. Add the egg yolk, prepared coffee, and melted chocolate and process until the mixture is smooth and forms a ball. If the ingredients are not completely incorporated knead briefly on a board or smooth work surface.

In the traditional manner: Place the sifted dry ingredients in a medium-size mixing bowl. Cut the butter into small pieces and add to the bowl. With a pastry blender cut in the butter until the particles are fine. Add the egg yolk, coffee, and melted chocolate. Stir with a fork until the ingredients are well mixed and the dough holds together. If it is not smooth knead it briefly on a board or smooth work surface.

Place small bits of the dough all over the bottom of the buttered pan. With your fingertips press on the pieces of dough to form a solid, smooth layer to cover the bottom, not the sides—it will be a thin layer.

Bake for 10 minutes.

Meanwhile, prepare the top layer.

TOP LAYER

3 ounces (¾ stick) sweet butter

2 teaspoons vanilla extract

¾ cup granulated sugar

2 eggs (graded large or extra-large)

8 ounces (2 generous cups) walnuts, cut into
  medium-size pieces

In the small bowl of an electric mixer cream the butter. Beat in the vanilla and sugar. Add the eggs one at a time, scraping the bowl with a rubber spatula and beating after each addition only until mixed. The mixture will look curdled but it is all right. Stir in the walnuts and set the mixture aside.

After the bottom layer has baked for 10 minutes, remove it from the oven. Sprinkle with the chocolate morsels and return to the oven for 2 more minutes. Remove from the oven again and immediately, while the chocolate is soft, use a rubber spatula to spread the chocolate into an even layer, spreading it all the way to the sides of the pan. Let stand for 2 or 3 minutes to allow the chocolate to set slightly.

Now place the batter for the top layer by large spoonfuls all over the chocolate and spread it to make an even layer touching the sides of the pan.

Return the pan to the oven and bake for 30 minutes until the top is a rich golden brown.

Let cool on a rack until the bottom of the pan has reached room temperature.

Then, to mark into even bars (unless you have a very keen eye), mark each side into four equal sections, using a 15-inch ruler and inserting toothpicks on the edges of the cake. Using the ruler as a guide, with a small, sharp knife score the top of the cake lightly in both directions from one toothpick to the one opposite. Remove the toothpicks and cut through the lines to make 16 pieces. Cut around the edges to release. With a wide metal spatula transfer the pieces to a cutting board. With a longer knife (wiping the blade occasionally) cut each piece into 2 or 3 bars or into quarters.

These are too fragile for a cookie jar. They may be stored in an airtight box, or on a tray and then covered with plastic wrap. Or wrap them individually in clear cellophane or wax paper. These may be frozen.

Raisin-Date-Nut Bars with Chocolate Chunks

32 Large Bars or 64 Small Bars

These soft and chewy bar cookies are full of chunky goodies. They keep well and mail well. Make them at Christmas or anytime.

1½ cups sifted all-purpose flour
1½ teaspoons baking soda
2 tablespoons powdered unsweetened cocoa
¼ teaspoon salt
3 eggs (graded large or extra-large)
1 teaspoon vanilla extract
1 cup granulated sugar

5 ounces (1 cup) raisins
16 ounces (2 cups, packed) pitted dates, cut into halves
8 ounces (2 generous cups) walnut and/or pecan halves or large pieces
8 ounces semisweet chocolate, cut into pieces (see Note for preparation)
Optional: confectioners sugar (to use after the cookies are baked)

Adjust rack to center of the oven and preheat oven to 325 degrees. With one large piece of aluminum foil line the bottom and sides of a 10½ x 15½ x 1-inch jelly-roll pan. Brush the foil with soft or melted butter and set the pan aside.

Sift together the flour, baking soda, cocoa, and salt and set aside.

In a large bowl beat the eggs, vanilla, and sugar just to mix—do not beat until light and fluffy. Add the sifted dry ingredients and beat only to mix.

With a heavy wooden spatula stir in the raisins, then the dates, nuts, and chocolate. The mixture will be very thick and it will look as though there isn't enough batter to cover the fruit, nuts, and chocolate. Just keep at it—there is enough, but barely.

Now spoon the mixture all over the bottom of the prepared pan. With the back of a metal spoon, spread, push, and move the pieces around to form an even layer completely covering the pan—again, just barely. Be sure that the corners are filled and that the mixture is not lower in the corners.

Bake for 30 to 35 minutes. After about 20 or 25 minutes of baking check the color of the cake; if the back is browning faster than the front, reverse the pan front to back. When the top is well-browned all over, remove the pan from the oven. Let the cake stand in the pan on a rack until it is cool.

Then cover it with a large rack or a cookie sheet and invert the rack and pan. Remove the pan and gently peel off the aluminum foil. Now cover it with a large cutting board or a cookie sheet and invert again, leaving the cake right side up.

Before cutting, the cake should be chilled to firm up the chocolate chunks. Place it in the freezer or the refrigerator until the chocolate is firm. Cut on the board or cookie sheet (or cut it into quarters and, with a wide metal spatula, transfer them to a cutting board). For cutting even pieces, use a ruler and mark the sides of the cake with toothpicks. With a long, thin, sharp knife cut into bars.

Wrap the cookies individually in clear cellophane or wax paper, or pack them in an airtight box with wax paper between the layers, or place them on a serving plate and cover with plastic wrap. They may be frozen.

If you wish, these may be sprinkled with confectioners sugar before serving. Place the cookies on wax paper and shake the sugar through a fine strainer held over the cookies.

NOTE: *Place the chocolate bars on a cutting board. Use a large, heavy knife. If the bars are thin, cut at about ½-inch intervals, first in one direction and then across. The chocolate will crack and will not cut evenly, don't expect it to. If you aim for pieces about ½ inch square, you will wind up with the correct assortment of sizes. If you use a thick bar, the pieces should be cut slightly smaller. But with any chocolate, what you want is rather generous-size pieces. And if you want to use more chocolate than the recipe calls for, do. And/or more nuts. And, if you wish, substitute some dried figs and/or prunes for some of the raisins and/or dates. This is a very flexible recipe.*

Prune-Oatmeal Chocolate Chip Cookies

60 LARGE COOKIES

These are large, old-fashioned, homey drop cookies. They are mildly spiced, wonderfully satisfying, crunchy crisp, and chewy.

2¼ cups sifted all-purpose flour
2 teaspoons baking powder
¾ teaspoon baking soda
Scant 1 teaspoon salt
1½ teaspoons cinnamon
1½ teaspoons ginger
12 ounces pitted, "ready to eat," soft dried prunes
½ pound (2 sticks) sweet butter
½ cup granulated sugar
1 cup light or dark brown sugar, firmly packed
1 egg
1 cup quick-cooking (not "instant") rolled oats
4 ounces (generous 1 cup) walnuts, cut or broken into medium-size pieces
12 ounces (2 cups) semisweet chocolate morsels

Adjust two racks to divide the oven into thirds and preheat oven to 375 degrees. Line cookie sheets with aluminum foil, or if you have the kind that have only one raised edge, just cut foil to fit the sheets and set aside.

Sift together the flour, baking powder, baking soda, salt, cinnamon, and ginger and set aside.

Cut the prunes (with scissors or a knife) into small pieces. You should have a generous 1½ cups, firmly packed, of cut prunes. Set aside.

In the large bowl of an electric mixer cream the butter. Add both sugars and beat well. Beat in the egg, then on low speed add the sifted dry ingredients and beat only to mix; it will be a stiff mixture.

Remove the bowl from the mixer and, with a heavy wooden spatula, stir in the rolled oats, prunes, nuts, and chocolate morsels. (It will be stiff and you will need strength.)

To shape the cookies (which will be rolled between your hands) first place a long piece of wax paper on the counter next to the sink. Using a rounded tablespoonful (make these large) of the dough for each cookie, place the mounds any which way on the wax paper. You should have about 60 mounds.

Wet your hands and shake off the water; they should be damp but not dripping wet. Pick up a mound of the dough, roll it between your hands into a ball, and place it on the aluminum foil. These must be at least 2 inches apart (they spread during baking); you should not place more than 8 or 9 balls of dough on a piece of foil.

Then, with the back of a wet fork (keep the fork wet) flatten the cookies by pressing first in one direction and then another; they should be flattened to a scant ½-inch thickness.

If the foil is not on cookie sheets, slide sheets under it. Bake two sheets at a time, reversing the positions top to bottom and front to back as necessary during baking to insure even browning. They

should be baked until they are well-colored all over; it will take about 17 or 18 minutes.

If you bake only one sheet at a time, slide an extra cookie sheet underneath; a single sheet has a tendency to burn on the bottom. Bake a single sheet on the higher rack. It will bake in a little less time, about 13 to 15 minutes.

With a wide metal spatula transfer the cookies to racks to cool. (These have a slight tendency to stick to the foil; usually it is a piece of prune. Press the spatula hard against the foil; if a few cookies still want to stick, leave them and remove the others. Then try the sticky ones again; the second time around they behave better.)

Chocolate Chip Wheat Germ Cookies

9 HUGE COOKIES

I am most grateful to Esther Starbuck, a veteran high-school teacher in Buena Vista, Colorado, for this great recipe. Mrs. Starbuck, who has a reputation for her baked goods, has been making these for many years—and I see why. If there were a Chocolate Chip Cookie Hall of Fame these would certainly be there.

They are huge, crisp, and chewy with a marvelously satisfying taste—and easy and fun to make, although they are not quick since they are so large that only three cookies can be baked on a sheet. The recipe may be multiplied by any number—just allow time for baking.

These are perfect for cookie jars (if they have a wide opening,), lunch boxes, picnics, etc. Or wrap them individually to fill a gift basket. Or whatever—they are just great!

¾ cup <u>unsifted</u> all-purpose flour (stir to aerate lightly before measuring)

1 teaspoon baking powder

½ teaspoon salt

¼ pound (1 stick) sweet butter

¾ teaspoon vanilla extract

½ cup granulated sugar

⅓ cup dark brown sugar, firmly packed

1 egg (graded large or extra-large)

¼ cup quick-cooking (not "instant") oatmeal

¾ cup untoasted wheat germ (natural, untreated, untoasted wheat germ is available at health-food stores)

1¾ ounces (⅔ cup, loosely packed) shredded coconut

6 ounces (1 cup) semisweet chocolate morsels

Adjust two racks to divide the oven into thirds and preheat oven to 350 degrees. Line cookie sheets with aluminum foil and set aside.

Sift together the flour, baking powder, and salt and set aside.

In the large bowl of an electric mixer cream the butter. Beat in the vanilla and both sugars. Add the egg and beat well. On low speed add the sifted dry ingredients, scraping the bowl and beating only until mixed. Mix in the oatmeal, wheat germ, and coconut. Then stir in the morsels.

Spread out a piece of wax paper. Use a ¼-cup metal or plastic measuring cup (made for dry ingredients) to measure the dough for each cookie. Form nine mounds of dough on the wax paper, each one a very slightly rounded ¼ cupful. A narrow rubber spatula (bottle scraper) is handy for removing the dough from the cup.

Wet your hands with cold water, shake the water off but do not dry your hands. Roll a mound of dough into a ball between your wet hands. These large balls of dough should be placed about 5 inches apart on the foil-lined sheets. The best way to do that is to place two on one long side of the sheet and one between them on the other long side. (That means only three on a 12 x 15½-inch sheet.)

With the back of the tines of a wet fork press the cookies in all directions to flatten them to ½-inch thickness. (If they crack on the edges use the fork to press them together.)

Bake two sheets at a time for 18 to 20 minutes, reversing the sheets top to bottom and front to back as necessary during baking to insure even browning. When they are done, the cookies will be lightly colored and the tops will spring back when lightly pressed with a fingertip. Time these carefully—do not underbake—to be sure they will be crisp on the edges and the bottoms when cool. The cookies will have spread out to 4½ inches in diameter when done. (If you bake only one sheet at a time, bake it on the upper rack.)

Let cool on the foil briefly only until the cookies are firm enough to be transferred. With a wide metal spatula transfer to racks to cool. Such large cookies must be cooled on racks that are raised to give more room for air to circulate underneath—just place each rack on any right side-up mixing bowl or cake pan.

When cool, store airtight.

VARIATION: *These can also be made with the above ingredients plus 1 cup of walnuts, cut into medium-size pieces. Due to the extra volume, you will make 11 cookies instead of 9.*

Chocolate Chip Honey Cookies

32 TO 36 COOKIES

These are plain, old-fashioned, homey drop cookies. They are light, soft, full of chocolate chips and nuts, quick and easy to make, and they keep well in a cookie jar.

1¼ cups sifted all-purpose flour
½ teaspoon baking soda
½ teaspoon salt
¼ pound (1 stick) sweet butter
½ teaspoon vanilla extract
½ cup honey
1 egg (graded large or extra-large)
4 ounces (generous 1 cup) pecans or walnuts, cut into medium-size pieces
6 ounces (1 cup) semisweet chocolate morsels

Adjust two racks to divide the oven into thirds and preheat oven to 375 degrees. Line cookie sheets with aluminum foil.

Sift together the flour, baking soda, and salt and set aside. In the large bowl of an electric mixer cream the butter. Add the vanilla and honey and beat to mix. Add the egg and beat to mix; the mixture will look curdled now—it is O.K., don't worry.

On low speed add the sifted dry ingredients and, scraping the bowl with a rubber spatula, beat only until incorporated.

Remove from the mixer and stir in the nuts and chocolate morsels.

Use a slightly rounded teaspoonful of the dough for each cookie. Place them about 2 inches apart on the foil-lined sheets.

Bake for 13 to 15 minutes, reversing the sheets top to bottom and front to back as necessary during baking to insure even browning. Bake until the cookies are nicely colored all over and spring back firmly when lightly pressed with a fingertip. (If you bake only one sheet at a time bake it on the higher rack.)

With a wide metal spatula transfer the cookies to racks to cool.

When cool, store airtight.

Chocolate Chip Whole-Wheat Cookies

52 COOKIES

These are easy-to-make drop cookies—they are marvelous. Thick and yummy, crisp on the outside, semi-soft in the middle, not too sweet. They have that deliciously satisfying and natural flavor of whole-wheat flour. Especially good for cookie jars, lunch boxes, picnics, or for mailing. The recipe comes from a ski lodge in Colorado where these were served with afternoon tea in front of a roaring fireplace. Huge wooden bowls of them disappeared in no time, most of the guests stashing away a few for a late-night snack.

½ pound (2 sticks) sweet butter

1 teaspoon vanilla extract

1½ cups dark brown sugar, firmly packed

3 eggs (graded large or extra-large)

½ teaspoon salt

1 teaspoon baking soda

⅓ cup dry instant powdered skimmed milk

2½ cups strained all-purpose whole-wheat flour (see Note)

6 ounces (1½ cups) walnuts or pecans, coarsely cut or broken

12 ounces (2 cups) semisweet chocolate morsels

Adjust two racks to divide the oven into thirds and preheat oven to 375 degrees. Line cookie sheets with aluminum foil.

In the large bowl of an electric mixer cream the butter. Add the vanilla and sugar and beat well. Add the eggs one at a time, beating well after each addition. Then

beat briefly until slightly lighter in color. Beat in the salt, baking soda, and then the dry powdered skimmed milk. On low speed gradually add the flour, scraping the bowl with a rubber spatula and beating only until incorporated. It will be a thick mixture. Remove it from the mixer and, with a heavy wooden spatula, stir in the nuts and then the chocolate morsels.

Use a rounded teaspoonful of the dough for each cookie (use another teaspoon to push it off) and place them in neat mounds about 1½ inches apart on the foil-lined sheets. (These do not spread out much in baking; you can place three rows, four cookies in each row, on a 12 x 15½-inch cookie sheet.)

Bake two sheets at a time for 12 to 14 minutes, reversing the sheets top to bottom and front to back once during baking to insure even browning. Bake until the cookies feel semi-firm to the touch and are slightly darkened—they should be well-baked but

watch them for burning. (If you bake only one sheet at a time, bake it on the higher rack—and one sheet bakes in less time than two.)

With a wide metal spatula transfer the cookies to racks to cool.

Store airtight with wax paper between the layers.

NOTE: *Whole-wheat flour has little particles of whole wheat in it, so before measuring you should press it through a large mesh strainer because it is too coarse to go through a sifter. Stir any bits of wheat back into the measured flour.*

VARIATION: *Shredded coconut and/or raisins may be used in place of all or part of the nuts.*

Chocolate Chip Health-Food Cookies

36 TO 40 LARGE COOKIES

These are from Key West, Florida. They are large, thick, semi-soft drop cookies loaded with chocolate chips and delicious health-food goodies. Great for filling a few cookie jars, or for packing in a box and mailing, or for a lunch box or picnic.

1½ cups sifted all-purpose flour

¾ teaspoon salt

½ teaspoon baking powder

½ teaspoon baking soda

1½ teaspoons cinnamon

¼ teaspoon allspice

¼ teaspoon ginger

2 tablespoons salad oil

1 cup regular or quick-cooking (not instant) rolled oats

¼ pound (1 stick) sweet butter

1 teaspoon vanilla extract

½ cup dark brown sugar, firmly packed

½ cup honey

1 egg (graded large, extra-large, or jumbo)

¼ cup wheat germ, raw or toasted

¼ cup milk

8 ounces (1 cup) pitted dates, coarsely cut

6 ounces (1½ cups) walnuts or pecans, cut or broken into large pieces

3½ ounces (1 firmly packed cup) shredded coconut

Optional: 2½ ounces (½ cup) sunflower seeds, either toasted and salted, or raw and unsalted (available in health-food stores)

12 ounces (2 cups) semisweet chocolate morsels

Adjust two racks to divide the oven into thirds and preheat oven to 350 degrees. Line cookie sheets with aluminum foil.

Sift together the flour, salt, baking powder, baking soda, cinnamon, allspice, and ginger, and set aside.

In any shallow cake pan (round or square), stir the salad oil into the rolled oats to mix. Bake for 15 minutes, stirring occasionally. Then set aside to cool.

In the large bowl of an electric mixer cream the butter. Add the vanilla, sugar, and honey and beat to mix. Add the egg and beat well (the mixture will look curdled). On low speed add the sifted dry ingredients and then the wheat germ, scraping the bowl with a rubber spatula and beating only until incorporated. Add the milk and beat to mix. Remove from the mixer.

With a wooden or rubber spatula stir in the rolled oats, dates, nuts, coconut, optional sunflower seeds, and then the chocolate morsels.

These should be large cookies; use a heaping teaspoonful or a well-rounded tablespoonful of the dough for each cookie. Place them about 1½ inches apart on the foil-lined sheets.

Bake two sheets at a time for about 18 to 20 minutes, reversing the sheets top to bottom and front to back as necessary during baking to insure even browning. Bake until the cookies are nicely colored all over and until they spring back when lightly pressed with a fingertip. (If you bake one sheet at a time, bake it on the upper rack.) Be very careful not to overbake these or the bottoms will burn.

With a wide metal spatula transfer the cookies to racks to cool. Then store airtight.

Colorado Cowboy Cookies

36 Cookies

In Colorado any oatmeal cookie that contains chocolate chips is called a Cowboy Cookie. I've had many versions and no two were alike. The cowboy who gave me this recipe said, "These are enough for a cowboy

and his horse." I divided his recipe (we don't have a horse) but you can multiply it by any number. These are deliciously crisp cookies that will keep very well in a cookie jar.

1 cup sifted all-purpose flour

½ teaspoon baking soda

¼ teaspoon baking powder

¼ teaspoon salt

¼ pound (1 stick) sweet butter

½ teaspoon vanilla extract

½ cup granulated sugar

½ cup dark brown sugar, firmly packed

1 egg (graded large or extra-large)

1 cup quick-cooking (not "instant") or regular rolled oats

3 ounces (½ cup) semisweet chocolate morsels

2 ounces (generous ½ cup) walnuts or pecans, cut or broken into medium-size pieces

Adjust two racks to divide the oven into thirds and preheat oven to 350 degrees. Line cookie sheets with aluminum foil.

Sift together the flour, baking soda, baking powder, and salt and set aside. In the large bowl of an electric mixer cream the butter. Add the vanilla and then both sugars and beat well. Add the egg and beat well. On low speed gradually add the sifted dry ingredients and beat, scraping the bowl with a rubber spatula, until incorporated.

Remove the bowl from the mixer. Stir in the oats and then the chocolate morsels and nuts. Transfer to a small bowl for ease in handling. (The dough will be rather stiff.)

Use a well-rounded (slightly less than heaping) teaspoonful of the dough to make each cookie. Place the mounds 2 inches apart on the aluminum foil. Bake for about 18 minutes until the cookies are golden-colored and completely dry. During baking reverse the sheets top to bottom and front to back to insure even browning.

If you bake only one sheet at a time, bake it on the upper rack.

With a wide metal spatula transfer the cookies to racks to cool. When completely cool, store them airtight.

Chocolate Chip-Coconut Macaroons

36 COOKIES

These are white cookies with chocolate chips and a layer of melted chocolate on the bottom. They are easy to make and they keep well.

⅓ cup sifted all-purpose flour

¼ teaspoon baking powder

⅛ teaspoon salt

1 tablespoon butter

¾ cup granulated sugar

2 eggs (graded large)

1 teaspoon vanilla extract

10½ ounces (4 loosely packed cups) shredded coconut

6 ounces (1 cup) semisweet chocolate morsels

Adjust two racks to divide the oven into thirds and preheat oven to 325 degrees. Line cookie sheets with aluminum foil.

Sift together the flour, baking powder, and salt and set aside.

Place the butter in a small pan over low heat to melt. Then set it aside to cool but do not let it harden—it must stay liquid.

Meanwhile, in the small bowl of an electric mixer add the sugar to the eggs and beat at high speed for 5 minutes until the mixture is almost white.

On lowest speed add the sifted dry ingredients, scraping the bowl with a rubber spatula and beating only until incorporated.

Remove from the mixer, fold in the liquid butter and then the vanilla. Then fold in the coconut and finally the chocolate morsels.

Use a well-rounded teaspoonful of the mixture for each cookie and place them 1½ inches apart on the aluminum foil.

Bake two sheets at a time, reversing the sheets top to bottom and front to back once during baking to insure even browning. Bake for about 18 minutes or until some parts of the tops of the cookies are lightly golden-colored—some parts of the cookies will still be white.

With a wide metal spatula transfer the cookies to racks to cool. If you bake one sheet at a time, bake it on the lower rack.

While the cookies are baking or cooling prepare the glaze.

GLAZE

6 ounces semisweet chocolate (see Note)

Break up the chocolate and place it in the top of a small double boiler over warm water on low heat to melt slowly. Cover until partially melted, then uncover and stir until completely smooth. Remove the top of the double boiler from the hot water.

Cover one or two cookie sheets with wax paper or aluminum foil.

With a small metal spatula spread some of the chocolate on the bottoms of the cookies, spreading it smoothly all the way to the edges in a rather thin layer.

After you spread the chocolate on a cookie, place it chocolate side down on the lined cookie sheet.

Refrigerate until the chocolate is firm and the cookies can be lifted easily. Place them in an airtight box.

These are best if they are stored in the refrigerator and served cold if you have used real chocolate.

NOTE: *If you use a compound chocolate (see page 5) for the glaze, it will dry quickly without refrigeration, the finished cookies may stand at room temperature, and the chocolate will not discolor. Otherwise, any real semisweet chocolate may be used, with the above directions for refrigerating.*

Icebox Cookies

Icebox cookies are fun. Prepare the dough ahead of time, store it in the freezer, then slice as many as you want and bake whenever you want.

Viennese Chocolate Icebox Cookies

48 COOKIES

Fragile, delicate, crisp, dark, delicious.

3 ounces (3 squares) unsweetened chocolate
½ pound (2 sticks) sweet butter
1 teaspoon vanilla extract
¼ teaspoon almond extract
⅔ cup granulated sugar
1 egg (graded large)
1½ cups sifted all-purpose flour
A few teaspoons crystal sugar (see page 7)
  or
A few tablespoons blanched almonds, coarsely
  chopped

Place the chocolate in the top of a small double boiler over hot water on moderate heat. Cover and let stand only until melted. Remove from the hot water, and set aside, uncovered, to cool slightly.

In the large bowl of an electric mixer cream the butter. Add the vanilla and almond extracts and the granulated sugar and beat to mix, then beat in the egg and then the melted chocolate. On low speed gradually add the flour, scraping the bowl with a rubber spatula and beating only until the mixture is smooth.

Tear off a piece of wax paper about 15 inches long. Place the dough by large spoonfuls down the length of the paper, forming a heavy strip of dough about 12 inches long.

Bring up both long sides of the paper. With your hands press against the paper, forming the dough into a roll about 2 inches in diameter, or a block

about 2½ inches by 1 inch—either shape should be about 12 inches long. Wrap the paper around the dough, smooth the sides and the ends.

Slide a cookie sheet under the paper and transfer the dough to the refrigerator at least until it is firm.

This dough may be kept in the refrigerator for a week or two, or it may be frozen. But it must be sliced at refrigerator temperature—it will crack if you slice it frozen.

When ready to bake adjust two racks to divide the oven into thirds and preheat oven to 375 degrees. Line cookie sheets with aluminum foil.

Place the dough on a board, open the top of the paper, and with a sharp, firm knife cut the dough into ¼-inch slices. (Wipe the blade of the knife whenever any of the dough sticks to it.)

Place the cookies about 1 inch apart on the aluminum foil.

Sprinkle the tops of the cookies with the crystal sugar or chopped almonds.

Bake for 10 to 12 minutes, reversing the sheets top to bottom and front to back once to insure even baking. Test by touching the tops with a fingertip—when they just feel firm they are done. Watch them carefully—chocolate burns easily if overbaked.

With a wide metal spatula, transfer the cookies to racks to cool.

Handle with care—these crack easily. Place them in layers on a tray or in a freezer box—not in a cookie jar. Cover airtight.

Chocolate-Nut Icebox Cookies

75 TO 100 COOKIES

These are thin, crisp, dark chocolate, speckled with coconut and nuts. They are easy to make and they keep well in a cookie jar. Or pack them in a container to give as a gift.

1½ cups sifted all-purpose flour

½ teaspoon baking soda

½ teaspoon salt

¼ pound (1 stick) sweet butter

½ teaspoon vanilla extract

1 cup dark brown sugar, firmly packed

1 egg (graded large or extra-large)

½ cup unsweetened cocoa powder (preferably Dutch process)

4 ounces (generous 1 cup) pecans or walnuts, cut into medium-size pieces

3½ ounces (1 to 1⅓ cups) shredded coconut

Sift together the flour, baking soda, and salt and set aside.

In the large bowl of an electric mixer cream the butter. Add the vanilla and brown sugar and beat to mix well. Add the egg and beat until smooth. On low speed gradually add the cocoa, and then the sifted dry ingredients, scraping the bowl with a rubber spatula and beating until well mixed.

Stir in the nuts and the coconut.

Lightly flour a large board or smooth work surface. Turn the mixture onto the floured surface. Lightly flour your hands. Form the dough into a compact ball and then shape it into a long roll about 14 inches long and about 1¾ inches in diameter. Smooth the sides.

Tear off a piece of wax paper or plastic wrap about 18 inches long and place it near the roll of dough. Roll the dough over onto the center of the paper. Wrap securely. Slide a cookie sheet under the roll of dough and transfer to the freezer for at least several hours or until frozen solid. The cookies slice best when the dough is frozen solid, and it may stay in the freezer for months.

When ready to bake, adjust two racks to divide the oven into thirds (or if you are baking only one sheet, adjust a rack to the center) and preheat oven to 400 degrees. Line cookie sheets with aluminum foil.

Unwrap the dough and place it on a cutting board. With a finely serrated knife, or any thin and sharp knife, slice the cookies a generous ⅛ inch thick. Place them 1 inch apart on the aluminum foil.

(If you don't bake all the cookies at one time, rewrap and refreeze the remainder of the dough.)

Bake for 8 to 10 minutes, reversing the sheets top to bottom and front to back as necessary during baking to insure even baking. The cookies should be baked until they are semi-firm to the touch, but they must be watched carefully—chocolate burns easily. If they have not been sliced exactly the same thickness (which would be quite a feat), the thinner ones will bake more quickly and should be removed individually as they are done.

With a wide metal spatula transfer the cookies to racks to cool.

Store airtight.

Mexican Chocolate Icebox Cookies

40 COOKIES

Extra-dark, extra-chocolaty, extra-crisp, plain, and bittersweet. These are from a friend who lives in Guatemala and says that this is the only recipe she bakes. She always has some unbaked in the freezer and some baked ones in a jar in the kitchen, and she makes them for a restaurant and for friends, and everyone loves them.

The original Spanish name for these means "raggedy edges." My friend said that during baking they ran slightly and the edges became raggedy. However, in my kitchen they hardly ever do that (only occasionally); they usually bake with quite neat edges. I don't know why.

1½ cups sifted all-purpose flour
¾ cup unsweetened cocoa powder (preferably Dutch process)
¼ teaspoon salt
Generous pinch of finely ground black pepper
Generous pinch of cayenne
¾ teaspoon cinnamon
6 ounces (1½ sticks) sweet butter
1½ teaspoons vanilla extract
1 cup granulated sugar
1 egg (graded large or extra-large)

Sift together the flour, cocoa, salt, pepper, cayenne, and cinnamon and set aside.

In the large bowl of an electric mixer cream the butter. Add the vanilla and sugar and beat to mix thoroughly. Beat in the egg, then on low speed gradually add the sifted dry ingredients, scraping the bowl with a rubber spatula and beating only until mixed. Toward the end of the mixing, if the dough starts to crawl up on the beaters, remove the bowl from the mixer and finish the mixing with a wooden or rubber spatula.

Lightly flour a large board. Turn the dough out onto the board. Lightly flour your hands and, with your hands, shape the dough into a cylinder about 10 inches long and about 2 inches in diameter.

Wrap the cylinder of dough in wax paper and place it in the freezer until firm. Or it may be kept frozen.

Before baking, adjust two racks to divide the oven into thirds and preheat oven to 375 degrees.

Unwrap the dough and place it on a board. With a sharp, heavy knife cut it into slices ¼ inch thick.

Place the slices 1½ to 2 inches apart (they will spread a little) on unbuttered cookie sheets.

Bake 10 or 11 minutes, reversing the sheets top to bottom and front to back once during baking to insure even browning. The cookies are done when they feel almost firm to the touch. Watch them carefully to be sure they do not burn. If you bake only one sheet at a time, bake it on the upper rack; the cookies will bake in a little less time than when there are two sheets in the oven.

Let them cool for a few seconds on the sheets until firm enough to be moved. Then, with a wide metal spatula, transfer the cookies to racks to cool.

Store airtight.

Chocolate Almond Sp-icebox Cookies

48 COOKIES

Crisp, dark, bittersweet chocolate spice cookies with slivers of almonds going every which way. Don't be startled by the list of spices—these are not sharp; they have a Christmasy taste but are superior cookies any time of the year. They may be prepared way ahead of time and frozen until you slice and bake them. A glass jar or a little box of these makes a lovely gift.

1¼ cups sifted all-purpose flour
1 teaspoon baking powder
½ teaspoon cinnamon
½ teaspoon dry powdered instant espresso or any other powdered (not granular) instant coffee
⅛ teaspoon salt
⅛ teaspoon ginger
⅛ teaspoon black pepper
⅛ teaspoon cloves
⅛ teaspoon allspice
⅛ teaspoon nutmeg
⅛ teaspoon dry mustard
3 ounces (3 squares) unsweetened chocolate
¼ pound (1 stick) sweet butter
⅔ cup granulated sugar
1 egg (graded large or extra-large)
2½ ounces (¾ cup) thinly sliced almonds, blanched or unblanched

Sift together the flour, baking powder, cinnamon, dry instant espresso, salt, ginger, pepper, cloves, allspice, nutmeg, and dry mustard and set aside.

Place the chocolate in the top of a small double boiler over hot water on low heat, cover until melted, then remove the top of the double boiler and set aside, uncovered, to cool slightly.

In the large bowl of an electric mixer cream the butter. Add the sugar and beat to mix well. Beat in the egg and then the melted chocolate. On low speed add the sifted dry ingredients and beat, scraping the bowl with a rubber spatula, only until incorporated. Remove from the mixer and stir in the almonds.

Tear off a piece of wax paper about 14 inches long. Place large spoonfuls of the dough down the length of the paper, forming a strip 12 inches long. Fold the sides of the paper together over the top and, pressing against the paper, form the dough into a smooth cylinder about 2½ inches wide, 1 inch high, and 12 inches long.

Wrap the dough in the paper. Slide a cookie sheet under it and transfer it to the freezer for at least several hours until it is firm, or much longer if you wish. (If it is going to stay frozen for more than a few hours or so, when it is firm wrap the package in aluminum foil for extra protection.)

When you are ready to bake adjust two racks to divide the oven into thirds and preheat oven to 375 degrees. Line cookie sheets with aluminum foil. (Or, if you prefer, these may be baked on unlined, unbuttered sheets.)

Unwrap the dough. With a sharp knife cut it into even slices ¼ inch thick. Place them 1 inch apart (these do not spread) on the cookie sheets.

Bake for 10 to 11 minutes, reversing the sheets top to bottom and front to back once to insure even baking. These should be baked long enough to be crisp when cool (they become crisp as they cool) but watch them carefully so they don't burn. When the cookies are done they will feel a little resistant to the touch.

With a wide metal spatula transfer to a rack to cool. Store airtight.

Rolled Cookies

When you use a cookie cutter always start cutting at the outside of rolled-out dough instead of in the middle. Or use a long, sharp knife and cut the dough into squares or triangles.

Chocolate Scotch Shortbread Cookies

35 TO 40 COOKIES

Traditionally, shortbread is not chocolate. Untraditionally this is very chocolate. These are thick, dry, crisp cookies that are buttery and plain. They keep well, mail well, and are lovely to package as a gift.

> 2 cups sifted all-purpose flour
> ½ cup strained unsweetened cocoa powder (preferably Dutch process)
> 1 cup confectioners sugar
> ¼ teaspoon salt
> ½ pound (2 sticks) sweet butter (see Note)
> 1 teaspoon vanilla extract

Adjust two racks to divide the oven into thirds and preheat to 300 degrees.

This may be prepared in a food processor (it's a breeze) or in an electric mixer. (I have also made it without either by first mixing all the ingredients together on a board with my bare hands.)

To use a processor: Fit it with a steel blade and place the dry ingredients in the bowl. Cut the cold butter into ½-inch slices over the dry ingredients. Add the vanilla. Cover and process until the ingredients hold together.

To use an electric mixer: Cream the butter in the large mixer bowl. Add the vanilla, sugar, and salt and beat to mix. On low speed add the flour and cocoa, scraping the bowl with a rubber spatula and beating only until the mixture holds together.

If the dough is not perfectly smooth, place it on a board or smooth work surface and knead it briefly with the heel of your hand.

Form the dough into a ball and flatten it slightly.

Flour a pastry cloth, rubbing the flour in well, and a rolling pin. Place the dough on the cloth and turn it over to flour both sides. With the floured rolling pin (reflour it as necessary) roll the dough until it is ½ inch thick (no thinner). It is important to make it the same thickness all over.

Use a plain round cookie cutter 1½ inches in diameter. Before cutting each cookie, dip the cutter in flour and tap it to shake off excess. Cut the cookies as close to each other as possible. Place the cookies 1 inch apart on unbuttered cookie sheets.

Press together leftover scraps of dough, reflour the cloth lightly if necessary, and reroll the dough.

Now each cookie should be pierced three times in a vertical row in the middle with the tines of a four-pronged fork, piercing all the way through the cookie each time. If the dough sticks to the fork, or if removing the fork causes the cookies to lose their shape, transfer the sheets of cookies to the refrigerator or freezer only until the dough becomes slightly firm—do not let it freeze or become too firm or the fork will crack the cookies.

Bake for 25 to 30 minutes or until the cookies are firm to the touch, reversing the sheets top to bottom and front to back once during baking to insure even baking. Watch these carefully—they could burn and become bitter before you know it unless you check them often. If you bake only one sheet, bake it on the higher rack; one sheet will bake in less time.

With a wide metal spatula transfer the cookies to racks to cool.

NOTE: *If you make this in a food processor, the butter should be firm and cold, right out of the refrigerator. If you make it in an electric mixer, the butter should be removed from the refrigerator about 20 or 30 minutes before using.*

VARIATIONS: *While working on this recipe I tried many variations and they were all good. Many of our friends like it better with the addition of 1 teaspoon of dry instant espresso or any other powdered (not granular) instant coffee. And it may be made without salt and/or vanilla. Some authorities claim that the chocolate flavor is stronger without vanilla.*

Stamped Shortbread

If you have a ceramic or wooden cookie stamp, or a little wooden form for stamping butter, use it to make stamped shortbread cookies. Follow the above recipe up to the direction for piercing the cookies with a fork. Do not pierce these. Instead, press the stamp onto each cookie, pressing firmly enough to imprint the design and, at the same time, to flatten the cookies slightly. Bake as above.

Chocolate Wafers

36 2³/₄-inch Cookies

Wonderful thin, crisp, plain cookies, the dough is rolled out and cut with a cookie cutter. The recipe can easily be doubled if you wish.

> 2 ounces (2 squares) unsweetened chocolate
> 1 cup plus 2 tablespoons sifted all-purpose flour
> ³/₄ teaspoon baking powder
> ¹/₄ teaspoon baking soda
> Pinch of salt
> 2 ounces (¹/₂ stick) sweet butter
> 1 teaspoon vanilla extract
> ¹/₂ cup granulated sugar
> 1¹/₂ teaspoons light cream or milk
> 1 egg (graded large)

Place the chocolate in the top of a small double boiler over hot water on moderate heat. Cover until partially melted, then uncover and stir until smooth. Remove from the heat and set aside to cool slightly.

Sift together the flour, baking powder, baking soda, and salt and set aside.

In the large bowl of an electric mixer cream the butter. Add the vanilla and sugar and beat to mix well. Add the melted chocolate and beat until incorporated. Then add the light cream or milk and the egg and beat to mix well. On low speed add the sifted dry ingredients, scraping the bowl with a rubber spatula and beating only until incorporated.

Place the dough on a piece of wax paper, fold the sides of the paper over the dough and press down on the paper to flatten the dough to a scant 1-inch thickness, wrap in the paper and refrigerate for 20 to 30 minutes—no longer or the dough will crack when you roll it out. (However, if you do refrigerate it for longer—even overnight—let it stand at room temperature for about an hour before rolling it out.)

Adjust two racks to divide oven into thirds and preheat oven to 400 degrees. Line cookie sheets with aluminum foil.

Flour a pastry cloth and place the dough on it. (If you have doubled the recipe, roll only half of the dough at a time.) With a floured rolling pin—which should be refloured frequently to avoid sticking—roll the dough out until it is only ⅛ inch thick (thin).

I use a round cookie cutter that is 2¾ inches in diameter—use any size you like, and cut the cookies as close to each other as possible.

Place the cookies ½ inch apart on the aluminum foil. (It might be necessary to transfer the cookies from the pastry cloth to the foil with a wide metal spatula—handle them carefully in order to keep them perfectly round and flat.)

Leftover pieces of the dough should be pressed together and rerolled.

Bake two sheets at a time for 7 to 8 minutes, reversing the sheets top to bottom and front to back once to insure even baking. Bake until the cookies feel almost firm to the touch. These are supposed to be crisp (they will become more crisp as they cool) and they should not be underbaked, but watch them carefully to be sure they do not burn. (If you bake one sheet at a time, bake it on the upper rack.)

With a wide metal spatula, transfer the cookies to racks to cool.

Store airtight.

NOTE: *These cookies may be crumbled to make a delicious chocolate-cookie crumb crust. If you make them for that purpose roll out the dough and then just cut it with a long knife into large squares; don't bother to use a cookie cutter.*

Old-Fashioned Chocolate Sugar Cookies

28 3-INCH COOKIES

These are extremely crisp/crunchy cookie-jar cookies with a bit of optional mace flavoring—it is not a strong flavor and is delicious with chocolate. (Mace and nutmeg come from the same fruit seed—the seed is nutmeg and the outside membrane is mace—they resemble each other in taste but mace is more pungent.) The dough is rolled with a rolling pin and cut with a cookie cutter, but if you wish it may be handled as ice-box cookies (see Notes). Either way, the dough has to be well chilled before it is baked.

2 ounces (2 squares) unsweetened chocolate
1½ cups sifted all-purpose flour
1 teaspoon baking powder
¼ teaspoon salt
1/16 teaspoon baking soda (see Notes)
Optional: ¼ teaspoon mace
¼ pound (1 stick) sweet butter
½ teaspoon vanilla extract
1 cup granulated sugar
1 egg (graded large)
Optional: additional granulated sugar or crystal sugar (see page 7), for sprinkling on the tops of the cookies

Place the chocolate in the top of a small double boiler over hot water on moderate heat, cover until partially melted, then uncover and stir until completely melted. Remove the top of the double boiler and set aside, uncovered, to cool slightly.

130

Sift together the flour, baking powder, salt, baking soda, and optional mace and set aside.

In the large bowl of an electric mixer cream the butter. Add the vanilla and the sugar and beat to mix well. Beat in the egg and then the chocolate. On low speed gradually add the sifted dry ingredients, scraping the bowl with a rubber spatula and beating only until everything is incorporated.

Transfer the dough to a large piece of wax paper or plastic wrap, flatten slightly, wrap airtight, and refrigerate for a few hours.

Before rolling, cutting, and baking the cookies, adjust two racks to divide the oven into thirds and preheat oven to 375 degrees.

Line cookie sheets with aluminum foil.

Flour a pastry cloth and a rolling pin. Work with half of the dough at a time (the other half may stand at room temperature unless the kitchen is very warm). Place the dough on the cloth and turn it over to flour both sides. If it is too stiff to roll, pound it with the rolling pin to soften slightly and/or let it stand at room temperature for awhile. Roll the dough until it is ⅛ inch thick and very even—reflour the rolling pin as necessary.

This dough may be rolled to a scant ¹⁄₁₆ inch to make extra-thin cookies. When it is that thin it is rather fragile; roll it slowly and carefully and keep the rolling pin floured. Bake less time and keep an eye on the cookies in order not to burn.

Using any cookie cutter you wish (I use a round 3-inch one) start cutting the cookies at the outer edge of the rolled dough and cut them touching each other in order not to have any more scraps than necessary. (Reserve the scraps and roll them all together—if the kitchen is warm it might be necessary to rechill them before rolling.)

With a wide metal spatula transfer the cookies to the aluminum foil, placing them 1 to 1½ inches apart.

Sprinkle the tops with the optional additional granulated sugar or crystal sugar.

Bake two sheets at a time for about 15 minutes or until the cookies feel semi-firm to the touch.

Reverse the sheets top to bottom and front to back once to insure even baking. They may begin to turn a slightly darker color on the edges, but watch them carefully—don't let them burn. (If you bake only one sheet at a time, bake it on the upper rack. When baking only one sheet it will take a bit less time.)

With a wide metal spatula transfer the cookies to racks to cool.

NOTES: *1. To measure ¹⁄₁₆ teaspoon baking soda, fill and level ¼ teaspoon, then with a small metal spatula or a table knife mark it into equal quarters, cut away three quarters (return it to the box) and use the remaining quarter.*

2. To use this dough for icebox cookies, after it is mixed transfer it to a large piece of wax paper, placing it by large spoonfuls touching each other down the middle of the paper. Bring up the sides of the paper and with your hands form the dough into a smooth roll, either rounded or squared, about 2 inches in diameter. Wrap in the paper and refrigerate or freeze until very firm (the dough can be sliced when it is frozen). Unwrap and cut into even slices ⅛ inch thick. Place them on the aluminum foil and bake as above.

Checkerboards

48 COOKIES

Checkerboard cookies must be neat and precise, therefore they are often thought of as a fancy petit four to be ordered from a fancy patisserie, or possibly as a fancy nibble served with the compliments of the chef in a fancy restaurant—not something that the average home cook would play around with. But believe me, you can make them—they are not difficult. Neat and precise, yes—but not difficult. Gorgeous is what they are.

½ pound (2 sticks) sweet butter
½ teaspoon vanilla extract
¼ teaspoon almond extract
½ cup granulated sugar
¼ teaspoon salt
2¾ cups sifted all-purpose flour
2 tablespoons unsweetened cocoa powder
   (preferably Dutch process)
1 egg, lightly beaten and strained

In the large bowl of an electric mixer cream the butter. Add the vanilla and almond extract and then the sugar and salt and beat to mix well. On low speed gradually add the flour and beat, scraping the bowl with a rubber spatula, for a few minutes. The mixture will be crumbly.

Turn it out onto a large board or smooth work surface, squeeze it between your hands and knead it until it holds together and is smooth. Extra kneading is good—work it well.

Now the dough has to be divided into two exactly equal halves. You have a scant 2½ cups of dough; carefully measure 1¼ cups minus one tablespoon of the dough, pressing it down in the cup (use the metal measuring cups that are made for measuring dry ingredients) and set it aside.

Add the cocoa to the remaining dough. Knead to incorporate the cocoa thoroughly. The mixture must be smooth. With the heel of your hand push off small amounts of the dough, pushing on the board and away from you; re-form the dough and push it off again. Repeat until the mixture is evenly colored. Now, with your hands shape each piece of dough into a flat square.

Then place one square on a lightly floured pastry cloth and, with a lightly floured rolling pin, roll it into a square shape ½ inch thick and 6 inches square (no smaller); keep the edges straight and the corners as square as you can. The edges may be pressed into a straight line by pushing a ruler or a long, heavy knife against them, or they may be trimmed with a long, heavy knife. Use your fingers to square-off the corners.

Carefully, with your hands or with two wide metal spatulas, temporarily transfer the square and roll out the remaining square.

Hold a ruler facing you against the farthest edge of one of the squares and, with the tip of a small, sharp knife, mark the dough into ½-inch lengths. (The strips must be cut straight; for extra insurance mark the opposite side of the square also.) With a long, heavy, sharp knife cut the square into ½-inch strips. You will need twelve perfect strips.

Repeat with the remaining square of dough.

(There might be some leftover scraps of dough; if so, set them aside until later.)

Tear off a piece of plastic wrap or wax paper (I think plastic wrap is better for this) about 10 inches long and place it near the strips of dough. To form the cookies: Place one strip of dark dough the long way on the paper or plastic. With a soft pastry brush, lightly brush one long edge of the strip with the beaten egg. Place a strip of light dough touching the egg-brushed edge. Brush the free long edge of the light dough with egg. Another dark strip, beaten egg, and then another light one. (You now have four strips of alternate colors touching each other, held together with a bit of beaten egg where they meet.)

Brush the top of the four strips lightly with the beaten egg. Place four more strips on top, placing dark over light and vice versa, and brushing a bit of egg between each strip as on the bottom layer. Be careful as you handle the strips and as you place them—they will not be easy to move because of the egg wash.

Brush the second layer with egg and then form a third layer, again dark over light, etc.

Now you have a three-layered bar, each layer made up of four narrow strips.

Wrap in the paper and refrigerate.

On a second piece of paper form another three-layered bar. (Most of the egg will be left over—you will not need it for the cookies.)

Wrap the second bar in the paper and refrigerate. The bars must be refrigerated for at least half an hour, or until they are firm enough to slice, but they may be refrigerated for several days or they may be frozen—if they are frozen they must be thawed before they are sliced.

When you are ready to bake: Adjust two racks to divide the oven into thirds and preheat oven to 350 degrees. Line cookie sheets with aluminum foil.

Unwrap one bar of dough. Cut a thin slice off one narrow end to make it perfectly straight.

With the ruler and the tip of a small, sharp knife, mark the bar into ¼-inch lengths. With a sharp knife cut the cookies. If the squares separate a bit as the cookies are cut, put them back in place where they belong—they will go together in baking. Place the cookies ½ inch to 1 inch apart on the lined cookie sheets.

(Leftover scraps of dough may be shaped now or later. Press them together lightly to form a marbleized dough. Roll it out ¼ inch thick on the pastry cloth and cut into shapes with a cookie cutter or cut into squares with a knife. Or roll pieces between your hands into little sausage shapes with tapered ends; place on cookie sheet and form into crescents.)

Bake 18 to 20 minutes, reversing the sheets top to bottom and front to back during baking to insure even browning. Bake until lightly colored.

With a wide metal spatula transfer to racks to cool.

Repeat with second bar, or reserve it to bake at some other time.

Macaroons

Chocolate Macaroons from Monte Carlo

24 MACAROONS

If these aren't the same as the ones I had on the Riviera, I can't tell the difference. Chocolate macaroons are one of my favorites. When I ate these I said they were the best ever. I could not get the recipe. This is the result of much experimenting. They are bittersweet and semi-soft/chewy. Almost like candy.

2½ ounces (2½ squares) unsweetened
   chocolate

5 ounces (1 cup) almonds, blanched or
   unblanched

1 cup granulated sugar

⅓ cup egg whites (from 2 to 3 eggs; measure
   carefully)

½ teaspoon vanilla extract

¼ teaspoon almond extract

About 1 teaspoon additional granulated sugar
   (for topping)

Optional: 6 candied cherries, cut into quarters

Adjust two racks to divide the oven into thirds and preheat oven to 325 degrees. These are traditionally baked on heavy brown paper. Cut two pieces (you can use grocery bags) to fit two 12 x 15 -inch cookie sheets, (The paper should be smooth; it can be ironed if necessary.)

Place the chocolate in the top of a small double boiler over hot water on moderate heat. Cover and let stand only until melted. Remove from the hot water, and set aside, uncovered, to cool.

The almonds must be ground to a fine powder. This can be done in a food processor, a blender, or a nut grinder. Place the ground almonds in a mixing bowl. Add the sugar and mix well.

Add the vanilla and almond extracts to the egg whites and stir into the almond mixture. Then add the melted chocolate. Stir thoroughly (The mixture should not be hard—or soft. It should be firm enough to hold a shape: semi-firm. It is a matter of proportion, and that is why it is important that the egg whites—and the other ingredients, too—be measured very carefully.) Now, if the mixture is runny or too sticky to handle, chill it briefly (that will harden the chocolate and make it easier to handle).

Place a large piece of wax paper in front of you, preferably near the sink because you will have to keep your hands wet while shaping the cookies.

Form 24 mounds of dough on the wax paper, using a rounded teaspoonful for each.

The macaroons should now be shaped into balls by rolling them between your hands, which must be wet. Wet your hands; shake off water but do not dry, pick up a mound of the macaroon dough (use a metal spatula to pick it up if that is easier), and roll it into a ball. Place the macaroons 2 inches apart on the brown paper, but if you have used a grocery bag do not place the macaroons on the seam where the paper is double—macaroons on that double section will stick to the paper. Keep your hands really wet.

Sprinkle the tops very lightly with a bit of the additional granulated sugar.

OPTIONAL: *Top each one with a quarter of a candied cherry, curved side up.*

Bake for about 20 minutes, reversing the sheets top to bottom and front to back once to insure even baking. When done, the macaroons should be dry (but slightly soft) on the outside, moist and soft in the centers. They will harden somewhat as they cool—don't overbake them.

Slide the papers off the cookie sheets. Let stand for about half a minute. Now the macaroons will be stuck to the paper. To remove them in the best classic manner, lift each piece of paper by holding two sides of it, and gently turn it upside down onto a work table or counter top. (Don't be afraid—it's O.K. Pastry chefs do it all the time.) Brush the paper with water, using a pastry brush or a wet cloth. Let it stand briefly. As you see the paper dry out over the cookies, wet it a second time. Let stand for a few minutes until the paper can be lifted off easily without tearing the bottoms of the macaroons. If necessary, wet the paper a third time. Place the cookies right side up on racks to cool.

Store airtight with wax paper between the layers. Macaroons will stay fresh and soft for weeks in an airtight container in the refrigerator; they will be all right for several days at room temperature; or they can be frozen.

Chocolate Coconut Macaroons

30 Macaroons

These are soft and chewy drop cookies, quick and easy to make, and they keep well.

4 ounces semisweet chocolate

1 ounce (1 square) unsweetened chocolate

2 egg whites (from eggs graded large or extra-large), at room temperature

Pinch of salt

½ cup granulated sugar

1 teaspoon vanilla extract

7 ounces (2⅔ cups, loosely packed) shredded coconut

Adjust two racks to divide the oven into thirds and preheat oven to 325 degrees. Line two 12 x 15 - inch cookie sheets with aluminum foil.

Break up the sweet chocolate. Place both chocolates in the top of a small double boiler over hot water on moderate heat. Cover until partially melted. Then uncover and stir until completely melted and smooth. Remove the top of the double boiler and set aside, uncovered, to cool to room temperature.

In the small bowl of an electric mixer beat the egg whites with the salt until they hold a firm peak when the beaters are raised. On moderately low speed add the sugar 1 to 2 tablespoons at a time, pausing about 10 seconds between additions. Add the vanilla. Then increase the speed to high and beat for about 5 minutes more until the meringue is very stiff.

Reduce the speed to low and add the cooled chocolate, scraping the bowl with a rubber spatula and beating only until mixed.

Remove the bowl from the mixer and, with a rubber or wooden spatula, fold in the coconut.

Use a moderately rounded teaspoonful of the mixture for each cookie. Place the mounds 1 inch apart on the aluminum foil, forming 15 cookies on each piece of foil.

Bake for about 16 minutes, reversing the sheets top to bottom and front to back once to insure even baking. When the macaroons are done they should feel dry on the outside but must remain soft in the centers.

With a wide metal spatula transfer the macaroons to racks to cool. Even if the racks have little feet to raise them, they should be raised still more; place them on any right-side-up pan or bowl. (These need plenty of room for air to circulate underneath, or steam forms on the bottom and keeps the bottoms of the cookies from being as dry as they should be.)

These may be stored airtight or only loosely covered. If they feel too soft/moist when they have cooled, let them dry out by storing them so the air can get to them.

VARIATIONS: *Chocolate-Nut Coconut Macaroons: Use about ½ to ¾ cup pecans, cut into medium-size pieces, and fold them in along with the coconut.*

Chocolate Coconut Macaroons with Chocolate Chips: Use about ¾ cup semisweet chocolate morsels and fold them in along with the coconut.

Bittersweet Chocolate Coconut Macaroons

24 MACAROONS

Soft and chewy drop cookies topped with toasted almonds—these are easily mixed in a saucepan.

24 whole blanched almonds
1 ounce (1 square) unsweetened chocolate
1 ounce semisweet chocolate
1 ounce (¼ stick) sweet butter
2 tablespoons granulated sugar
2 eggs graded large
Pinch of salt
½ teaspoon vanilla extract
7 ounces (2⅔ cups, loosely packed) shredded coconut

Adjust two racks to divide the oven into thirds and preheat oven to 325 degrees. Line two cookie sheets with aluminum foil.

Place the almonds in a small, shallow pan and bake, shaking the pan occasionally to stir the almonds, for 20 to 25 minutes until they are golden brown. Set aside to cool.

Coarsely chop both chocolates and place them in a 6- to 8-cup saucepan. Cut up the butter and add it to the saucepan. Stir frequently over low heat until chocolate and butter are melted and smooth.

Remove from the heat and let stand for about 2 minutes. Stir in the sugar and then the eggs one at a time, stirring until smooth after each addition. Stir in the salt, vanilla, and coconut.

Form 24 cookies (12 on each sheet) using a rounded teaspoonful of the dough for each cookie, mound them high (do not flatten the tops), and place them about 1 inch apart (these do not spread) on the aluminum foil.

Push a toasted almond, pointed end down, into each cookie, and press the almond to insert it at least halfway or more (or it may fall out after baking).

Bake two sheets at a time for 25 minutes, reversing the sheets top to bottom and front to back once to insure even baking. The cookies will still feel soft—that is right; as they cool they will become crisp on the outside and should be soft in the centers.

With a wide metal spatula transfer to racks to cool.

NOTE: *For a sweeter cookie eliminate the unsweetened chocolate and use 2 ounces instead of 1 of semisweet.*

Black and White Coconut Macaroons

Follow the above recipe, eliminating the whole almonds. Place the cookies on the aluminum foil, and then prepare the white coconut mixture—or prepare it ahead of time if you wish and let it stand.

WHITE COCONUT MIXTURE

3 ounces cream cheese, at room temperature
¼ teaspoon almond extract
¼ cup granulated sugar
3½ ounces (generous 1 cup, loosely packed) shredded coconut
2 ounces (generous ½ cup) pecans, finely chopped

Mix the cheese with the almond extract and the sugar, then stir in the coconut and pecans.

With the back of a small spoon (a ¼- or ½-teaspoon measuring spoon works well) shape a deep and wide impression in the center of each mound of chocolate macaroon.

Place a rounded teaspoonful of the white mixture in the impression, mounding it high—it will not run; it will stay where you put it.

Bake and cool as in above recipe.

Other Cookies

Florentines

24 Cookie Sandwiches

These candy-like cookies are a classic European delicacy, elegant and swanky. They are the thinnest and crispest of all lace cookies. This version has two cookies sandwiched together with chocolate in the middle.

The dough is mixed in a saucepan; you will need a candy thermometer. Baking these takes quite a while because they must be baked with only a few on each cookie sheet or they run together. The finished cookies must be refrigerated (or they may be frozen).

¼ **pound (1 stick) sweet butter**

⅔ **cup granulated sugar**

2 **tablespoons milk**

2 **tablespoons honey**

½ **teaspoon vanilla extract**

4 **ounces (generous 1 cup) almonds, blanched or unblanched, and thinly sliced**

4 **ounces (¾ cup) candied orange peel, diced**

¼ **cup plus 2 tablespoons sifted all-purpose flour**

Adjust two racks to divide the oven into thirds and preheat oven to 350 degrees. Line cookie sheets with aluminum foil. (The foil must be smooth and unwrinkled. It is best if you use cookie sheets that are flat on three sides and have only one raised rim. If not, just be very careful that you do not wrinkle the foil.)

You will need a saucepan with about a 6-cup capacity; it should be narrow rather than wide for the thermometer to register correctly. Place the butter, sugar, milk, and honey in the saucepan over moderate heat. Stir occasionally until the mixture comes to a boil. Place a candy thermometer in the saucepan and cook without stirring until the thermometer registers 232 degrees (the "thread" stage).

Immediately remove the saucepan from the heat and stir in vanilla, almonds, orange peel, and flour.

Now place the saucepan over the lowest possible heat and stir occasionally to keep the mixture from hardening.

Use a level or slightly rounded teaspoonful of the mixture (do not use more) for each cookie, placing the mounds 3 to 4 inches apart on the foil-lined sheets. (These spread into large wafers; you will be able to make only 5 or 6 cookies on a 12 x 15-inch cookie sheet.)

Bake two sheets at a time for 10 to 12 minutes, reversing the sheets top to bottom and front to back as necessary to insure even browning. Bake until the cookies are browned all over; do not underbake. (A few of the nuts might remain lighter, but the cookies must be well done.) If you bake one sheet at a time bake it on the higher rack.

Now the cookies must stand on the foil until they are *completely cool*. If you are using cookie sheets with three flat sides you can slide the foil with the cookies off the sheet (be careful to keep it smooth so the cookies will cool and harden perfectly flat). Then you can slide the cookie sheet under another piece of foil that has unbaked cookies on it, and continue baking. (If you reuse the foil it must be wiped dry and spread out completely smooth, or the cookies will run into any creases in the foil and will lose their round shape.)

When the cookies are completely cool, gently peel the foil away from the backs of the cookies. Do not let them stand around or they will lose their wonderful crispness. Sandwich them immediately and refrigerate.

CHOCOLATE FILLING

3 to 4 ounces semisweet chocolate (see Note)

Break up or coarsely chop the chocolate (morsels may be used as is) and place it in the top of a small double boiler over hot water on low heat. Cover until partially melted. Then uncover and stir until completely melted and smooth. Remove the top of the double boiler.

With a small, narrow metal spatula spread a thin layer of the chocolate on the bottom of a cookie, leaving an uncovered border about ½ inch wide. Cover the cookie with another one, placing it so that both flat sides meet in the middle. Gently press the two cookies together. You will see some of the chocolate oozing out of the lacy holes in the cookies. That is as it should be, but there should not be much. And the chocolate should not spread out all the way to the rims of the cookies—so don't use too much.

As you sandwich the cookies place them on a tray in the freezer or refrigerator only until the chocolate is set. Then package airtight in a strong box with plastic wrap or wax paper between the layers. (I wrap them individually in cellophane and then package them in a box.) Refrigerate or freeze. (If you freeze Florentines the box with the cookies should be transferred to the refrigerator for a few hours before the cookies are unwrapped and served.)

Serve Florentines cold or at room temperature. But don't unwrap them until just before they are served; humidity will make them lose their crispness.

NOTE: *Any semisweet chocolate may be used. I have used many different ones and they all worked well—the cookies were always delicious. But Florentines deserve the best chocolate you can get.*

A Date with Chocolate

36 LARGE COOKIES

Old-fashioned and homey chocolate drop cookies, each one with a pecan-stuffed date inside and a thin, clear glaze over the top.

36 large pitted dates
36 large pecan halves
3 ounces (3 squares) unsweetened chocolate
¼ pound (1 stick) sweet butter
½ teaspoon vanilla extract
⅛ teaspoon salt
1 cup granulated sugar
2 eggs (graded large)
¾ cup sifted all-purpose flour
1 tablespoon prepared coffee

With a small, sharp knife cut through one long side of each date. Open them enough to insert a pecan half in each, and then press each one firmly closed around the nut (it is all right if they don't close completely). Set the prepared dates aside.

Adjust two racks to divide the oven into thirds and preheat oven to 325 degrees. Line cookie sheets with aluminum foil.

Place the chocolate in the top of a small double boiler over hot water on low heat, cover only until melted, then remove from the hot water and set aside uncovered.

In the large bowl of an electric mixer cream the butter. Add the vanilla, salt, and sugar and beat to mix. Add the melted chocolate and beat to mix. Then add the eggs one at a time, beating until incorporated after each addition. On low speed add the flour and beat, scraping the bowl with a rubber spatula and beating only until incorporated. Add the liquid coffee and beat again only until incorporated.

Transfer to a medium-size shallow bowl for easier handling.

Place a few of the stuffed dates on top of the dough. Using 2 teaspoons to work with, push one of the dates down into the dough, turn it around to coat it completely, then pick up the date with a rather generous coating of the dough and place it on the aluminum foil. Continue with the remaining dates, placing them 2 inches apart.

Bake two sheets at a time, reversing the sheets top to bottom and front to back once to insure even baking. Bake for 20 minutes until the cookies feel semi-firm to the touch.

While the cookies are baking, prepare the glaze.

GLAZE

1 cup strained confectioners sugar
Boiling water

Place the sugar in a small bowl. Add the water slowly—just a few drops at a time (it won't take much)—and stir with a rubber spatula until smooth and the consistency of a heavy cream sauce.

The glaze must be covered airtight with plastic wrap or aluminum foil except when you are working with it.

As soon as the cookies are done, use a pastry brush to quickly spread a bit of the glaze over each cookie—do not spread it all the way to the edges of the cookies. The heat of the cookies will melt the glaze into an almost transparent film which will dry quickly.

Use a wide metal spatula to transfer the cookies to racks to cool.

If you bake one sheet at a time, it should be placed on the lower rack.

These keep well but should be packed in an airtight container with wax paper between the layers.

NOTE: *If you have any leftover cookie dough, make plain drop cookies, using a rounded teaspoonful of the dough for each cookie. Or you can stir some chopped nuts and/or raisins into it before shaping.*

Whoopies

13 VERY LARGE COOKIE SANDWICHES

These are chocolate drop cookies—large and cake-like—sandwiched together—with a thick layer of creamy vanilla filling. They are monster cookies for cookie monsters.

I remember them as Whoopie Pies when I was growing up and going to school in New York. My husband remembers them as Moon Pies in Texas. They were also known as Cowboy Pies, Cobs, and Devil's Delights. But under any name all children were crazy about them.

Until recently I never thought of making them at home. This recipe gives a large yield of large cookies that take a lot of room in the kitchen while you are baking. And a lot of time, since they are baked only five at a time on each cookie sheet.

If you are looking for something for a children's party, try these—but if the children are small you might want to cut each cookie sandwich into two or three pieces before serving. Teenagers and husbands devour them whole in no time.

3 cups sifted all-purpose flour

1½ teaspoons baking powder

1½ teaspoons baking soda

3 teaspoons cream of tartar

½ teaspoon salt

6 ounces (1½ sticks) butter

1½ teaspoons vanilla extract

1½ cups granulated sugar

2 eggs (graded large or extra-large)

½ cup plus 1 tablespoon unsweetened cocoa
powder (preferably Dutch process)

1 cup plus 2 tablespoons milk

Adjust two racks to divide the oven into thirds and preheat oven to 375 degrees. Cut aluminum foil to fit cookie sheets (you will need six pieces of foil, or you can wipe it off and reuse it between batches).

Sift together the flour, baking powder, baking soda, cream of tartar, and salt and set aside. In the large bowl of an electric mixer cream the butter. Add the vanilla and sugar and beat to mix well. Add the eggs one at a time, scraping the bowl with a rubber spatula and beating until incorporated after each addition. On low speed add the cocoa and then the sifted dry ingredients in three additions, alternating with the milk in two additions, scraping the bowl with the spatula and beating only until smooth after each addition. (Before all the dry ingredients are added the mixture might look curdled—it's all right.)

It is important for these cookies to be shaped evenly and as close to the same size as possible. Use a ¼-cup measuring cupful of the dough for each

cookie. Use a narrow rubber spatula to fill the cup, level it off, and then to transfer the dough to the aluminum foil. Shape each mound of dough as round as possible—they will run and you want them to run into even circles. Place only five mounds of dough on one piece of foil—one in the center and one toward each corner. (During baking the cookies will spread to about 4 inches in diameter.)

Slide a cookie sheet under each piece of foil. Bake for 20 minutes, reversing the sheets top to bottom and front to back once to insure even baking. The cookies are done when they spring back very quickly and surely when lightly pressed in the center with a fingertip.

Slide the foil off the sheet and let stand for a minute or two. Then, with a wide metal spatula, loosen the cookies carefully from the foil and transfer them to large racks to cool. (The racks should be raised from the surface to make room for air to circulate underneath. Just place each rack on any right-side-up cake pan or mixing bowl.) If you don't have enough racks, as soon as some of the cookies have cooled they may be transferred to wax paper or foil.

You will have 27 very large cookies. If they are not all the same size, pick out the ones that match each other most closely and form them into pairs—there will be one cookie left over. Now lay them out in pairs, opened, with the flat sides up.

CREAMY WHITE FILLING

⅓ cup plus 3 tablespoons sifted all-purpose
flour

1½ cups milk

¾ pound (3 sticks) butter

Generous pinch of salt

1½ teaspoons vanilla extract

3¾ cups strained confectioners sugar

Place the flour in a 1-quart saucepan. Add the milk gradually, stirring with a rubber spatula. If the mixture is not smooth, strain it before cooking. Place it over moderate heat. Cook, stirring and scraping the bottom constantly with a rubber spatula, until the mixture becomes very thick and bubbles slightly. Simmer, stirring, for about 2 minutes. If necessary, beat with a small wire whisk to make the mixture smooth.

Stir in 1 tablespoon of the butter and set the mixture aside to cool to room temperature—stir it occasionally while it is cooling.

Place the remaining butter in the large bowl of an electric mixer and beat until it is slightly softened. Add the salt, vanilla, and sugar (gradually) and beat well for about 2 minutes, scraping the bowl as necessary with a rubber spatula. Gradually, 1 large spoonful at a time, add the cooled flour and milk mixture. Then beat at high speed for a minute or two until the filling is smooth, light, and fluffy.

Now place a generous heaping tablespoonful of the filling on the center of one of each pair of the cookies—use all of the filling. With the back of the spoon spread the filling out to about ½ inch from the edges. The filling will be almost ½ inch thick. Top the filling with another cookie, flat side down. With the palm of your hand press down gently on the top cookie.

Then hold a sandwich in your hands and with your fingertips press gently all around to spread the filling almost, but not completely, to the edges.

The filled sandwiches may be layered in a large shallow box or on a large tray with wax paper or plastic wrap between the layers and over the top. (Or they may be packaged individually in cellophane or wax paper, or in plastic sandwich bags, but it is best

to do this after they have been refrigerated.) Store in the refrigerator or freezer.

These may be served either cold from the refrigerator, or at room temperature. When they are cold, both the cookies and the filling will be firmer. At room temperature they will be quite soft, like the ones I used to buy.

Chocolate Oatmeal Cookies

22 LARGE COOKIES

I have made enough varieties of chocolate oatmeal cookies (which have always intrigued me) to qualify as a self-proclaimed connoisseur of chocolate oatmeal cookies. I think these are the best of all. So does my husband, and he claims to have eaten enough varieties of chocolate oatmeal cookies to put him in the Guinness Book of Records.

These are very oatmealy, coarse, crisp, and crunchy, with soft and chewy centers. They are east to make, and are sturdy but they must be stored airtight or they become limp.

⅔ cup sifted all-purpose flour
2 teaspoons baking powder
½ teaspoon salt
¼ cup plus 1 tablespoon unsweetened cocoa
    powder (preferably Dutch process)

144

2⅔ ounces (5⅓ tablespoons) sweet butter
1½ teaspoons vanilla extract
1¼ cups granulated sugar
1 egg (graded large or extra-large)
⅓ cup milk
2½ cups quick-cooking (not "instant")
    oatmeal (see Note)

Adjust two racks to divide the oven into thirds and preheat oven to 350 degrees. Line cookie sheets with aluminum foil and set aside.

Sift together the flour, baking powder, salt, and cocoa and set aside. In the large bowl of an electric mixer cream the butter. Add the vanilla and sugar and beat well. Add the egg and beat until smoothly mixed. On low speed add half of the dry ingredients, then the milk, and then the remaining dry ingredients, scraping the bowl with a rubber spatula and beating only until smooth after each addition. Add the oatmeal and mix until evenly incorporated.

Use a rounded tablespoonful of the dough for each cookie; they should be moderately large. Place the mounds of dough about 2½ inches apart on the foil-lined sheets.

Bake two sheets at a time, reversing the sheets top to bottom and front to back once to insure even baking. The cookies will rise as they bake and then flatten. Bake for 22 to 24 minutes until the tops of the cookies feel semi-firm to the touch. Do not underbake. These will crisp as they cool. (If you bake only one sheet at a time, bake it on the upper rack. One sheet of cookies bakes in slightly less time than two.)

Let the cookies cool for a minute or so on the foil. Then, with a wide metal spatula, transfer them to racks to finish cooling.

Store airtight. I store them in the freezer (thaw before unwrapping) to keep them as crisp as possible.

NOTE: *I especially like Shiloh Farms rolled oats from health food stores.*

Chocolate Spritz Cookies

60 TO 70 COOKIES

This recipe is for a cookie press, although you can shape the cookies many other ways (see directions below). They are rich, tender, fragile, and delicate.

3 ounces semisweet chocolate
½ pound (2 sticks) sweet butter
¼ teaspoon salt
½ teaspoon vanilla extract
⅔ cup granulated sugar
3 egg yolks
2½ cups sifted all-purpose flour

Adjust two racks to divide the oven into thirds and preheat oven to 400 degrees.

Place the chocolate in the top of a small double boiler over warm water on low heat. Cover and let stand until melted. Then remove the top of the double boiler and set aside, uncovered, to cool slightly.

In the large bowl of an electric mixer cream the butter. Add the salt, vanilla, and sugar and beat to mix well. Add the egg yolks and beat to mix, then the chocolate, and on low speed, gradually add the flour. Beat only to mix after each addition.

Now place the dough in a cookie press; or place as much of it as will fit at one time in a cookie press and then repeat. Shape the cookies ½ to 1 inch apart on unbuttered, unlined cookie sheets.

Or with your hands roll the dough into small balls, flatten the balls, place them on a cookie sheet, and then press with a fork to form deep ridges going in one direction. Or, instead of a fork, press with a cookie stamp or a butter mold. Or shape the dough with butter paddles and flatten slightly. Or with your hands shape the dough into crescents and flatten slightly. Or roll the dough into long, thin tube shapes and then twist into pretzel shapes (see Note) or other curlicues. The cookies should not be more than about one-third inch thick; they may be thinner.

Bake for 8 to 10 minutes, reversing the sheets top to bottom and front to back once during baking to insure even baking. If you bake one sheet at a time, bake it on the upper rack.

With a wide metal spatula transfer the cookies to racks to cool.

Package these carefully, they are fragile. Store them airtight.

NOTE: *These may be sprinkled before baking with crystal sugar (see page 7), especially appropriate for pretzel shapes. For other shape cookies you might use chopped nuts, or glazed cherries.*

Brownies

*Someone once asked, "How can you write a whole
book on just cookies?" and without thinking I
answered, "1 could write a whole book on just
Brownies." In fact, I have written two other books
which have ten Brownie recipes. Two of them are
included here and I would have liked to reprint all the
others as well.*

*It is important to time Brownies with the utmost
care—two or three minutes can make a huge difference. If they are baked too long they will be dry instead
of moist, but if they are not baked long enough they
will be too wet. Start to test them a few minutes before
the baking time is up. Test them carefully several times
in different spots. Perfectly timed Brownies are a great
accomplishment!*

*Here is a list of the additional Brownie recipes in
my other books.*

Petites Trianons
Greenwich Village Brownies
Cream Cheese Brownies
Fudge Brownies
Chocolate Mint Sticks
Dark Rocky Roads
Butterscotch Brownies
Brownie Crisps

Brownies

24 OR 32 BROWNIES

This is from my dessert book. These are the Brownies with which I started my reputation as a pastry chef when I was about ten years old. People who barely knew me, knew my Brownies. Since I always wrapped them individually I usually carried a few to give out. I occasionally meet people I never knew well and haven't seen in many years, and the first thing they say is, "I remember your Brownies." Sometimes they have forgotten my name—but they always remember my Brownies.

5 ounces (5 squares) unsweetened chocolate

5⅓ ounces (10⅔ tablespoons)
   sweet butter

1 tablespoon powdered (not granular)
   dry instant coffee

½ teaspoon salt

4 eggs (graded large or extra-large)

2 cups granulated sugar

1 teaspoon vanilla extract

¼ teaspoon almond extract

1 cup sifted all-purpose flour

10 ounces (2½ generous cups)
   walnut halves or large pieces

Adjust rack one-third up from the bottom of the oven and preheat oven to 450 degrees. Butter a 10½ x 15½ x 1-inch jelly-roll pan. Line the bottom and sides with one long piece of wax paper, butter the paper lightly, dust it with flour, and invert over a piece of paper to tap lightly and shake out excess flour.

Place the chocolate and the butter in the top of a small double boiler over hot water on moderate heat. Cover until melted, stirring occasionally with a small wire whisk. Add the powdered dry instant coffee and stir to dissolve. Remove the top of the double boiler and set aside, uncovered, to cool slightly.

Meanwhile, in the small bowl of an electric mixer, add the salt to the eggs and beat until slightly fluffy. Gradually add the sugar and beat at medium-high speed for 15 minutes. Transfer to the large bowl of the mixer.

Stir the vanilla and almond extracts into the chocolate mixture. On lowest speed add the chocolate to the eggs, scraping the bowl with a rubber spatula and beating *only enough to blend*. Still using lowest speed and the rubber spatula, add the flour, beating *only enough to blend*. Fold in the nuts, handling the mixture as little as possible.

Turn into the prepared pan and spread very evenly.

Place in the oven and *immediately* reduce the oven temperature to 400 degrees. Bake 21 to 22 minutes or until a toothpick gently inserted in the middle just barely comes out clean. Do not overbake. These should be slightly moist.

Remove from the oven and immediately cover with a large rack or cookie sheet and invert. Remove the pan and wax paper. Cover with a large rack and invert again. After 10 or 15 minutes cover with a rack or cookie sheet and invert only for a moment to be sure that the Brownies are not sticking to the rack.

Cool completely. The cake will cut more neatly if it is chilled first—it is even best if it is partially frozen. (It may be cut in half and partially frozen one piece at a time if you don't have room in your freezer for the whole thing.)

Transfer to a cutting board. To mark portions evenly, measure with a ruler and mark with toothpicks. Use a long, thin, very sharp knife or one with a finely serrated edge. Use a sawing motion when you cut in order not to squash the cake.

Wrap the Brownies individually in clear cellophane or wax paper (not plastic wrap, which is too hard to handle) or package them any way that is airtight—do not let them stand around and dry out.

West Coast Brownies

32 BROWNIES

I heard about Brownies called "Brownie Points" that are being sold in leading stores across the country. I was told they are very, very good. They are made in a bakery in Venice, California, by a young man named Richard Melcombe. I was delighted one day recently to open a California newspaper and see both the recipe and a picture of the baker, who calls himself Richmel.

This is my version of "Brownie Points." Although they are rather thin (only ½ inch thick), they are extra chewy and moist. And the coffee and Kahlúa or Cognac give them an unusually delicious and exotic flavor, but one probably more appreciated by adults than by children.

1½ cups sifted all-purpose flour
1 teaspoon salt
1 teaspoon baking soda

2 ounces (2 squares) unsweetened chocolate
½ pound (2 sticks) sweet butter
¾ cup granulated sugar
¾ cup dark or light brown sugar,
　firmly packed
2 eggs (graded large or extra-large)
2 tablespoons Kahlúa or Cognac
1 tablespoon vanilla extract
¼ cup dry instant espresso or other powdered
　(not granular) instant coffee
6 ounces (1 cup) semisweet chocolate morsels
3 ounces (⅔ cup) walnut halves or large pieces
3 ounces (⅔ cup) pecan halves or large pieces

Adjust rack to the center of the oven and preheat oven to 375 degrees. Butter a 15½ x 10½ x 1-inch jelly-roll pan. Carefully line the pan with one long piece of wax paper. Then butter the paper and set the prepared pan aside.

Sift together the flour, salt, and baking soda and set aside.

Place the chocolate in the top of a small double boiler over hot water on moderate heat. Stir occasionally until melted. Remove the top of the double boiler and set it aside, uncovered.

Place the butter in the large bowl of an electric mixer. Cream the butter, add both sugars and beat well, then add the eggs, Kahlúa or Cognac, vanilla, and dry instant espresso. Now add the melted chocolate and beat until blended. On low speed mix in the sifted dry ingredients.

Remove the mixture from the mixer and stir in the morsels and nuts.

Turn into the prepared pan and smooth the top.

Bake for about 25 minutes until a toothpick inserted in the center comes out clean and dry. The cake will feel very soft. Do not overbake.

Cool in the pan, then cover with a large rack or a large cookie sheet. Invert, remove the pan and the paper, cover with a cookie sheet and invert again, leaving the cake right side up.

Cut the cake into quarters. If the edges need to be trimmed (and they probably will) do it now after cutting the cake into quarters. Then cut each quarter into eighths.

Wrap each Brownie individually in cellophane or wax paper. Or package them in an airtight box with wax paper between the layers.

All-American Brownies

16 Squares, or 12 to 24 Bars

This is from my cookie book. It is a classic recipe for what has to be the most popular of all home-made American cookies.

¼ **pound (1 stick) sweet butter, cut into pieces**
2 **ounces (2 squares) unsweetened chocolate**
1 **cup granulated sugar**
½ **teaspoon vanilla extract**
2 **eggs (graded large or extra-large)**
½ **cup sifted all-purpose flour**
Pinch of salt
2 **ounces (generous ½ cup) walnuts, broken**
  into medium-size pieces

Adjust rack one-third up from the bottom of the oven and preheat oven to 350 degrees. Prepare an 8-inch square cake pan as follows: Turn the pan upside down. Tear off a 12-inch square of aluminum foil, center it over the inverted pan, fold down the sides and the corners, and then remove the foil and turn the pan right side up. Place the foil in the pan. In order not to tear the foil, use a pot holder or a folded towel and, pressing with the pot holder or towel, smooth the foil into place. Lightly butter the bottom and halfway up the sides, using soft or melted butter, and spreading it with a pastry brush or crumpled wax paper. Set aside.

Place the butter and the chocolate in a heavy 2- to 3-quart saucepan over the lowest heat. Stir occasionally with a rubber or a wooden spatula until the butter and chocolate are melted and smooth. Set aside to cool for about 3 minutes. Then stir in the sugar and the vanilla, and then the eggs, one at a time, stirring until smooth after each addition. Add the flour and salt and stir until smooth. Mix in the nuts.

Turn into the prepared pan and smooth the top.

Bake for 20 to 25 minutes until a toothpick gently inserted into the center of the cake barely comes out clean but not dry. Do not overbake. These should be soft and slightly moist.

Set aside to cool until the pan reaches room temperature. Then cover with a rack, invert, and remove the pan and the aluminum foil. The bottom of the cake should look slightly moist in the center. Cover with another rack and invert again, leaving the cake right side up. (It will be about ¾ inch thick.)

Transfer the cake to a cutting board. With a long, thin, sharp knife cut into squares or oblongs. (If the cake doesn't cut neatly, transfer it to the freezer or refrigerator until firm and then cut it. I always chill it before cutting.)

Wrap the Brownies individually in cellophane or wax paper (not plastic wrap—it is too hard to handle), or arrange them on a tray and cover with plastic wrap. Either way, do not let them dry out.

They may be frozen, and may be served either at room temperature or frozen, directly from the freezer (delicious).

Black Pepper Brownies

12 SMALL OR 24 LARGE BROWNIES,
OR 16 DESSERT-SIZE PORTIONS

These are old-fashioned Brownies pepped up with black pepper (this amount is not too much—it will just give the Brownies a little zing). The Mexicans have been using pepper and chocolate together in hot chocolate drinks and in entrees for hundreds of years. After tasting these you might decide to add a dash of pepper to all dark, rich, sweet chocolate recipes. Or, if you do not want to use the pepper, just leave it out and you will have yummy Brownies—rich, dark, and moist. These are thicker, more chocolaty, and less sweet than the recipe for All-American Brownies.

4 ounces (4 squares) **unsweetened chocolate**

6 ounces (1½ sticks) **sweet butter**

⅛ teaspoon **salt**

1 teaspoon **dry instant espresso or any other powdered (not granular) instant coffee**

1 teaspoon **black pepper, finely ground**

1 teaspoon **vanilla extract**

1¼ cups **dark or light brown sugar, firmly packed**

3 **eggs (graded large or extra-large)**

¾ cup **sifted all-purpose flour**

4 ounces (generous 1 cup) **walnuts or pecans, broken into large pieces**

Adjust the oven rack one-third up from the bottom and preheat oven to 375 degrees. Prepare a 9-inch square cake pan as follows: Turn the pan upside down. Cut a 12-inch square of aluminum foil, center it over the inverted pan, and fold the sides and corners down. Remove the foil, turn the pan upright, and place the foil in the pan. In order not to tear the foil use a folded towel or a pot holder to press the foil firmly into place in the pan. Brush with very soft or melted butter. Set the prepared pan aside.

Place the chocolate in the top of a small double boiler over hot water on moderate heat. Cover until partially melted, then uncover and stir until completely melted. Remove the top of the double boiler and set it aside, uncovered, to cool slightly.

In the large bowl of an electric mixer cream the butter. Add the salt, instant coffee, black pepper, vanilla, and then the sugar and beat until blended. Add the eggs one at a time, scraping the bowl with a rubber spatula and beating only until incorporated after each addition. On low speed add the chocolate and then the flour, scraping the bowl with a rubber spatula and again beating only until incorporated.

Remove the bowl from the mixer and stir in the nuts.

Turn into the prepared pan and smooth the top.

Bake for 25 to 30 minutes; a flat toothpick inserted into the middle of the cake should come out barely moist—not wet but not completely dry. Begin to test before the time is up and do not overbake.

Cool the cake in the pan for 15 to 20 minutes. Then cover with a rack and invert the pan and the rack. Remove the pan and peel off the aluminum foil. Cover with another rack and invert again, leaving the cake right side up to cool.

It is best to chill the cake before cutting it. Place it in the freezer or the refrigerator until it is firm. Then transfer it to a cutting board. With a finely serrated knife or a long, thin, sharp knife, cut it into bars or squares, wiping the blade with a damp cloth whenever some of the cake sticks to it. If you are serving these as cookies, cut the cake in half, then cut each half into thirds, and cut each piece into four bars. To serve it as a cake dessert, cut it into 16 squares and serve with vanilla and/or coffee ice cream and chocolate sauce. To serve as small petit fours, cut it into quarters, cut each quarter in half, and then cut each piece into four bars.

Spice Brownies

Follow the above recipe for Black Pepper Brownies (see page 152) with the following additions. Sift the flour together with 1½ teaspoons cinnamon, ½ teaspoon ginger, ½ teaspoon cloves, and ½ teaspoon allspice. And add ½ cup raisins along with the nuts.

Date-Nut Brownies

Chocolate and dates are a delicious combination. This recipe is another variation of the previous Black Pepper Brownies. Make the following changes.

Omit the black pepper. Where the recipe calls for brown sugar, use brown or white (granulated) sugar. Before stirring in the nuts, stir in 8 ounces (1 cup) coarsely cut pitted dates.

Ginger Brownies

Follow the recipe for Black Pepper Brownies (see page 152) with the following changes: In place of the pepper use ¾ teaspoon ground ginger. Add ¾ cup diced crystallized (candied) ginger; it should be in pieces about ¼ inch square or a bit larger—it is nice to bite into a chunk. Add the ginger with the nuts.

The nuts may be left out of this recipe—it is good either way.

Palm Beach Brownies

16 HUGE OR 24 OR MORE EXTRA-LARGE
BROWNIES

These are the biggest, thickest, gooiest, chewiest, darkest, sweetest, mostest-of-the-most chocolate bars with an almost wet middle and a crisp-crunchy top. It is best to bake these a day before—they can not be cut into bars when they are too fresh.

8 ounces (8 squares) unsweetened chocolate
8 ounces (2 sticks) sweet butter
5 eggs (graded large or extra-large)
1 tablespoon vanilla extract
1 teaspoon almond extract
¼ teaspoon salt
2½ tablespoons dry instant espresso or other
    powdered (not granular) instant coffee
3¾ cups granulated sugar
1⅔ cups sifted all-purpose flour
8 ounces (2 generous cups) walnut halves or
    large pieces

Adjust rack one-third up from the bottom of the oven and preheat oven to 425 degrees. Line a 9 x 13 x 2-inch pan as follows: Invert the pan, cover it with a long piece of aluminum foil, and with your hands press down on the foil around the sides and the corners to shape it like the pan. Remove the foil. Turn the pan right side up, and place the foil in the pan. Very carefully (without tearing it) press the foil into place in the pan.

Now butter the foil with soft or melted butter. The easiest way is to place a piece of butter in the pan, place the pan in the oven while it is warming up, and when the butter is melted use a pastry brush to spread it all over the sides and bottom of the foil. Set the prepared pan aside.

Place the chocolate and the butter in the top of a large double boiler over hot water on moderate heat, or in a 4- to 6-cup heavy saucepan over very low heat. Stir occasionally until the chocolate and butter are melted. Stir to mix. Remove from the heat and set aside.

In the large bowl of an electric mixer, beat the eggs with the vanilla, almond extract, salt, dry instant coffee, and sugar at high speed for 10 minutes. On low speed add the chocolate mixture and beat only until mixed. Then add the flour and again beat only until mixed. Remove from the mixer and stir in the nuts.

Turn into the prepared pan and smooth the top.

Bake for 35 minutes, reversing the pan front to back as necessary during baking to insure even baking. Cover loosely with foil for about the last half of the baking time to prevent overbrowning. At the end of 35 minutes the cake will have a thick, crisp crust on the top, but if you insert a toothpick into the middle it will come out wet and covered with chocolate. Nevertheless it is done. Do not bake it anymore.

Remove the cake from the oven and let stand at room temperature until cool. Then cover with a rack or a cookie sheet and invert. Remove the pan and the foil lining. Cover with a cookie sheet and invert again, leaving the cake right side up.

It is best to refrigerate the cake overnight before cutting (at room temperature it is too sticky to cut). Use a serrated French bread knife. It will be necessary to wash and dry the blade several times while cutting. First cut the cake in half, cutting through the long sides. If the cake was baked correctly the edges will be too dark and dry; trim about ¼ inch or so as necessary from the edges.

The cake will be 1¼ inches thick. Cut into 24 huge Brownies, or 32 large ones. (See Note.)

Either wrap the Brownies individually in clear cellophane, aluminum foil, or wax paper, or package them in an airtight container.

Refrigerate and serve cold.

NOTE: *I cut the Brownies into 24 bars, and then often, just before serving, I cut each bar in half the long way.*

Chocolate Oatmeal Brownies

24 COOKIES

These taste like soft, moist macaroons. They are chewy, nutty, not-too-sweet chocolate oatmeal bar cookies, made without flour. They are easily mixed in a saucepan (children can make them), they keep well and mail well, and are extremely popular.

3 ounces (3 squares) unsweetened chocolate
¼ pound (1 stick) sweet butter
½ teaspoon salt
¾ cup dark or light brown sugar, firmly
   packed
⅓ cup honey
1 teaspoon vanilla extract
1 egg, lightly beaten
2⅔ cups quick-cooking (not "instant") rolled
   oats
4 ounces (generous 1 cup) walnut halves or
   large pieces

Adjust rack to the center of the oven and preheat oven to 425 degrees. Prepare a 9-inch square cake pan as follows: Turn the pan upside down, cut a

12-inch square of aluminum foil and center it over the inverted pan. Fold down the sides and the corners and then remove the foil and turn the pan right side up. Place the foil in the pan. In order not to tear the foil, use a pot holder or a folded towel and, pressing gently against the pot holder or towel, smooth the foil into place. Butter the bottom and the sides, using soft or melted butter and a pastry brush or crumpled wax paper. (I put a piece of butter in the lined pan and place it in the warming oven first to melt. Then I spread it with a pastry brush.) Set the prepared pan aside.

Place the chocolate and butter in a heavy 2- to 3-quart saucepan over the lowest heat. Stir occasionally until completely melted. Remove from the heat and stir in the remaining ingredients in the order listed.

The mixture will be thick. Pack it firmly and smoothly into the prepared pan.

Bake for 15 minutes.

Cool in the pan on a rack for 15 to 20 minutes. Then cover with a rack and invert carefully, remove the pan and the foil, cover with another rack and invert again, leaving the cake right side up to cool completely.

The cake may be cut into finger-shaped bars when it is cool, or it may be chilled a bit first in the freezer or refrigerator to make the cutting easier and neater.

With a long, thin, sharp knife cut the cake into halves. Cut each half crossways into thirds. Then cut each piece the short way into four strips.

These may be placed on a serving tray and covered with plastic wrap, or they may be packed in a box with wax paper between the layers, or they may be wrapped individually in clear cellophane or wax paper.

Whole-Wheat Brownies

16 BROWNIES

I baked these and served them to my husband without saying what they were. He said, "I know these are Brownies, but they have a whole different taste. They have more oomph." (I had used whole-wheat flour and brown sugar. And some spices.)

1 ounces (2 squares) unsweetened chocolate
½ cup plus 2 tablespoons strained all-purpose whole-wheat flour (see Notes)
½ teaspoon cinnamon
½ teaspoon ginger
½ teaspoon allspice
4 ounces (1 stick) sweet butter
Scant ½ teaspoon salt
½ teaspoon vanilla extract
¼ teaspoon almond extract
1 cup light or dark brown sugar (see Notes), firmly packed
2 eggs (graded large or extra-large)
4 ounces (generous 1 cup) walnuts, cut or broken into medium-size pieces
½ cup raisins

Adjust rack one-third up from the bottom of the oven and preheat oven to 350 degrees. Prepare an 8-inch square cake pan as follows: Place the pan upside down. Cut a 12-inch square of aluminum foil and center over the inverted pan. Fold down the sides and corners, and then remove the foil and turn the pan right side up. Place the shaped foil in the pan and press it smoothly and firmly into place. In order not to tear the foil, place a pot holder in the pan and press against the pot holder. Then butter the bottom and sides of the foil, using soft or melted butter and a pastry brush or crumpled wax paper. Set the prepared pan aside.

Melt the chocolate in the top of a small double boiler over hot water on moderate heat, and then remove it from the hot water and set aside to cool.

Sift the flour with the cinnamon, ginger, and allspice, and set aside.

In the small bowl of an electric mixer cream the butter. Add the salt, and vanilla and almond extracts. Then add the sugar and beat until well mixed. Add the eggs one at a time, scraping the bowl with a rubber spatula and beating only until smooth after each addition. Add the chocolate and beat only until smooth. Add the sifted dry ingredients and beat on low speed, continuing to scrape the bowl with the spatula, and beating only until incorporated. Stir in the walnuts and raisins.

Turn the mixture into the prepared pan and spread it to make an even layer.

Bake for about 30 minutes or until a toothpick gently inserted in the center of the cake comes out barely clean and dry—there may be a few specks of chocolate clinging to the toothpick. Do not overbake.

Remove the pan from the oven and let it stand until it reaches room temperature (this might take up to an hour).

Cover the pan with a rack and invert pan and rack. Remove the pan and the aluminum foil. Cover with another rack and invert again, leaving the cake right side up.

It will be easier to cut neat squares if you place the cake in the freezer until it is quite firm. Then transfer it to a cutting board. Use a long, sharp knife or, preferably, a long, finely serrated one, and cut the cake into 16 squares.

These may be arranged on a tray and covered with plastic wrap. Or they may be wrapped individually in clear cellophane or wax paper. They may be frozen and may be served either at room temperature or straight from the freezer.

NOTES: *1. There is a slight difference in the taste of light and dark brown sugar. However, since chocolate is the strong taste in these I doubt if you will notice any difference between the light and dark. But just for the record, I have been using dark in this recipe.*

2. All-purpose whole-wheat flour is too coarse to be sifted—it is better to strain it. Shake it through a large, fine strainer set over a large bowl. Any pieces that are too coarse to go through the strainer should be stirred into the strained flour.

3. These will be very thick Brownies—about 1¼ inches thick.

Chocolate Honey Bars

32 BARS

These are a cross between Brownies and honey cake. They get better if you freeze them for a few days or longer before serving.

4 ounces (4 squares) unsweetened chocolate

2 ounces (½ stick) sweet butter

4 eggs (graded large or extra-large)

1½ teaspoons vanilla extract

1 cup granulated sugar

1 cup honey

½ teaspoon salt

1 cup plus 2 tablespoons sifted all-purpose flour

3 ounces (generous ½ cup) raisins

8 ounces (2 generous cups) walnut halves or large pieces

Optional: 4 ounces (½ cup) diced candied orange or lemon peel

Adjust rack to the center of the oven and preheat oven to 325 degrees. Prepare a 9-inch square cake pan as follows: Invert the pan and center a 12-inch square of aluminum foil over the pan. Fold down the sides and the corners of the foil to shape it like the pan. Remove the foil, turn the pan right side up, and place the foil in the pan. In order not to tear the foil with your fingernails, place a pot holder or folded towel in the pan and press it gently to press the foil into place in the pan. With a pastry brush coat the foil with soft or melted butter. Set the pan aside.

Place the chocolate and the butter in the top of an uncovered small double boiler over hot water on moderate heat, or in a heavy saucepan over low heat, and stir occasionally until melted and smooth. Remove from the heat and set aside.

In the small bowl of an electric mixer beat the eggs with the vanilla and sugar at high speed for about 5 minutes until very pale and thick. On low speed gradually add the honey, then the chocolate and butter, and then the salt and flour, scraping the bowl with a rubber spatula and beating only until each addition is incorporated. Stir in the raisins, nuts, and the optional peel.

Turn into the prepared pan. Smooth the top.

Bake for 1 hour and 5 minutes or until a toothpick gently inserted into the middle of the cake just barely comes out clean and dry.

Let the cake cool in the pan until it reaches room temperature.

Cover with a rack, invert pan and rack, remove the pan and the foil, cover with another rack leaving the cake right side up. Let stand for a few hours or refrigerate briefly before cutting.

Transfer the cake to a cutting board. With a finely serrated knife or a long, thin, sharp knife, cut the cake into quarters. Cut each quarter in half and then cut each piece into four narrow bars.

Wrap each piece individually in cellophane or wax paper, or place them in an airtight box with wax paper between the layers.

VARIATIONS: *A mildly spiced version of these Honey Bars calls for ½ teaspoon of each, ginger, cinnamon, and cloves, sifted together with the flour. I have also made this spiced version with about ½ cup diced candied ginger.*

A Brownie Sundae

A Brownie Sundae has long been a popular all-American dessert (just watch them fly to the tables and counters at Howard Johnson's).

Cut the Brownies (any Brownies) into squares larger than you would if you were going to serve them as cookies, top each one with a scoop of ice cream, then a generous amount of the World's Best Hot Fudge Sauce (see page 258) or any other chocolate sauce and a large spoonful of whipped cream.

PASTRIES

Individual Pastries

Chocolate Serendipity

20 PORTIONS
(SEE NOTE)

This is a most unusual dessert—chic, simple, elegant, and absolutely delicious. If they serve chocolate and whipped cream in heaven this has to be on the menu.

It takes time and patience to put together but is great fun and can all be done a day ahead.

Plan it for a dinner party or a luncheon and once you have made it you won't be able to wait to make it again.

It consists of a thin, thin layer of almost flourless chocolate cake, covered with a thick, thick layer of whipped cream, covered with a paper-thin coating of bittersweet chocolate glaze. It is then cut into squares before serving. And is refrigerated until it is served.

You will need a long, narrow metal spatula—mine has an 8-inch blade.

CAKE

5 ounces semisweet chocolate
7 tablespoons (1 stick less 1 tablespoon) sweet
    butter
½ cup granulated sugar
4 eggs (graded large), separated
1 tablespoon plus 1½ teaspoons sifted all-
    purpose flour
Pinch of salt

Adjust rack to the center of the oven and pre-heat oven to 350 degrees. Butter a 10½ x 15½ x 1-inch jelly-roll pan. Dust it with flour, invert and tap to shake out excess flour. Set the pan aside.

Place the chocolate in the top of a small double boiler over hot water on moderate heat. Cover until partially melted. Uncover and stir until completely melted and smooth. Remove the top of the double boiler and set aside, uncovered, to cool slightly.

In the small bowl of an electric mixer cream the butter. Add the sugar and beat to mix well. Beat in the egg yolks all at once, scraping the bowl with a rubber spatula and beating well. On low speed add the melted chocolate and beat until smooth. Add the flour and beat only to mix. Remove from the mixer.

Add the salt to the egg whites in a small, clean bowl and beat until they hold a definite shape but are not dry.

Fold about one-quarter of the whites into the chocolate mixture. Then fold in half of the remaining whites, and finally the balance of the whites, being careful not to handle any more than necessary.

Turn into the prepared pan. Very gently and carefully spread the mixture to make a smooth and even layer—it will be very thin.

Bake for 18 minutes. If the cake puffs up in a few places during baking don't worry about it—it will settle down.

Let the cake cool completely in the pan. It will be only ⅓ inch thick (thin). If you want to do this ahead of time, the cake can be covered in the pan and frozen or refrigerated. It is best if the cake is really cold or even frozen when the whipped cream is put on.

WHIPPED CREAM

1½ teaspoons unflavored gelatin
2 tablespoons cold water
½ cup strained confectioners sugar
1 teaspoon vanilla extract
Optional: 1 tablespoon rum or brandy
3 cups heavy cream

Chill the large bowl of an electric mixer and the beaters in the freezer or refrigerator before whipping the cream.

Sprinkle the gelatin over the cold water in a small glass custard cup. Let stand for 5 minutes. Then place the cup in shallow hot water in a small pan over low heat. Let stand until the gelatin is dissolved. Remove from the hot water and set aside.

While the gelatin is melting, add the sugar, vanilla, and optional rum or brandy to about 2¾ cups of the cream (reserve about ¼ cup) in the chilled large bowl of the electric mixer. With the chilled beaters, beat until the cream barely starts to thicken.

Stir the reserved ¼ cup cream into the dissolved gelatin and, with the mixer going, add it all at once to the partially whipped cream and continue to beat until the cream holds a firm and definite shape. (In order to beat it enough and still avoid overbeating, which would turn it to butter, I suggest that you finish the beating at the end with a large balloon-type wire whisk.)

Place the stiffly whipped cream over the top of the cold cake and spread it evenly. With a long, narrow metal spatula spread it very smooth—it will just reach the top of the cake pan, and must be smooth.

Refrigerate the cake now for at least 1 hour, but it may be several hours if you wish.

About half an hour before glazing the cake, prepare the glaze.

GLAZE

1 teaspoon dry instant coffee

½ cup boiling water

⅓ cup granulated sugar

1 tablespoon vegetable shortening (such as Crisco)

1 ounce (1 square) unsweetened chocolate

4½ ounces semisweet chocolate

In a small saucepan dissolve the coffee in the water. Add the sugar and shortening. Place over moderate heat and bring to a boil. Add both chocolates and stir until they are melted—don't worry about making it smooth.

Transfer to the small bowl of an electric mixer and beat briefly on low speed only until smooth. Then let the glaze stand until it cools to room temperature. Again beat briefly on low speed only until smooth.

Now, to cover the cream with a very thin layer of the glaze: Starting a few inches from one of the narrow ends of the pan, pour a thick ribbon of the glaze (about one-third of the total amount) over the whipped cream along the narrow end of the pan. With a long, narrow metal spatula quickly spread it into a smooth, thin, even layer covering about one-third of the whipped cream. (You will find it best to rest the edge of the spatula blade on the rim of the pan as you spread the glaze. The glaze will actually be spread on the rim of the pan in some places.) Then immediately pour on the remaining glaze and spread that, covering all of the cream and smoothing the glaze evenly. This is not difficult, just unusual. The main thing is to work quickly and do not work over the chocolate any more than is absolutely necessary.

Refrigerate at least until the chocolate is firm enough to be cut. That will take only a few minutes, but it can wait longer if you wish—several hours or even overnight. Or place it in the freezer—this will cut more neatly if it is frozen or partially frozen. However, frozen or not . . . superb!

With a small, sharp knife cut around the outside of the cake to release. With toothpicks mark a long side of the cake into five 3-inch lengths. With the small, sharp knife cut through the cake forming five 3-inch strips—wipe the knife blade after making each cut. Then, along a short side, cut down the middle, and then cut both halves in half again. (If this sounds complicated just cut it any way you wish, cutting the cake into about 20 portions. Cut carefully, and remember to wipe the blade after each cut.)

With a wide metal spatula transfer the portions to a large serving platter. Refrigerate until serving time.

NOTE: *Although this makes 20 portions, I have found that it is not too much for eight or ten people.*

Chocolate Pasticcios

The dictionary definition of pasticcio *is "In music, art, or writing, a medley made up of fragments of other works connected so as to form a complete work." These came about when I had a wonderful pastry and a delicious filling, both unrelated, and I put them together.*

These are chic, elegant little pastries—they are finger-food. Serve them at a tea party or as dessert for a luncheon. Or on a buffet. They are like miniature pies. The crust is a classic French pastry, the filling is a smooth, soft chocolate fudge. (How rich and creamy, dark sweet/bittersweet, etc., can chocolate be? From 1 to 10, this filling rates 12.)

This is not a quickie. On the contrary, it takes time and qualifies as a hobby or pastime.

You will need small, round (not fluted) tartlet pans. Mine are French. They measure 2⅜ (just over 2¼) inches across the top and they are ⁷⁄₁₆ (just under ½) inch in depth. These are generally available in specialty kitchen stores. In New York they are at The Bridge Company, 214 East 52nd Street, New York, N.Y. 10022. You will also need a plain, round cookie cutter 2¾ inches in diameter.

PASTRY

It is best to make this ahead of time. It should be refrigerated at least one hour before using, but it may wait in the refrigerator for a few days or it may be frozen.

> 1¼ cups sifted all-purpose flour
> ¼ cup granulated sugar
> ¼ pound (I stick) sweet butter, cut into small pieces
> 1 egg yolk
> 2 tablespoons ice water

This pastry may be put together in a food processor or in the traditional manner. To make in the processor fitted with the steel blade, place the flour and sugar in the bowl. Add the butter which should be cold and process until the mixture resembles coarse meal. Add the yolk and water and process only until the mixture forms a ball.

To make in the traditional manner, place the flour and sugar in a medium-size mixing bowl. With a pastry blender, cut in the butter until the mixture resembles coarse meal. Stir the yolk and water together, add to the flour mixture, and stir with a fork until the mixture holds together.

Wrap the pastry airtight and refrigerate it for at least an hour, or even a few days if you wish, or freeze it.

The pastry crusts will be baked empty first and then again with the filling. When you are ready for the first baking line up your little tartlet pans. This recipe is for 30 tartlets but if you don't have enough pans the remaining pastry (and the filling) can wait (see Note).

Flour a pastry cloth and a rolling pin. Work with half of the dough at a time—reserve the balance in the refrigerator.

Place the pastry dough on the floured cloth. Flatten it slightly and turn it over to flour both sides. With the floured rolling pin roll out the dough until it is very thin—it should be about ¹⁄₁₆ of an inch.

(During the rolling, roll the pastry up on the pin and then unroll it upside down in order to keep both sides floured.)

Cut into rounds with a 2¾-inch plain, round cookie cutter, cutting them as close to each other as possible and making 50 rounds. As you cut each round, place it over a tartlet pan, ease it gently into place, and press lightly so that it touches the pan all over. (If your fingernails are in the way, use a few scraps of the dough to form a little ball, dip the ball into flour, and press the ball all over the pastry to insure that the dough is completely in place.) Press scraps together and reroll.

Place the pastry-lined pans on a jelly-roll pan or a cookie sheet and transfer to the freezer until the dough is firm. (If you want to leave it overnight or longer at this stage, cover with plastic wrap or aluminum foil.)

While the tartlet shells are freezing, cut 30 small squares of aluminum foil, each one about 3 inches square.

Now, adjust a rack one-third up from the bottom of the oven and preheat oven to 400 degrees.

Line each tartlet shell with a square of the foil and press it firmly into place—keep the lined shells on the jelly-roll pan or cookie sheet. In order to keep the pastry in place and keep it from puffing up, fill the foil with dried beans. (You can use any kind. Save them to use again for the same purpose.) Or use pie pellets (see page 179).

Bake the tartlets for about 12 minutes, reversing the pan front to back once during baking to insure even browning.

After about 10 or 11 minutes check on one of the shells—gently lift the square of foil with the beans in it. The shells should be baked until they are golden-colored. When done, remove from the oven and reduce the oven temperature to 300 degrees.

Gently remove the foil and beans by lifting two opposite sides of each piece of foil.

Either cool the shells completely or fill them while they are still slightly warm.

FILLING

3 ounces (¾ stick) butter, cut into pieces
12 ounces (2 cups) semisweet chocolate morsels
¼ cup light corn syrup
8 egg yolks (the whites may be frozen for some other use)
A few teaspoons of chopped, unsalted green pistachio nuts, walnuts, or pecans

Place the butter and chocolate in the top of a large double boiler over hot water on moderate heat. Cover for a few minutes until almost melted. Then uncover and stir until smooth. Stir in the corn syrup.

In a bowl stir the yolks briefly just to mix and then gradually stir in a few spoonfuls of the hot chocolate mixture. Gradually stir the egg mixture into the remaining chocolate. Reduce the heat to low and cook, stirring constantly, for 5 minutes.

Remove the top of the double boiler from the hot water. Transfer the mixture to a small bowl for easier handling. For best results use this filling while it is still warm.

Place a well-rounded teaspoon of the filling in each baked shell, placing it evenly in the center. (It is not necessary to spread the filling—it will run during baking. But place it carefully in the center. I find this is easiest to do by using two demitasse spoons, one for picking up and one for pushing off. But the amount should be the same as a well-rounded regular teaspoon—or 2 well-rounded demitasse spoonfuls.)

With your fingertips, sprinkle a few of the chopped nuts on the center of each Pasticcio.

Make sure that the oven temperature has reduced to 300 degrees—if not, the pastries can wait.

Bake for 12 minutes, reversing the pan front to back once to insure even baking. The tops will feel dry to the touch but the centers will still be soft. Do not overbake!

Remove from the oven. Let stand until cool enough to handle, then use your fingertips to ease them gently out of the pans and place them on racks until completely cool.

These may stand at room temperature or they may be refrigerated or frozen. And they may be served either at room temperature or chilled or frozen. Try them each way and see which you like best. (The filling will be softer at room temperature, but even when these are frozen it will not be too hard. Of course, if it is too soft chilling will firm it.)

If you are serving Pasticcios as dessert, plan on 3 to a portion.

NOTE: *A tip from a cateress friend who often makes these in large quantities: Bake the shells as directed, cool slightly, remove them from the tartlet pans and place them on a cookie sheet before filling them. In this way you can make many Pasticcios without so many tartlet pans.*

Viennese Chocolate Squares

16 SMALL SQUARES

These are small squares (petits fours) of almost flourless chocolate almond cake with a thin top layer of buttery dark chocolate icing. They are moist, not too sweet (they have no sugar), and are both light and rich. They are easy, quite professional-looking, and delicious. You will like making them and will be proud to serve them. The recipe makes a small number, just right for a few people. If you double it, it must be baked in two pans.

4 ounces semisweet chocolate

1½ ounces (⅓ cup) almonds, blanched or unblanched

5⅓ ounces (10⅔ tablespoons) sweet butter

2 teaspoons dry powdered (not granular) instant espresso or other powdered instant coffee

1 teaspoon vanilla extract

1 tablespoon dark rum, Cognac, or whiskey

4 eggs (graded large or extra-large), separated

2 tablespoons <u>un</u>sifted all-purpose flour

¼ teaspoon salt

Optional: 2 or 3 tablespoons apricot preserves

Adjust rack one-third up from the bottom of the oven and preheat oven to 350 degrees. Prepare a shallow 8-inch square metal baking pan as follows: Invert the pan, cover with a 12-inch square of aluminum foil, turn down the sides and the corners of the foil. Then remove the foil, turn the pan right side up, place the foil in the pan, and press it smoothly into place. Butter the foil using soft or melted butter and a pastry brush or crumpled wax paper. Set the prepared pan aside.

Place the chocolate in the top of a small double boiler over hot water on moderate heat. Cover until partially melted; then uncover and stir until completely melted and smooth. Remove the top of the double boiler and set aside, uncovered, to cool slightly.

The nuts must be ground to a fine powder. It may be done in a food processor, a nut grinder, or a blender. Set aside.

In the large bowl of an electric mixer cream the butter. Add the coffee, vanilla, rum, and the melted chocolate and beat until smooth. Add the egg yolks all at once and beat until smooth. Add the flour and then the almonds and beat until incorporated. Remove from the mixer.

In the small bowl of the electric mixer add the salt to the egg whites and, with clean beaters, beat only until the whites barely hold a firm shape, not until they are stiff or dry.

Gradually, in several additions, small at first, fold the whites into the chocolate mixture.

Turn into the prepared pan and smooth the top.

Bake for 30 minutes.

Cool in the pan for about 15 minutes.

Cover with a rack and invert. Remove the pan and foil, cover with another rack and invert again, leaving the cake to cool right side up. (The cake will be a scant 1 inch high.)

OPTIONAL: *Spread the top of the cooled cake with 2 or 3 tablespoons of warm, melted, and strained apricot preserves. Let stand while you prepare the icing.*

CHOCOLATE BUTTER ICING

4 ounces semisweet chocolate (see Note)
2 ounces (½ stick) sweet butter
½ teaspoon dry powdered (not granular) instant espresso or other powdered instant coffee

Place the chocolate and the butter in the top of a small double boiler over hot water on moderate heat. Cover until partially melted. Then uncover and stir until completely melted and smooth. Stir in the coffee. If the mixture is not smooth, stir it briskly with a small wire whisk. Remove from the hot water and set aside to cool to room temperature.

Then let stand at room temperature or refrigerate, stirring occasionally, until only slightly thickened or thick enough so it will spread without running down the sides.

Place the cake upside down on a small board.

When the icing is ready, stir it well and turn it out onto the cake. With a long, narrow metal spatula spread smoothly.

Let stand until the icing is set (it will not take long).

After the cake is cut into squares they may be served as they are, or each one may be topped with a walnut or pecan half, a whole, toasted blanched hazelnut, or a chocolate coffee bean (candy).

If you plan to leave them plain, when the icing is set use a long, thin, sharp knife to trim the edges and then cut the cake into 16 small squares.

If you are going to decorate the squares use a long knife but only score the cutting lines, first the four sides and then the cutting lines for the squares.

OPTIONAL DECORATION

½ ounce semisweet chocolate
16 walnut or pecan halves, or 16 whole, toasted blanched hazelnuts, or 16 chocolate coffee beans (candy)

Coarsely chop the ½ ounce chocolate, place it in a small cup in a small pan of shallow hot water over low heat. Stir occasionally until melted.

Meanwhile, make a small paper cone (see page 266). Place the melted chocolate in the tip of the cone, cut a tiny bit off the tip to make a small opening, and press out just a small dab of the chocolate on the top (right in the middle) of each square. (The chocolate is only to serve as a paste to hold the nut or coffee bean; it should not show—do not use too much.) Place the nut or coffee bean on the chocolate.

Now trim the edges and cut the cake into squares.

Let stand at room temperature and serve at room temperature.

To store these overnight or to freeze them, pack in a single layer in a box or on a tray. Cover the squares airtight with plastic wrap. It you have frozen them, thaw before unwrapping.

NOTE: *If you prefer a less sweet flavor, use 1 ounce of unsweetened and 3 ounces of semisweet for the icing.*

Chocolate Éclairs

12 TO 14 DESSERT-SIZE ÉCLAIRS

Homemade éclairs are not an everyday dessert—they are special. And with all the steps involved I consider them a creative art. Although they are not really difficult, I congratulate you when you make them.

The éclair shells are easy and fun if you can handle a pastry bag and they may be made way ahead of time and frozen (see Note). The filling and icing should be done the day they are served—or the filled and iced éclairs may be frozen. (This filling is unconventional—it is a combination chocolate pastry cream and chocolate bavarian.)

CREAM-PUFF PASTRY
(Pâte à Choux)

This mixture may be shaped and baked as soon as it is prepared, or it may be covered and may stand either at room temperature or in the refrigerator for an hour before using.

For shaping the éclairs you will need a 10- to 16-inch pastry bag and a #8 plain, round tube which has a ⅝-inch opening.

¼ pound (1 stick) sweet butter, at room temperature
1 cup boiling water
Pinch of salt
1 cup sifted all-purpose flour
4 eggs (graded large—no larger or smaller)

Adjust a rack to the center of the oven and preheat oven to 425 degrees. Line a 12 x 15-inch or larger cookie sheet with aluminum foil. Place the cookie sheet on another, unlined one of the same size—the double sheets will prevent the bottoms of the éclairs from browning too much. (They will be a beautiful, smooth, shiny, pale golden color.) Set aside.

Place the butter, boiling water, and salt in a heavy 2- or 3-quart saucepan over high heat. Stir with a heavy wooden spatula (cutting the butter as you stir) until the butter is melted and the mixture boils hard. (Do not boil unnecessarily or too much water will evaporate.)

Remove from the heat and immediately add the flour all at once, stirring vigorously with the wooden spatula until the mixture forms a ball and leaves the sides of the pan. If that does not happen within about half a minute, stir over low heat for a few seconds.

Turn the mixture into the small bowl of an electric mixer. Add the eggs one at a time—beating on low-medium speed after each addition until incorporated. After adding the last egg beat for one half minute more, scraping the bowl with a rubber spatula.

Fit a 10- to 16-inch pastry bag (large is better than small) with a #8 plain, round tube. Fold down a deep cuff on the outside of the bag. To support the bag, place it in a tall, narrow jar or glass and transfer the warm (or cooled) pastry to the bag. Then unfold the cuff and twist the top of the bag closed.

(It is easier to work with a pastry bag at table height rather than at counter height.) Place the prepared cookie sheet on a table. Hold the pastry bag at an oblique angle to the sheet with the tube almost touching the sheet. Press on the top of the bag to press out 12 to 14 finger-shaped strips 5 inches long and ¾ to 1 inch wide (keep them narrow). Place them about 1½ inches apart—at the end of each strip retrace your direction with a quick jerk in order to cut off the pastry neatly.

Bake for 20 minutes (at which time the éclairs should have finished rising—the oven door should not be opened until they have finished rising or even a little longer).

Then reduce the oven temperature to 350 degrees and bake for an additional 30 to 35 minutes (total baking time is 50 to 55 minutes). The éclairs should be golden brown and crisp all over (including the sides, which are the last part to dry out and become crisp).

About 5 or 10 minutes before they are done reach into the oven and, with a small, sharp knife, cut a few small slits in the top of each éclair to let the steam escape.

If they are underbaked the éclairs will collapse as they cool—but it will not hurt to overbake them a bit.

As soon as they are done, with your fingers peel them carefully from the foil and place them on racks to cool. (If they cool on the foil they might stick.)

When they are cool, use a serrated knife and slice each one horizontally, cutting about one-third from the top, which will leave a deep bottom to hold the filling. Do not mix up the tops and bottoms—keep them in their original pairs.

With your fingers remove any excess soft dough from the inside of each half. Now either package them airtight and freeze, or fill them. Do not let them stand around or they may become limp. (They can wait for the length of time it takes to make the filling.)

CHOCOLATE ÉCLAIR FILLING

2 ounces (2 squares) unsweetened chocolate
1 tablespoon (1 envelope) unflavored gelatin
¼ cup cold water
2 tablespoons <u>un</u>sifted flour
1 cup milk
Pinch of salt

⅓ cup granulated sugar
4 egg yolks
1 teaspoon vanilla extract
1 tablespoon sweet butter
1 tablespoon strong prepared coffee, rum, Cognac, or crème de cacao
1 cup heavy cream

Place the chocolate in the top of a small double boiler over warm water on low heat; cover and let stand until the chocolate is melted. (If the chocolate melts before you are ready to use it, uncover the pot and remove from the hot water.)

Sprinkle the gelatin over the cold water in a small custard cup and let stand.

Sift or strain the flour into a 1½- or 2-quart heavy saucepan. Add ¼ cup of the milk and stir well with a rubber spatula until smooth—if there are any lumps press against them with the spatula. When smooth, gradually stir in the remaining milk and then the salt and sugar.

Place over moderate heat and cook, stirring and scraping the pan with the rubber spatula, until the mixture thickens to the consistency of a thin white sauce and comes to a boil. Let boil, stirring, for one minute.

In a medium-size bowl stir the yolks lightly just to mix. Gradually stir in about half of the hot sauce and then stir the yolks into the remaining sauce.

Cook over very low heat, stirring constantly, for two minutes. Do not let it get too hot or cook too long.

Remove from the heat. Stir in the melted chocolate and the softened gelatin. Beat with a wire whisk, electric mixer, or egg beater until smooth. If the mixture is not smooth, strain it. Then mix in the vanilla, butter, and coffee or liquor.

Partially fill a large bowl with ice and water. Set

the bowl or saucepan of filling into the bowl of ice water and stir occasionally until cool and partially thickened.

Meanwhile, whip the cream until it holds a soft shape—it should be semi-firm, not stiff.

When the chocolate mixture starts to thicken to the consistency of a heavy mayonnaise, stir it briskly with a wire whisk and then fold the whipped cream into it.

Use right away or refrigerate briefly (if it is not firm enough to hold its shape and be pressed out of a pastry bag, it must be refrigerated to stiffen it a bit).

The filling will be put into the shells with a pastry bag; if the shells are on a slippery surface they will slide away from you while you fill them. I place them, open sides up, in matched pairs on a kitchen towel.

To fill the shells, fit a 15- or 18-inch pastry bag with a #8 plain, round tube. Fold down a deep cuff on the outside of the bag. To support the bag place it in a tall narrow jar or glass and transfer the cold filling to the bag.

Unfold the top of the bag, twist it closed, and press out a heavy strip of the filling into the bottom half of each éclair. Then repeat, so you have two heavy strips of filling, mounded high, in the bottom halves.

Cover with the tops of the éclairs, pressing the tops down firmly so they stay in place—the filling should show on the sides.

Place on a tray and refrigerate while you prepare the glaze.

CHOCOLATE GLAZE FOR ÉCLAIRS

2½ ounces (2½ squares) unsweetened chocolate

½ cup granulated sugar

3 tablespoons plus 1½ teaspoons water (be very careful not to use too much—less is better than more)

Place the chocolate in the top of a small double boiler over hot water on moderate heat. Cover until partially melted. Uncover and stir until completely melted. Add the sugar and water and stir to mix.

Remove the top of the double boiler and place it over direct heat. Stir until it comes to a boil.

Remove from the heat and stir briskly with a small wire whisk for a few seconds until the mixture is very smooth and only slightly thickened.

This should not be thick or stiff, but it should not be so thin that it runs down the sides of the éclairs. If it is too thick, add a few drops of hot water and stir well. If it is too thin, let it cool briefly and stir well. When it is right it will spread evenly and smoothly over the tops and will stay where you put it. Use the glaze immediately while it is still warm.

Hold an éclair in your left hand. With your right hand use a teaspoon to pick up a rounded spoonful of the glaze, place it on the éclair and spread it with the back of the spoon. Use just enough to make a rather thin layer all over the top.

If the glaze thickens while you are working with it, replace it over warm water, or stir in a few drops of warm water.

Return the glazed éclairs to the refrigerator.

Serve the same day, or chill until the glaze is dry and firm, then wrap individually in plastic wrap and freeze. Thaw in the refrigerator for a few hours before unwrapping. If the éclair stands too long after it has thawed the shell will lose its crispness.

NOTE: *If the éclair shells have been frozen unfilled (they should be split before they are frozen), thaw them as follows: Place them, frozen, on a cookie sheet in a 350-degree oven for about 8 minutes to thaw and crisp. Cool on a rack.*

Profiteroles

8 TO 12 PORTIONS

When I was going to school (Pratt Institute) I was invited to lunch at the old Stork Club on 53rd Street in New York. Sherman Billingsley, the owner, sent profiteroles (and perfume and cigarette lighters) to our table with his compliments. Since then I have always thought of profiteroles as an elegant dessert to be served in a swank place with headwaiters and captains watching for a nod of approval.

The fact is they are one of the simplest and easiest (and most fun) things you can do for dessert. They are made ahead of time and served directly from the freezer. They are small cream puffs filled with ice cream and served with chocolate sauce.

THE PUFFS

Follow the preceding éclair recipe for cream-puff pastry (pâte à choux). When it is mixed, the directions change. Instead of a pastry bag, these are shaped with teaspoons (like drop cookies). Use a well-rounded teaspoonful of the mixture for each puff (each one should be slightly larger than a walnut in the shell), and place it neatly (try to keep them rather round and without peaks) on the aluminum foil on double cookie sheets—see preceding recipe. Use half of the pastry to make twelve mounds on one foil-lined sheet. (Cover the remaining pastry and set it aside at room temperature.)

Bake in the middle of a 425-degree oven for 15 minutes. Then reduce the oven temperature to 350 degrees and bake for an additional 30 minutes (total baking time is 45 minutes). Do not open the oven door until 5 minutes before the baking time is up. Then reach into the oven and insert a small, sharp knife into the top and/or sides of each puff in two places to allow steam to escape. Bake for the final 5 minutes.

Remove the puffs from the oven and, with your fingers, gently peel them away from the foil and place them on racks to cool.

Repeat with the remaining half of the pastry.

When all the puffs are baked and cooled, use a serrated knife to cut the top third off each. With your fingers pick any soft, undercooked dough out of the centers. Be sure to keep each top with its own bottom in order to be able to match them up neatly when they are filled.

THE ICE-CREAM FILLING

One pint of ice cream will fill about 9 puffs. You should have 3 pints to fill 24 puffs, although you might not use it all. Use any flavor you like, or an assortment (vanilla is traditional). The ice cream must not be so hard that it cracks the puffs, nor so soft it runs. Use a spoon or a very small ice-cream scoop; I have a tiny one that measures only 1½ inches in diameter and works very well. (I have seen them in specialty kitchen shops and in wholesale restaurant supply stores.) Work right next to the freezer; as you fill a puff, place it directly in the freezer on a tray. Fill the bottom half of each puff, mounding it moderately high. Replace the top, pressing it gently onto the ice cream. A bit of ice cream should show around the middle.

Freeze the puffs until the ice cream is hard. Then package in any airtight container, or simply cover the tray airtight with aluminum foil.

THE STORK CLUB'S PROFITEROLE SAUCE

A few years after my first profiteroles at The Stork Club, I started making silver stork pins and cuff links for Mr. Billingsley to include in his generous balloon-night giveaways. Then I was in and out of the place frequently, usually in the mornings before it was open for business. One day the chef let me shape the cream puffs (there it was done with a pastry bag) and let me watch him make the sauce, which could not be easier.

> 6 ounces semisweet chocolate
> 1 ounce (1 square) unsweetened chocolate
> 2 cups water
> ½ cup granulated sugar
> ½ teaspoon vanilla extract

Coarsely cut up both chocolates and place them in the top of a small double boiler over hot water on moderate heat. Cover until partially melted, then uncover and stir until completely melted and smooth.

Meanwhile, place the sugar and water in a 6- to 8-cup saucepan over high heat. Stir with a wooden spatula until the sugar is dissolved and the mixture comes to a boil. Let boil without stirring for 5 minutes.

Remove from the heat, stir in the melted chocolates, return to the heat, and bring to a low boil. Adjust the heat so it simmers and let simmer, stirring occasionally, for 10 minutes.

Remove from the heat and stir in the vanilla.

This may be served warm or at room temperature. (The Stork Club served it warm.) It may be reheated over hot water.

Serve the profiteroles on individual flat dessert plates or shallow soup plates, two or three to a portion, with sauce poured over and around them. Eat with a knife and fork.

These amounts will yield 2 cups of sauce, enough for 24 puffs.

Chocolate Profiteroles

These are made with chocolate cream-puff pastry (chocolate pâte à choux). This bakes to a rich chocolate color and may be used for any recipe that uses pâte à choux.

CHOCOLATE CREAM-PUFF PASTRY
(Chocolate Pâte à Choux)

Follow the recipe for Cream-Puff Pastry (see page 167) with the following changes: Finely chop 1 ounce (1 square) of semisweet chocolate. Add it to the saucepan along with the butter and melt it with the butter in the boiling water. Reduce the amount of flour to 1 cup minus 3 tablespoons.

Now follow the recipe for Profiteroles (see page 170).

Just before serving these dark chocolate profiteroles, sprinkle the tops with confectioners sugar through a fine strainer. Serve with any chocolate sauce. (When I taught this recipe in demonstrations that I gave around the country, I used the World's Best Hot Fudge Sauce [see page 258] and everyone raved.)

French Fudge Squares

16 Squares or 32 Small Bars

So rich, dark, dense, moist, these are more like fudge candy than like cake. With a divine, shiny dark chocolate glaze. The mixture is baked in a square pan and, before serving, is cut into small squares. (The ingredients are similar to Brownies with additional chocolate—the technique is a bit different.)

Don't decide to make this for tonight; the cake should stand to mellow before it is served. Bake it a day or two before serving, or way before and freeze it. But the glaze should be put on early in the day for serving that night; it takes only a few minutes to make the glaze.

8 ounces (8 squares) **unsweetened chocolate**
4 **eggs** (graded large, extra-large, or jumbo),
    separated
½ pound (2 sticks) **sweet butter**
2 cups **granulated sugar**
2 cups sifted **all-purpose flour**
Pinch of salt

Adjust rack one-third up from the bottom of the oven and preheat oven to 350 degrees. Line a 9-inch square cake pan as follows: Invert the pan, tear off a 12-inch square of aluminum foil and center it over the inverted pan, fold down the sides and corners, remove the foil and turn the pan right side up. Place the foil in the pan. In order not to tear it, use a pot holder or a folded towel and, pressing gently with the pot holder or towel, smooth the foil into place. Lightly butter the bottom and sides, using soft or melted butter and a pastry brush or crumpled wax paper. Set aside.

Place the chocolate in the top of a small double boiler over hot water on low heat. Cover until partially melted, then uncover and stir occasionally until completely melted. Remove the top of the double boiler and set aside, uncovered, to cool slightly.

In the small bowl of an electric mixer beat the yolks until they are pale lemon-colored. Set aside.

Place the butter in the large bowl of the electric mixer. You can use the same beaters without washing them to cream the butter. Add 1¾ cups (reserve ¼ cup) of the sugar and beat well. Add the egg yolks and beat to mix, then add the chocolate and beat to mix again. On low speed gradually add the flour and beat, scraping the bowl with a rubber spatula, and beating only until thoroughly incorporated. Remove from the mixer.

Now you need a clean, small mixer bowl and clean beaters. Place the egg whites in the bowl, add the salt, and beat until the whites thicken so they barely hold a soft shape. Reduce the speed to moderate and gradually add the reserved ¼ cup sugar. Increase the speed to high again and beat only until the whites hold a definite shape but not until they are stiff or dry.

The chocolate mixture will be quite stiff. First stir in about half a cup of the beaten whites. Then fold in half of the remaining whites—do not be too thorough—and then fold in the balance of the whites. The chocolate mixture will seem too stiff, but don't worry—first continue to fold until the whites disappear. It will be O.K.

Turn into the prepared pan. Smooth the top as well as you can—the mixture does not run as it bakes.

Place the pan in a larger shallow pan and pour hot—not boiling—water into the larger pan to about half the depth of the cake pan.

Bake for 50 minutes (there is no test for doneness—just time it).

Remove the cake pan from the hot water and let stand until completely cool.

Cover with a rack, invert, remove the pan and the foil lining, and then transfer the cake, upside down, to a board, flat platter, or a cookie sheet. (The cake will be 1¼ inches high.)

Wrap in plastic wrap and refrigerate for a day or two, or freeze for a longer time. Bring to room temperature before glazing.

FUDGE GLAZE

2 tablespoons unsweetened cocoa powder
   (preferably Dutch process)
¼ cup granulated sugar
¼ cup water
I ounce (1 square) unsweetened chocolate,
   coarsely chopped
1 ounce (¼ stick) sweet butter, cut into pieces
1 tablespoon vegetable oil

In a small, heavy saucepan stir the cocoa, sugar, and water to blend. Place over moderate heat and cook, stirring, until the mixture comes to a boil. Let boil slowly, still stirring, for 1 minute. Add the chocolate and stir until it melts.

Remove the pan from the heat and add the butter, one piece at a time, stirring until smooth after each addition. Add the oil and stir until completely blended.

Now, immediately, while the glaze is hot, pour it onto the top of the cake. With a long, narrow metal spatula spread it over the top only; if a bit runs down on the sides just leave it. (Isn't this glaze gorgeous?)

Let stand at room temperature for at least sev-
eral hours. If the cake is refrigerated the glaze will become dull—the taste and texture will still be delicious but different from the way they are at room temperature. (The consistency will be firmer and the taste will be slightly less sweet.) As a matter of fact, if I weren't so intrigued by the shine of the glaze, I would say that I prefer the cake chilled.

With a long, thin, sharp knife, first trim a thin slice from each of the four sides so they will look the same as the cut interior sides. If necessary, wipe the blade after making each cut. Then cut into 16 squares. Or cut each square in half, making 32 small bars if you are serving these as finger-food.

Chocolate Madeleines

12 3-INCH MADELEINES

Madeleines are small French cakes (or are they cookies?) baked in shell-shaped forms. They are traditionally white cakes—these are untraditionally and unequivocally chocolate—extra-bittersweet, dark, dense, soft, rich, and very spongy.

This recipe is for twelve-inch Madeleines—see Notes for doubling.

¼ cup sifted all-purpose flour

¼ cup unsweetened cocoa powder (preferably Dutch process)

1 teaspoon powdered (not granular) instant coffee

½ teaspoon baking powder

Pinch of salt

2 ounces (½ stick) sweet butter

½ teaspoon vanilla extract

1 teaspoon dark rum or brandy

¼ cup granulated sugar

1 egg (graded large) plus 2 egg yolks

Confectioners sugar (for topping)

Adjust rack one-third up from the bottom of the oven and preheat oven to 375 degrees. You will need a Madeleine pan with twelve 3-inch shell-shaped forms (see Notes). To prepare the pan: Use soft (not melted) sweet butter and, with a pastry brush, brush it thoroughly all over the forms—be careful not to leave any unbuttered spots—make it a thin, even coating. Set the prepared pan aside.

Sift together the flour, cocoa, coffee, baking powder, and salt and set aside.

In the small bowl of an electric mixer cream the butter. Add the vanilla, rum, and granulated sugar and beat well. Add the egg and the yolks and beat to mix (the mixture will look curdled—it's O.K.). On low speed add the sifted dry ingredients and beat only to mix.

Place a rounded teaspoonful of the mixture in each of the buttered shell forms. Do not spread, it will run by itself. Use all of the mixture for the twelve 3-inch forms.

Bake for about 12 minutes until the Madeleines spring back when lightly pressed with a fingertip.

Remove from the oven and immediately cover with a rack and invert. If the cakes do not slip out easily tap the inverted pan sharply on a counter top or board to knock the cakes out. Cool them patterned side up on a rack.

Place the rack over paper. Sprinkle the shell-patterned sides of the cooled Madeleines with confectioners sugar, shaking the sugar through a fine strainer held over the cakes. If the flat side is sticky, sugar both sides.

Store airtight with wax paper between the layers.

NOTES: *1. This recipe may be doubled for two pans if they will both fit on the same oven rack. (It is best not to bake these one pan over another.) They should be baked as soon as they are mixed, so do not double the recipe unless you have two pans and a large oven or two ovens.*

2. French tinned-steel Madeleine pans with twelve 3-inch forms (they are also available with six forms, but for this recipe only a twelve-form pan will do) are generally available at fine kitchen equipment shops. Or they may be ordered by mail from Williams-Sonoma, (877) 812-6235. In New York City they are at Bridge Kitchenware, 214 East 52nd Street, New York, New York 10022.

3. Never clean Madeleine pans with anything rough (just wash them with soap and water and a dishcloth) or the cakes might stick.

Pies

General Directions for a Crumb Crust

The following directions for how to line a plate with aluminum foil, shape and bake a crumb crust, then how to remove the foil are from my dessert book. Follow them to insure that the crust does not stick to the plate.

Although the crumb mixture may be pressed into place directly in the pie plate, I prefer to line the plate with foil first and then remove the foil before filling the crust. This guarantees easy serving–the crust can't stick to the plate. It's a bit more work (or play), but I think well worth it.

For a 9-inch pie plate, use a 12-inch square of foil. Place the plate upside down on a work surface. Place the foil over the plate and, with your hands, press down on the sides of the foil, pressing it firmly against the plate all around. Remove the foil. Turn the plate right side up. Place the shaped foil into the plate. Now, to press the foil firmly into place in the plate, use a pot holder or a folded towel; place the pot holder or towel in the plate and press against it all around, making sure that the foil touches all parts of the plate. Fold the edges of the foil down over the rim of the plate.

Turn the crumb-crust mixture into the plate. Using your fingertips, I distribute the mixture evenly and loosely over the sides first and then the bottom. Then press the crust firmly and evenly on the sides, pushing it up from the bottom to form a rim slightly raised over the edge of the plate. Be careful that the top of the crust is not too thin. To shape a firm edge, use the fingertips of your right hand against the inside and press down against it with the thumb of your left hand. After firmly pressing the sides and the top edge, press the remaining crumbs evenly and

firmly over the bottom. There should be no loose crumbs.

Bake in the center of a preheated 375-degree oven for 8 minutes, or until very lightly browned on the edges.

Cool to room temperature.

Freeze for at least 1 hour, longer if possible. It must be frozen solid.

Remove from the freezer. Raise the edges of the foil. Carefully lift the foil (with the crust) from the plate. Gently peel away the foil as follows: Support the bottom of the crust with your left hand and peel the foil, a bit at a time, with your right hand. As you do so, rotate the crust gently on your left hand.

Supporting the bottom of the crust with a small metal spatula or a knife, ease it back into the plate very gently so as not to crack it. It will not crack or break if it has been frozen sufficiently.

Baked Pie Shell

Whoever said "As easy as pie"? Making a proper pie crust takes patience, practice, experience, and a thorough knowledge of the subject. Instructions teach you not to use too much or too little flour, too much or too little shortening and butter, too much or too little ice water. And especially not to handle the mixture any more than necessary. And to chill it properly. And to roll it very carefully. Etc., etc., etc. I hope the following will help you. Just follow the directions, and make a few crusts to practice before planning a finished pie. It will get easier.

This recipe will make a single 9-inch crust. (For a 10-inch crust, see Notes.) I recommend using an ovenproof glass pie plate.

1 cup sifted all-purpose flour
Scant ½ teaspoon salt
3 tablespoons vegetable shortening (such as Crisco), cold and firm

3 tablespoons sweet butter, cold and firm, cut
    into small pieces
About 3 tablespoons ice water

(If the room is warm it is a good idea to chill the
mixing bowl and even the flour beforehand.)

Place the flour and salt in a large mixing bowl.
Add the shortening and butter. With a pastry
blender cut in the shortening and butter until the
mixture resembles coarse crumbs—when partly cut
in, raise the bowl with both hands, quickly move it
away from you, up, and then toward you in a jerky
motion to toss the bottom ingredients to the top.
Search out any large pieces of butter and cut them
individually with a knife. It is all right to leave a few
pieces about the size of small peas.

Sprinkle 1 tablespoon of the ice water by small
drops all over the surface. Mix and toss with a fork.
Continue adding the water only until all the flour is
barely moistened. (Too much water makes the pastry
sticky-soggy-tough.) Do not ever dump a lot of the
water in any one spot. When the water is partly
added, with both hands raise the bowl, quickly move
it away from you, up, and then toward you in a jerky
motion to toss the dry flour to the top. (I know one
cook who uses a laundry-sprinkling container and
another who uses a salt shaker to add the water; that
way they distribute it in a fine spray all over.)

When adequate water has been added the mixture
will still be lumpy, but with practice you will know by

the look of it that it will form a ball when pressed
together. I have occasionally had to add a little more
water, but very little—about 1 to 2 teaspoons.

The shortening and butter must not melt (they
should remain in little flour-coated flakes) so do not
handle now any more than necessary. Turn the mixture out onto a board or smooth work surface and,
with your hands, just push the mixture together to
form a ball. (My mother never touched the dough
with her hands at this stage—she turned it out onto
a piece of plastic wrap, brought up the sides of the
plastic, and squeezed them firmly together at the top,
pressing from the outside and letting the mixture
form a ball without actually touching it.) If the
dough is too dry to hold together do not knead it, but
replace it in the bowl and use a knife to cut it into
small pieces again and add a few more drops of water.

Lightly flour your hands, round the ball of dough,
then flatten it slightly and smooth the edges. (Or, if
you have formed it into a ball in a piece of plastic wrap
as my mother did, open the top of the plastic briefly
and close it again loosely. Flatten the dough slightly
with your hands, smooth the edges, and rewrap it in
the plastic wrap.) Wrap the dough in plastic wrap and
refrigerate overnight or at least for a few hours. It may
stay in the refrigerator for up to a week, or if you are in
a rush it may be used after a few hours. Or it may be
frozen now, airtight, for up to two months.

Rolling out the dough is much easier if you use a
pastry cloth to work on and a stockinette cover for the
rolling pin. Flour the cloth by rubbing in as much
flour as the cloth will absorb, then lightly scrape off
loose excess flour. Rub flour into the covered rolling
pin. (I use a French style rolling pin that is long and
narrow and tapered at both ends. It is too long and
narrow to wear a stockinette cover. Just keep it lightly
floured while you roll with it.)

Place the flattened ball of dough on the cloth. If
the dough is very firm, pound (whack) it sharply in
all directions with the rolling pin to flatten it to a circle about 7 inches in diameter. If it is not too firm,
just press down on it gently in all directions with the

rolling pin to form a 7-inch round. With your fingers, smooth the edges and pinch together any small cracks at the edges.

Now start to roll, always from the center out. Do not roll back and forth and do not turn the dough over during rolling. Roll first in one direction and then another, trying to keep the shape round. If the edges crack slightly, pinch them together. If the dough cracks anywhere other than the edges, or if the circle is terribly uneven, do not reroll the dough; simply cut off uneven edges and use the scraps as patches. The piece used as a patch should be turned upside down when it is put in place. Then roll over that area lightly to seal.

It may be necessary to reflour the pin occasionally. It should not be necessary to reflour the pastry cloth, but if there is any hint that the dough might stick, reflour it very lightly. The less flour you use the better—too much flour toughens pastry.

Roll the dough into a circle 13 inches in diameter for a 9-inch plate; 13½ or 14 inches for a 10-inch plate—the dough should be a scant ⅛ inch thick. It is important that the rolled-out pastry be exactly the same thickness all over so it will brown evenly.

Now, if you have a cake-decorating turntable or a lazy Susan to place the pie plate on, you will find it much easier to trim and shape the crust.

Roll the dough up loosely around the rolling pin to transfer it to the pie plate. Then unroll it, centering it evenly over the plate. With your fingers, ease the sides of the dough down into the plate—it is important not to stretch the dough or it will shrink during baking.

The dough must touch the plate all around—press the bottom where the sides and bottom meet. Then press gently against the sides. If your fingernails are in the way, cut a small portion of the dough from an uneven edge, form it into a small ball, flour it lightly, and use it as a tamping tool to press the dough into place.

With scissors cut the edge of the crust evenly, leaving about a ½-inch overhang. With floured fingertips fold the edge to the outside and down, forming a hem that extends about ½ inch over the rim. Press the hem lightly together between your thumb and forefinger knuckle, making it stand upright. (While you are handling the edges, if the kitchen is warm and the pastry becomes sticky, refrigerate it briefly.)

Now, with lightly floured fingertips, form a decorative edge on the pastry. There are many ways of doing this. Here's one. You will be moving clockwise around the rim, starting at three o'clock. Place your left forefinger at a right angle across the rim of the pastry. Your hand will be over the inside of the plate with your finger sticking over to the outside. Move your right arm so the elbow is up, then with your right hand grip the pastry rim using the thumb and forefinger knuckle. Grip slightly ahead (clockwise) of your left finger, and twist the pastry edge toward the center of the plate. Remove both hands, then replace your left forefinger just ahead (clockwise again) of the twist you have just formed. This will be at about four o'clock on the rim. Repeat the twists all around the edge. Check and reshape any uneven spots.

Then, with your fingertips, press the sides of the pastry firmly against the sides of the plate.

With a fork prick the bottom all over at ¼-inch intervals.

Place the shell in the freezer for 15 minutes or more until it is frozen firm. (This helps prevent shrinking.)

About 15 minutes before you bake, adjust oven rack one-third up from the bottom and preheat oven to 450 degrees.

In order to keep the pastry shell in place during baking, cut a 12-inch square of aluminum foil. Place the foil, shiny side down, in the frozen shell. Press it into place all over. If your fingernails are in the way, place a pot holder or a folded dish towel against the foil while you press it. Do not fold the edges of the foil over the rim of the crust; let the corners of the foil stand up. Fill the foil at least three-quarters full with dried beans or with the aluminum pellets that are made for this purpose. (If you use beans, reserve them to use again for the same purpose.) Aluminum pie weights (pellets) are available by mail from Williams-Sonoma, (877) 812-6235, and in New York from Bridge Kitchenware, 214 East 52nd Street, New York, New York 10022.

Bake the frozen shell for 12 to 13 minutes until it is set and lightly colored on the edges. Remove it from the oven. Reduce the heat to 400 degrees. Gently remove the foil and beans by lifting the four corners of the foil. Replace the shell in the oven and continue to bake about 7 or 8 minutes more, or longer if necessary. Watch it almost constantly; if it starts to puff up anywhere, reach into the oven and pierce the puff with a cake tester or a fork to release trapped air. Bake until the edges are richly colored—a too-pale crust is not as attractive as one with a good color. The bottom will remain paler than the edges. (During baking, if the crust is not browning evenly reverse the position of the pan.)

Place on a rack and cool to room temperature.

NOTES: *1. For a 10-inch crust, increase the amounts to 1¼ cups flour, generous ½ teaspoon salt, 3¾ tablespoons vegetable shortening, 3¾ tablespoons butter, and 3¾ tablespoons ice water.*

2. The ingredients for the crust may easily be doubled for two shells.

3. Here's a hint for freezing: Roll out each round of dough. Place it on wax paper on cookie sheets and freeze. Then wrap the flat rounds of dough airtight in plastic wrap and return them to the freezer. When you want to use one, let it thaw until it is soft enough to be placed in the pie plate and shaped. This way you can freeze as many as you want even if you don't have many pie plates and they won't take up much room.

Or, if you don't plan on that many pies, it is a great luxury to have just one unbaked shell in the freezer. I try to keep one frozen, all ready for the oven, in the pie plate with the aluminum foil lining in place. I wrap it in plastic wrap or a freezer bag. Then I only have to fill it with the dried beans when I am ready to bake it. (I think it is

better that way, but some people like to keep one already baked, frozen.)

VARIATION: *For a chocolate crust follow the above directions using the following ingredients: 1 cup sifted all-purpose flour; ¼ teaspoon salt; 1 tablespoon unsweetened cocoa powder; 1 tablespoon confectioners sugar (sift together the flour, salt, cocoa, and sugar); 1½ tablespoons vegetable shortening; 4 tablespoons sweet butter; 3 to 4 tablespoons ice water.*

Chocolate Pecan Pie

8 TO 10 PORTIONS

The non-chocolate version of this pie is one of the most famous of all truly American recipes. The classic Southern pecan pie, often described as "utterly deadly," is rich, gooey, sweet-sweet-sweet. The unsweetened chocolate and rum in this recipe cut the sweetness to just right. This is one of the best of all pies.

Traditionally, the filling is poured into an unbaked crust and then it is baked. I have never had one made that way that had a really crisp bottom crust. I like a crisp bottom crust, so the procedure for this is different. In this recipe the crust is partially baked "blind" (without the filling), then it is baked again with the filling. It will have a crisp bottom crust.

And, traditionally, this amount of filling is used for a 10-inch crust or even for two 9-inch crusts. I like a thicker filling; this is baked in one 9-inch crust and it will be a thick filling.

When just right, the crust should be flaky, crisp, and buttery, and a rich golden color. The filling should be semi-firm in the middle with a consistency somewhere between a thick fudge sauce and smooth caramel; and the pecans, which rise during baking, should form a crunchy layer on the top.

PIE CRUST

Prepare a 9-inch baked pie shell (see page 176), but because this pie has such a generous amount of filling it is important to form an even, high rim with no low spots, so the filling can't run over. And make a change in timing (since this will have additional baking after the filling is poured in): When you remove the aluminum foil and the dried beans and reduce the temperature to 400 degrees, bake for only 4 minutes (instead of 7 or 8), or until the bottom of the crust is completely dry but still pale and the edges are just beginning to color.

Let the partially baked crust cool slightly (or completely if you wish) and then prepare the filling.

FILLING

2 ounces (2 squares) **unsweetened chocolate**

2 ounces (½ stick) **sweet butter**

4 **eggs** (graded large)

1 cup **granulated sugar**

1¼ cups **dark corn syrup**

1 teaspoon **vanilla extract**

2 tablespoons **dark rum**

7 ounces (2 cups) **pecan halves or large pieces**

Adjust rack one-third up from the bottom of the oven and preheat oven to 350 degrees.

Place the chocolate and the butter in the top of a small double boiler over hot water on moderate heat; cover until partially melted, then uncover and stir until completely melted. Remove from the hot water and set aside, uncovered, to cool slightly.

In a large bowl (you can use an electric mixer, a manual egg beater, or a wire whisk) beat the eggs lightly just to mix, then beat in the sugar and syrup just to mix. Add the vanilla, rum, and then the melted chocolate/butter, and mix. Now stir in the pecans.

Carefully pour the filling into the partially baked crust, watching the edges as you pour; if the rim is not high enough, or has any low spots, do not use all of the filling or it will run over.

Bake for 40 to 50 minutes. If you bake until a knife inserted in the filling comes out clean, the pie will be overdone. The top should still feel soft to the touch, and the middle should wiggle and shake if you move the pan slightly. Do not be alarmed—and do not bake any longer. The filling will set and firm as it cools. Longer baking would spoil the sensational quality of the filling. (During baking the top will rise and crack; it will settle down as it cools.)

Remove the pie from the oven, place it on a rack, and cool to temperature.

Southerners are emphatic about the fact that pecan pie is best when it is still slightly warm (it takes about 3 hours to cool to room temperature). However, I think this particular pie is much better when it is cold—very cold. I refrigerate it and serve it cold.

OPTIONAL: *Whipped cream is traditional with pecan pie. If you use it, whip 1 cup heavy cream with only 1 tablespoon of granulated or confectioners sugar, ½ teaspoon of vanilla extract and/or 1 tablespoon of rum or bourbon for 5 portions—double the amounts to serve 10. Whip only until the cream holds a soft shape, not stiff. Pass it separately.*

Chocolate Fudge Pie

10 PORTIONS

This is dense, dark, moist, chewy, and rich, rich, rich! It is best to make the pie early in the day for serving that night; it should be cooled and refrigerated before serving.

PIE CRUST

Prepare a 10-inch baked pie shell (see page 176). Note that for this pie it is important to form a high rim with no low spots to hold all the filling. And make a change in timing since this will have additional baking when the filling is poured in. After you remove the aluminum foil and the dried beans and reduce the temperature to 400 degrees, bake for only 3 or 4 minutes (instead of 7 or 8) until the bottom of the crust is dry but not brown.

Let the partially baked crust cool slightly (or completely, if you wish) while you prepare the filling.

FUDGE FILLING

¼ pound (1 stick) sweet butter
3 ounces (3 squares) unsweetened chocolate
4 eggs (graded large or extra-large)
Scant ¼ teaspoon salt
1½ cups granulated sugar
3 tablespoons light corn syrup
¼ cup milk
1 teaspoon vanilla extract
Optional: 1 tablespoon Cognac or rum

Adjust rack one-third up from the bottom of the oven and preheat oven to 350 degrees.

Place the butter and the chocolate in the top of a small double boiler over warm water on low heat.

Cover until partially melted, then uncover and stir until completely melted and smooth. Remove the top of the double boiler and set it aside, uncovered, to cool slightly.

Meanwhile, in the large bowl of an electric mixer, beat the eggs well. Except for the chocolate and butter mixture add all the remaining ingredients and beat well. Then beat in the chocolate and butter mixture.

Turn into the prepared, partially baked pie crust; the filling will come almost to the top of the crust. Handle very carefully and place in the preheated oven.

Bake for 50 minutes. Do not bake any longer even if the filling appears soft. Turn the oven heat off, prop the oven door partially open, and let the pie stand in the oven until it is completely cool. (The filling will puff up during baking and then will settle down to a thin layer that will crack while cooling. O.K.)

Refrigerate for several hours.

WHIPPED CREAM

2 cups heavy cream
1 teaspoon vanilla extract
Optional: 1 tablespoon Cognac or rum
¼ cup confectioners sugar

In a chilled bowl with chilled beaters, whip the cream with the remaining ingredients until it will just hold a shape.

Shortly before serving spread the cream in a thick layer over the top of the pie.

Chocolate Angel Pie

12 TO 14 PORTIONS

This is from my good friend Janet Chusmir, who is a wonderful cook and Editor of The Miami Herald.

An Angel Pie has a meringue crust and a rich and creamy mousse-like filling. This filling is the best I've ever had for this type dessert. You will love it.

This is a large, dramatic dessert, made in a 10-inch ovenproof glass pie plate, with a filling more than 3 inches deep. The meringue shell and the filling must be made the day before serving, or the meringue will be sticky and difficult to cut. And the filling will be firmer and more delicious after standing. The whipped cream topping should be put on shortly before serving ("shortly before" may be anywhere from about 1 or 2 hours up to immediately before).

MERINGUE SHELL

(You can use leftover egg whites that have been frozen and thawed)

½ cup egg whites (from 3 to 4 eggs, depending on their size), at room temperature
¼ teaspoon salt
¼ teaspoon cream of tartar
1 cup granulated sugar
1 teaspoon vanilla extract

Adjust rack one-third up from the bottom of the oven and preheat oven to 275 degrees. Lightly butter a 10-inch ovenproof glass pie plate and set it aside.

In the small bowl of an electric mixer at moderate speed beat the egg whites for a few seconds or just until they are foamy. Add the salt and cream of tartar. Beat at moderate speed for a minute or so until the whites hold a soft shape. Continue to beat at moderate speed and start adding the sugar, 1 rounded tablespoonful at a time. Beat for half a minute or so between additions. When about half of the sugar has been added, add the vanilla and then continue adding the sugar as before. When all of the sugar has been added, increase the speed to high and beat for 7 or 8 minutes more until the sugar is dissolved—test it by rubbing a bit between your fingers. If it feels grainy, beat some more. The meringue will be very stiff. (Total beating time from start to finish is 15 to 18 minutes.)

The meringue will be a little sticky and hard to handle. Use a spoon to pick it up and a rubber spatula to push it off the spoon. Place well-rounded tablespoonfuls of the meringue touching one another around the sides of the plate and then place the remainder on the bottom of the plate and spread it to make a shell almost 1 inch thick and extending about ¾ of an inch above the rim of the plate. The meringue should be fairly smooth on the bottom and sides, but the top of the rim should be shaped into irregular peaks. Try not to spread the meringue over the edge of the plate—it rises and spreads during baking and if it has been spread over the edge too much it might run over the sides and be difficult to serve. I use a teaspoon on the inside of the plate to bring the meringue up into peaks, forming a high shell without letting it spread over the rim.

Bake for 1¼ to 1½ hours until the meringue is a pale, sandy color. The meringue should dry out in the oven as much as possible, but the color should not become any darker than a pale gold. Then turn off the heat, open the oven door slightly, and let the meringue cool in the oven. It will probably crack during cooling—don't worry, that's O.K.

CHOCOLATE MOUSSE FILLING

12 ounces semisweet chocolate (see Note)

6 eggs (graded large or extra-large), 4 of the eggs should be separated and 2 should be left whole

2 cups heavy cream

Pinch of salt

Place the chocolate in the top of a double boiler over hot water on moderate heat. Cover until the chocolate is partially melted. Then uncover and stir until completely melted and smooth. Remove from the hot water and set aside, uncovered, briefly.

Place the 4 egg yolks and 2 whole eggs in a large mixing bowl. Stir with a wire whisk to mix well (they should be thoroughly mixed but not beaten until airy). Then gradually add the warm chocolate, stirring constantly with the whisk, until smooth. Set aside.

In a chilled bowl with chilled beaters whip the cream only until it holds a definite shape but not until it is stiff (stiff cream will make the filling heavy and buttery instead of light and creamy). Set aside.

In the small bowl of an electric mixer add the salt to the 4 remaining egg whites and beat until the whites hold a shape or are stiff but not dry. In 2 or 3 additions add the whites to the chocolate/egg mixture and fold them in using a rubber spatula. Then in 2 or 3 additions, add the whipped cream and fold that in. Do not handle any more than necessary to blend the ingredients.

Turn the filling into the cooled meringue shell. Smooth the top. Refrigerate overnight.

The next day prepare the whipped cream topping.

WHIPPED CREAM TOPPING

2 cups heavy cream

⅓ cup strained confectioners sugar

1½ teaspoons vanilla extract

In a chilled bowl with chilled beaters whip the cream with the sugar and vanilla only until the cream holds a shape. (It should hold a shape but it is nicer if it is not too stiff.) Place the cream by large spoonfuls over the filling. Then spread it to cover the filling; it may be spread smoothly or swirled into peaks. Or, if the mousse filling is too deep (that will depend on how you shaped the shell) serve the cream separately. Refrigerate.

OPTIONAL: *Cover the top of the pie generously with Chocolate Shavings (see page 263). You can work either directly over the pie, letting the curls fall on the cream, or work over wax paper and then transfer the curls with a spoon; or, holding the two narrow sides of the paper, lift it and funnel the curls over the top.*

TO SERVE THE PIE: *Place the pie plate on a folded napkin on a large platter. When you cut the meringue it might crumble and the platter will catch any overflow. And the folded napkin will keep the pie plate from slipping. Use a large, sharp knife.*

NOTE: *Janet uses semisweet chocolate morsels for the filling and her word to describe this pie is "exceptional." I have used the morsels and have also made it with Tobler Tradition and with Lindt Excellence. There is a difference in flavor, but no matter what the chocolate, the word is "exceptional." (If you use bar chocolate, break or cut it into pieces before using.)*

Chocolate Pecan Angel Pie

10 Portions

This is somewhat similar to the previous Chocolate Angel Pie with these differences: this crust has nuts in it, this filling has no eggs and is easier to make, and this one has a coffee flavor.

MERINGUE SHELL

Prepare the meringue shell as in the Chocolate Angel Pie (above), but just before placing the mixture in the pie plate gently fold in ¾ cup pecans cut into medium-small pieces. Then continue with the directions for shaping and baking the meringue shell.

FILLING

8 ounces semisweet chocolate

2 tablespoons dry instant coffee

6 tablespoons boiling water

2 scant teaspoons vanilla extract

1 pint (2 cups) heavy cream

Optional: 2 tablespoons whiskey, rum, or Cognac

Break up or coarsely chop the chocolate and place it in a medium-size saucepan. Dissolve the coffee in the boiling water and pour it over the chocolate. Stir over low heat until the chocolate is melted and the mixture is

smooth. Set aside until completely cooled. (This may be stirred briefly over ice and water to save time.) Test the temperature by dropping a bit of the mixture on the inside of your wrist. When it is cool, stir in the vanilla.

In a chilled bowl with chilled beaters whip the cream with the optional liquor until the cream just holds a shape—do not beat until it is really stiff.

Fold half of the whipped cream into the chocolate and then fold the chocolate into the remaining cream.

Turn the filling into the cooled meringue shell and smooth the top. After a few hours the top may be loosely covered with plastic wrap.

Although the optional toppings may be put on shortly before serving, the meringue shell and the filling must be refrigerated overnight.

OPTIONAL: *Cover the filling either now or later with a generous topping of Chocolate Shavings (see page 263). Or shortly before serving cover the top with a generous amount of whipped cream as in the previous recipe (see page 183). Or form a border of whipped cream. (To make just a border, whip ½ cup heavy cream with ½ teaspoon vanilla extract and 2 tablespoons of strained confectioners sugar until the cream holds a shape. Then either use a pastry bag fitted with a medium-size star tube and form small rosettes, touching one another, around the rim of the chocolate, or use a teaspoon and place the cream around the rim in small mounds.) The cream may be decorated with pecan halves or pieces or with chocolate coffee beans (candy).*

Chocolate Pie with Graham Crust

8 TO 10 PORTIONS

When my friend Cecily Brownstone, the Associated Press food editor, made Graham Crackers from my cookie book, she said she was going to make a pie crust with them. She meant that she was going to make crumbs and a regular crumb crust. I misunderstood and thought that she meant to use the rolled-out dough to line a pie plate. I tried it and it turned out to be a wonderful idea—a whole graham cracker crust in one piece, not made from crumbs. (The dough handles beautifully.)

The crust seemed to call for a rich chocolate filling, and whipped cream topping. (The filling is a walnut version of one often used in a pie called French Silk Pie.)

GRAHAM CRUST
(see Notes)

½ cup sifted all-purpose white flour
½ teaspoon baking powder
¼ teaspoon baking soda
⅛ teaspoon salt
½ teaspoon cinnamon
2 ounces (½ stick) butter
½ teaspoon vanilla extract
¼ cup dark brown sugar, firmly packed
2 tablespoons honey
1 cup <u>unsifted</u> all-purpose whole-wheat flour
   (stir lightly to aerate before measuring)
¼ cup milk

Sift together the white flour, baking powder, baking soda, salt, and cinnamon and set aside.

In the small bowl of an electric mixer cream the butter. Add the vanilla, brown sugar, and honey and beat to mix well. On low speed add the whole-wheat flour and the sifted dry ingredients in three additions, alternating with the milk in two additions. Scrape the bowl as necessary with a rubber spatula and beat only until smooth after each addition. If the mixture is not completely smooth, turn it out onto a board or smooth work surface and knead it briefly with the heel of your hand.

Divide the dough in half. Form each half into a round ball, flatten slightly, wrap airtight, and refrigerate for at least 2 to 3 hours. It may be refrigerated for several days or frozen.

When ready to prepare the crust, adjust a rack to the center of the oven and preheat oven to 350 degrees.

Have a 9-inch pie plate ready. Flour a pastry cloth and a rolling pin.

Place one piece of the dough on the cloth and turn it over to flour both sides lightly. Roll out the dough into a circle at least 12½ or 13 inches in diameter (it will be very thin).

Roll the dough up loosely around the rolling pin and unroll it over the pie plate, centering it as evenly as you can. Gently ease it into place in the plate. If you have a cake-decorating turntable or a lazy Susan, place the pie plate on it.

With scissors trim the crust 1 inch beyond the edge of the plate. Fold the crust edge back on itself to the outside forming a ½-inch hem. Pinch the folded-over dough lightly with thumb and index finger into a rim standing about ½ inch all around. With your fingers press gently against the crust to make sure it touches the plate all over. And with your fingers flute the rim around the edge of the crust. With a fork, pierce holes at about ½-inch intervals over the bottom and sides of the crust.

Chill the crust briefly in the freezer or refrigerator—a few minutes will be enough—or if you wish you can keep it chilled longer and bake it later.

Bake the crust for 16 or 17 minutes until it is lightly colored all over and slightly darker at the edge.

Place on a rack until completely cool.

Meanwhile, prepare the filling. Or the baked crust may be frozen and filled much later.

FRENCH SILK FILLING

3 ounces (3 squares) unsweetened chocolate
6 ounces (1½ sticks) butter
1 teaspoon vanilla extract
1 cup light brown sugar, firmly packed
4 eggs
½ cup walnuts, cut into medium-size pieces

Place the chocolate in the top of a small double boiler over hot water on moderate heat. Cover and let stand only until melted. Remove from the hot water and set aside, uncovered, to cool.

In the small bowl of an electric mixer cream the butter until it is soft. Add the vanilla and sugar and beat well for several minutes. Add the melted chocolate and beat to mix. Now add the eggs one at a time, beating for 5 (*five*) minutes after each addition. For the first egg you can use high speed, but as you add the remaining eggs and the mixture thins, reduce the speed as necessary to avoid splashing. Total beating time for the eggs is 20 minutes.

Stir in the walnuts and pour the mixture into the baked and cooled crust.

Refrigerate for several hours or overnight.

The following whipped cream may be prepared just before serving or early in the day to use that night—the little bit of gelatin will keep it from separating.

WHIPPED CREAM TOPPING

1 teaspoon unflavored gelatin
2 tablespoons cold water
2 cups heavy cream
½ cup strained confectioners sugar
Scant 2 teaspoons vanilla extract
Optional: coarsely grated chocolate

In a small heatproof cup sprinkle the gelatin over the cold water and let stand for a few minutes. Then place the cup in a small pan of shallow hot water on low heat. Let stand until the gelatin is dissolved.

Reserve about 3 tablespoons of the cream and place the rest in the small bowl of an electric mixer. (If the room is very warm the bowl and beaters should be chilled.) Add the sugar and vanilla and beat until the cream increases in volume and barely holds a soft shape. Quickly stir the reserved cream into the dissolved gelatin and, beating constantly, pour all at once into the whipped cream. Continue to beat only until the cream holds a shape and is just firm enough to be a topping—don't overbeat.

Place the whipped cream, one large spoonful at a time, around the outer edge of the pie. Then fill in the center. Place any remaining cream on the center. With a rubber spatula spread the cream to cover the pie and then to form swirls.

Sprinkle with the optional grated chocolate and then refrigerate until serving time.

Serve in small portions—really!

NOTES: *1. The recipe for the graham crust will make two crusts. You can either divide the recipe in half to make only one, or bake two crusts, or freeze the remaining dough or use it for cookies. I recommend making the full amount; it is no more work and it is nice to have it on hand.*

You can use this crust for any recipe that calls for a baked crust or a crumb crust, and you can make cookies with any leftover scraps of the dough. Press them together, wrap airtight, and chill until firm enough to roll. Then, on a floured pastry cloth with a floured rolling pin, roll the dough until it is a scant ¼-inch thick. Cut into squares or circles, transfer to an unbuttered cookie sheet, and with a fork prick the cookies at ½-inch intervals. Bake above the center of a 350-degree oven for about 12 minutes or until the cookies are lightly colored. Transfer them to a rack to cool.

2. This French Silk Filling may of course also be used in a regular baked pie shell (see page 176) or a crumb crust (see page 176).

Chocolate Chiffon Pie

8 PORTIONS

This is a beautiful and important pie. The filling is airy, creamy dark chocolate, mounded 2 ¼ inches high. The crust may be prepared ahead of time but the filling should be made early in the day for that night; it is more delicate if it does not stand overnight.

PIE CRUST

Prepare a pie shell and bake it in a 9-inch pie plate (see page 176). Cool it completely.

CHOCOLATE FILLING

7 ounces semisweet chocolate
1 cup milk
1 tablespoon (1 envelope) unflavored gelatin

⅔ cup granulated sugar
2 eggs (graded extra-large or jumbo), separated
1 teaspoon dry instant coffee
1½ cups heavy cream
Pinch of salt

The chocolate must be finely ground. It may be ground in a food processor, a blender, or a nut or chocolate grater. (If you use a food processor or a blender, it should be chopped or broken into small pieces first.) When the chocolate is finely ground, set it aside.

Place the milk in the top of a large double boiler. Sprinkle the gelatin over the milk and let it stand for 2 or 3 minutes. Add ⅓ cup of the sugar (reserve remaining ⅓ cup), the egg yolks, and the chocolate. Stir to mix thoroughly. Place over hot water on moderate heat and stir constantly until the chocolate, sugar, and gelatin are dissolved. (Do not overcook or the yolks will curdle.) Add the dry instant coffee and stir to dissolve. Remove from the hot water.

Place the top of the double boiler in a large bowl of ice and water and stir the chocolate mixture until it reaches room temperature (test it on the inside of your wrist). Remove from the ice water and set aside.

In a chilled bowl with chilled beaters whip the cream until it barely holds a shape (if it is too stiff it will make the filling heavy). Set aside.

Beat the egg whites and the salt in the small bowl of the electric mixer until the whites have increased in volume and started to thicken. On moderate speed, while beating, add the reserved sugar very gradually. Then increase the speed to high and beat only until the whites barely hold a peak when the beaters are raised, or when the whites are lifted with a rubber spatula. (Do not beat the whites too stiff and dry or it will be difficult to fold them in.) Set them aside.

Now replace the chocolate mixture in the ice water and stir constantly with a rubber spatula, scraping around the bottom and sides until the mixture has barely started to thicken. (Do not wait until it actually stiffens. The ideal conditions for folding are to have the chocolate, whites and cream, all the same consistency.)

Fold about one-third of the chocolate into the beaten whites and fold another third into the whipped cream. Then, in a large bowl, fold together the whites, the cream, and the remaining chocolate. (Do not handle any more than necessary.)

Pour the chiffon mixture into the prepared shell but watch the rim carefully—you will possibly have more filling than the shell will hold, and you must be careful not to let it run over the edges. Pour in only as much as the shell will safely hold. Place the filled shell in the freezer for a few minutes (leaving the remaining filling at room temperature) just until the filling in the shell is slightly set. Then mound the remaining filling high in the center.

Refrigerate the filled shell for at least an hour or more until completely set.

TOPPING

Optional: ¾ teaspoon unflavored gelatin
Optional: 1½ tablespoons cold water
1½ cups heavy cream
⅓ cup strained or sifted confectioners sugar
1 teaspoon vanilla extract
Optional: 1 ounce or less semisweet chocolate

If the whipped cream topping stands for an hour or more it may separate slightly—the watery liquid will run out. To avoid that, add the gelatin. However, if you put the whipped cream on just before serving, the gelatin may be omitted.

Sprinkle the gelatin over the cold water in a small heatproof cup. Let stand for 5 minutes. Then place the cup in shallow hot water over moderate heat until the gelatin is dissolved. Remove from the heat.

Place all but about 2 tablespoons of the cream in the chilled small bowl of the electric mixer. Add the sugar and vanilla. With chilled beaters whip the cream until it is slightly thickened.

Quickly stir the reserved 2 tablespoons of cream into the dissolved warm gelatin and, with the beater going, add the gelatin mixture all at once to the partially whipped cream. Continue to beat until the cream holds a shape. (Do not overbeat. Stiff whipped cream is buttery and not so attractive or delicious. But if it is to be used decoratively with a pastry bag and a star tube it should be stiff enough to hold the design.)

Now the cream may be spread evenly all over the pie, or it may be piped on with a pastry bag fitted with a large, star-shaped tube. (A suggestion; With the tube form eight large, high rosettes around the pie, about an inch from the edges. To form a rosette, move the pastry bag in a small spiral. Make the outside loop about 2 to 2½ inches in diameter. Keep spiraling toward the center and up until the rosette stands 1½ to 2 inches high.)

The optional chocolate is for decoration. It may be grated, or shaved with a vegetable peeler. Sprinkle it over the top of the pie or over the rosettes.

Refrigerate and serve very cold.

Chiffon and Velvet Pie

6 TO 8 PORTIONS

The "chiffon" is coffee sour-cream meringue, the "velvet" is smooth, dark chocolate filling, and there is a crunchy crumb crust. It is an elegant combination of textures and flavors.

The crust may be made way ahead of time (it

has to be made somewhat ahead of time)—the filling and topping may be made early in the day for that night or the day before.

CRUST

1 cup graham-cracker crumbs
¼ cup granulated sugar
½ cup walnuts, finely chopped (not ground)
2 ounces (½ stick) butter, melted

Adjust rack to the center of the oven and preheat oven to 375 degrees. Stir the crumbs, sugar, and nuts in a mixing bowl. Add the melted butter and stir with a rubber spatula, pressing the mixture against the sides of the bowl until thoroughly mixed. The mixture will be crumbly but it will hold together when it is pressed into the pie plate.

Use a 9-inch ovenproof glass pie plate and follow the directions for crumb crust (see page 176).

FILLING

8 ounces semisweet chocolate
2 tablespoons granulated sugar
1 cup light cream
4 egg yolks (reserve the whites for the topping)
1 teaspoon vanilla extract

Break up the chocolate and place it in the top of a large double boiler. Add the sugar and cream. Place over hot water on moderate heat. Cook, stirring occasionally, until the chocolate is melted and the mixture is smooth. If it does not get smooth, stir it briskly with a small wire whisk.

Stir the yolks slightly in a mixing bowl just to mix. Gradually add about half of the chocolate to the yolks, stirring constantly, and then add the yolks to the remaining chocolate. Add the vanilla and stir well.

Remove from the hot water and set aside for 5 to 10 minutes, stirring occasionally.

Pour the filling (which may be warm) into the prepared crust. Cool to room temperature, then place in the refrigerator for about half an hour.

Meanwhile, prepare the top layer.

TOPPING

2 tablespoons dry instant coffee
¼ cup boiling water
1 teaspoon unflavored gelatin
    (this is ⅓ of an envelope)
4 egg whites
½ cup granulated sugar
½ cup sour cream

In a small cup dissolve the dry instant coffee in the boiling water. Let stand until completely cool (refrigerate if necessary).

Sprinkle the gelatin over the cooled coffee. Let stand for about 5 minutes. Then place the cup in a small pan of shallow hot water over low heat until the gelatin is dissolved (stir with a metal teaspoon in order to see any undissolved crystals). Remove from the hot water and set aside to cool to room temperature.

In the small bowl of an electric mixer beat the egg whites until they hold a very soft shape. Reduce the speed to medium and gradually add the sugar. Then increase the speed to high and beat until the whites are really stiff and hold a firm shape.

On low speed, very gradually add the cooled coffee-gelatin mixture, scraping the bowl with a spatula and beating until smooth.

In a mixing bowl stir the sour cream with a rubber spatula until it is smooth and soft. Fold about 1 cup of the whites into the cream and then fold the cream into the remaining whites.

Spread the topping over the pie, mounding it high in the middle and thinner on the edges (the edges should not be heavy or they might run over the crust).

Refrigerate for at least 4 hours or overnight.

Gulf Coast Chocolate Pie

This was served to us (after bowls of steamed shrimp) overlooking the Gulf of Mexico. Our hostess, originally from Alabama, said that it was a family recipe she had used for many, many years.

The filling is like a bavarian made without whipped cream. It is smooth, light, velvety, and delicious. It should be served the day it is made.

PIE CRUST

Prepare a baked pie shell in a 10-inch pie plate (see page 176); cool completely.

CHOCOLATE FILLING

6 ounces semisweet chocolate
1 tablespoon (1 envelope) **unflavored gelatin**
¼ cup cold water
3 eggs (graded large or extra-large), **separated**
¾ cup granulated sugar
1½ cups milk
1 teaspoon vanilla extract
⅛ teaspoon salt

If you use bars or squares of chocolate, chop them rather small; if you use morsels, leave them as they are. Set aside.

In a small cup sprinkle the gelatin over the cold water and let stand.

Place the egg yolks in the top of a large double boiler off the heat. Stir them lightly with a wire whisk.

Stir in ¼ cup (reserve remaining ½ cup) of the sugar. Gradually stir in the milk, quite slowly at first.

Place over hot water in the bottom of the double boiler and cook on moderate heat, stirring frequently, with a rubber spatula, until the mixture thickens enough to coat a metal spoon lightly (that will be 180 degrees on a candy thermometer).

Add the softened gelatin and stir to dissolve. Then add the chocolate and stir to melt. Remove from the hot water.

Beat the mixture briskly with a wire whisk or a beater only until it is smooth. Stir in the vanilla.

Partially fill a large bowl with ice and water. Place the top of the double boiler in the ice water and stir frequently until the mixture is cold (test it by dropping a bit on the inside of your wrist).

Temporarily remove it from the ice water and set aside.

In the small bowl of an electric mixer add the salt to the egg whites and beat until they barely hold a soft shape. Reduce the speed to moderate and gradually add the reserved ½ cup of sugar. Increase the speed to high again and continue to beat only until the whites hold a soft shape; they must not be stiff or dry, they should resemble marshmallow whip. Remove the whites from the mixer and set aside.

Now return the top of the double boiler to the ice water and stir constantly until the chocolate mixture begins to thicken.

Fold about one-third of the chocolate mixture into the whites, and then fold the whites into the remaining chocolate mixture, folding only until incorporated.

Turn the mixture into the baked pie shell. Refrigerate for a few hours; 2½ or 3 hours is enough, but it can be longer if you wish.

WHIPPED CREAM TOPPING

2 cups heavy cream
1 teaspoon vanilla extract
¼ cup confectioners or granulated sugar

In a chilled bowl with chilled beaters, whip all of the above ingredients until the cream is just firm enough to hold its shape but not until it is really stiff.

Whipped cream separates as it stands. If you put it on the pie more than an hour or so before serving, a bit of thin, watery cream will run out toward the edges so do try to put the cream on soon before serving time. However, you can whip it ahead of time, refrigerate, and then stir briefly with a wire whisk just before using.

Place the whipped cream by large spoonfuls all over the top of the filling, spread it to cover, and then, with a rubber spatula, form large swirls in a daisy or sunburst pattern.

I leave it alone—no further decoration. But of course you can top it with Grated Chocolate or Chocolate Shavings (see page 263), or whatever. Our hostess, who gave me this recipe, was most apologetic about not having large pecan halves to trim the top.

COLD AND HOT DESSERTS

Refrigerator Desserts

Chocolate Mousse Heatter

6 PORTIONS

The following recipe is reprinted here from my dessert book.

This is one of the desserts I made daily for my husband's restaurants and I always made it with Tobler Tradition or Lindt Excellence chocolate (available from Paprikas Weiss, see page 11). Either one is great for this mousse. However, since they are not generally available all over the country many people have told me about excellent results with a variety of other chocolates.

Our friends generally make this when they invite us to dinner (they know I love it).

It has been said that chocolate is the sexiest of all flavors. If so, this is the sexiest of all desserts.

8 ounces semisweet, bittersweet, or
    extra-bittersweet chocolate
1 tablespoon dry instant coffee
⅓ cup boiling water
5 eggs (graded large or extra-large), separated
Pinch of salt

Coarsely chop or break up the chocolate and place it in a small, heavy saucepan. Dissolve the coffee in the boiling water and pour it over the chocolate. Place over low heat and stir occasionally with a small wire whisk until smooth. Remove from the heat and set aside to cool for about 5 minutes.

Meanwhile, in the small bowl of an electric mixer, beat the egg yolks at high speed for 3 to 4 minutes until they are pale lemon-colored. Reduce the speed to low, gradually add the slightly warm chocolate, and beat, scraping the bowl with a rubber spatula. Beat only until smooth. Remove from the mixer.

Add the salt to the egg whites and beat with clean beaters only until they hold a definite shape but not until they are stiff or dry (see Notes).

Without being too thorough, gently fold about one-quarter of the beaten whites into the chocolate mixture, then fold in a second quarter, and finally fold the chocolate into the remaining whites, folding only until no whites show.

Gently transfer the mousse to a wide pitcher and pour it into six large wine glasses, each with about a 9-ounce capacity. Do not fill the glasses too full; leave generous headroom on each. (I always prepared this mousse in individual glasses and thought it had to be best that way. But it has been served to me many times at other people's homes from one large serving bowl, and it was fine.)

Cover tightly with aluminum foil and refrigerate for 3 to 6 hours. (The mousse may stand longer—12 to 24 hours if you wish. The texture will become more spongy and less creamy. Delicious both ways.)

MOCHA CREAM

1 cup heavy cream
¼ cup confectioners sugar
1 tablespoon instant coffee

In a chilled bowl with chilled beaters, beat the above ingredients only until the cream thickens to the consistency of a heavy custard sauce—not stiff.

Pour or spoon the cream onto the mousse to completely cover the top of each portion.

Refrigerate until serving time.

OPTIONAL: *Top with a light sprinkling of shaved or coarsely grated semisweet chocolate. Or place a few large Chocolate Slabs (see page 263) standing upright into the cream. Refrigerate until serving time.*

NOTES: *1. I beat the egg whites with the salt in the large bowl of the mixer, beating at high speed only until the whites thicken or hold a very soft shape. Then I finish the beating with a large wire whisk so that there is less chance of overbeating.*

2. This recipe may easily be doubled if you wish.

Mint Chocolate Mousse

The taste of this will remind you of creamy white mints covered with dark bittersweet chocolate.

This recipe is the same as the above mousse with the following changes:

Do not use the instant coffee—use just plain water. And, while beating the chocolate into the egg yolks, add a generous ½ teaspoon peppermint extract.

Instead of the mocha cream topping, use plain whipped cream, made with 1 cup heavy cream, ¼ cup confectioners sugar, and ½ teaspoon vanilla extract.

Another Chocolate Mousse

6 to 8 Portions

Chocolate Mousse Heatter (see page 195) depends almost completely on the chocolate you use for its flavor—it has no sugar and no vanilla.

Here is a delicious, rich, dense mousse made with unsweetened chocolate. This is a traditional French recipe.

It must be made 24 hours before serving.

4 ounces (4 squares) unsweetened chocolate
1 teaspoon dry instant espresso or other dry instant coffee
¼ cup plus 1 tablespoon boiling water
¾ cup granulated sugar
5 eggs (graded large or extra-large), separated
1 teaspoon vanilla extract, or 1 tablespoon rum, brandy, bourbon, kirsch, or Grand Marnier
Pinch of salt

Chop the chocolate coarsely and set it aside.

In a heavy saucepan with a 1- to 2-quart capacity, add the coffee to the water and stir to dissolve. Add ½ cup (reserve ¼ cup) of the sugar and place over moderate heat. Stir until the sugar is dissolved and the mixture barely begins to simmer. Reduce the heat to low, add the chocolate, and stir constantly until melted. Remove from the heat and set aside for a few moments.

In a large mixing bowl stir the egg yolks with a wire whisk just to mix. Gradually stir in about half of the warm chocolate, and then stir the yolks into the remaining chocolate. Stir in the vanilla or liquor, return to the large mixing bowl, and set aside.

In the small bowl of an electric mixer add the salt to the egg whites and beat until they barely hold a soft shape. Reduce the speed to moderate and gradually add the reserved ¼ cup of sugar. Increase the speed to high again and beat briefly only until the whites hold a shape but not until they are stiff or dry.

One at a time, stir two or three tablespoonfuls of the whites into the chocolate, fold about half of the whites into the chocolate—do not be too thorough—and finally fold in the remaining whites.

The mousse may be poured into one large serving dish (it must have at least a 6-cup capacity but it may be larger), or gently pour it into a wide-mouthed pitcher and then pour into six to eight glasses with a 6- to 8-ounce capacity, or eight individual soufflé dishes. (Do not fill them all the way to the top.) Cover the serving dish or individual portions airtight with aluminum foil.

Refrigerate for about 24 hours.

WHIPPED CREAM

1 cup heavy cream
2 tablespoons confectioners sugar
½ teaspoon vanilla extract, or 2 to 3 teaspoons
  of whichever alcohol you used in the
  mousse

If you love whipped cream, double the above ingredients.

In a chilled bowl with chilled beaters, whip the above ingredients only until the cream holds a soft shape—not stiff. If you whip the cream ahead of time, refrigerate it. If so, it will probably separate while standing. Just stir/beat it a bit with a wire whisk before using.

Pour or spoon it over the mousse or pass it separately as a sauce.

OPTIONAL: *Chocolate Shavings (see page 263) may be sprinkled over the mousse whether the whipped cream is on it or not. Or the mousse may be served without any decoration.*

NOTE: *If the mousse is served at the table from one large bowl, it should be spooned onto chilled flat dessert plates.*

P.S. *As with all chocolate desserts, the flavor of the chocolate itself is quite important and is frequently a matter of your own taste. I like this mousse flavored with vanilla, rather than with liquor; it will have a more unadulterated, undiluted, pure chocolate taste. And if you don't use either vanilla or liquor, the chocolate flavor will be even stronger.*

Pots de Chocolat (mousse)

4 PORTIONS

This recipe comes from Oxford University in England where it was taught in a "Cordon Bleu" cooking course. I was told that this was a special favorite of Prince Rainier of Monaco.

It is a very dense mousse (more chocolate per egg than the usual) so the portions should be small. Prepare it in pots de crème cups, demitasse cups, or small wine glasses. The cups or glasses should have about ½-cup capacity and should not be filled all the way to the top.

Make this early in the day for that night, or the day before. The recipe may be divided to make only 2 portions or it may be multiplied by any number.

4 ounces semisweet chocolate
1 tablespoon butter
2 tablespoons light rum or prepared coffee
2 eggs (graded large or extra-large), separated
Pinch of salt

Break up the chocolate and place it with the butter and rum or coffee in the top of a small double boiler over hot water on moderate heat. Cover until partially melted. Then uncover and stir until completely melted and smooth. If necessary, stir briskly with a small wire whisk to make the mixture smooth. Remove from the hot water. Let stand for 2 or 3 minutes to cool slightly.

Add the egg yolks one at a time, stirring until smooth after each addition.

In a small bowl add the salt to the egg whites and beat until they hold a firm shape or are stiff but not dry. The whites must be folded into the chocolate gradually; it is all right if the chocolate is still warm. First fold in one rounded tablespoonful, then another, and then a third. Now fold in all the remaining whites—do not handle any more than necessary. Gently transfer to a small, wide-mouthed pitcher and gently pour into four small cups or glasses, cover, and refrigerate for 6 to 8 hours, or overnight. It will be soft and creamy after 6 to 8 hours and will become more firm after standing overnight. (Good both ways, but if you do let these stand overnight be sure to cover them securely with plastic wrap or aluminum foil—or with the covers of the pots de crème cups—otherwise the tops dry out too much.)

These are traditionally served as is, that is to say with no topping or decoration. However, if you would like a small rosette of whipped cream, and maybe a candied rose or violet petal, or a bit of grated or shaved chocolate, use it.

It is best to eat these with demitasse or other small spoons.

Baked Chocolate Custard

6 5-OUNCE CUPS

A beautiful custard is not only for invalids or children—it is an exquisite dessert for anyone at any time. But making a perfect, plain, baked chocolate custard is an accomplishment—it takes care and attention, although it can be put together in just a few minutes. If you are not careful, the eggs in a custard can become scrambled or tough or watery. Success depends on the heat that the eggs are exposed to—the hot milk must be added to the eggs slowly, and the custard must be baked at a low temperature. And it must not be overbaked.

It is best if this does not stand overnight. Make it during the day to serve that night. The recipe may be divided in half or it may be multiplied by any number.

1½ cups milk
2 ounces semisweet chocolate

1 ounce (1 square) unsweetened chocolate

½ cup water or prepared coffee

2 eggs plus 2 yolks (graded large, extra-large, or jumbo)

¼ cup granulated sugar

1 teaspoon vanilla extract

Generous pinch of salt

Adjust rack one-third up from the bottom of the oven and preheat oven to 300 degrees.

Heat the milk uncovered in a small, heavy saucepan over low heat (high heat will scorch it) until a slightly wrinkled skin forms on the top.

Meanwhile, place both chocolates and the water or coffee (which may be hot or cold) in the top of a large double boiler over hot water on moderate heat. Stir occasionally until the chocolate is melted and smooth.

While the chocolate is melting, place the eggs and yolks in a medium-size mixing bowl and stir with a wire whisk just to mix thoroughly (do not beat until airy), and then stir in the sugar. Set aside.

When the milk and the chocolate are both ready, pour the hot milk all at once into the chocolate and stir until smooth.

Then, very gradually, add the hot chocolate/milk to the eggs, stirring constantly and adding the milk only a little at a time at the beginning.

Return the mixture to the top of the double boiler over warm water on low heat and cook, stirring constantly and scraping the bottom and the sides, for 5 minutes (see Note).

Pour the custard through a fine strainer into a pitcher. Stir in the vanilla and salt.

Place six 5-ounce custard cups in a shallow baking pan—it must not be deeper than the cups. Divide the custard evenly among the cups—do not fill the cups all the way but leave a bit of room at the top of each. Then pour very hot water into the shallow pan to about half the depth of the cups. (If the shallow pan is aluminum, add about ½ teaspoon of cream of tartar to the hot water. It is not necessary to stir it

around—just put it in. It will not affect the custard but it will keep the aluminum from turning dark.)

Place in the oven and cover with a cookie sheet or a large piece of aluminum foil.

Bake for 40 to 45 minutes or until a small, sharp knife gently inserted (not too deep—about ½ to ¾ of an inch is enough) comes out clean. The knife should be inserted halfway between the center and the rim. Test carefully. Correct timing is very important and can mean the difference between success and failure of the custard. (The baking time will vary according to the cups—heavy or thin, deep or shallow.) Do not overbake—custard continues to cook slightly from its own heat after it is removed from the oven.

Carefully remove the cups from the hot water and let them stand uncovered until they cool to room temperature. Then refrigerate; they may be covered in the refrigerator if you wish.

Custard should be served cold; it may be refrigerated for about 3 hours or overnight, but not longer than 24 hours. (Aside from the growth of bacteria, it begins to shrink in the middle and is not as attractive.)

This custard is served in the cups—not inverted or unmolded—with no topping.

NOTE: *If you are an experienced custard baker, you might wonder why this recipe says to cook it on the stove before baking. Here's why: During baking the chocolate rises to the top, and without some stove cooking first to thicken it a bit the mixture may separate into two layers, a light-brown one at the bottom and a thin darker one on top.*

Chocolate Pots de Crème

---

*Another creamy, smooth, extra-rich baked custard—
this is one of the most classic and popular of all
French chocolate desserts (my favorite!). It is quick
and easy to prepare. Make it just a few hours before
serving or make it in the morning for that night. It
may be served with a simple salad luncheon or a
swanky dinner, and, since it is made in individual
dishes, it is easy to handle for a buffet. It may be
made in pots de crème cups with covers, but I think
those portions are too small—I use individual soufflé
dishes (1/2-cup capacity). This recipe makes six 1/2-cup
servings but it may be multiplied to make nine,
twelve, or more.*

2 cups light cream
4 ounces semisweet chocolate
6 egg yolks (from eggs graded large or extra-
   large)
2 tablespoons granulated sugar
Pinch of salt
1½ teaspoons vanilla extract

Adjust rack to the center of the oven and preheat oven to 325 degrees.

Place 1½ cups of the cream in a small, heavy
saucepan over low heat. Place the remaining ½ cup
cream and the chocolate in the top of a large double
boiler over hot water on moderate heat. In a mixing
bowl stir the yolks lightly just to mix—do not beat
until foamy.

When the cream is scalded (a slight skin formed
on the top) stir in the sugar and salt and remove
from the heat.

Stir the chocolate mixture with a small wire
whisk until perfectly smooth. Off the heat, very
gradually add the hot cream to the chocolate, stirring constantly to keep the mixture smooth. Then
gradually stir the chocolate mixture into the yolks
and stir in the vanilla.

Return the mixture to the top of the double
boiler over hot water on low heat and cook, stirring
constantly with a rubber spatula, for 3 minutes.

Pour the mixture through a fine strainer into a
pitcher. Then pour it into the individual soufflé
dishes or pots de crème cups—do not fill them all
the way, leave a bit of headroom.

Place in a shallow baking pan. Pour in hot water
to about half the depth of the cups. Place a cookie
sheet over the top to cover the cups or if you have
used pots de crème cups put their covers on.

Bake for 22 minutes (individual soufflé dishes and
pots de crème cups both take the same time). The usual
test for baked custard is to insert a small, sharp knife
halfway between the middle and the edge; when it
comes out clean the custard is done. However, with this
recipe, if you bake it until the knife comes out clean the
custard will be too heavy and firm by the time it is
chilled. If your oven is right, 22 minutes is correct. The
custard will look too soft but it will become firmer as it
chills, and it is best if it is still slightly creamy in the center when it is served.

Remove the cover or covers, remove the cups
from the water and place on a rack to cool. Then
refrigerate for a few hours.

Serve as is or with a spoonful of sweetened and
flavored whipped cream on top.

Abby Mandel's Boule de Neige (snowball)

8 TO 12 PORTIONS

This is a dense, dark, moist chocolate mixture completely covered with tiny rosettes of whipped cream. It is in a class by itself—not a pudding, not a mousse, not a cake, yet vaguely like all three. It looks elegant, tastes divine (Abby calls this her "most favorite chocolate"), and is easy.

It should be made at least a day before serving, or it may be refrigerated for 4 or 5 days, or it may be frozen, but the whipped cream should be put on the day it is served.

8 ounces semisweet chocolate

2 teaspoons dry instant coffee

½ cup boiling water

1 cup granulated sugar

½ pound (2 sticks) sweet butter, at room
    temperature

4 eggs (graded large)

1 tablespoon Cognac or dark rum

Adjust rack one-third up from the bottom of the oven and preheat oven to 350 degrees. You will need a round, ovenproof mixing bowl (for baking this dessert) with a 6- to 8-cup capacity; it may be glass, pottery, or metal, and it should preferably be deep and narrow rather than wide and shallow (I use a stainless steel bowl that measures 4½ inches high by 6 inches across the top, and has an 8-cup capacity— although a smaller bowl would do).

To line the bowl with aluminum foil, turn the bowl upside down, tear off a 12-inch square of foil

and center it over the inverted bowl, and with your hands press down on the sides all around to form the foil into a bowl shape. Then remove the foil, turn the bowl right side up, and place the bowl-shaped foil into the bowl. Press it firmly into place and set aside.

Break up the chocolate and place it in a small saucepan. Dissolve the coffee in the boiling water and add it along with the sugar. Stir over moderate heat until the chocolate is melted—the mixture does not have to be smooth.

Transfer to the large bowl of an electric mixer and beat on low speed until smooth. Gradually add the butter and continue to beat on low speed until smoothly blended. Add the eggs one at a time, beating until smooth after each addition. Add the Cognac or rum and beat on moderate speed for about a minute.

Pour the mixture into the lined bowl and bake for 55 minutes. When done the top will be puffy with a thick, cracked crust. (If you have used a bowl with an 8-cup capacity, the mixture will not rise to the top.)

Let the bowl stand at room temperature until the dessert is cool—it will shrink as it cools and will shrink more in the center than around the rim. This will leave a hollow in the middle which should be eliminated. The following directions will seem unusual, but follow them. A few minutes after the dessert has been removed from the oven, place a piece of wax paper on top of the bowl, touching the dessert. With your fingertips, press down on the edges of the paper to flatten the raised rim of the dessert (the crust will crack—that's all right). Repeat several times while the dessert is cooling in order to flatten the top as much as possible.

When the dessert is cool, cover airtight and refrigerate overnight or for a few days, or freeze.

A few hours before serving, when you are ready to unmold the dessert and mask it with whipped cream, remove its covering. Invert a flat dessert plate over it (since the dessert will be solid white, a colored or clear glass plate will look better than an all-white one), invert the plate and bowl, remove the bowl, and then peel off the aluminum foil. Refrigerate.

WHIPPED CREAM

1 cup heavy cream
2 tablespoons granulated sugar
2 teaspoons Cognac or dark rum

You will need a pastry bag about 13 inches long and a medium-small star tube, or about a #4. Insert the tube in the bag, fold down a deep cuff on the outside of the bag, and set aside.

In a chilled bowl with chilled beaters, whip the cream until it holds a soft shape. Add the sugar and Cognac or rum and continue to beat until the cream holds a definite shape, but be careful not to make it too stiff or it might curdle while you press it out of the pastry bag.

Transfer the cream to the pastry bag, unfold the cuff, and twist the top of the bag closed.

Now you will completely cover the dessert with small pointed rosettes of whipped cream. Start at the center top and squeeze out one small rosette right in the middle. Then make a circle of rosettes touching one another around the one on top. Then another circle, etc.—the last circle should touch the plate.

Refrigerate.

(Traditionally, a Boule de Neige is decorated with a few crystallized violets and/or rose petals—if you use them, press them into the cream just before serving or they may run and discolor the cream.)

Serve small portions.

NOTE: *Abby Mandel, the beautiful and talented Machine Cuisine® cooking teacher, makes this in a food processor (in about a minute) as follows: Break up the chocolate and place it with the coffee and sugar in*

the processor bowl that has been fitted with the steel blade. Turn the machine on and off four times to start the processing and then let the machine run until the chocolate is finely chopped. With the machine running, add the boiling water through the feed tube and process until the chocolate is melted. Add the butter in small pieces and process until blended. Add the eggs and Cognac or rum and process about 15 seconds until well-combined.

Pour into the foil-lined bowl and continue the recipe as above.

Pavé au Chocolat

10 TO 12 PORTIONS

The translation of the French pavé is "paving-stone." In this case it refers to the shape of this dessert: brick-shaped. This is a classic French recipe, deliciously semisweet, and the quickest and easiest of all icebox cakes. Icebox cakes are generally made by lining a form with lady fingers or sponge cake to make a shell which is then filled with a rich filling. In this recipe the ladyfingers and chocolate filling are simply layered over each other directly on a serving plate.

This can be made early in the day for that night or a day ahead, or it can be frozen (see Note). The recipe can be divided in half to make a cake half as long—or it can be multiplied by any number. (I once made this Pavé to serve fifty people. It was huge and a huge success.)

You will need a long, narrow platter or serving

board; a chocolate-roll board works perfectly. The fin-ished "paving-stone" will be 13 inches long, 3 inches wide, 2 inches high. And you will need room for it in the refrigerator.

6 ounces (2 3-ounce packages) ladyfingers
6 ounces (6 squares) unsweetened chocolate
6 ounces (1½ sticks) sweet butter
1 cup strained confectioners sugar
6 egg yolks
2½ tablespoons light rum, kirsch, or
    framboise
⅓ cup water

A 3-ounce package of ladyfingers has four rows of ladyfingers, six fingers to a row. Separate the strips of ladyfingers but do not separate each individual finger; it is easier to make this if the fingers are fas-tened to each other. Packaged ladyfingers are soft and squashy and absorbent; they work better in this recipe if you dry them out before using. Preheat the oven to 300 degrees. Place the ladyfingers on a cookie sheet. Heat them in the center of the oven for 6 or 7 minutes. Turn them over and bake for 6 or 7 minutes more, until they are almost crisp and dry—they will become crisper as they cool—they *should* be crisp. Let them cool while you prepare the chocolate filling.

Place the chocolate in the top of a small double boiler over hot water on moderate heat. Cover until partially melted, then uncover and stir until com-pletely melted and smooth. Remove from the hot water and set aside to cool slightly.

In the small bowl of an electric mixer cream the butter. Add the sugar and beat well. Add the egg yolks one or two at a time, beating until thoroughly incor-porated after each addition. Beat well for a minute or so. On low speed add the chocolate and beat only until smooth. Remove it from the mixer and set aside.

Mix the rum, kirsch, or framboise with the water.

Now, pick up a whole strip of ladyfingers. Using a pastry brush, lightly brush the liquor-water over the flat side of the strip. Place it on the serving plat-ter flat side down. Brush another strip of ladyfingers and place it end to end with the first, forming a row of twelve. Then brush the tops lightly with the liquor-water.

Use a long, narrow metal spatula to spread a layer of the chocolate over the ladyfingers; it should be about ⅛ inch thick. Continue brushing both sides of the ladyfingers lightly and placing them directly over the first row, with chocolate sandwiched between. There will be four layers of ladyfingers, and enough chocolate left to coat the top and sides. Don't make the ladyfingers too wet, but if you run out of the liquor-water, prepare a bit more. Spread the chocolate smoothly all over, and make the surface as smooth and even as you can.

That's it. It does look like a brick.

However if you have trouble spreading the out-side smoothly enough, or if you just can't resist the temptation, decorate it any way you want: chocolate curls; grated chocolate; chopped, unsalted, green pistachio nuts; or toasted sliced almonds. Fauchon in Paris makes a dessert that looks like this and they cover the whole thing, top and sides, with uneven pieces of Chocolate Slabs (see page 263) overlapping each other. They do not attempt to form straight or even edges where the sides meet the top. Or if you love to use a pastry bag, spread the chocolate thinner in order to have some left over and use the leftover chocolate in a pastry bag fitted with a star tube to decorate to your heart's content.

Refrigerate for about 4 hours or longer.

This is generally served as is, but it is wonderful with fruit and cream. If you wish, serve it with fresh strawberries or raspberries that have been marinated in a bit of rum, kirsch, or framboise. Or with brandied cherries. Or stewed pears. And whipped cream.

NOTE: *To freeze, chill until firm, then wrap airtight. Thaw, wrapped, for an hour or longer in the refrigerator.*

Chocolate Regal

12 PORTIONS

The ultimate chocolate extravaganza! WARNING: This should be served only to avowed chocolate lovers, preferably in small portions after a light luncheon or dinner. This looks like a cake and cuts like a cake, but there any similarity ends. Call it what you will, but it is simply wonderful and wonderfully simple. And easy and foolproof to make. It tastes somewhat like a rich pot de crème, only more so.

It may be made a day or two before serving. But before you start, you will need a 9-inch spring-form pan; it can be deep or shallow, but the sides and the bottom of the pan must fit securely or the mixture, which is thin, might run out. (If you doubt your pan, place it on a square of aluminum foil and bring the sides of the foil securely up around the outside of the pan. Unless the pan is really bad, probably very little will run out anyhow.)

1 pound semisweet chocolate, broken into pieces

1 cup milk

Pinch of salt

¾ pound (3 sticks) sweet butter, at room temperature (it must be soft, but don't melt it or cream it first) and cut into pieces

6 or 7 egg yolks (6 from eggs graded extra-large or jumbo; 7 from smaller eggs)

Adjust rack one-third up from the bottom of the oven and preheat oven to 350 degrees. Cut a round of baking-pan liner paper or wax paper to fit the bottom of a 9-inch spring-form pan. Butter the sides (not the bottom) of the pan and one side of the round of paper. Place the paper in the pan, buttered side up.

Place the chocolate, milk, and salt in the top of a large double boiler over hot water on moderate heat, or in a heavy 1½- to 2-quart saucepan over low heat. Stir frequently with a rubber spatula, scraping the bottom and sides, until the chocolate is completely melted—don't worry if the mixture isn't smooth.

Transfer to the large bowl of an electric mixer and beat on low speed only until smooth. Then let stand for 4 or 5 minutes to cool slightly.

On low speed alternately add pieces of the butter and the egg yolks, scraping the bowl with a rubber spatula and beating only until incorporated after each addition. Do not beat on high speed and do not beat any more than necessary—the mixture should not lighten in color.

When it is smooth, pour the mixture into the prepared pan.

Bake for 25 minutes, no longer. It will still be soft and shiny and will not look done. Remove it from the oven!

Let stand until it reaches room temperature. Then refrigerate for a few hours until completely firm. It may be kept refrigerated for a day or two if you wish.

With a small, sharp knife cut around the sides to release—press the blade firmly against the pan in order not to cut into the dessert. Remove the sides of the spring form. Cover the dessert with a flat cake plate and invert. Remove the bottom of the pan. (If it doesn't lift off, insert a narrow metal spatula or a table knife between the paper and the pan and gently and carefully work it around to release the pan.) Peel off the paper lining. The Chocolate Regal will be 1 inch high.

Now cover it generously with the following whipped cream, or refrigerate it and whipped-cream it later on.

REGAL WHIPPED CREAM

2 tablespoons cold water
1 teaspoon unflavored gelatin
2 cups heavy cream
1 teaspoon vanilla extract
¼ cup honey

Place the cold water in a small heatproof cup. Sprinkle the gelatin over the top and let stand for 5 minutes. Then place the cup in a small pan of shallow hot water over low heat to melt the gelatin.

Meanwhile, in the small bowl of the electric mixer (the bowl and beaters should be chilled) whip about 1¾ cups (reserve about ¼ cup) of the cream and the vanilla. While beating, gradually add the honey and scrape the bowl with a rubber spatula—the honey might settle to the bottom. Whip only until the cream has increased in volume and thickened, but not until it is firm enough to hold a shape.

When the gelatin is dissolved, remove the cup from the hot water. Stir the reserved ¼ cup of cream into the gelatin and immediately, while beating, add it all at once to the partially whipped cream. Continue to beat until the cream holds a shape and is stiff enough to spread. But remember that it is always more delicious if it is a bit soft and creamy instead of stiff.

The cream may be put on simply and smoothly in a thick layer, or it may be swirled with a rubber spatula or the back of a large spoon. Or spread only a thin coating to cover the dessert, then use a pastry bag fitted with a star tube and, using the remaining cream, form either a lattice design on the top or decorate with rosettes or swirls.

OPTIONAL: *A bit of shaved chocolate may be sprinkled over the top. Or a few chopped, unsalted green pistachio nuts. But there is something regal about keeping the decoration at a minimum.*

Brandied black bing cherries go well with dense chocolate desserts. They may be served with this, placing a spoonful of them alongside each portion. Use the bought ones or prepare your own as follows: A day or two before using, drain a can of plain pitted black bing cherries. Add 2 tablespoons of Cognac and 2 tablespoons of kirsch. Let stand, covered, stirring occasionally—they may either be refrigerated or at room temperature.

Gelatin Desserts

Gelatin mixtures are best if they have only as much gel-atin as necessary to help them hold their shape. More than that makes them stiff and tough. And they are best when they have chilled only long enough to set the gel-atin. After that they become heavy. As soon as they become firm, they should be covered airtight to prevent evaporation. They should be unmolded enough ahead of time so you aren't rushed, but no sooner than that.

Chocolate Bavarian

6 PORTIONS

This is a classic French Crème Bavaroise au Chocolat. If you attend a class at the Cordon Bleu Cooking School in Paris, you might make it just this way. It is a creamy gelatin mixture, traditionally made in a mold and turned out before serving. It is best to make this early in the day for that night, but if it is well-covered in the mold it may stand overnight. This recipe may be doubled for a larger mold.

1 cup milk
2 ounces (2 squares) unsweetened chocolate
2 teaspoons unflavored gelatin
¼ cup cold water
4 egg yolks
½ cup granulated sugar
2 teaspoons dry instant coffee
Pinch of salt
1 teaspoon vanilla extract
2 tablespoons dark rum
1 cup heavy cream

You will need a 5- to 6-cup thin metal mold. It is best to use a very light-weight tin mold—the heavier the mold, the slower and more difficult it is to unmold. It may be a plain shape or it may have a design.

Place the milk in a small saucepan, uncovered, over moderate heat to warm slowly (it burns over high heat).

Meanwhile, place the chocolate in the top of a small double boiler, covered, over hot water on moderate heat. Heat only until the chocolate is melted, then uncover, remove from the hot water and set aside to cool.

Sprinkle the gelatin over the cold water in a small custard cup and let stand.

Place the egg yolks in the top of a large double boiler off the heat. Add the sugar and beat with a hand-held electric mixer or stir briskly with a small wire whisk for a minute or two until the mixture lightens a bit in color and is smooth and creamy.

When a slightly wrinkled skin forms on top of the milk, add the milk gradually, very little at a time at first, to the egg-yolk mixture, beating or whisking as you add to keep the mixture smooth.

Pour hot (not boiling) water into the bottom of the double boiler and put the top, with the custard mixture, over it. Add the dry instant coffee and stir to dissolve. Cook, scraping the sides and bottom with a rubber spatula, for about 8 minutes until the mixture thickens enough to coat a metal spoon (a candy thermometer will register about 175 degrees).

Remove the top of the double boiler, add the softened gelatin, and stir to dissolve. Then add the melted chocolate and stir to mix. Stir in the salt, vanilla, and rum. The chocolate will have a slightly speckled appearance. Beat briskly with an egg beater or an electric mixer until very smooth.

Set the chocolate mixture aside for a moment. Whip the heavy cream only until it holds a semi-firm shape—not until it is stiff. (If it is stiff it will make the Bavarian heavy.)

Now, put some ice and water in a large mixing bowl. Place the saucepan with the chocolate mixture into the ice water and scrape the bottom and sides constantly with a rubber spatula until the mixture is completely cool and starts to thicken slightly to the consistency of a heavy cream sauce. (It is best if the chocolate mixture and the whipped cream are the same consistency.) Remove the pot from the ice water, if necessary beat again briskly with an egg beater or electric mixer until very smooth, and then quickly and carefully fold the chocolate all at once into the whipped cream. Fold only until thoroughly blended. If necessary, pour back and forth gently from one bowl to another to insure thorough blending.

Quickly rinse a 5- to 6-cup thin metal mold with ice water, pour out the water but do not dry the mold. Pour the Bavarian into the wet mold—do not fill it all the way to the top or it will be difficult to dip into hot water to unmold. Refrigerate for about 3 hours (a larger mold may take a little longer). When the top is firm, cover it airtight with plastic wrap.

This may be unmolded a few hours before serving. Fill a large bowl or dishpan with hot (not boiling) water. With a small, sharp knife cut about ½ inch deep around the upper edge of the mold to release. Dip the mold for 10 seconds (no longer) into the hot water. Remove it, dry quickly, cover with a chilled dessert platter, and invert. If the Bavarian does not slip out easily, dip it again as necessary but for only a few seconds at a time—a heavy mold will take longer to release than a thin one.

Refrigerate.

This beautiful unmolded dessert does not need any decoration—but it lends itself to whatever you want. Try a border of small whipped cream rosettes, each one topped with a chocolate coffee bean candy. Or surround it with any brandied fruit and serve soft whipped cream on the side.

Cold Chocolate Soufflé

8 PORTIONS

This is an incredibly light and airy gelatin dessert made in a soufflé dish and extending generously above the top of the dish. It is especially dramatic in a clear glass dish, but is equally delicious and attractive in a classic white china soufflé dish. It may be made early in the day for that night, or the day before.

⅓ cup cold water
1 tablespoon (1 envelope) unflavored gelatin
I teaspoon dry instant coffee
⅓ cup boiling water
1 cup milk
1 ounce semisweet chocolate
4 ounces (4 squares) unsweetened chocolate
5 eggs (graded extra-large or Jumbo or 6 eggs graded medium or large), separated
1 cup granulated sugar
1 tablespoon vanilla extract
Generous pinch of salt
Optional: 1 ounce semisweet chocolate (for sprinkling on top)

First, prepare a straight-sided soufflé dish. In order that the soufflé rise 1½ inches over the top, the dish should not have more than a 5-cup capacity. (My glass one measures 6 inches in diameter and 3 inches in depth. The closest white china soufflé dish measures 6½ (across the top) x 3 inches—and it works fine.) Prepare an aluminum foil collar: Tear off a piece of foil large enough to wrap around the dish and overlap a few inches. Fold it in half the long way. With a paper towel, brush tasteless salad oil over half of one of the long sides, brushing it along the half that has two open sides, not the folded edge. Wrap the foil tightly around the dish, oiled side to the top and inside. Fasten tightly with a string. Set aside.

Place the cold water in a small bowl or a cup with at least 1-cup capacity. Sprinkle the gelatin over the top and let stand for 5 minutes. Then dissolve the coffee in the boiling water, quickly add it to the gelatin and stir to dissolve. Set aside.

Place the milk and both chocolates in the top of a small double boiler over hot water on moderate heat. Stir occasionally with a small wire whisk until the chocolate is melted and the mixture is smooth. Remove the top of the double boiler and set it aside.

In the small bowl of an electric mixer, beat the egg yolks with ½ cup of the sugar (reserve remaining ½ cup). Beat for a few minutes at high speed until the mixture is creamy and pale-colored. Beat in the vanilla and then, on low speed, gradually add the warm chocolate mixture, scraping the bowl with a rubber spatula and beating until smooth. Gradually beat in the dissolved gelatin. Transfer to a medium-size mixing bowl (preferably metal) and set aside.

Prepare a large mixing bowl partly filled with ice and cold water and have it ready.

In the large bowl of the electric mixer (with clean beaters) beat the whites and the salt until the mixture increases in volume and starts to thicken. Gradually, while beating on moderate speed, add the reserved ½ cup sugar. Then increase the speed to high and beat only until the mixture holds a soft peak—one that bends over slightly when the mixture is lifted with a rubber spatula. (If the whites are beaten until stiff or dry, it will be impossible to fold the chocolate into them without losing most of the air that has been beaten in.) Remove from the mixer and set aside.

Place the bowl of chocolate mixture in the ice and water and stir frequently until the mixture thickens to the consistency of a medium cream sauce. (This is an important step; if the chocolate mixture is too thin when it is folded into the whites, the chocolate will sink to the bottom—if it is too thick, it will

become lumpy and the mixture will not be smooth. So pay close attention to it. Stir constantly after it starts to thicken slightly. It might take about 10 minutes, or a bit more. Actually, the chocolate mixture and the beaten whites should be of the same consistency—or as close as possible—for easy folding.)

Just as soon as the chocolate is ready, remove it from the ice water and fold a few large spoonfuls into the beaten whites. Repeat two or three times, folding in about three-fourths of the chocolate. Then fold the whites into the remaining chocolate. If necessary, pour gently back and forth from one bowl to another to insure thorough blending.

Gently pour the soufflé into the prepared dish and place it in the refrigerator. To keep the air out, place a piece of plastic wrap over the top, letting it rest on the foil collar, not touching the soufflé. Let stand for about 8 to 10 hours or overnight.

OPTIONAL: *Finely grate 1 ounce of semisweet chocolate and sprinkle it over the soufflé before removing the collar.*

Do not remove the collar until shortly before serving. Peel it off very gently or, if it sticks, cut between the soufflé and the collar with a small, sharp knife. Wipe the sides of the soufflé dish and place it on a folded napkin on a flat plate.

Serve with a side dish of whipped cream.

WHIPPED CREAM

2 cups heavy cream
⅓ cup strained confectioners sugar
1 teaspoon vanilla extract

Beat the above ingredients to make soft whipped cream and serve a large spoonful over each portion. (If the cream is whipped ahead of time it may separate slightly; if so, first stir it a bit to blend before serving.)

NOTE: *The effect will not be so dramatic, but this may also be prepared in any serving bowl or in individual-wine glasses or dessert bowls.*

Molded Chocolate Mousse

8 TO 10 PORTIONS

A gelatin-chocolate mousse made in an 8-cup loaf pan. Make it early in the day for that night, or make it the day before. The recipe may be doubled for a larger loaf pan or for two pans, but if you double it you will need a very large bowl for folding the egg whites and chocolate together.

6 ounces (6 squares) **unsweetened chocolate**

¼ cup cold water

1 tablespoon (1 envelope) **unflavored gelatin**

6 eggs (graded large, extra-large, or jumbo), separated

1½ cups granulated sugar

1 tablespoon dry instant coffee

1 cup boiling water

1½ teaspoons vanilla extract

2 tablespoons light rum (see Note)

Pinch of salt

Prepare an 8-cup (9 x 5 x 3-inch) loaf pan as follows (for miraculously easy unmolding): Tear off two long pieces of wax paper, one to cover the length of the pan and the other the width. Fold each one lengthwise as many times as necessary for it to fit the pan exactly—it works best if there is more than one thickness of paper. Put each strip into place in the pan, allowing them to extend slightly above the rim on all sides.

Place the chocolate in the top of a small double boiler over hot water on moderate heat. Cover and let stand only until the chocolate is melted. Then uncover, remove the top of the double boiler and let stand until cool.

Pour the cold water into a mixing bowl with about a 2- to 3-cup capacity. Sprinkle the gelatin over the water and let stand for about 5 minutes. (It does not hurt if it stands longer.)

Meanwhile, in the small bowl of an electric mixer beat the egg yolks with 1 cup (reserve ½ cup) of the sugar at high speed for 5 minutes until very pale.

On the lowest speed add the cooled melted chocolate, scraping the bowl with a spatula and beating only until smooth. Let stand.

Add the dry instant coffee and the boiling water to the gelatin and stir to dissolve. (Stir with a metal spoon so you can see when the gelatin is dissolved.) You may transfer this to a small pitcher for ease in handling if you wish.

The chocolate mixture will be very stiff; on lowest speed, very gradually (just a few drops at a time at first) add the coffee/gelatin mixture. Scrape the bowl almost constantly with a rubber spatula to keep the mixture smooth—it must be smooth.

Mix in the vanilla and the rum.

Transfer the mixture to a large mixing bowl and place it in a larger bowl of ice and cold water. Stir constantly, scraping the bottom and sides, with a rubber spatula for only 2 or 3 minutes until very cold, but not long enough for it to start to thicken. Remove from the ice water temporarily and set aside.

Add the salt to the egg whites in the large bowl of the electric mixer. With clean beaters, beat until the whites increase in volume and barely hold a soft shape. Reduce the speed to moderate and gradually add the reserved ½ cup of sugar. Then increase the speed to high and beat until the whites thicken to a marshmallow-like consistency, or like soft whipped cream. Not stiff.

Replace the bowl of chocolate mixture in the ice water and stir constantly for 2 or 3 minutes until the chocolate barely starts to thicken. Remove the bowl from the ice water.

Fold about half of the chocolate into the beaten whites and then fold the whites into the remaining chocolate. Do not handle any more than necessary. Pour gently from one bowl to another to insure thorough blending.

Pour the mixture into the prepared loaf pan.

Refrigerate for 8 to 10 hours or overnight. (After an hour or so the top may be covered with plastic wrap.) Before the 8 hours are up the texture will be sticky and will cling to the knife when you serve—after 8 hours it changes to a drier, spongier texture that does not cling as much.

To remove the mousse from the pan: Since most loaf pans flare at the top, there will probably be a section, depending on how much the pan flares, where the wax paper does not line the corners. With a small, sharp knife cut the corners to release the mousse. Then invert a flat serving platter over the loaf pan and invert pan and platter. Remove the pan and gently peel away the paper.

WHIPPED CREAM

2 cups heavy cream
⅓ cup strained confectioners sugar
1 teaspoon vanilla extract

In a chilled bowl with chilled beaters whip the above ingredients until the cream is thick and sauce-like. (The cream may be prepared ahead of time and refrigerated. It will probably separate slightly—it's O.K. Just before serving whip it a bit with a wire whisk.)

Spoon a generous amount of the cream over each slice of the mousse, (Although the mousse may be decorated with the whipped cream and with chocolate decorations, it is elegant and lovely if the mousse is left plain and the cream served separately. However, if you do want to decorate it, whip the cream a bit longer until it is stiff enough and then pipe it through a pastry bag with a large star-shaped tube. This mousse wants a generous amount of cream with it.)

NOTE: *The light rum will barely be a noticeable taste. If you would like to really taste it, use dark rum. Or you can use Cognac, bourbon, or whiskey.*

Chocolate Breeze

4 PORTIONS

I learned to make this in Home Ec. class in elementary school on Long Island—1 think I was about 10 or 12 years old at the time. My teacher was a wonderful and brave woman to teach a room full of thirty or so girls, all cooking at once, how to handle gelatin, how to beat and fold in egg whites, and how to whip cream. I have had the recipe ever since and have used it often.

It is lighter and airier than most chocolate desserts, and quick and easy to make—it is a breeze in more ways than one. It may be made in individual glasses or in a mold. Like all gelatin desserts it is at its best within a few hours after the gelatin has set, but I have made this a day ahead and it was still delicious. The recipe may be doubled.

2 ounces (2 squares) unsweetened chocolate
1 tablespoon (1 envelope) unflavored gelatin
¼ cup cold water
3 eggs (graded large, extra-large, or jumbo), separated
½ cup granulated sugar
Boiling water
1 teaspoon vanilla extract
⅛ teaspoon salt

Place the chocolate in the top of a small double boiler over hot water on moderate heat; cover until partially melted, then uncover and stir until completely melted.

While the chocolate is melting, sprinkle the gelatin over the cold water in a glass measuring cup and let stand.

Also meanwhile, with a wire whisk, beat the egg yolks and the sugar together in a medium-size mixing bowl, whisking briskly for about half a minute.

Add the warm melted chocolate and whisk until thoroughly mixed.

Add boiling water to the softened gelatin up to the 1-cup line. Stir with a metal spoon to dissolve the gelatin and then gradually stir into the chocolate mixture. Stir in the vanilla.

Partially fill a large bowl with ice and water. Place the bowl of chocolate mixture in the ice water and stir occasionally until the mixture begins to thicken. Remove it from the ice water and beat with an electric mixer or an egg beater until smooth.

In a small bowl, add the salt to the egg whites and beat until they hold a definite shape, but not until they are stiff or dry.

Fold about one-third of the chocolate mixture into the whites and then fold the whites into the remaining chocolate mixture.

If necessary, pour gently from one bowl to another to insure thorough blending.

Pour into four 7- or 8-ounce wine glasses or dessert bowls leaving a bit of head room on each.

Or, if you want to make a molded dessert, rinse a 4-cup thin metal mold (loaf pan, ring mold, melon mold) with cold water, shake out the water but do not dry the mold, and pour in the Breeze.

Cover glasses or mold with aluminum foil or plastic wrap (it should not touch the dessert), and refrigerate for at least a few hours.

If you have made this in a mold, shortly before serving cut around the top to loosen the edge, dip the mold in hot (not boiling) water for a few seconds, dry the mold quickly, cover with a flat serving plate and unmold. If the Breeze does not slip out easily, dip it again.

WHIPPED CREAM

1 cup heavy cream
½ teaspoon vanilla extract
2 tablespoons confectioners or granulated sugar

In a chilled bowl with chilled beaters, whip all the ingredients only until the cream holds a shape, but not until it is stiff.

Shortly before serving, place a large spoonful of the cream over each portion in a glass. Or, if you have made this in a mold, either place large spoonfuls of the cream around the unmolded dessert, or whip the cream a little longer and use a pastry bag fitted with a star tube and apply the cream in a decorative pattern either around or on top of the dessert.

VARIATION: When I grew up I started adding things to this original recipe. To make an Espresso Breeze, add 1 tablespoon of dry instant espresso or other instant coffee to the hot dissolved gelatin, and, if you wish, add a teaspoon or two of rum or Cognac to the chocolate mixture before folding in the egg whites.

Chocolate Charlotte

6 PORTIONS

This is a chocolate Charlotte Russe—an icebox cake. Wonderfully light, airy, delicate, delicious. The recipe is written for a loaf pan (which makes it very easy to form and then to unmold) with an 8-cup capacity—generally that is 9 x 5 x 3 inches, but they vary. This may be doubled for a larger pan or for 2 pans. It may be made just about 4 hours before serving or the day before.

2 3-ounce packages soft, fresh lady fingers
  (you will need about 18 double lady fingers)
1 tablespoon (1 envelope) unflavored gelatin
¼ cup cold water
½ cup milk
4 ounces semisweet chocolate
¼ cup plus 2 tablespoons
  granulated sugar
4 eggs (graded large or extra-large), separated
2 tablespoons dark rum
1 teaspoon vanilla extract
½ cup heavy cream
Pinch of salt

Prepare a loaf pan with an 8-cup capacity by tearing off two pieces of aluminum foil, one for the length and one for the width—they should both be long enough to extend several inches over the edges of the pan. Fold the pieces of foil lengthwise and put them in place in the pan.

Separate the ladyfingers into rows but not into individual fingers—leave them attached to each other in a strip. Line the bottom of the pan with ladyfingers, placing them rounded side down and touching each other across the bottom, not lengthwise. (This will be the top of the cake and it will look better if the ladyfingers go across the cake the short way.) Then place a row of ladyfingers standing upright, rounded side out, along each of the long sides of the pan—not on the short ends. (Reserve enough ladyfingers for a final layer on the top.) Set aside.

Sprinkle the gelatin over the cold water in a small cup and let stand.

Place the milk and the chocolate in the top of a small double boiler over hot water on moderate heat. Stir with a small wire whisk until the chocolate is melted and the mixture is smooth.

Add ¼ cup of the sugar (reserve the remaining 2 tablespoons) and stir to mix.

In a small bowl stir the egg yolks lightly just to mix. Add a few spoonfuls of the hot chocolate milk mixture, stir together, and then add the egg-yolk mixture to the remaining chocolate milk. Stir constantly over hot water for about 2 minutes.

Remove the top of the double boiler, add the softened gelatin, and stir to dissolve. Mix in the rum and vanilla.

Pour the chocolate mixture into a large mixing bowl. Place it in a larger bowl partially filled with ice and water. Stir until it is completely cool and then remove it from the ice water temporarily.

In a small bowl whip the cream only until it holds a soft shape and set aside.

In the small bowl of an electric mixer add the salt to the egg whites and beat until they barely hold a soft shape. Reduce the speed to moderate and

gradually add the reserved 2 tablespoons sugar. Then increase the speed and beat briefly only until the whites are slightly thicker and barely hold a point. Set aside.

Replace the bowl containing the chocolate mixture in the ice water and stir constantly with a rubber spatula until the chocolate barely begins to thicken to the consistency of a light cream sauce. (It is best if the whipped cream, beaten whites, and chocolate mixture are all the same thickness.)

Remove the bowl from the ice water and immediately add the beaten whites and whipped cream and fold all together.

Pour the mixture into the ladyfinger-lined pan.

Then cover the top with another layer of ladyfingers going in either direction (this will be the bottom).

There will be ladyfingers left over.

Fold the aluminum foil extensions over the top to cover the ladyfingers.

Refrigerate for 3 to 4 hours (if the recipe is doubled and made in one large pan it should be refrigerated for 5 to 6 hours) or overnight.

Shortly before serving, uncover the top. Cover with a serving platter. Invert and remove the pan and the aluminum foil. Refrigerate.

Serve with whipped cream which may be served separately as a sauce (that's my preference) or may be applied to the Charlotte with a pastry bag fitted with a star-shaped tube.

WHIPPED CREAM

1 cup heavy cream
¼ cup strained confectioners sugar
2 tablespoons dark rum

In a chilled bowl with chilled beaters, whip the above ingredients. If you plan to serve the cream separately, whip it only until it thickens to the consistency of a sauce. For decorating whip it longer until it holds a shape.

(If the cream is to be served as a sauce, it may be whipped ahead of time and refrigerated. If so, it will separate slightly—just stir it a bit with a small wire whisk before serving. If the cream is to be put on with a pastry bag it may be done a few hours before serving.)

NOTE: *If you wish, the rum may be left out of the Charlotte and the whipped cream—substitute ½ teaspoon vanilla extract in the cream.*

Chocolate Prune Whip

6 GENEROUS PORTIONS

This could be called a mousse—it is light, airy, creamy—an elegant version of an old-time classic. It is made in individual portions, either 6 to 8 hours ahead or the day before.

1 17-ounce jar cooked prunes (see Note)
4 ounces semisweet chocolate
1 tablespoon (1 envelope) unflavored gelatin
½ cup granulated sugar
¼ teaspoon cinnamon (that is enough—
     do not use more)
Pinch of salt
1⅓ cups milk
3 eggs (graded large or extra-large), separated
Optional: 2 tablespoons Cognac
½ cup heavy cream
½ cup walnuts, cut into medium-size pieces

Drain the prunes in a strainer or a colander, remove the pits, and cut or chop the prunes into rather small pieces—they should not be mashed or pureed, but the pieces should not be large. Let the chopped prunes stand in a strainer.

Break up the chocolate and place it in a heavy 2-quart saucepan. Add the gelatin, ¼ cup of the sugar (reserve remaining ¼ cup), cinnamon, salt, and milk. Place over medium heat and stir for about 5 minutes until the chocolate is melted and the mixture is smooth. If it is not smooth, stir it briefly with a small wire whisk.

In a bowl beat the egg yolks just to mix. Stirring constantly, add about half of the hot chocolate milk mixture. Then stir the yolk mixture into the remaining chocolate milk. Cook, stirring constantly, for 1 minute. Set aside to cool, stirring occasionally. Stir in the optional Cognac.

Meanwhile, in a small bowl whip the cream until it holds a shape, and set it aside.

And, in the small bowl of an electric mixer, beat the whites until they barely hold a soft shape. Reduce the speed to moderate and gradually add the reserved ¼ cup of sugar. Increase the speed to high and beat until the whites hold a definite shape but not until they are stiff and dry. Set aside.

Now transfer the chocolate milk to a large mixing bowl. Place it in a larger bowl of ice and water. Stir constantly until the mixture begins to thicken. Beat it briefly with an egg beater or an electric mixer.

Then stir in the chopped prunes and the nuts. Fold in the whipped cream and the beaten egg whites.

Spoon the mixture into 6 wine glasses or dessert bowls.

Refrigerate for most of the day or overnight.

OPTIONAL: *If you wish, sprinkle the tops with grated or shaved chocolate, or place a few Chocolate Slabs (see page 263) upright into the top of each portion.*

NOTE: *You may use dried prunes and stew them yourself. They should be cooked until they are really soft. After they are pitted and chopped, you should have 1¼ cups.*

Harlequin

8 PORTIONS

This is an adaptation of a recipe by Craig Claiborne and Pierre Franey originally printed in The New York Times *and called Harlequin Mousse. It was made in a fancy mold. This version is prepared in individual portions in glasses with at least 12-ounce capacity—most attractive if the glasses are clear, plain, stemmed wine glasses.*

It is a sort of chiffon-mousse-bavarian: light, creamy, and dreamy—a two-tone dessert, one layer chocolate and one vanilla. Make it the day you serve it or a day ahead (see Note).

You will prepare two separate recipes; the bases of each are prepared individually, but the whipped cream and the egg whites are beaten at one time for both bases. Just take it one step at a time; it is not hard work and, although it does use more mixing bowls than the usual, it is worth it.

4 cups cold milk

2 tablespoons (2 envelopes) unflavored gelatin

1½ cups granulated sugar

2 ounces (2 squares) unsweetened chocolate

1 tablespoon dry instant coffee

2 tablespoons cornstarch

3 tablespoons dark rum

5 eggs (graded large, extra-large, or jumbo), separated (when you separate the eggs, place 2 yolks in one small mixing bowl and 3 in another)

Salt

1 tablespoon cold water

2 tablespoons Amaretto, or 1 teaspoon vanilla extract

1 cup heavy cream

Set out two saucepans, preferably heavy, each with about a 6- to 8-cup capacity (larger is O.K.). Pour 2 cups of the milk into each saucepan. Sprinkle 1 envelope of the gelatin over each. Stir ½ cup granulated sugar (reserve remaining ½ cup) into each.

Add the chocolate to one of the saucepans and place it over moderate heat. Cook, stirring frequently, until the chocolate is melted and the mixture begins to simmer. Stir in the dry instant coffee. Beat with an electric mixer (on low speed or it will splash) or an egg beater until the chocolate is smooth. Reduce the heat to low.

Place 1 tablespoon of the cornstarch (reserve remaining 1 tablespoon) in a small cup. Add 2 tablespoons of the rum (reserve remaining 1 tablespoon) and stir until smooth. Then gradually, while stirring, mix it into the hot chocolate mixture. Cook, barely simmering, stirring gently for about 2 minutes.

Gradually stir a few large spoonfuls of the hot chocolate into the 2 egg yolks, and then stir the yolks

into the remaining chocolate. Stir over low heat for about a minute.

Pour through a fine-meshed strainer set over a medium-size bowl.

Stir in the reserved 1 tablespoon rum. Stir occasionally until cool.

Meanwhile, prepare the vanilla mixture.

Add a pinch of salt to the other saucepan and place over moderate heat. Cook, stirring frequently until the mixture begins to simmer. Reduce the heat to low.

Place the reserved 1 tablespoon of cornstarch in a small cup. Add 1 tablespoon cold water and stir until smooth. Gradually, while stirring, mix it into the hot milk mixture. Cook, barely simmering, stirring gently for about 2 minutes.

Gradually stir a few spoonfuls of the hot milk mixture into the 3 egg yolks, and then stir the yolks into the remaining milk. Stir over low heat for about a minute.

Pour through a fine-meshed strainer set over a medium-size bowl.

Stir in the Amaretto or vanilla. Stir occasionally until cool.

When both mixtures have cooled they must be chilled until they thicken slightly. Partially fill a large bowl with ice and water; place the bowl of chocolate mixture in the ice water and stir it frequently until it thickens slightly, or enough to barely show a mound when a spoonful of it is lifted and then dropped back onto the chocolate.

Meanwhile, place the vanilla mixture in the freezer or the refrigerator and stir occasionally until it thickens to the consistency of a heavy cream sauce.

While the two mixtures are chilling, whip the cream until it holds a soft shape. Gradually add ¼ cup of the reserved sugar (you will still have another ¼ cup for the egg whites) and beat slightly. The cream should only hold a soft shape, it should not be stiff. Set aside.

In the small bowl of the electric mixer add ⅛ teaspoon of salt to the egg whites and beat until they hold a soft shape. Reduce the speed to moderate and gradually add the reserved ¼ cup sugar. Increase the speed again and continue to beat only until the whites barely hold a shape—they should not be stiff or dry.

When the chocolate mixture has thickened enough, stir it gently to be sure it is smooth. Fold in half of the whipped cream (it is not necessary to measure—it does not have to be exact) and then fold in half of the beaten whites.

Set out eight glasses, each with a capacity of 12 ounces or more. Pour the mixture gently into a large, wide-mouthed pitcher and pour it into the glasses, filling each one about halfway.

Now, to set the chocolate mixture quickly, place the glasses in the freezer for about 10 minutes or in the refrigerator a few minutes longer.

Meanwhile, look at the vanilla mixture occasionally; if it starts to thicken too much in the refrigerator, let it stand at room temperature. If it is not thick enough, place the bowl in the ice water and stir almost constantly. When it is thick enough, fold half of it into the remaining whipped cream and then fold that back into the remaining vanilla mixture. Then fold about one-fourth of it into the remaining beaten egg whites and fold that back into the remaining vanilla mixture.

Gently transfer to a large, wide-mouthed pitcher. When the chocolate mixture is partially set, pour the vanilla mixture on top.

The dessert will be ready to serve in a few hours. Refrigerate until then.

This does not need any topping, but if you would like, spoon a bit of whipped cream over each Harlequin shortly before serving, and/or sprinkle the tops with a bit of shaved chocolate (see page 263) or a chunk of Chocolate Slab (see page 263).

NOTE: *If you make this a day before serving, each glass should be covered airtight or it may dry out a bit in the refrigerator. That means that the glasses should*

not be filled up to the rims; use slightly larger glasses, or just do not fill them all the way.

Crème de la Crème

8 PORTIONS

This is an elegant, dome-shaped, molded white cream covered with a paper-thin coating of chocolate—a most impressive and delicious dinner-party dessert that is not difficult to make, but you must allow at least 6 hours for the refrigeration and freezing. It may be made the day before serving or in the morning for that night. It must be frozen for half an hour to an hour just before serving.

2 ounces (½ cup) unsalted green pistachio nuts (other nuts may be substituted)
½ cup cold water
1 tablespoon (1 envelope) unflavored gelatin
3 ounces (¾ stick) sweet butter
1 teaspoon vanilla extract
½ cup granulated sugar
3 egg yolks
¼ cup Amaretto, or 3 tablespoons Cognac or kirsch
1½ cups heavy cream

You will need a plain, round 6-cup metal bowl to mold this dessert—it must be plain and round. (The small metal bowl from my electric mixer is a little larger but it works nicely.) Just have the bowl ready to use later.

Chop the nuts into small pieces and set aside.

Place the water in a small heatproof glass cup and sprinkle the gelatin over the top. Let stand for about 5 minutes. Then place the cup in shallow hot water in a small pan over low heat; stir occasionally with a metal spoon until the gelatin is dissolved. Remove from the water and set aside to cool.

In the small bowl of an electric mixer cream the butter. Add the vanilla and sugar and beat well. Then add the egg yolks and beat thoroughly. On low speed gradually add the gelatin and then the Amaretto or other liquor, scraping the bowl with a rubber spatula and beating only until thoroughly mixed.

Whip the cream only until it holds a soft shape—not stiff—and set aside.

Now chill the Amaretto mixture only until it thickens to the consistency of a thin cream sauce. It may be chilled in the freezer or the refrigerator, stirring occasionally. Or over ice and water, stirring constantly. Either way, watch it carefully—it will thicken quickly.

Stir in the chopped nuts and then fold into the whipped cream. If necessary, pour back and forth gently from one bowl to another to insure thorough blending.

Rinse the plain, round 5- to 6-cup metal bowl with cold water—shake it out lightly, do not dry it. (Do not oil the bowl or the icing will run off the dessert after it is unmolded.)

Pour the dessert into the wet bowl and smooth the top. Cover and refrigerate for 4 hours or longer. (If the dessert reaches the top of the bowl, chill it until set before covering.)

Just before unmolding, prepare a flat serving plate by spreading it with a very thin coating of tasteless salad oil—it is easy to spread the oil with a paper towel. (The oil will make it possible to move the dessert slightly if necessary, and it will also make it easier to clean the sides of the plate after the icing is applied.)

Have a large bowl or a dishpan full of hot but not boiling water as deep as the dessert bowl. With a small, sharp knife cut around the top of the dessert to release it. Then dip the bowl for only a few seconds into the hot water. Quickly dry the bowl and place the dessert plate upside down over the bowl—see that it is centered. Invert the plate and bowl and then remove the bowl. If the dessert doesn't slip out easily, dip the bowl into the hot water a second time.

Refrigerate while you prepare the icing.

CHOCOLATE ICING

3 ounces semisweet chocolate, ground or
    finely chopped; or ½ cup semisweet
    morsels, left whole
2 tablespoons light corn syrup
1 tablespoon water or prepared coffee

Place all the ingredients in the top of a small double boiler over hot water on moderate heat. Stir constantly with a rubber spatula until the chocolate has melted. Remove from the hot water and stir briskly until completely smooth. If you have used morsels, the mixture will be thick enough to spread immediately. Other chocolates may be a bit too thin. If it is thin, let stand for 5 to 10 minutes, stirring occasionally to thicken but only very slightly—you want it thin enough to flow and form a smooth, thin layer.

Now, to coat the dessert with a thin layer of the chocolate, pour it slowly and gradually in a spiral starting at the top to completely cover the dessert. (If the top is flat, in order not to have the icing thicker there pour icing over that section, then use a small metal spatula to spread it a bit thinner. Continue pouring to cover the sides.) When necessary, use a small metal spatula to spread the icing over any small areas that are not covered. Don't worry about excess icing that runs down on the plate—that will be removed later; and don't worry about an uneven edge on the bottom—it will be covered with whipped cream.

Refrigerate for at least one hour or more until the icing is firm enough to be cut. Then with a small, sharp knife carefully cut the chocolate around the bottom of the mold. With the small metal spatula remove excess chocolate that has run onto the plate. Wipe around the sides with a paper towel to clean and dry the plate. Refrigerate.

WHIPPED CREAM DECORATION

½ cup heavy cream
2 tablespoons confectioners sugar
¼ teaspoon vanilla extract

Place the above ingredients in a small bowl and beat just until the cream holds a shape.

Fit a small pastry bag with a medium-size (#4) star-shaped tube. Fold down a cuff on the outside of the bag and place the bag upright in a glass or jar. Transfer the cream to the bag. Unfold the cuff and close the top of the bag. Press out small rosettes of the cream touching one another all around the base of the dessert, concealing any uneven edges on the chocolate.

Refrigerate, and then *freeze for ½ to 1 hour* before serving. It should not freeze any longer— just put it in the freezer right before you sit down to dinner.

Freezer Desserts

4-STAR FRENCH CHOCOLATE
   ICE CREAM 222

GLACÉ AU CHOCOLAT 223

DORIS DUKE'S BITTERSWEET
   CHOCOLATE ICE MILK 224

MEXICAN CHOCOLATE SHERBET
   (water ice) 225

MOCHA CHOCOLATE PARFAIT 226

FROZEN CHOCOLATE MARQUISE
   WITH MOCHA CREAM 227

FROZEN CHOCOLATE MOUSSE 228

MOUSSE BRILLAT-SAVARIN 230

TOBLERONE MILK CHOCOLATE
   MOUSSE 232

PONTCHARTRAIN MILE-HIGH
   ICE CREAM PIE 233

MISSISSIPPI MUD PIE 235

FROZEN CHOCOLATE PIE 236

ICE CREAM EN ROBE 237

CHOCOLATE CHIP-COGNAC-COFFEE
   ICE CREAM 239

TO SOFTEN ICE CREAM

Freezer temperatures vary. (Zero degrees Fahrenheit is considered correct.)

Howard Johnson's has two freezers for ice cream—one for storage, which is set at 10 degrees below zero, and one they serve from (they call it the dipping box), which is set for 8 to 12 degrees above zero. At that temperature their ice cream stays firm but soft enough to serve easily.

Some of these frozen desserts may be a little too firm if they are served directly from the freezer. Check them ahead of time; if they are too firm transfer them to the refrigerator for 15 to 30 minutes (the time will depend on the temperature of your refrigerator and the size of the container of the dessert).

Although a frozen dessert that is too firm to serve may stand at room temperature to soften, it is better if it stands in the refrigerator. At room temperature it might melt on the outside and still be too hard inside. In the refrigerator the dessert will soften more uniformly, although it may take longer.

It is better to let your guests wait than to serve a frozen dessert that is too hard.

If ice cream has been frozen too firm, either wait for it to soften or, better yet, cut it into small pieces and process it (about two cupfuls at a time) in a food processor fitted with a steel blade, stopping the machine frequently and, with a wooden spatula, pushing the ice cream down. Or in a blender (about 1 cup at a time), stopping the machine frequently and pushing the ice cream down. (If you do a small amount at a time, return each batch to the freezer immediately.) Or soften it in the large bowl of an electric mixer (the bowl and beaters should be chilled); in the mixer you can do it all at once. Process, blend, or mix only to the consistency of soft-frozen ice cream. Serve immediately or return to the freezer, where it should remain soft-frozen for an hour or two.

4-Star French Chocolate Ice Cream

ABOUT 3½ QUARTS

This is luxuriously and extravagantly smooth/ creamy/rich. It is French ice cream times ten. It must be made in an ice-cream churn. If you have never made real ice cream in a churn, you are in for an exciting good time and a delicious treat. If you don't have a churn, beg, borrow, buy, or steal one to make this great ice cream. You will need a 4-quart churn to make the full recipe, but it may be divided to make half (see Notes). (It is no more work to make the full amount; if you have a large enough churn, make it all—you will be glad you did.)

Like all homemade ice creams, this is at its best a few hours after it is made, or just as soon as it becomes firm. It will keep well for a few weeks but it doesn't keep as long as commercial ice cream; no preservatives in this.

7 cups heavy cream

12 ounces semisweet chocolate (see Notes)

2 ounces (2 squares) unsweetened chocolate

1 cup granulated sugar

½ cup water

Pinch of salt

6 yolks (from eggs graded large, extra-large, or jumbo)

2 teaspoons vanilla extract

Place 2 cups of the cream (reserve 5 cups) in a 6- to 8-cup heavy saucepan. Add both chocolates, place over low heat, and stir occasionally until the chocolate is melted.

Remove from the heat and beat briefly with a wire whisk, an electric mixer, or an egg beater until smooth. Set aside.

Place the sugar and water in a very small saucepan over moderate heat. Stir with a wooden spatula until the sugar is dissolved and the syrup becomes clear and comes to a boil. Wash down the sides with a brush dipped in cold water to remove any undissolved granules. Increase the heat to high and let boil without stirring for 5 minutes—a candy thermometer should reach 230 degrees.

Meanwhile, in the small bowl of an electric mixer add the salt to the yolks and beat for about a minute.

When the syrup is ready add it gradually—in a thin stream—to the yolks, beating at high speed. Then continue to beat for several minutes until the mixture is pale and thick and forms a ribbon when the beaters are raised.

Transfer the mixture to the large bowl of the electric mixer. On low speed add the warm chocolate cream and beat only until mixed, scraping the bowl frequently with a rubber spatula.

Add the vanilla and on low speed add the reserved 5 cups of cold heavy cream, scraping the sides and bottom of the bowl as you add the cream to keep the mixture smooth.

You may pour the mixture into a churn now and freeze it, or refrigerate it for several hours or overnight (it will become very thick) before freezing. Carefully follow the freezing directions for your churn. Because this is so rich you should use a little less ice cream salt than usual for your churn or the ice cream will harden too quickly; it is best if it hardens slowly.

Check the ice cream before serving; if it is too firm, place it in the refrigerator for 15 to 30 minutes or longer if necessary. Or, better yet, process, blend, or mix it (after doing each many times I think I prefer to mix in the electric mixer) as described in To Soften Ice Cream (see page 221). To serve, scoop or spoon into chilled dessert cups or bowls.

NOTES: *1. For the semisweet chocolate I have used Maillard's Eagle Sweet, Tobler Tradition, and Lindt Excellence. Each one is delicious, but Lindt Excellence has a flavor that I especially love. You can use any semisweet. If you use a bar chocolate, break it up; if you use 1-ounce squares, they may be chopped coarsely or left whole.*

2. If you divide the recipe to make only half, the syrup will be too shallow to test with a thermometer— just time it; this smaller amount will need only 3 minutes of boiling. And for this smaller amount of ice cream, it will not be necessary to transfer the mixture to a larger bowl—it can all be mixed in the small bowl of the electric mixer.

VARIATIONS: *This is perfect as it is; however, it lends itself to many variations. For a mocha flavor, add instant coffee to the hot cream. For a liquor flavor, add rum, bourbon, Cognac, Amaretto, Grand Marnier, Tia Maria, Kahlúa, crème de menthe, etc., to the cooled mixture before churning it, Or add nuts to the churned ice cream when you remove the dasher; stir them in thoroughly. (Toasted whole unblanched almonds are delicious.) Ground toasted blanched hazelnuts may be added before or after it is churned. To make Rum-Raisin Chocolate Ice Cream, place about 1 cup of raisins in a jar with a tight cover, add about ½ cup dark rum, cover and let stand for a few days, turning the jar occasionally to keep all the raisins wet, or marinate in a closed plastic bag. Stir raisins and any unabsorbed rum into the ice cream after churning. Or do the same thing with chopped dates, using rum or brandy. For Chocolate-Chip Chocolate Ice Cream, finely chop (do not grind or grate) about 4 ounces of semi-sweet chocolate and stir it into the ice cream after it is churned. If you feel really exotic, use a liquor and nuts and chopped chocolate. Etcetera.*

Glacé au Chocolat

1 SCANT QUART

This is a French chocolate ice cream—extraordinarily and outrageously smooth, rich chocolate. It is prepared without an ice-cream churn and is not stirred during the freezing—it will need several hours to freeze, then it can be served right away or kept frozen for days.

The flavor of this cream depends completely on your choice of chocolate, as there is no other flavoring. The recipe may be doubled.

6 ounces semisweet chocolate
1½ cups heavy cream
3 egg yolks
⅓ cup water
¼ cup granulated sugar

Chop the chocolate into rather small pieces and set aside.

In a chilled bowl with chilled beaters, whip the cream only until it holds a soft shape—not until it is stiff—and let stand at room temperature. (It should not be too cold when it is folded into the chocolate.)

In the small bowl of an electric mixer beat the egg yolks until they are light lemon-colored.

Meanwhile, stir the water and sugar together in a 4- to 6-cup saucepan over high heat until the sugar is dissolved and the mixture comes to a boil. Boil without stirring for 3 minutes (no longer or too much water will evaporate).

Add the chopped chocolate to the sugar syrup, remove from the heat, and stir until the chocolate is melted. It will be very thick.

Now, gradually, on low speed, add the hot chocolate mixture to the egg yolks and beat until very smooth. It will be thick. Remove from the mixer and stir occasionally until cooled to room temperature.

If the whipped cream has separated a little, stir or beat it a bit with a wire whisk only to make it smooth but not long enough to thicken it any more.

With a rubber spatula stir a large spoonful of the whipped cream into the cooled chocolate. One at a time stir in two or three more spoonfuls until the chocolate is smooth and about the same consistency as the whipped cream. Then add the chocolate to the remaining cream and fold together. If necessary, pour gently from one bowl to another to insure thorough blending.

Pour the mixture into an ice-cube tray or an 8- or 9-inch metal loaf pan (or any covered container), cover tightly with aluminum foil, and freeze for a few hours until firm.

Serve like any ice cream, but this is richer so make the portions small.

Doris Duke's Bittersweet Chocolate Ice Milk

3 QUARTS PLUS ¹/₂ PINT

NOTICE: *This is definitely for the bittersweet division of the Chocolate Lovers Association—dense, dark, really bittersweet, extravagantly rich in chocolate, fabulously delicious, a luxurious and sophisticated dessert for the simple name "ice milk." (Actually,*

it slightly resembles a sherbet, is closer to an ice cream, but is different from both.)

This is made in an ice-cream churn. And you will need a 4-quart size. Or it may be divided in half for a 2-quart churn.

> 1 tablespoon dry powdered instant espresso or other powdered instant coffee
> ¼ cup boiling water
> 1 cup strained unsweetened cocoa powder (preferably Dutch process)
> 7 cups milk
> 2 pounds semisweet chocolate (see Note)
> 4 yolks (from eggs graded large, extra-large, or jumbo)
> 2 tablespoons vanilla extract
> 1 tablespoon Cognac

Dissolve the instant coffee in the boiling water.

Place the cocoa in a heavy 3-quart saucepan. Add 2 cups of the milk (reserve remaining 5 cups) and the dissolved coffee. Stir/mix with a wire whisk until the mixture is smooth.

Break up or coarsely chop the chocolate and add it to the cocoa mixture. Place over moderately low heat and stir frequently until the chocolate is melted. Stir/mix with the wire whisk until the mixture is smooth.

Place the yolks in a large mixing bowl and stir just to mix. Gradually, stirring constantly, add about half of the hot chocolate mixture. Then add the yolk mixture to the remaining chocolate and stir well.

Place over low heat and stir constantly for about 2 minutes.

Remove from the heat and transfer the mixture to a large mixing bowl. Stir in the vanilla and Cognac. Then gradually whisk in the reserved 5 cups of cold milk, scraping the sides occasionally with a rubber spatula to keep the mixture smooth.

(For best freezing results I transfer the bowl to the freezer or refrigerator for about half an hour or more to chill before freezing.)

Now freeze in an ice-cream churn, following the directions for your particular churn.

Check the firmness some time before serving. If it is too firm, plan to transfer it to the refrigerator for about 15 minutes or so, depending on the size of the container, or, better yet, process, blend, or mix it as described in To Soften Ice Cream (see page 221).

NOTE: *Doris Duke used a semisweet chocolate that she said was a "must" for this recipe. It is from Li-Lac Candies, Inc., 40 8th Ave., New York City.*

Mexican Chocolate Sherbet (water ice)

3 QUARTS

This is extra-chocolaty, extra-dark, slightly exotic, yet light and refreshing. You will need a 3- to 4-quart ice-cream churn (see Note).

3 cups granulated sugar
1½ cups strained unsweetened cocoa powder (preferably Dutch process)
½ teaspoon salt
½ teaspoon cinnamon

3 tablespoons dry instant coffee
7½ cups cold water
1 tablespoon vanilla extract
1½ tablespoons dark rum

You will need a 5- to 6-quart saucepan. Place the sugar, cocoa, salt, cinnamon, and instant coffee in the saucepan and stir to mix. Stir in the water. Place over moderate heat and stir until the sugar is dissolved and the mixture comes to a boil. Adjust the heat so it does not boil over (watch it carefully) and let boil, uncovered, for 5 minutes.

Remove from the heat and let cool to room temperature.

Mix in the vanilla and rum.

Place in the freezer or refrigerator to chill a bit before freezing in the churn.

Freeze according to manufacturer's directions for the churn. (This mixture will take longer to freeze than rich ice cream does. Also it will probably need more salt with the ice in the churn since it will not freeze as hard as ice creams do. It will also melt sooner at room temperature than rich ice creams.)

Serve it quickly in well-chilled bowls or glasses.

NOTE: *To make 2 quarts of this sherbet use 2 cups sugar, 1 cup cocoa, ¼ teaspoon salt, ¼ teaspoon cinnamon, 2 tablespoons dry instant coffee, 5 cups water, 2 teaspoons vanilla, and 1 tablespoon rum.*

Mocha Chocolate Parfait

6 PORTIONS

With all the chocolating that went on while this book was being written, this was one of my husband's favorites—he could not get enough. It is a creamy coffee-chocolate dessert frozen in individual wine or parfait glasses. It may be served the day it is made or it may be frozen for a few weeks.

You will need a candy thermometer.

2 ounces (2 squares) unsweetened chocolate
¾ cup granulated sugar
2 tablespoons dry powdered instant espresso
    or other powdered instant coffee
⅓ cup water
4 egg yolks
2 cups heavy cream
1 teaspoon vanilla extract
1 teaspoon dark rum

Chop the chocolate into medium-small pieces and set them aside on a piece of wax paper.

Place the sugar, espresso, and water in an 8-cup saucepan (it must have at least an 8-cup capacity or the syrup will boil over). Stir over high heat until the sugar is dissolved and the mixture comes to a boil. Insert candy thermometer and let boil without stirring until the thermometer registers 230 degrees—the thread stage. (The mixture will rise to the top of the pan and bubble hard—if necessary reduce the heat slightly to keep the mixture from spattering.)

Meanwhile, place the yolks in the small bowl of an electric mixer and beat at high speed until they are pale lemon-colored.

When the sugar syrup is ready add the chopped chocolate to it, remove from the heat, and stir until the chocolate is melted.

Then, very gradually, beating at a rather low speed, add the hot chocolate mixture to the yolks, scraping the bowl with a rubber spatula and beating until smooth. Remove from the mixer.

Let stand, stirring occasionally, until the mixture cools to room temperature. Test against the inside of your wrist. (If it is the least bit warm it will deflate the whipped cream.)

Meanwhile, in a chilled bowl with chilled beaters, whip the cream only until it holds a soft shape—not stiff. Let it stand at room temperature until you are ready for it. (If it separates a bit while standing, stir lightly with a wire whisk until reincorporated, but not until it becomes any stiffer.)

When the chocolate has cooled to room temperature stir in the vanilla and rum. Stir in one large spoonful of the whipped cream. Stir in another spoonful and then fold in half of the remaining cream. Transfer to a larger mixing bowl and fold in the remaining cream.

You will need six 8-ounce wine glasses or tall, narrow parfait glasses. Either spoon the mixture into the glasses or transfer it to a wide-mouthed pitcher and pour it into the glasses. Do not fill them all the way—leave a bit of headroom so the glasses can be covered without disturbing the top of the dessert.

Cover each glass tightly with aluminum foil. Freeze for about 2 to 3 hours until firm (although this is equally delicious, if not more so, before it is completely firm). Or freeze much longer, if you wish.

Freezer temperatures vary. If yours is down to zero the parfait may become too firm. Check the parfait ahead of time and if it is too firm transfer it to the refrigerator for about an hour or two before serving. It should have the consistency of a firm ice cream, but as this does not melt the way ice cream does, a little softer or a little harder is O.K.

Serve as is, or top each portion with Chocolate Shavings (see 263) or a few Chocolate Cigarettes (see page 267).

A bottle of Amaretto may be passed with this—a small amount poured over each portion is delicious.

Frozen Chocolate Marquise with Mocha Cream

6 TO 8 PORTIONS

A chocolate Marquise is a rich, thick, chocolate mousse—one of the richest—generally prepared in a dome-shaped mold. This recipe, originally called Bonbon Chocolate, is really a frozen Marquise made in a loaf pan (see Note). It has a sensational consistency, similar to a rich, dense ice cream, but smoother. It may be served 5 or 6 hours after it is made or it may wait for a few days. The recipe, which does not take long to prepare, may easily be increased.

8 ounces semisweet chocolate
4 ounces (1 stick) sweet butter
½ teaspoon vanilla extract
½ cup granulated sugar
4 eggs (graded large or extra-large), separated
Pinch of salt

Prepare a 4-cup metal loaf pan (8 x 4 x 2 inches) as follows: Cut or tear two strips of aluminum foil, one for the length and one for the width, each one long enough to extend a bit over the rim of the pan. Press them into place in the pan. Brush with a thin layer of tasteless salad oil, and set the pan aside.

Break up the chocolate and place it in the top of a small double boiler over hot water on moderate heat. Cover and let stand for a few minutes until the chocolate is partially melted. Remove the cover and stir the chocolate with a rubber spatula until it is completely melted and smooth. Remove the top of the double boiler from the hot water and set aside to cool.

In the small bowl of an electric mixer cream the butter. Add the vanilla. Set aside 2 tablespoons of the sugar and add the rest of it to the butter. Beat well for several minutes. Then add the egg yolks one at a time, scraping the bowl with a rubber spatula and beating well after each addition. After adding the last yolk, beat for 4 to 5 minutes until the mixture is very creamy. Then add the cooled chocolate and beat only until blended.

Transfer the mixture to a medium-size mixing bowl.

Wash and dry the mixer bowl and beaters. Now, in the clean, dry small bowl of the mixer add the salt to the egg whites and beat until they increase in volume and barely hold a soft shape. Add the reserved 2 tablespoons of sugar and continue to beat only until the whites hold a shape when the beaters are raised—they should not be beaten until completely stiff and/or dry.

In several additions, small at first, fold the whites into the chocolate mixture.

Turn the dessert into the prepared pan. Smooth the top and cover it with wax paper or plastic wrap—the foil that extends over the top of the pan should be folded down on the outside.

Freeze for 5 or 6 hours, or it may be stored in the freezer for several days.

This may be unmolded an hour or so before dinner (or earlier if you cover it with plastic wrap).

Remove the wax paper from the top. If the foil lining does not cover the corners of the pan, cut between the dessert and the pan to release it. Invert a chilled platter over the pan. Holding carefully, invert the platter and the pan. Hold the edges of the foil to help release the pan. Remove the pan and peel off the foil. If necessary, with a small metal spatula smooth over the top and sides of the loaf and return it to the freezer.

This may be served as is; it doesn't need any decoration or sauce. Or the loaf may be decorated with whipped cream, using a pastry bag and a star-shaped tube. Or the following Mocha Cream and/or brandied cherries or other brandied fruit may be passed.

Serve on chilled dessert plates, cutting through as you would slice a cake. Make the portions small.

MOCHA CREAM

1 cup heavy cream
¼ cup confectioners sugar
1 tablespoon dry powdered (not granular) instant coffee
½ teaspoon vanilla extract

Place all of the ingredients in a chilled small mixer bowl. With chilled beaters whip only until the cream holds a soft shape—think "sauce" instead of "whipped cream."

If the cream is prepared ahead of time, refrigerate it. It may separate slightly—if so, whip it briefly with a small wire whisk just before serving.

NOTE: If you wish, this frozen cream may also be prepared in an ice-cube tray or any covered container and spooned out for serving. And it behaves very nicely in a fancy mold. (Oil the mold lightly with tasteless salad oil before filling it.)

Frozen Chocolate Mousse

12 TO 16 PORTIONS

My friend Joan Borinstein, of Los Angeles, is a prize-winning chocolate dessert-maker and a full-fledged chocolate dessert addict who recently fulfilled a lifelong dream fantasy: She gave a New Year's Eve dessert-and-champagne party for which she prepared 72 desserts for 100 guests. Her apartment that night was wall-to-wall desserts. This is Joan's smooth and creamy chocolate mousse (it tastes like ice cream), made with a chocolate-cookie crumb crust. It is a beautiful and delicious creation for an important occasion. It may be made up to two weeks before serving.

CRUST

8 ounces chocolate wafer cookies (The bought ones are sometimes called icebox wafers. Better yet, make your own Chocolate Wafers, page 129.)
3 ounces (¾ stick) sweet butter

Adjust rack one-third up from the bottom of the oven and preheat oven to 375 degrees. Separate the bottom from the sides of a 9 x 3-inch spring-form pan; butter the sides only (if you butter the bottom the crust will stick to the bottom and it will be difficult to serve), and then replace the bottom in the pan and set aside.

Crumble the cookies coarsely and place them in a food processor or a blender (or place them in a plastic bag and pound and roll them with a rolling pin) to make fine crumbs; you should have 2 cups of crumbs. Place them in a mixing bowl. Melt the butter and stir it into the crumbs until thoroughly distributed. Pour about two-thirds of the mixture into the prepared pan.

To form a thin layer of crumbs on the sides of the pan: Tilt the pan at about a 45-degree angle and, with your fingertips, press a layer of the crumbs against the sides, pressing from the bottom up toward the top of the pan and rotating the pan gradually as you press on the crumbs—they should reach the top of the pan all the way around. Then place the pan upright on its bottom; pour in the remaining crumbs and, with your fingertips, distribute them over the bottom of the pan to cover it. Press them firmly to make a compact layer.

Bake for 7 to 8 minutes, remove from the oven, and cool completely.

CHOCOLATE MOUSSE

1 tablespoon dry instant coffee
½ cup boiling water
1¼ cups granulated sugar
12 ounces semisweet chocolate chopped
4 eggs (graded large or extra-large), separated
3 cups whipping cream
Pinch of salt
⅛ teaspoon cream of tartar

Dissolve the coffee in the water in a heavy 2-quart saucepan. Add ½ cup (reserve ¾ cup) of the sugar and stir over moderate heat to dissolve. Adjust the heat to low, add the chocolate, and stir until it is melted and smooth. Remove from the heat and let stand for a few minutes to cool slightly. Add the egg yolks one at a time, stirring them in with a wire whisk. Set aside to cool completely.

In the large bowl of an electric mixer whip the cream until it holds a shape but not until it is really stiff. Set it aside.

In the small bowl of an electric mixer, with clean beaters, beat the egg whites until they are foamy. Add the salt and the cream of tartar and continue to beat until the whites hold a soft shape. Reduce the speed to moderate and gradually add the reserved ¾ cup sugar, one large spoonful at a time. Beat briefly between additions. Then increase the speed to high again and beat for a few minutes until the meringue is quite firm, but not stiff or dry.

Gradually, in two or three additions, fold most of the chocolate into the whites and then fold the whites into the remaining chocolate.

In a very large mixing bowl fold together the whipped cream and the chocolate mixture.

Pour into the chocolate-cookie crumb crust, smooth the top or form a swirling pattern, and place in the freezer. After about an hour or so cover the top airtight with plastic wrap. Freeze overnight or for up to 2 weeks.

The mousse may be removed from the pan just before serving or days before. With a firm, sharp, heavy knife, cut around the sides of the crust, pressing the blade firmly against the pan as you cut. Then release and remove the sides of the pan. Now, use a firm (not flexible) metal spatula (either a wide one or a long narrow one): Insert the spatula gently and carefully under the crust and ease it around to release the

dessert completely from the bottom of the pan. The dessert will be firm and sturdy and easy to transfer. If you are serving it soon, place it on a large, flat dessert platter; if you are going to store it again in the freezer, place it on a large piece of plastic wrap and wrap airtight. In either case, return it to the freezer until serving time. It does not freeze too firm, and will cut beautifully and easily. Use a sharp, heavy knife.

OPTIONAL DECORATION

Just before serving, cover the top of the mousse with whipped cream and/or a layer of overlapping Chocolate Leaves (see page 264), and surround the whole dessert with a generous ring of large Chocolate-Covered Strawberries (see page 252). When Joan made this for me and my husband, she made some of the leaves with dark chocolate, some with lighter milk chocolate, and some with white chocolate, and alternated them on top—it was gorgeous. I have made it with one shiny leaf almost large enough to cover the top.

Or you can serve the mousse as is, and pass softly whipped cream as a sauce. Or serve it without whipped cream—it is wonderful just by itself.

VARIATION: *White Chocolate Mousse: This creamy white mousse is made from the Frozen Chocolate Mousse recipe. With the dark chocolate crumb crust, white mousse filling, dark chocolate leaves, and red and green strawberries it makes a fabulous picture. And with or without the leaves and berries, it is a sensational dessert.*

Make the following, changes in the preceding recipe:

1. Eliminate the instant coffee.

2. Do not add the ½ cup sugar to the water at the beginning. (Use only the ¾ cup that is added to the egg whites—therefore, use only a total ¾ cup instead of 1¼ cups.)

3. Use 12 ounces white chocolate instead of semisweet chocolate.

4. After melting the chocolate in the water, beat it with an electric mixer until smooth.

5. Add 2 tablespoons of white or natural crème de cacao to the cooled melted chocolate and egg-yolk mixture.

Mousse Brillat-Savarin

10 TO 12 PORTIONS

This is a frozen white chocolate mousse adapted from a recipe created by Michel Fitoussi, head chef at the famous Palace Restaurant in New York City. (It is one of the desserts on a $500 dinner menu.) Frankly, I take a dim view of white chocolate compared to brown, but this is delicious regardless of its color, and is an original and beautiful dessert.

It is a white, creamy, marshmallow-like sweet mousse that reminds me of soft-frozen ice cream, with little pieces of crunchy white chocolate throughout. It is served frozen, and may be made way ahead of time. But the strawberries that are served with it, and are an important part of the dessert, must be fresh; so wait for fresh berries to serve it.

You will need a candy-making thermometer.

12 ounces white chocolate
1 cup granulated sugar
¼ teaspoon cream of tartar

⅓ cup water

Pinch of salt

4 egg whites (½ cup or a little more,
  depending on the size of the eggs)

2 tablespoons kirsch

2 cups heavy cream

The chocolate must be chopped very fine (after the mousse is frozen, if the pieces are too large they become hard to eat). But because white chocolate is almost pure cocoa butter, if you chop it in a blender or a food processor it will quickly form a solid mass—which is not what you want. I do not recommend a blender; a food processor is all right if you are very careful not to overdo it. The best way, unfortunately, takes more time: that is to chop the chocolate with a long, heavy knife on a board. Then set it aside.

Place the sugar, cream of tartar, and water in a 1- to 1½-quart saucepan (the pan should be deep and narrow, not wide, or the thermometer will not reach the mixture). Cook over moderate heat, stirring constantly with a wooden spatula, until the sugar is dissolved and the mixture comes to a boil. Wash down the sides of the saucepan with a brush dipped in water to remove any undissolved sugar granules— undissolved granules may prevent a smooth syrup.

Increase the heat to high, insert a candy thermometer, and let boil without stirring until the syrup reaches the soft-ball stage, which is from 234 to 240 degrees on the thermometer.

Meanwhile, in the small bowl of an electric mixer, add the salt to the egg whites and beat until they hold a shape or are stiff but not dry.

While beating at high speed, very gradually, in a thin stream, pour the syrup into the whites. While you are adding the syrup, if the whites reach the top of the bowl transfer the mixture to the large bowl of the mixer and continue to add the syrup. Then beat at high speed for about 3 minutes until the mixture is very thick. (This mixture is called Italian meringue.)

Remove from the mixer. If you have not already transferred the mixture to a larger bowl, do so now.

(The mixture will still be warm.) Add the chopped white chocolate and fold together.

Now, if the meringue is still warm, let it stand until it reaches room temperature—test it on the inside of your wrist; it must be completely cool or it will deflate the whipped cream.

Add the kirsch to the cream in the small bowl of an electric mixer and whip until it holds a soft shape—the mousse will be more delicate if the cream is not whipped really stiff.

Add the whipped cream to the cooled meringue and fold together.

Now, you can pour this into a large serving bowl, cover, and freeze if you plan to serve it at the table from the bowl. Or pour it into any covered container, freeze, and scoop or spoon out portions in the kitchen. It will not freeze too hard to serve easily.

Prepare the following strawberries during the day for that night.

STRAWBERRIES

When I measure a little basket of strawberries from the market I find that it measures almost 1 quart in volume, although frequently food stores and recipes refer to that amount as 1 pint. Actually, it should weigh 1 pound. For serving about 10 or 12 portions, use 5 baskets; or, if you measure them, almost 3 quarts—or 3 pounds. (But since the dessert is frozen and may be kept for some time in the freezer, if you plan to serve only part of it, use 1 basket of berries for 4 portions of mousse—and 1 tablespoon of sugar and 1 of kirsch.)

3 baskets of fresh strawberries
3 tablespoons granulated sugar
3 tablespoons kirsch

Wash the berries quickly—don't let them soak. Wash either in and out of a bowl of cold water, or under cold running water. Remove the hulls and spread the strawberries out on paper towels to drain and dry. Then, on a large flat plate, crush them coarsely with a large fork (they should not be fine or mushy); or slice them. Place the berries in a bowl, add the sugar and kirsch, and let stand at room temperature, stirring occasionally, for about an hour.

Then cover and refrigerate until serving time.

Pass the strawberries separately or spoon a generous amount over each portion. (Or, to serve it as they do at the Palace, spoon some of the berries and their sauce into the bottoms of individual dessert cups and spoon the mousse over them.)

Toblerone Milk Chocolate Mousse

4 PORTIONS

In order to have the very special flavor of this chocolate, this recipe must be made with Toblerone, a triangular Swiss bar of sweet milk chocolate with chopped almonds and honey nougat. It comes in 3-ounce or 14-ounce bars and is generally available at fine-food stores and some candy shops. The mousse will be a

light chocolate in color and creamy-firm. It is prepared in individual portions and must be made at least a few hours before serving, but it can be made a few days ahead. This recipe makes 4 portions but can easily be multiplied.

7 ounces Toblerone milk chocolate, broken
    into small pieces
6 tablespoons boiling water
½ cup heavy cream
2 egg whites
Pinch of salt
2 tablespoons granulated sugar
Optional: additional Toblerone for shaving
    over the top

Place the chocolate and boiling water in a small, heavy saucepan over the lowest heat. Stir occasionally with a small wire whisk until the chocolate is melted. (You will see little bits of almonds and melting nougat.) Do not overheat the chocolate. As soon as it is melted remove it from the heat and set aside until completely cool.

In a small bowl whip the cream until it holds a definite shape and set it aside.

In the small bowl of an electric mixer beat the egg whites with the salt until they hold a soft shape. Gradually add the sugar and continue to beat until the mixture holds a firm shape but is not stiff or dry.

Meanwhile, chill the chocolate briefly, either in the freezer, stirring occasionally, or over ice and water, stirring constantly. The chocolate should be cold enough to thicken very slightly but do not let it start to harden.

In a medium-size mixing bowl fold the chocolate, beaten egg whites, and whipped cream together only until incorporated.

Pour the mousse into four individual dessert bowls or wine glasses.

Cover and freeze for at least a few hours or for a few days.

This does not need whipped cream on top. But you may sprinkle the top with little curls of Toblerone milk chocolate made by shaving it with a vegetable peeler.

Pontchartrain Mile-High Ice Cream Pie

8 TO 10 PORTIONS

This is from a friend, Mr. Lysle Aschaffenburg, creator and owner of the Pontchartrain Hotel in New Orleans, which has one of the most famous dining rooms (the Caribbean Room) in a city of famous dining rooms.

It is one of the most startling, dramatic, and impressive pies I have ever seen. Your guests will swoon.

Most of it can and should be made way ahead of time; the rest, which does not take long, should be done early in the day for that night (or, possibly, the night before—see Note). It is related to a Baked Alaska, but read on. It has a baked pie shell which is filled with ice cream (that is the ahead-of-time part), and it is covered with a FOUR-inch topping of meringue which is baked to a golden honey color. Now, delightfully, instead of rushing it to the table, the whole thing goes into the freezer. On top of all that, it is served with a marvelous thick, dark chocolate sauce.

Plan it for an occasion—Thanksgiving, Christmas, a graduation, an anniversary—something special. The pie serves 8 to 10, but you can make two or more if you have room in the freezer—and a lot of egg whites.

Save (freeze) leftover egg whites from other recipes for this one.

PIE CRUST

Prepare a baked pie shell in a 9-inch ovenproof glass pie plate (see page 176) and cool it completely.

FILLING

3 pints chocolate ice cream

Use a good-quality commercial ice cream. Homemade ice cream (mine) might freeze too firm for comfortable serving, and you would not know it (because it is covered with meringue) until you served it.

Actually, this is quite flexible. I use 3 pints of chocolate ice cream—you could use 4. Or you could use more than one flavor, and place them in layers in the pie shell; the Pontchartrain uses peppermint, vanilla, and chocolate. Or coffee and chocolate are delicious.

Spread the ice cream in the pie shell, mounding it in the middle if you use more, and freeze it very well. It must be frozen solid. If you do this part way ahead of time, and it is good if you do, cover airtight and let stand in the freezer. (It is helpful if you turn the freezer temperature to coldest for a while before proceeding with the meringue.)

PONTCHARTRAIN MERINGUE

¼ teaspoon salt

1½ cups egg whites (about 10 or 12 whites, depending on their size; they may be whites that have been left over from other recipes, frozen, and then thawed)

1½ teaspoons lemon juice

1 cup granulated sugar

1 tablespoon vanilla extract

Adjust rack one-third up from the bottom of the oven and preheat oven to 450 degrees. Make room in the freezer—the pie will be at least 5 inches high. And set the freezer control to coldest.

In the large bowl of an electric mixer add the salt to the egg whites and beat at high speed until they are foamy. Add the lemon juice and beat only until the whites barely hold a soft shape. Reduce the speed to moderate and beat, adding the sugar about 1 tablespoon at a time, pausing for 10 or 15 seconds between additions. (It should take about 5 or 6 minutes of beating from the time you begin until all the sugar is added.) Now increase the speed to high again, add the vanilla, and beat for 4 or 5 minutes longer—the meringue should really be quite stiff. Remove from the mixer.

Take the frozen pie from the freezer, and, if you have a cake-decorating turntable or a lazy Susan, place it on it.

Work quickly now! Transfer this enormous amount of meringue you have made onto the top of the ice cream any quick way. Then, with a rubber or long, narrow metal spatula, quickly shape it—it should be so stiff that you actually have to force it— to cover the top of the ice cream and touch the pastry all around the sides. Then with a long, narrow metal spatula form it into a dome. Still working quickly (you do not want the ice cream to melt), flatten the top, forming a smooth, flat plateau about 6 inches in diameter, smooth the sides (they will taper

in toward the top and will stand 4 inches above the top of the pie plate), and IMMEDIATELY place the pie in the oven.

Bake for 5 minutes—the meringue will turn a luscious smooth, golden honey color—and then immediately place the pie in the freezer.

Freeze for 2 to 8 hours or more. It must be frozen long enough rechill the ice cream, which may have softened during baking; the time required will depend on how cold your freezer is. But the dessert may be frozen longer without hurting the meringue (see Note following Pontchartrain Chocolate Sauce recipe below).

PONTCHARTRAIN CHOCOLATE SAUCE

2 CUPS

This super sauce can be used for any other dessert.

¾ cup heavy cream

½ cup granulated sugar

8 ounces semisweet chocolate, broken up

2 ounces (2 squares) unsweetened chocolate, coarsely chopped

Place the cream in a 6- to 8-cup heavy saucepan over moderate heat. Stir occasionally until it barely begins to simmer. Add the sugar and stir over heat until completely dissolved. Reduce the heat to low; add the chocolates and stir until melted. When melted, stir briskly with a small wire whisk until perfectly smooth. It will be very thick.

The sauce should be warm but not hot when it is served.

If you make it ahead of time, cover it—let it cool covered. Then reheat slowly, stirring occasionally, over low heat.

If before serving it seems to be too thick (although it should be thick), gradually stir in some additional cream or water.

TO SERVE: *Place the pie plate on a folded napkin on a flat dessert platter.*

Use a rather long, sharp, heavy knife to cut portions, and serve them on large dessert plates. Pour or spoon a few spoonfuls of the sauce over each portion.

NOTE: *After about 6 to 8 hours the meringue starts to evaporate and shrink, and therefore becomes less airy. But the process is slow. It is best to serve the pie within about 6 to 8 hours after the meringue is baked; however, if it must stand longer—even overnight—the pie will still taste good and the meringue will still look sensationally high (but if you measure it with a ruler after it has stood overnight you will see a difference).*

Mississippi Mud Pie

8 to 10 Portions

We had this popular pie at the Chart House, a restaurant in Aspen, Colorado. It consisted of an unbaked crumb crust made of chocolate sandwich cookies (the kind with a white filling—such as Oreos or Hydrox), a thick filling of coffee ice cream, and a thin chocolate glaze topping. In Aspen it was served with a generous amount of bourbon-flavored whipped cream and toasted, sliced almonds.

It is best to make the crust a day before filling it or at least several hours before; the pie should be completed at least a day before serving, or it may be frozen for days. Or longer.

CRUST

7½ ounces (21 cookie sandwiches) chocolate
   sandwich cookies (such as Oreos or Hydrox)
2 ounces (½ stick) sweet butter, melted

To prevent the crust from sticking to the plate when the pie is served, line the plate with aluminum foil as follows: Place a 12-inch square of foil into a 9-inch ovenproof glass pie plate—press the foil firmly into place by pressing against it with a folded towel or a pot holder; fold the edges of the foil tightly out over the rim of the plate. Set aside.

Break the cookies into pieces and place them in a food processor or a blender and process or blend until the crumbs are fine—you should have a scant 1¾ cups of crumbs.

In a bowl, mix the crumbs thoroughly with the melted butter.

Turn the mixture into the lined pie plate. With your fingertips distribute the crumbs evenly and loosely over the sides first and then over the bottom. Then press the crumbs firmly against the sides—be careful that the top edge of the crust is not too thin—and then press it firmly against the bottom. It must all be very firm—no loose crumbs.

Place in the freezer for at least several hours or overnight; it must be frozen firm.

FILLING

2 pints coffee ice cream (of course you can use
   any other flavor you prefer)

The ice cream should be softened slightly so you can transfer it to the pie plate. Place it in the refrigerator for about 10 minutes or so, depending on the firmness of the ice cream and the temperature of the refrigerator.

Meanwhile, to remove the foil from the pie plate, raise the edges of the foil and carefully lift the foil (with the frozen crust) from the plate. Gently peel away the foil (it will come away easily in one piece) by supporting the bottom of the crust with your left hand and peeling the foil slowly—a bit at a time—with your right. As you peel, rotate the crust gently on your left hand.

Support the bottom of the crust with a small metal spatula or a knife and ease it back into the plate very gently so as not to crack it—it will not crack if it has been frozen sufficiently.

Now turn the slightly softened ice cream into the crust. Spread it smoothly, mounding it a bit higher in the middle.

Return to the freezer until the ice cream is very firm.

Meanwhile, make the chocolate glaze.

CHOCOLATE GLAZE

1 ounce (1 square) unsweetened chocolate
2 ounces semisweet chocolate
1 tablespoon plus 1½ teaspoons water
2 tablespoons light corn syrup
1½ tablespoons sweet butter, cut into small
   bits

Chop both chocolates into small pieces and set aside.

Place the water, corn syrup, and butter in a small saucepan over moderate heat. Stir occasionally until the mixture comes to a boil.

Add the chopped chocolate and remove from the heat immediately. Stir with a small wire whisk until the chocolate is melted and the mixture is smooth.

Set aside to cool to room temperature.

Pour the cooled glaze carefully over the frozen ice cream to cover the top completely—be careful not to let any run over the sides of the crust. If it is necessary to spread the glaze, do it quickly before it hardens. It will be a very thin layer of glaze.

Return the pie to the freezer for at least a few hours or more.

When the glaze is frozen firm, the pie may be wrapped airtight with plastic wrap and may be frozen for any reasonable time.

This may be served as is, or with whipped cream (sweetened and flavored with vanilla extract or rum, bourbon, Kahlúa, etc.) and toasted, sliced almonds or other nuts. And/or with the World's Best Hot Fudge Sauce (see page 258).

NOTE: *Mississippi Mud (a cold drink) was originally a mixture of vanilla ice cream, strong, cold prepared coffee, and a lot of bourbon, with a sprinkling of nutmeg on top. In honor of the original Mud, and because it tastes so good, I pass a bottle of bourbon to be sprinkled or poured over individual portions.*

Frozen Chocolate Pie

8 TO 12 PORTIONS

This is extremely rich and dense. WARNING: It should be served only to avowed chocolate lovers. It may be made early in the day for that night, or days or weeks ahead. It is served frozen.

1 9-inch baked and cooled pie shell (see page
   176)
2 ounces (2 squares) unsweetened chocolate
4 ounces semisweet chocolate
¼ pound (1 stick) sweet butter
1 teaspoon vanilla extract

Optional: 1 tablespoon rum, Cognac, or
strong prepared coffee
¾ cup strained confectioners sugar
4 eggs (graded extra-large or jumbo)

Place both chocolates in the top of a small double boiler over hot water on moderate heat. Cover until partially melted. Uncover and stir until completely melted and smooth. Remove the top of the double boiler and set aside to cool to room temperature.

In the small bowl of an electric mixer cream the butter until it is soft. Add the vanilla, optional rum, Cognac, or coffee, and the confectioners sugar and beat until very smooth and creamy. Add the cooled melted chocolate and beat at moderate speed, scraping the bowl with a rubber spatula, until smooth. Add the eggs one at a time, scraping the bowl with the spatula and beating until thoroughly incorporated after each addition. After the last egg has been added, beat for 1 minute more.

Turn the mixture into a prepared pie shell. Spread it to make an even layer, or swirl it with the back of a spoon, and place in the freezer.

After about 15 minutes or so, when the top is firm, wrap it in plastic wrap and return it to the freezer. Freeze for about 4 hours, or much longer if you wish.

Remove from freezer and let stand at room temperature for 15 to 20 minutes before serving.

TOPPING

About ½ ounce semisweet or milk chocolate
1 cup heavy cream
Scant 1 teaspoon vanilla extract
3 tablespoons strained confectioners sugar

Make shaved chocolate curls (they can be made as much ahead of time as you wish and stored in the refrigerator or freezer if the kitchen is warm). Working over wax paper, with a vegetable peeler scrape the side of the chocolate, forming curls and

letting them fall on the wax paper. Set aside until you are ready to serve the pie.

The whipped cream may be made just before serving or a few hours before. (If it has to stand, refrigerate it; it will separate slightly and should be stirred with a wire whisk just before using.)

Place the cream, vanilla, and sugar in a chilled small bowl. With chilled beaters whip until the cream is stiff enough to hold a shape.

Immediately before serving spread the cream over the top of the pie and, with a large spoon, sprinkle the chocolate curls over the top.

Use a sharp, heavy knife and serve in small portions.

Ice Cream en Robe

This is a fascinating company or family dessert. The ingredients are simply ice cream and chocolate. But the handling of them is unusual, creative, and great fun.

They may be prepared an hour or so before serving or they may wait in the freezer for as long as you would store ice cream. If this dessert is going to be frozen for a long time you will need roomy, shallow boxes—these shells are fragile and must be stored without crowding.

You will need a round ice-cream scoop that measures 2½ inches in diameter to form balls like those used in ice-cream cones.

You will need 1 pint of ice cream for 3 portions. Use any flavor you like, but this is especially fine made with pistachio or coffee ice cream, or you can use a variety of flavors. And you will need 1 ounce of semisweet chocolate for each portion. Any semisweet chocolate may be used.

Before you start, make some room in the freezer where things can rest on a flat surface. And line a shallow pan (for holding scoops of ice cream) with wax paper or aluminum foil.

With the ice-cream scoop, form large, round balls of ice cream mounded high (as though you were scooping it for cones). Place the balls in the lined pan and immediately place the pan in the freezer—the ice cream must be frozen hard before you proceed.

While the balls are freezing, cut a round of wax paper for each ball (it must be wax paper—not foil or plastic wrap). Do it as follows: Tear off as many pieces of wax paper as you will need (each piece should be at least 7½ inches wide). Place them in a pile on a counter or table top. Find something round that measures 7½ inches in diameter—a small plate, or use a compass. Trace around the plate to mark a circle on the top piece of paper. Place your left hand flat on the pile of papers to keep them in place and, with scissors, cut through six to eight papers at once. (If you are making more, cut one pile and then another.) The edges do not have to be cut exactly or evenly.

Now coarsely chop the semisweet chocolate (1 ounce for each portion). Place it in the top of a small double boiler over warm water on low heat. Stir occasionally until the chocolate is melted and smooth—do not let it become warmer than tepid. Remove the top of the double boiler and let stand, stirring occasionally, until the chocolate reaches room temperature.

Place one round of wax paper on a work surface close to the freezer. Place a generous tablespoonful (about 1 ounce) of the chocolate in the center of the wax paper. Now work quickly. With the back of a large spoon or with a rubber spatula spread the chocolate out over the paper into a thin round, leaving an uncovered border of wax paper about 1 inch wide all around. The chocolate layer should be thin and the edges should be neat and even, but don't worry about the surface being perfectly smooth.

Quickly, with a wide metal spatula, transfer a ball of ice cream to the center of the soft chocolate layer. Place it rounded side up. With your fingers bring up two opposite sides of the wax paper and the chocolate. The cold ice cream will quickly harden the chocolate and keep it in place. Immediately bring up the other two opposite sides, forming a four-sided cup (or robe) around the ice cream, with four folded corners pointing out.

Don't fuss with it. Don't try to make the corners all exactly alike. Just make sure that the four sides of the chocolate are up and that they meet in the corners. (The top of the ice cream will remain uncovered.)

Immediately place the En Robes, still in the wax paper, in the freezer.

If the chocolate starts to thicken too much while you are working with it, replace it over warm water and stir briefly only to soften it.

Continue to prepare as many as you want. When they are firm, carefully place them in a box or on a tray and cover with plastic wrap.

Now, this is the fun part. Sometime before serving (a day before if you wish—or right before), when it is quiet and you are not rushed, peel off the wax paper. Do this carefully and slowly but don't keep the ice cream out of the freezer so long it starts to melt. It is best to begin on a side instead of at a corner, and gently peel the paper away. The corners are the most fragile part—handle them with care. If it seems difficult to remove the wax paper all in one piece, tear it anywhere that seems to make it safer—or give you less chance of breaking the chocolate—and then remove the paper in pieces.

Return the desserts to the freezer until serving time. Serve these on flat plates with a fork and a spoon.

Chocolate Chip-Cognac-Coffee Ice Cream

1 QUART

I got this recipe from Rita Leinwand, food editor of Bon Appétit *Magazine, when she came to our home for lunch. She told me that she got it from Sam Aaron, wine connoisseur, writer, and owner of the Sherry-Lehmann Wine and Liquor store in New York City. Now you've got it. It is FAN-TAS-TIC!!! Thank you, Rita. Thank you, Sam.*

2 ounces semisweet chocolate
1 quart coffee ice cream (see Note)
2 teaspoons dry powdered (not granular)
     instant espresso
4 ounces (½ cup) Cognac

On a board, with a large, heavy knife, chop the chocolate into fine pieces. The pieces do not all have to be the same size, some may be a little larger or smaller.

The rest of the instructions for this recipe are simply mix all the ingredients.

It is necessary to soften the ice cream slightly, but no more than necessary—do not allow it to melt! (When ice cream is churned it absorbs a certain amount of air which makes it light and creamy. If you allow it to melt it will lose that air.)

Place the ice cream in the refrigerator for 15 or 20 minutes, just until it can be stirred. Or cut the firm ice cream into pieces and, very briefly, mix it in an electric mixer or process it in a food processor. Quickly stir in the chocolate, espresso, and Cognac and refreeze immediately.

NOTE: *Rita said that Sam said the ice cream must be Haagen-Dazs®. I can buy that brand easily here so that is what I have been using. If you have trouble buying it, please use whatever good coffee ice cream you can get.*

Hot Soufflés

Correct oven temperature is especially critical when baking soufflés. If it is too hot the soufflé will overbake, will probably be too dry, and will possibly burn on the outside. If it is not hot enough the soufflé will not rise properly, will probably be too soft inside, or will have to bake much longer and will then become too well done in the middle. Please check your oven temperature carefully (see page 11).

L'Escoffier's Cappuccino Soufflé

4 PORTIONS

This is from the elegant L'Escoffier restaurant in Beverly Hills, California. It is a wonderful soufflé with a sensational flavor. You will need a soufflé dish with a 5- to 6-cup capacity—6¾ inches across by 3 inches deep.

It will take 40 minutes to bake and must be served IMMEDIATELY, so plan accordingly. (Part of it may be prepared ahead of time.)

This recipe makes 4 servings; if you want to double it, it must be made in two dishes or the outside will be too dry and the inside too soft. If you do make more than one soufflé, have someone help you serve so that neither has to wait and fall.

½ ounce (½ square) unsweetened chocolate
1 cup milk
1 tablespoon dry instant coffee or espresso
3 tablespoons sweet butter
¼ cup sifted all-purpose flour
2 tablespoons Grand Marnier
1 tablespoon Cognac
¼ cup granulated sugar
4 eggs (graded large or extra-large), separated,
    plus 1 additional egg white
1 teaspoon vanilla extract
Pinch of salt

Adjust a rack very low in the oven. Prepare a 5- to 6-cup soufflé dish as follows: Butter the inside of the dish. Tear off a piece of aluminum foil long enough to wrap around the dish and overlap slightly. Fold it in half the long way. Run the foil firmly over the edge of a counter to make it more flexible. Then butter one half of one long side along the open edge (not the folded edge). Wrap the foil securely around the dish with the buttered side in and the folded edge even with the bottom of the dish. Wrap a piece of string around just below the top of the dish and tie it tightly. Shake some granulated sugar (additional to that called for) around in the dish to coat the inside and the foil, invert to shake out excess. Set the prepared dish aside.

Coarsely chop the ½ ounce of chocolate and place it in a small heatproof cup in a small pan of shallow hot water over low heat. Let stand until the chocolate is melted and then remove it from the water and set aside. (Be very careful not to get a drop of water in the chocolate.)

Meanwhile, in a small saucepan over moderate heat, scald the milk just until it is very hot. Add the dry instant coffee and stir to dissolve.

While the milk is heating, place the butter in a heavy 2-quart saucepan over moderate heat to melt. Add the flour and stir over heat for about 2 minutes.

Remove the saucepan containing the butter/flour mixture from the heat, add the hot milk all at once, and immediately stir well with a small wire whisk. Add the melted chocolate, Grand Marnier, Cognac, and half of the sugar (reserve 2 tablespoons of the sugar). Stir until smooth and replace over moderate heat, stirring constantly until the mixture comes to a low boil. Let it boil slowly, continue stirring, for about 1 minute. Remove from the heat.

In a mixing bowl stir the yolks lightly just to mix. Gradually add the hot milk mixture, stirring constantly. Stir in the vanilla.

Now this chocolate mixture should cool slightly—5 to 10 minutes is enough, or longer if you wish. While it is cooling it must be stirred frequently to prevent a skin from forming on the top. (The recipe may be prepared hours ahead of time up to this point. When the mixture is cool, cover it airtight and let it stand at room temperature. Then, just before going on with the recipe, stir this chocolate mixture briefly in the top of a small double boiler over hot water to reheat until it is just barely warm.)

Preheat the oven to 350°.

To complete the soufflé, place the 5 egg whites and the salt in the small bowl of an electric mixer (or beat them in a copper bowl with a balloon wire whisk) and beat until they hold a soft shape. Then gradually add the reserved sugar and continue to beat (or whisk) until the whites hold a definite shape or are stiff but not dry.

Fold about half of the chocolate mixture into the whites and then fold the whites into the remaining chocolate—handle as little as possible in order to retain the air beaten into the whites.

Gently pour the soufflé into the prepared dish (it will come just to the top of the dish).

Bake for 40 minutes. At that time the soufflé will be firm enough to hold its shape for a few minutes but it will still be slightly creamy in the center, as it should be. (The soufflé will have risen several inches above the top of the dish.)

Reach into the oven to cut the string and carefully peel away the foil collar. Work, quickly. (Handle the dish carefully—it will be slippery on the outside from the buttered aluminum foil.) Place the soufflé dish on a folded napkin on a tray and serve immediately.

Or place the soufflé dish, with the aluminum foil, on a folded napkin on a tray, bring it to the table, and cut the string and remove the foil at the table; you will feel a little safer and the guests will enjoy the show.

This is delicious as it is, or it may be served with the following: whipped cream or Grand Marnier Custard Sauce. (Serve the cold cream or sauce alongside—not over—each portion.)

WHIPPED CREAM

1 cup heavy cream
¼ cup confectioners sugar
1 tablespoon Grand Marnier
¼ teaspoon vanilla extract

In a chilled bowl with chilled beaters, whip above ingredients, beating only until the cream has thickened to the consistency of a sauce. (If the cream is whipped ahead of time it will separate slightly on standing; if so, stir it briefly with a wire whisk just before serving.)

GRAND MARNIER CUSTARD SAUCE

1 cup milk
¼ cup heavy cream
4 egg yolks
½ cup granulated sugar
Pinch of salt
1 teaspoon vanilla extract
3 tablespoons Grand Marnier

Place the milk and cream in a heavy saucepan over moderate heat. Let stand uncovered until a slight skin forms on the top.

Meanwhile, in the top of a large double boiler off the heat, stir the yolks lightly with a small wire whisk just to mix. Gradually stir in the sugar and the salt.

Then gradually stir the hot milk/cream into the egg-yolk mixture.

Place over hot water, which must not touch the upper section of the double boiler and should not be hot enough to boil. Stir the custard mixture constantly with a rubber spatula, scraping the sides and bottom, until the mixture thickens slightly or enough to coat a metal spoon. It might take about 10 minutes, and will register 180 degrees on a candy thermometer.

Strain into a small bowl and let stand, stirring occasionally, until the custard reaches room temperature.

Stir in the vanilla and Grand Marnier. Cover, refrigerate, and serve cold. This can be made early in the day for that night. (Stir briefly before using.)

Hot Chocolate Soufflé Alice

4 PORTIONS

This is a soufflé, but when you read the ingredients you will recognize that it is really a baked chocolate mousse.

This is an extremely easy, quick, dark soufflé. It serves four but is not too much for two or three generous portions. To double the recipe, double the ingredients but bake in two separate 1-quart soufflé dishes. (In one large dish it becomes too dry on the outside before the center is baked.) If you have made more than one soufflé, have someone help you serve so neither has to wait and fall.

This does not rise as high as the previous soufflé.

4 ounces semisweet chocolate, broken into
    small pieces
Generous ½ teaspoon dry instant coffee
1 tablespoon boiling water
2 ounces (½ stick) sweet butter, at room
    temperature, cut into small pieces
4 eggs (graded extra-large or jumbo), or 5 eggs
    (graded large or medium), separated
½ teaspoon vanilla extract
Pinch of salt

Adjust rack one-third up from the bottom of the oven and preheat oven to 475 degrees. Butter a 1-quart soufflé dish (6 to 6½ inches x 3 inches) and dust it with granulated sugar; invert the dish and tap it to shake out excess sugar—it should be a very thin coating.

Dissolve the coffee in the boiling water and pour it over the chocolate in the top of a small double boiler over warm water on low heat. Cover. Let

stand briefly only until the chocolate is melted. With a small wire whisk stir until smooth.

With the whisk, stir in the butter one piece at a time, stirring until smooth after each addition. Remove from the hot water.

Place the yolks in a medium-size mixing bowl and stir them briefly just to mix. Gradually add the warm chocolate mixture, stirring well with the whisk until smooth. Stir in the vanilla. Set aside.

(The soufflé may be prepared ahead of time to this point and may wait for an hour or two to be completed. Let both the chocolate mixture and the whites stand at room temperature. Then, during the salad course, or after it, finish the soufflé. Or if salad has been served as a first course, serve coffee and let your guests wait a few minutes for dessert—this doesn't take long.)

In a small bowl add the salt to the whites and beat until they just barely hold a firm shape when the beaters are raised or when the whites are lifted with a rubber spatula. Do not beat them until they are dry.

Gradually, in about three additions (small at first), fold half of the whites into the chocolate and then fold the chocolate into the remaining whites—do not be too thorough; handle as little as possible. If there are a few small bits of white that have not been folded in, leave it that way. They don't matter, and it is better than handling the mixture too much.

Turn into the prepared soufflé dish. Smooth the top.

Bake for 6 minutes. Then reduce the heat to 425 degrees and bake 7 minutes more. Total baking time is 13 minutes. (With this timing the soufflé will have, and should have, a slightly soft interior which serves as a sauce and is much more delicious than a soufflé that has been baked until it is firm all the way through.) The top of the soufflé will be rounded slightly above the top of the dish. Do not bake any longer for it to rise higher or it will become too dry in the center.

Serve immediately! A hot soufflé will collapse if it stands for more than a minute or two.

Serve with an optional side dish of softly whipped cream. The cream (follow preceding recipe on page 241, substituting rum or Cognac for Grand Marnier) may be prepared ahead of time and refrigerated until you are ready. But if it stands for long it might separate slightly; if so, just stir it briefly with a wire whisk.

At the table, serve the soufflé with two large serving spoons or with a large fork and spoon, serving some of the soft center with each portion. Place a large spoonful of the optional whipped cream alongside each portion, or pass the cream.

OTHER

Confections

Fudge

1¹/₄ POUNDS

2 cups granulated sugar

½ cup strained unsweetened cocoa powder (preferably Dutch process)

⅛ teaspoon salt

⅔ cup heavy cream

2 tablespoons light corn syrup

2 tablespoons sweet butter

1 teaspoon vanilla extract

2 ounces (generous ½ cup) walnuts, cut or broken into medium-size pieces

One day recently in Palm Springs, California, I spotted a most attractive shop that sold only homemade fudge. The decor was all blue and white and in the window there was a huge shiny copper cauldron full of boiling fudge. I watched a man make the fudge right there in the window. It was a treat and I was so excited I could hardly wait for him to finish before I asked, "What causes fudge to be grainy?" He answered, "Cooking." So I said, "What do you mean?" And he said, "You either cooked it too long or not long enough or you cooked it too fast or too slowly. Or you didn't dissolve the sugar. Or it could be the weather."

"Thanks, Mister."

When I decided to write a fudge recipe for this book, I called on my friend Virginia Heffington, the food editor of the Independent Press-Telegram in Long Beach, California. I was thrilled to hear that fudge was one of her favorites; she has made it since she was a child in Iowa, and she calls herself "the fudge lady." She was quite casual about saying that it is not difficult if you follow the rules. Here is Virginia's favorite recipe.

It begins with an emphatic warning. CAUTION: Humidity causes fudge disasters. Pick a dry day!!!

It is safer to make a small amount of fudge at a time. Unless you are an experienced fudge-maker do not increase the recipe. But if you are, and if you do, increase it only by half. (In which case cook it in a 3½-to 4-quart saucepan.)

Use a candy thermometer.

Generously butter the sides of a 2- to 3-quart saucepan. Mix the sugar, cocoa, salt, cream, and corn syrup in the pan. Stir over moderate heat slowly and carefully to avoid splashing the mixture on the sides of the pan until the sugar is dissolved and the mixture comes to a boil. Cover the saucepan for 2 or 3 minutes. (Covering the pan causes steam to form, which dissolves any sugar granules that may cling to the sides—one grain of sugar can start a chain reaction and turn the whole thing granular. And the buttered pan helps; incidentally, it also keeps the fudge from boiling over. If the pan has a spout and is therefore not airtight when you cover it, carefully hold a pot holder over the opening.)

Now uncover, and place a candy thermometer in the pan. Boil without stirring until the thermometer reaches 236 degrees or the soft ball stage. (Professionals advise 234 to 236 degrees during cold weather; 236 to 238 degrees during warm weather.)

It is important now not to stir, mix, shake, or disturb the mixture. Very carefully and gently remove the saucepan from the heat. Do not remove the thermometer. Add the butter by simply placing it in the pan and letting it melt; do not stir it.

Let stand until the temperature drops to 110 degrees.

While the fudge is cooling, prepare a pan for it. I like to use a small loaf pan, which makes a 1¼-inch-thick layer of fudge. Mine is called an 8 x 4-inch pan, which measures 7 x 3½ inches on the bottom of the pan. If you use a larger pan the fudge will be just as good but not as thick. Fold two pieces of aluminum foil to fit the loaf pan, one for the length and one for the width. Press them into place in the pan.

When the fudge has cooled to 110 degrees (at that temperature the bottom of the saucepan will feel comfortably warm on the palm of your hand) remove the thermometer. Add the vanilla. Now, to beat the fudge, use a moderately heavy wooden spatula or wooden spoon. Virginia's system, which works very comfortably, is to sit and grip the pan between your knees, leaving both hands free to grapple with the spatula. First stir gently to incorporate the melted butter. Then start to stir steadily or to beat, and once you do, do not stop until the fudge is finished.

I think that knowing just how long to beat, and just when to pour, are the most important things in this recipe. And the most difficult to describe. To quote Virginia, "When the candy stiffens and loses its shine you are on borrowed time." But I think that if you beat until it is stiff or dull, it is too late. Beat until the fudge becomes very thick, or falls in thick gobs, or is thick enough almost to hold its shape when a little is dropped from the spatula. At this stage it should barely begin to lose its shine, but only barely. It should still be slightly glossy.

Quickly stir in the nuts and quickly, with the spatula, push the mixture into the lined pan. It will be too thick to pour. And Virginia says that you should not scrape the pan too well; scraping encourages grainy fudge. Quickly push the fudge into a smooth layer in the pan; it may be easiest to use your fingertips or your knuckles.

The fudge may be ready almost immediately (even while it is still slightly warm) to be cut into individual portions. As soon as it feels firm, but before it hardens, remove it from the pan by lifting the foil, and with a long, sharp knife cut the fudge into portions. I like to make 12 large squares, but you can make 24 or more.

Do not let the fudge dry out. Wrap the squares immediately, individually, in cellophane or wax paper. Or package them in an airtight box.

Fudge is best the day it is made, but it will keep for a few days at room temperature if it is well wrapped. For longer storage, freeze it. It can be frozen for months.

FIRST AID: *If your fudge turned to sugar, or if it stiffened in the saucepan, or if it crumbled when you cut portions (because you beat too long), add 2 tablespoons of cream and stir over very low heat (cutting up the fudge with the wooden spatula while you stir). Cook and stir only until warm and slightly softened but not until it is hot or thin. Remove from the heat, beat again until smooth and thick, and then turn it out of the saucepan again. (Some cooks think that this twice-cooked fudge is creamier and more smooth than otherwise.)*

If you have the opposite problem of fudge that didn't set, you didn't cook it long enough or you poured it too soon. If you think that you did not cook it long enough, add ¼ cup of milk or cream, then cook and stir constantly until it reaches 236 degrees again. Cool as above, and beat again.

But if you think that you cooked it enough and simply poured it too soon, transfer the mixture to a marble, tile, or Formica countertop. Then squeeze it between your hands and knead it as though it were bread dough until it is firm enough to hold a shape. Then roll it into a sausage shape, or form it into a square about 1 inch thick. Let stand for just a few moments and then slice the sausage shape or cut the square into portions. (Many fudge-makers think that kneaded fudge is smoother, creamier, better than fudge that has not been kneaded, so they plan accordingly to knead.)

Unless someone wants to lick the pan, the fudge that remains in the pan can be scraped out, kneaded with your hands until it is smooth and creamy, and then rolled between your hands into marble-size balls.

VARIATIONS: *Fudge may be varied in many ways. When the nuts are added you can also add ½ to 1 cup of raisins, cut-up dates, candied cherries, diced candied pineapple, diced candied ginger, or minced candied orange peel. Raisins or dates may be marinated in a bit of rum or bourbon. The nuts can be left out, or you can use any other kind of nuts (if you use almonds they are best if lightly baked), or a variety, or sunflower or pumpkin seeds. A spoon or two of liquor or liqueur can be added along with the vanilla. (A friend makes it with Grand Marnier and candied orange peel.) Rocky Road Fudge has about a cup of miniature marshmallows mixed in with the nuts. Rum Raisin Fudge has 2 tablespoons of dark rum in place of the vanilla and about ½ cup of raisins in place of the nuts (marinate for a few hours or overnight). Apricot Fudge is made with whole dried apricot halves, and then there is prune and apricot—*

Place the chocolate in the top of a small double boiler over warm water on moderate heat. Cover until partially melted. Then uncover and stir occasionally until completely melted. Remove the top of the double boiler and set aside uncovered.

In the small bowl of an electric mixer, mix the cream cheese (or stir it by hand in a bowl) until soft and smooth. Add the vanilla and salt. Gradually beat in the sugar and then add the chocolate and beat until smooth. Mix in the nuts.

Now, either line an 8-inch square pan with foil or wax paper and press the fudge into the pan, or shape the fudge by hand on a piece of plastic wrap or wax paper into an even shape about 1 inch thick and 6 inches square, or roll the fudge into a sausage shape about 1½ inches in diameter.

Wrap and refrigerate until firm. It may chill longer. Cut into squares or slices and wrap individually or package airtight.

Refrigerate or store at room temperature. Serve cold or at room temperature. (I like it cold.)

Phudge

1½ POUNDS

This uncooked cream cheese fudge is quick, foolproof, smooth, dark, delicious, and so easy that children can make it.

    4 ounces (4 squares) unsweetened chocolate
    6 ounces cream cheese, at room temperature
    ½ teaspoon vanilla extract
    ⅛ teaspoon salt
    1 pound (4 loosely packed cups) strained
        confectioners sugar
    3½ ounces (1 cup) walnuts or pecans, cut or
        broken into medium-size or large pieces

Chocolate Raisin Clusters

1 Pound

These are so easy it is ridiculous. But they are delicious. You can make them in 5 minutes (so can a five-year-old), but they must harden for a few hours before serving.

8 ounces semisweet chocolate
⅔ cup sweetened condensed milk
5 ounces (1 cup) raisins

Break up the chocolate and place it in the top of a double boiler over hot water on moderate heat. Stir occasionally until melted and smooth.

Remove the top of the double boiler. Add the condensed milk and stir until smooth, then stir in the raisins.

Use a rounded teaspoonful of the mixture for each cluster, forming 24 clusters and placing them on a piece of aluminum foil.

Let stand at room temperature for about 3 hours until they are firm. Then release each cluster and turn it over to let the bottom dry; they will dry quickly.

Store airtight. Do not let these dry out. They may be frozen. (If you freeze them be sure to let them thaw before unwrapping or they will sweat.)

Rocky Roads

1⅓ Pounds

Here's another quick, easy, and foolproof candy.

1 pound milk chocolate
12 large-size (regular) marshmallows (see Note)
6 ounces (1½ cups) pecan halves or large pieces

Prepare an 8-inch square cake pan as follows: Invert the pan and cover it with a 12-inch square of aluminum foil. Fold down the sides and corners of the foil. Remove the foil, turn the pan right side up, put the shaped foil in the pan and gently press it into place.

Cut or break the chocolate into coarse pieces and place it in the top of a double boiler over warm water on low heat. (Milk chocolate must be melted very slowly, the slower the better—it should not ever get really hot.) Cover until partially melted.

Meanwhile, cut the marshmallows into quarters. (Some people use scissors; if they stick to the marshmallows, moisten them slightly in cold water.) Set the marshmallows aside.

Uncover the chocolate and stir until completely melted and smooth. Pour about half of the chocolate into the foil-lined pan and spread it to cover the bottom of the pan; it will be a thin layer. Sprinkle with about half of the nuts and then place the marshmallow pieces evenly over all. Stir the remaining chocolate well and drizzle it over the top. It will not cover the top completely but it should be drizzled on so that it holds the nuts and marshmallows in place. Now top with the remaining nuts.

Refrigerate until firm. Remove from the pan and peel off the foil. With a long, thin, sharp knife cut the candy into 16 or 24 large squares. Wrap them individually in cellophane or wax paper. Or wrap the whole block securely in plastic wrap or aluminum foil and do not cut into squares until serving time. Or gift-wrap the whole block in one piece.

This should be stored in the refrigerator to keep the chocolate fresh-looking and to avoid any discoloring (it will keep for weeks). I think it is best to remove it from the refrigerator for a while before serving so the chocolate is not too brittle, but that is a matter of taste.

NOTE: *1⅔ cups of miniature marshmallows may be substituted for the cut-up large marshmallows, but Rocky Road connoisseurs like it better with larger pieces. Some even cut the marshmallows only into halves. And some leave them whole.*

VARIATIONS: *Walnuts or cashews are frequently substituted for pecans. And whole dried apricot halves (unchopped) or dried pitted prunes (unchopped) are often used in place of the nuts. I think any dried or candied fruits would be good either in place of or along with the nuts.*

French Chocolate Mint Truffles

20 TRUFFLES

These are dense, bittersweet chocolate candies flavored with mint, shaped to resemble natural truffles. They are easy fun to prepare and should be made at least a day before serving. Many truffle candies must be refrigerated until serving—these must not. They are served at room temperature. They may be served as dessert, with dessert, after dessert, or between meals. They are especially good after dinner with espresso and/or Cognac.

6 ounces semisweet chocolate

2 ounces (½ stick) sweet butter, cut into small bits

2 egg yolks

Approximately ¼ teaspoon peppermint extract

Unsweetened cocoa powder (preferably Dutch process)

Approximately 2 ounces additional semisweet chocolate (for coating the finished candies)

Break or chop the chocolate into medium-size pieces. Place it in the top of a small double boiler over hot water on low heat. Cover and let stand until partially melted. Uncover and stir until completely melted.

Remove the top of the double boiler temporarily. Add the butter, a few pieces at a time, and stir with a small wire whisk after each addition until smooth.

In a small bowl stir a bit of the chocolate into the yolks and then stir the yolks into the chocolate.

Replace over the hot water on low heat and stir gently with a rubber spatula for about 2 minutes.

Now, remove the top of the double boiler. Stir in the peppermint extract, adding just a few drops at a time. Taste it—make it as minty as you like (I make it strong), but add it slowly and taste it carefully. Some mint extracts taste unpleasant if you use too much.

Place the top of the double boiler in a bowl of ice and water. Stir constantly with a small wooden spatula until the mixture is firm enough to hold a definite shape.

Place a piece of wax paper in front of you. Use a slightly rounded teaspoonful of the mixture for each truffle. Place them in mounds on the wax paper, forming 20 mounds.

If the mixture is firm enough, the truffles may be rolled into shape immediately. But if it is too soft, let it stand uncovered at room temperature for about half an hour or until firm enough to handle.

Spread out two more large pieces of wax paper. Onto one, strain a generous amount of unsweetened cocoa. Coat the palms of your hands well with the cocoa.

Pick up a mound of the chocolate mixture, roll it between your hands to form an uneven ball (real truffles are very uneven), then roll it around in the cocoa and place it on the other piece of wax paper. Continue to shape all of the truffles, coating your hands with cocoa before shaping each truffle.

Let the truffles stand overnight at room temperature, uncovered or loosely covered, so the outsides dry a bit.

The 2 ounces of additional chocolate must be ground to a fine powder; it may be done in a food processor, a blender, a nut grinder, or on a fine metal grater. Spread the ground chocolate on wax paper and roll the truffles around in it to coat them again.

These are best when they are very fresh, before they dry out too much and while they are still creamy soft in the centers. They may be kept at room temperature for a day or two but they should be refrigerated or frozen for longer storage. (Bring them back to room temperature before serving.)

VARIATIONS: *Truffle variations are endless. Here are just a few. To make plain chocolate truffles simply omit the mint. Then, if you wish, vary some by adding ground or very finely chopped nuts (toasted hazelnuts are special) or chopped shredded coconut. Or rum-soaked raisins or dates, or cut up soft, dried apricots. Or some diced candied (or drained preserved) ginger. Or chopped candied chestnuts. And/or a teaspoon or two of rum, Cognac, bourbon, Grand Marnier, Amaretto, whiskey, etc. For a coffee flavor add coffee extract. Or roll the shaped truffles in very finely chopped nuts or coconut in place of the cocoa and ground chocolate. Etcetera.*

Chocolate-Covered Strawberries

1¹/₄ POUNDS OF DIPPED BERRIES

This is fun!

Chocolate-covered strawberries have become very popular in the last few years with a group of elite food people. Although they are the simplest thing imaginable—any child can make them—they are featured by some of the country's most expensive/exclusive/posh candymakers, where they cost a fortune.

Since they are made with only strawberries and chocolate, their quality depends entirely on the quality of the berries and the chocolate.

Naturally these will be more dramatic if you use large berries, although small berries are very cute and are often more delicious. If possible, use berries with stems (which I have seen in other parts of the country but have never been able to buy in Florida). The berries must be ripe but not soft—do not use any berries that have soft spots. Do not wash the berries; just brush them gently with a dry pastry brush. (But if you would feel better about washing them, swish them around quickly in a large bowl of cold water and then drain on several thicknesses of paper towels for hours until they are completely dry.)

Some chocolate dippers refrigerate the berries for a few hours before dipping them: "If the berries are cold the chocolate sets faster and there is less chance that it will streak or discolor." Others let them stand on a rack at room temperature for a few hours before dipping: "To dehydrate the surface." I've tried both and I don't see any difference.

You can use any kind of sweet, semisweet, bittersweet, or milk chocolate. It may be real chocolate or compound chocolate (see page 5).

These may be served as dessert, with dessert, or as a decoration for some other dessert. Or serve them as candy.

They are perishable but they do keep for the better part of a day.

Line the bottom of a tray large enough to hold the dipped berries with wax paper or aluminum foil.

One small "pint" box of berries will be enough to serve four people if you are serving these as a dessert. The strawberries in such a box will measure almost 4 cups and will weigh 1 pound. For one such box you will need 4 ounces of chocolate.

Break up or coarsely chop the chocolate and place it in the top of a small double boiler over warm water on low heat. Cover until the chocolate is partially melted. Then uncover and stir until the chocolate is all melted and completely smooth.

Remove the top of the double boiler for easy handling but if the chocolate starts to thicken replace it over warm water.

Hold a berry by the stem or by the green leaves (the hull) and dip it to about three-quarters length (not all the way—let some of the red berry show at the top). The chocolate coating should not be too thick and heavy nor should it be as thin as on a Good Humor. Wipe excess chocolate off against the rim of the pot (but don't wipe so much that you leave that section uncovered). Place the dipped berry on its side on the lined tray. (If the chocolate gets too low to dip the last few berries, transfer it to a small custard cup or a small wine glass.)

If you have used compound chocolate it will set quickly at room temperature and will not have to be refrigerated. If you have used real chocolate place the tray of dipped berries in the refrigerator only until the chocolate is firm, no longer. Then gently lift each berry by the stem or leaves to release it from the paper.

Now, do not refrigerate these. They should be stored and served (within 24 hours) at room temperature. If they are refrigerated the chocolate will sweat when returned to room temperature. And if they are cold when they are served, the chocolate will be brittle and the berries will be difficult to eat.

(If you have some leftover melted chocolate, save it and melt it again the next time you dip berries. Or use it to make Chocolate Slabs (see page 263) for some other dessert.)

NOTE: *Candymakers also dip orange sections—you must be sure that the membrane is not broken and that they are seedless oranges; dip them to cover about two-thirds of the section. Or place toothpicks into 1-inch pieces of banana, and dip to cover all or part of the banana. Or dip individual seedless green grapes on small stems. Or, or, or . . .*

Stuffed Figs au Chocolat

These are more like candy than dessert but whatever they are, they are delicious, unusual, elegant, beautiful-looking, and fun to make. The figs are stuffed with one chocolate and then coated with another chocolate. They are finger-food, like chocolate-covered cherries. There is very little cooking involved, but quite a bit of hand-work—all of which goes quickly.

They may be refrigerated for a week or so, or they may be frozen.

> 1 pound (about 24) dried brown figs (although they are dried, they must be soft and moist, not hard and dry; and, although I have used only brown figs to stuff, I don't see any reason why black ones would not be equally good)

It is best to use figs that have been packed loosely rather than those that have been pressed into an almost solid mass. (However, I have used the pressed ones—it is just a bit more work.)

Press each fig between your fingers to shape it so it will stand upright when stuffed.

With a small, sharp knife cut a slit through the bottom of each fig opposite the stem. Extend the slit about halfway up to the stem on both sides.

With your fingers, open each fig and form a large pocket to hold the stuffing.

Prepare a tray that will hold the stuffed figs by lining it with wax paper or aluminum foil, and make room for it in the refrigerator or freezer.

CHOCOLATE STUFFING

> ¼ cup heavy cream
> 4 ounces semisweet or bittersweet chocolate (see Note)
> 1 tablespoon butter
> 1 egg yolk

Place the cream in a small saucepan over moderate heat until it just barely comes to a boil.

Meanwhile, coarsely chop or break up the chocolate.

Add the chocolate to the hot cream and stir until the chocolate is melted and the mixture is smooth. Remove from the heat. Add the butter and stir until the butter is melted. Let stand to cool slightly—about 2 or 3 minutes. Stir in the egg yolk until smooth.

Transfer to a small bowl for easy handling. Place in the freezer, stirring occasionally until the stuffing is about as stiff as chilled whipped butter.

With a small metal spatula or a table knife, fill the figs with the chocolate mixture. It is best to fill each half and then press the cut bottom together to close and reform the fig—each fig will hold about a teaspoon or a bit more of the stuffing.

Place the filled figs stem up on the prepared tray and refrigerate or freeze while you make the glaze—the figs must be cold when they are glazed.

CHOCOLATE GLAZE

> 6 ounces semisweet or bittersweet chocolate (see Note)
> 1 tablespoon vegetable shortening

Coarsely chop or break the chocolate and place it in the top of a small double boiler over warm water on low heat. Add the vegetable shortening. Cover until partially melted. Then uncover and stir until completely melted and smooth. Remove the top of the double boiler, dry the underside of the pot (a drop of water would spoil the chocolate), and transfer the chocolate to a small custard cup for easy handling.

Line another tray or a cookie sheet with aluminum foil or wax paper to hold the glazed figs.

Hold a chilled stuffed fig by the stem and dip it in the chocolate almost but not quite up to the stem. Hold it briefly over the custard cup for the excess chocolate to run off, wipe the bottom of the fig against the side of the cup to remove excess chocolate, and place it stem up on the prepared tray. (There should not be so much chocolate on any fig that it runs down and forms a heavy layer on the bottom.) Continue to glaze all of the figs.

Refrigerate until the glaze is completely firm. Then carefully remove the figs from the aluminum foil or wax paper.

Place them on a serving dish and cover with plastic wrap.

Refrigerate for at least a few hours or several days if you wish. Or freeze them (thaw overnight in the refrigerator or for an hour or so at room temperature before unwrapping).

Although these may be served either cold or at room temperature, I like them better cold.

NOTE: *Use any semisweet or bittersweet chocolate. I have made these with many different chocolates—I especially like them with extra-bittersweet.*

Chocolate Fondue

6 to 8 Servings

Fondue is French for melted; a fondue is a melted food. Originally it was a melted cheese dish served with chunks of bread. It is probably the most popular dish from Switzerland. The recipe has come a long way to this chocolate version—a fun dessert. It is especially good for a casual party.

To serve it properly you need a fondue pot or some other way of keeping the chocolate warm. And it must be within comfortable reach of all the guests; on a very long table you need more than one fondue pot. (It is most cozy to serve this on a round table with a lazy Susan in the middle.)

You will serve the warm chocolate mixture and an assortment (few or many—it's up to you) of dunkable foods. The dunkables may be on one large platter, or many small ones, or each guest can be served a plate with an assortment. Most commonly they are well-drained pineapple chunks which may be fresh, canned, or frozen and thawed. (Some fonduers rave about the delicious quality of frozen pineapple chunks dipped in the warm chocolate. If you want to try that, the pineapple, which may be fresh, canned, or frozen and thawed, should be well drained. Each chunk should have a toothpick stuck in it to lift it with. The pieces should be frozen—not touching each other—on a foil-covered tray.) Fresh strawberries are wonderful. So are orange sections, apple wedges, banana chunks, lady fingers, graham crackers, chunks of angel food or pound cake. And marshmallows, candied orange and grapefruit peel. Dried figs, dried apricots, pitted dried prunes and dates. And most especially (seriously, these are divine), saltines, pretzels, and plain salted but unflavored matzohs.

Long-handled fondue forks might or might not

be necessary depending on the dippers you serve. *Some of them (saltines, pretzels, graham crackers) are finger-food. But some fresh fruits, some dried fruits, marshmallows, or squares of pound cake will require a fondue fork for each person.*

I think it is best to make the chocolate mixture in the kitchen and transfer it to the fondue pot just before serving. Fondue recipes are very flexible. You can vary the chocolates and the liquors. Just remember to keep the mixture thick; it should coat the dunkable items heavily. Here are three different popular recipes.

Toblerone Fondue

12 ounces Toblerone milk chocolate (see Note)
½ cup heavy cream
3 tablespoons light rum, kirsch, or Grand Marnier

Break up the chocolate or chop it coarsely. Place it in a small saucepan with the cream over low heat. Stir frequently until melted and smooth. If necessary, stir briskly with a small wire whisk. (This may be done ahead of time and kept warm over warm water on low heat. Or it may be reheated.) Just before serving stir in the liquor or liqueur and transfer to the fondue pot. The mixture should be thick, but if it is too thick add a bit more cream.

NOTE: *To make a semisweet fondue, substitute Toblerone bittersweet chocolate for half of the milk chocolate.*

Hershey Fondue

1 pound Hershey's milk chocolate
4 ounces Hershey's Special Dark chocolate
¾ cup light cream
3 tablespoons kirsch, or ½ teaspoon almond extract

Follow the directions for the above Toblerone Fondue.

Maillard's Fondue

2 cups heavy cream
4 ounces cream cheese
6 or 8 ounces Maillard's Eagle Sweet chocolate or any other semisweet chocolate
Optional: 1 or 2 tablespoons Cognac

In a heavy saucepan over moderate heat bring the cream to a boil. Add the cream cheese and stir until melted and smooth. Break up the chocolate or chop it coarsely, add it to the cream and cream cheese, and stir until melted and smooth. If necessary, stir briskly with a small wire whisk. Just before serving stir in the optional Cognac and transfer to the fondue pot. The mixture should be thick but if it is too thick add a bit of milk.

Sauces

The World's Best Hot Fudge Sauce

1 Cup

This is very thick, coal black, as shiny as wet tar, and not too sweet. It will turn chewy and even thicker when it is served over cold ice cream—great! It may be served hot or warm, but at room temperature or chilled it will be too thick. It may be refrigerated for a week or two before serving.

½ cup heavy cream
3 tablespoons sweet butter, cut into small pieces
⅓ cup granulated sugar
⅓ cup dark brown sugar, firmly packed
Pinch of salt
½ cup strained unsweetened Dutch-process cocoa powder (it must be Dutch process to have the right color and flavor)

Place the cream and butter in a heavy 1-quart saucepan over moderate heat. Stir until the butter is melted and the cream just comes to a low boil. Add both sugars and stir for a few minutes until they are dissolved. (The surest test is to taste; cook and taste until you do not feel any undissolved granules in your mouth.)

Reduce the heat. Add the salt and cocoa and stir briskly with a small wire whisk until smooth. (If the sauce is not smooth—if there are any small lumps of undissolved cocoa—press against them, and stir well, with a rubber spatula.) Remove from the heat.

Serve immediately or reheat slowly, stirring frequently, in the top of a double boiler over hot water, or in a heavy saucepan over the lowest heat.

This should be thick, but if it is reheated it may be too thick. If so, stir in a bit of hot water, adding very little at a time.

NOTE: *If you plan to store the sauce in the refrigerator, use a straight-sided glass jar or any covered container that flares out at the top. The sauce will become too firm when it is chilled to be spooned out of a jar. It is best to place the jar in hot water until the block of sauce melts on the outside and can be poured out of the jar. Then place the sauce in the top of a small double boiler over hot water, or in a small heavy saucepan over the lowest heat. With a wooden spatula cut the sauce into pieces as you stir until completely melted.*

Milk-Chocolate-with-Almonds-Bar Sauce

1 Cup

Everyone loves this—be prepared with enough. One cup should be enough for four portions if it is served over ice cream, but I have seen times when two cups was not too much. Yes, it is as easy as it sounds.

½ pound milk chocolate bar with almonds.
¼ cup boiling water

Break up the chocolate and place it in the top of a small double boiler.

Milk chocolate must be melted very slowly or it may become lumpy, so place the top of the double boiler over warm water on low heat. Cover and let stand until melted. Milk chocolate holds its shape when melted—the only way you will know it is melted is by stirring it; stir with a rubber spatula.

When the chocolate is melted, add the boiling water all at once and continue to stir with a rubber spatula until the chocolate and water are smoothly blended.

Serve right away, or keep warm over warm water, or let cool and serve at room temperature, or reheat slowly over warm water.

If the sauce thickens too much while standing, stir in a few drops of water. (The thought that a chocolate sauce could be too thick reminds me of an old saying that Grandma Heatter used when someone complained about something that was too good: She would say, "The bride was too beautiful.")

This is especially popular served slightly warm over vanilla and/or coffee ice cream. Or anything.

Rum Mocha Chocolate Sauce

2¹/₃ CUPS

This is marvelous!

¼ **pound (1 stick) butter**
1 **cup granulated sugar**
¹/₃ **cup strained unsweetened cocoa powder**
2 **tablespoons dark rum**
1 **cup heavy cream**
¹/₈ **teaspoon salt**
1 **teaspoon dry instant coffee**
1 **teaspoon vanilla extract**

In a medium-size heavy saucepan over low heat melt the butter. Add the sugar, cocoa, rum, heavy cream, and salt. Stir over moderate heat until the mixture comes to a boil. Add the instant coffee and stir to dissolve. Reduce the heat and let simmer for 5 minutes. Remove from the heat and stir in the vanilla.

This may be served hot, warm, at room temperature, or cold. It may be kept warm or reheated over hot water. If may be refrigerated for weeks. It's wonderful over ice cream—it does not harden.

Michael Guérard's French Chocolate Sauce

SCANT 2 CUPS OF SAUCE

Paula Wolfert, who has written delicious cookbooks on Mediterranean and Moroccan food, gave this recipe to me as one of her favorites when I told her I was writing this book. It is quick and easy, dark and delicious. Serve it hot over ice cream. Monsieur Guérard serves it with honey ice cream. It will keep in the refrigerator for two or three weeks.

> ¾ cup strained unsweetened cocoa powder (Use Dutch-process cocoa for the right flavor—I use Droste's.)
> ¾ cup granulated sugar
> Pinch of salt
> 1 cup cold water
> 2 tablespoons sweet butter

In a 6-cup saucepan stir the cocoa, sugar, and salt to mix. Add the water and stir until smooth (a small wire whisk will blend them quickly). Place over moderate heat and stir with a rubber or wooden spatula until the mixture comes to a low boil. Let it simmer for 3 minutes. Add the butter, stir until melted, and simmer again for 3 minutes more.

Serve immediately or set aside and reheat.

Store in a covered jar in the refrigerator.

Basic Chocolate Sauce (with 8 variations)

2 CUPS

This will not harden over cold ice cream—it will remain saucy. It may be kept for many weeks in the refrigerator.

> 4 ounces (4 squares) unsweetened chocolate
> 1 cup granulated sugar
> ⅛ teaspoon salt
> 1 tablespoon butter
> ½ pint (1 cup) light cream
> ½ teaspoon vanilla extract

Chop the chocolate coarsely and place it over the lowest possible heat in a heavy saucepan with about a 4- to 6-cup capacity. (Remember that chocolate burns easily. If you don't have a really heavy pan, do this step in a double boiler, in which case the chocolate does not have to be chopped.) Stir frequently until the chocolate is melted. Stir in the sugar, salt, butter, and then gradually add the cream, stirring until smooth. (If you have used a double boiler, remove the bottom now and place the top over direct heat.)

Increase the heat slightly to low-medium and stir constantly for 4 or 5 minutes until the sauce thickens slightly. Do not boil.

Remove from the heat and stir in the vanilla.

Serve this either warm or at room temperature— it may be kept warm in the top of a double boiler over hot water. If it is too stiff at room temperature, either warm it slightly or stir in a bit of cream, milk, coffee, or water. To reheat after refrigerating, stir it in the top of a double boiler over hot water.

Variations Using Basic Chocolate Sauce

LIQUOR

Add a spoon or two or more of any liquor or liqueur to the finished sauce. Rum, Cognac, and whiskey are the most common additions. Bourbon is good. Grand Marnier is good. Crème de menthe or crème de cacao or crème d'almond are all good. Amaretto is sensational with chocolate. Whichever you choose, add it slowly, tasting often.

MARMALADE

Melt about ¼ to ½ cup of orange marmalade. Add it to the sauce and, if you like, add a dash of Grand Marnier or Curaçao.

MINT

Along with the vanilla add a few drops of peppermint extract. Add very little at a time, taste it often and carefully, and make it as minty as you like.

CARAMEL

Use semisweet chocolate instead of unsweetened, and firmly packed dark or light brown sugar instead of granulated.

NUT

Add about ⅓ cup of coarsely cut or broken walnuts or pecans, or whole unblanched almonds. Or add toasted whole blanched or unblanched almonds. (To toast the almonds, place them in a small, shallow tin in the middle of a 350-degree oven. Shake the pan occasionally until the nuts are lightly toasted, about 10 minutes.)

MOCHA

Add 1 to 2 teaspoons dry powdered instant coffee or espresso while stirring the hot sauce.

EXTRA-BITTERSWEET

This is strong, dense, thick, and *really* bittersweet. Use only ½ cup of sugar instead of 1 cup. (That will reduce the yield to 1⅔ cups.) Since this is so dense, it should be served in small quantities.

BLACK FOREST SAUCE

Chocolate, cherries, and kirsch are a magnificent combination. Use any kind of canned or frozen pitted cherries, well drained. Or use fresh ones if you have a cherry pitter. Add the cherries and add kirsch, to your taste, to the basic sauce.

Chocolate Decorations

All of the following decorations may be made well ahead of time. They should be stored in the refrigerator or the freezer. They should be brought to room temperature before they are unwrapped or uncovered. Otherwise, they sweat when the air hits them and moisture forms on them. They should be cold when you place them on a dessert, and should be handled as little as possible to avoid fingermarks.

If they are made with real chocolate that has not been tempered, they will discolor after several hours at room temperature. They will not discolor in the freezer or the refrigerator. Therefore, if you use real chocolate, refrigerate the decorated dessert until serving time.

Compound chocolate (see page 5) will not discolor.

Grated Chocolate

Use any kind of semisweet chocolate, and grate it against a coarse grater, in a small Mouli rotary grater, or with a swivel-bladed vegetable peeler. Work over paper, then use a spoon to sprinkle the chocolate over the dessert. To transfer the chocolate to a jar for storage, lift the paper and funnel the chocolate into the jar.

Chocolate Shavings

Chocolate shavings are made with a swivel-blade vegetable peeler. They will vary in size and shape depending on the chocolate you use; compound chocolate (see page 5) will be softer and will form larger shavings than a dry or brittle chocolate. And a thick piece of chocolate will make larger and more dramatic shavings than a thin one. Candy stores often sell chunks of chocolate by the pound, and this chocolate frequently has a better quality for shaving than many other chocolates do. Milk chocolate is soft and flexible and will not crack when it is shaved (although some may actually be so soft that shavings will not curl—pieces will wave and bend more than curl). White chocolate generally behaves quite well for shavings, and may look most attractive (sometimes startling) on a dark chocolate dessert.

If the room is cold and the chocolate is too brittle, sometimes it is possible to soften the chocolate slightly by holding it firmly for a minute or so between the palms of your hands; the heat of your hands will warm the surface of the chocolate and soften it a bit. It may be necessary to repeat warming it in your hands constantly while working with it.

The pressure you put on the vegetable peeler will also affect the results.

Work over wax paper. Try different chocolates,

different amounts of pressure. Hold the chocolate in your left hand; as you move the vegetable peeler toward yourself, press it very firmly against a side (either the wide or narrow side) of the chocolate.

If you are not going to use the shavings right away, slide a cookie sheet under the paper and transfer to the freezer or refrigerator until firm. Then gently lift the paper and funnel the shavings into a container. Store them indefinitely in the refrigerator or the freezer.

When you are ready to use the shavings, gently transfer them with a large spoon to the top of a dessert, or pour them carefully right from the container onto the dessert.

Chocolate Slabs

Coarsely chop or break up 2 ounces of any semisweet chocolate. Place it in the top of a small double boiler over hot water on moderate heat. Cover until partially melted, then uncover and stir until completely melted and smooth. Remove the top of the double boiler.

Tear off a piece of wax paper about 12 inches square. Pour the chocolate out onto the paper. With a long, narrow metal spatula spread the chocolate into a thin layer about 10 inches square. Work quickly before the chocolate starts to harden. Do not worry about making it perfectly smooth and do not fuss with the edges, but do try to keep them as thick as the rest.

Slide a cookie sheet under the paper and place in the freezer, or in the refrigerator.

When the chocolate is firm quickly peel the paper away from the chocolate. Handling as little as possible, break the chocolate into large, irregular pieces.

Store the slabs in a box in the refrigerator.

TO USE: *Handle as little as possible. Place the slabs upright in whipped cream on top of pies or other desserts. They will be different shapes, different sizes, and will look dramatic.*

Refrigerate the dessert until serving time. These crisp slabs will soften and fold over on themselves if they are left standing on a dessert in a room that is very warm.

Chocolate Leaves

You will need fresh green leaves, preferably gardenia, ivy, or rose leaves. Although I have used much larger leaves with great success. Try to select leaves that are firm rather than soft (if the leaf is too thin and delicate, it will tear while you are working with it). And especially select leaves that have markedly raised veins on the underside of the leaf.

Separate the leaves, but keep enough stem on each leaf to hold it with (⅛ inch is enough if that is all there is). Wash and dry thoroughly, patting both sides of each leaf with a towel.

You can use any kind of chocolate, real or compound (see page 5). Leaves made with real chocolate will have to be refrigerated or they will discolor after a while. I usually use 1-ounce squares of Baker's Semisweet, and I store the leaves in the refrigerator. The amount of chocolate to use depends on the number of leaves you want, but a few ounces should be enough for a moderate number of leaves.

Coarsely chop the chocolate and place it in the top of a small double boiler over hot water on low heat. Cover until the chocolate is partially melted, then uncover and stir until it is completely melted and smooth. Remove the top of the double boiler.

Hold a leaf upside down in your left hand. With a small, narrow metal spatula or with a pastry brush spread a thin and even layer of the chocolate over the underside (the veined side) of the leaf. Be careful not to let the chocolate run onto the front of the leaf;

with a fingertip, wipe the edges of the front to make sure there is no chocolate there. Place the leaf, chocolate side up, on a small plate in the freezer or refrigerator for a few minutes only until the chocolate is completely set and firm. Then, gently and carefully, peel away the green leaf, starting at the stem end and handling the chocolate leaf as little as possible. Immediately put the chocolate leaf on a small tray. (If the chocolate in the pot begins to harden while you are working with it, replace it over warm water.)

If the green leaf has not been torn it may be reused.

Continue to make as many leaves as you want. Store in a covered box in the refrigerator or the freezer.

Use these leaves to top any dessert, either standing them on an angle or placing them flat on whipped cream, cake icing, or ice cream. Although I make these only with dark semisweet chocolate, I have friends who use a variety of chocolates: dark semisweet chocolate, lighter milk chocolate, and white chocolate. (They usually lay the different colored leaves overlapping each other in a circular design around the top of a cake, or stand them upright around the sides of a cake.)

Chocolate Curls

You can make these curls with any semisweet chocolate: I have used many and they all worked equally well. But if you use real chocolate, it is best to use the curls only for refrigerated desserts. If the curls stand at room temperature for more than a few hours they discolor, although they keep indefinitely in the refrigerator or the freezer.

You can make these curls only in a cool, dry, room. If the room is warm and humid, the chocolate may be too sticky to handle. If your kitchen is not air-conditioned, wait for a cool, dry day and then make a lot of these.

For 16 to 20 1½-inch curls—moderately sensational—coarsely chop 3 ounces semisweet chocolate and place it in the top of a small double boiler over warm water on low heat. Stir occasionally until the chocolate is partially melted. Then stir constantly until it is completely melted and smooth.

Tear off two pieces of wax paper, each about 12 inches long. Place one on a smooth work surface. Dry the underside of the section of the double boiler containing the chocolate so that no water drips. Pour the chocolate onto the middle of the wax paper and cover it with the other piece of wax paper. With your fingers gently smooth over the top piece of wax paper, spreading the chocolate into a 6- or 7-inch squarish shape—don't worry about an even surface or exact edges, just make it rather square.

Then, with a rolling pin, preferably one that is not too heavy, gently roll over the top piece of paper several times in each direction to spread the chocolate into about a 10-inch square shape. Again, don't worry too much about the edges but now the chocolate must be as smooth and level as you can make it, and about ¹⁄₁₆ inch thick (thin).

Slide a cookie sheet under the bottom paper and transfer it to the freezer for a few minutes until the chocolate is set and the paper can be peeled away easily. Peel off the top piece just to release and then replace it. Invert both pieces of paper with the chocolate between them. Peel off the other piece of paper and do not replace it. Let stand for just a few minutes until the chocolate has reached room temperature and is flexible but not wet or sticky. (Don't walk away and leave it until later; if it stands too long the curls

might crack as you roll them. It sounds as though it would be the opposite, but that is what happens.)

With a small, sharp knife and a ruler trim one side of the chocolate square to make an even edge; remove excess. With the knife and the ruler cut strips 1½ inches wide, parallel with the trimmed side. Then cut the strips into 2½-inch lengths.

Using the knife as a spatula, transfer one of the strips to the edge of your work surface (the edge closest to you). Now use the handle of a large wooden spoon—the handle must be round and should be about ³⁄₈ to ½ inch in diameter. A smaller diameter will make a tighter, less dramatic curl.

Don't touch the chocolate any more than necessary or the heat of your hands may melt it. Place the end of the handle along the 1½-inch edge of the chocolate nearest you. With your fingers, start the curl by loosely curling the end of the chocolate over the handle. Then roll the handle toward the other end of the chocolate, rolling the chocolate as you do. Do not roll too tightly or the curl will not slide off the handle easily.

Carefully slide the curl off the handle and place it on wax paper, seam down. Shape all of the curls.

Slide a cookie sheet under the wax paper, transfer to the freezer or refrigerator until firm, and then place the curls in a small freezer box. Store the curls in the refrigerator or the freezer.

NOTES: *1. If the chocolate is sticky when you start to form a curl, let it stand at room temperature for just a few minutes.*

2. If the chocolate doesn't behave beautifully, the room is too warm or you have rolled it too thin or not thin enough. It may be remelted and rerolled. (Leftover scraps may be remelted, if you wish.)

3. After you have tried these you will see that they can be made any length, shorter or longer, and they can be made fatter or thinner.

4. Don't attempt more than 3 ounces of chocolate at a time, or the last pieces of chocolate will have stood too long and may crack while they are being formed.

Chocolate Cones

These take time and patience, and an ability to work with something small. Making them can be a delightful way to spend a spare hour or so; then they can be stored indefinitely in the freezer or refrigerator. It is a luxury to have these on hand for decorating a dessert in the most elegant, but simple, style. They are tiny, hollow cones of chocolate, and they do look very special. The smaller they are, the more chic and classy; also, the more difficult to make.

Cut wax paper into squares measuring 4 to 5 inches. Cut each square in half to form two triangles. Roll each triangle into a cone by rolling the two outer points, one around the other, to the center point. Then double-fold the points to hold it all in place securely (see illustrations). The tip must be tightly closed or the chocolate will run out. (Several people have told me that they find it helpful to secure the cone with a piece of Scotch tape over the seam and around the cone before the points are double-folded.) You will need one paper cone for each chocolate cone.

These can be made with any semisweet chocolate (real or compound, see page 5). A few ounces of chocolate will be enough for a moderate number of cones. Coarsely chop the chocolate and place it in the top of a small double boiler over hot water on low heat. Cover until partially melted, then uncover and stir until completely melted and smooth. Remove the top of the double boiler.

With a small, pointed paring knife, spread the inside of a cone with the chocolate. Coat it completely, making sure that you do not leave any empty spots, or any spots that are so thin that the chocolate will break when you remove the paper. The chocolate should not run over the top of the cone onto the outside of the paper.

Place the chocolate-lined cone on its side on a small plate in the freezer or the refrigerator for a few minutes only until the chocolate is set and firm.

Then gently and carefully, with a light touch, peel off the wax paper, handling the cone as little as possible. (Sometimes it seems easiest to unfold the double-folded point and then unroll the paper. Or you might prefer to start a small tear anywhere in the top of the cone, and unroll from there.) If you have used Scotch tape it should be cut first with small scissors.

Repeat to make additional cones. Pack them carefully in a small, strong box. Store in the refrigerator or the freezer.

To use these, place them on a cake before the icing is dry—one cone to a portion. Place them on their sides with the open ends pointing out and the pointed ends toward the center. Resist the temptation to fill them with a squirt of whipped cream or buttercream; it would hide their thinness and delicacy.

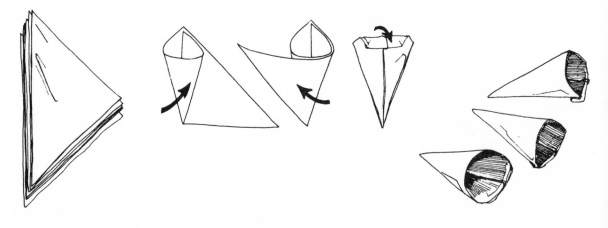

Chocolate Cigarettes

These are long, thin, cigarette-shaped curls; dramatic and professional. They must be made with a compound chocolate (see page 5), and you will need a marble surface to work on.

To make a very generous amount (you can make much less) coarsely chop about 8 ounces of a compound chocolate. Place it in the top of a double boiler over hot water on low heat. Cover until partially melted, then uncover and stir until completely melted and smooth. Do not allow the chocolate to get any hotter than necessary. Remove it from the heat, stir gently for a minute or so to cool a bit, and then pour it out onto the marble, forming a strip about 10 inches long and 3 to 4 inches wide. The chocolate strip will be about ¼ to ⅜ inch thick. Let stand at room temperature until the chocolate is no longer soft or sticky to the touch.

To shape the cigarettes, use a long, heavy knife—I use a Sabatier cook's knife with a 12-inch blade. Hold the knife straight across the 3- to 4-inch width of the chocolate, very close to (almost against) the right-hand end of the chocolate, with the blade of the knife tilted at a 45-degree angle (the sharp edge of the blade against the right-hand end; the top of the blade tilted toward the opposite end).

Cut down slowly and firmly. The chocolate will roll around itself as it is cut. Repeat, each time plac-ing the blade close to the cut end; the curls should be paper-thin.

Gently transfer the curls with a wide metal spatula to a tray or a firm box. Cover the tray with plastic wrap, or cover the box. Store in the refrigerator or the freezer.

Drinks

BONANZA CHOCOLATE DRINK,
   HOT OR COLD   269

MOCHA-BRANDY-
   CHOCOLATE THICK SHAKE   269

HOMEMADE CHOCOLATE SYRUP
   (with 19 different drinks and
   suggested variations)   270

Bonanza Chocolate Drink, Hot or Cold

5 CUPS

This is smooth/rich/creamy/flavorful/satisfying—it is the ultimate hot or cold chocolate drink. Mocha-flavored. Serve it any time, from breakfast to a midnight supper; take a thermos of it, hot or cold, on a trip, on a picnic, or to a sporting event. It may be made a day or two ahead.

1½ cups milk
6 ounces semisweet chocolate (see Note)
¼ cup granulated sugar
⅛ teaspoon salt
2 cups strong, hot coffee (I use 4 tablespoons of instant coffee dissolved in 2 cups of boiling water)
1 cup heavy or light cream
1 teaspoon vanilla extract

Place the milk and chocolate in a 2- to 3-quart heavy saucepan over moderate heat. Stir occasionally until the chocolate is melted. Stir with a wire whisk until smooth; if the mixture is not perfectly smooth—if there are little flecks of chocolate—beat it with an electric mixer or an egg beater. (It might be necessary to transfer the mixture to the small bowl of an electric mixer to beat it.)

Add the sugar and salt, stir, and bring the mixture to a boil. Reduce the heat and let simmer for 5 minutes, scraping the pan occasionally with a rubber spatula. Stir in the coffee and cream; then let it just come to a simmer again. Stir in the vanilla.

Serve immediately. Or keep it warm, stirring occasionally, over low heat. Or let it cool, stirring occasionally to prevent a skin from forming.

It may be refrigerated and served very cold (in chilled glasses). Or it may be refrigerated and then reheated before serving, and served very hot. If you serve this hot you may, if you wish, beat or whisk it until foamy before serving.

NOTE: *You can use any semisweet. If you use a thin bar chocolate, break it up; if you use 1-ounce squares, chop them coarsely; if you use morsels, use them as they are.*

VARIATION: *To make a rich, rich milkshake with this chocolate drink, use 1 scoop of chocolate ice cream (bought or homemade, see page 222) for each cup of the cold drink; blend in a blender until foamy, and serve immediately in glasses that have been chilled in the freezer. Serve with straws. SENSATIONAL!*

Mocha-Brandy-Chocolate Thick Shake

Wonderful things can happen with chocolate ice cream, Cognac, and coffee. This extra-thick drink can be served after dinner (dessert, coffee, and brandy all in one), or almost any time of the day or night.

For each serving, in a glass measuring cup dissolve 1 teaspoon instant espresso or other instant coffee in a few spoonfuls of hot cream (heavy or light), or milk, or water. Add cold milk or cream to the ¼-cup line. Transfer to a blender. Add 1 extra-large scoop of chocolate ice cream, or half chocolate and half coffee ice cream—it is best to cut the ice cream into pieces—and 1 ounce (2 tablespoons) of Cognac (see Note). Blend only until smooth, or even leave a few little pieces of ice cream. Serve immediately in a chilled glass, with an optional spoonful of whipped cream on top, and a straw.

VARIATION: *A Chocolate Tom and Jerry Shake is the same recipe made with half Cognac and half rum.*

NOTE: *Cognac and brandy may be used interchangeably. They are both brandy. Cognac is an extra-fine brandy that comes from the Cognac section of France.*

Homemade Chocolate Syrup

(with 19 different drinks and suggested variations)

3¹/₂ CUPS OF SYRUP

This is thinner than chocolate sauce and is used for making hot or cold chocolate milk drinks. Store it in the refrigerator and it will keep indefinitely. Use it to make either one portion at a time, or many.

Following this recipe are 19 different drinks and suggested variations, all of which call for the syrup. In this drink department you can be especially creative and make up your own. Any drink made with your own homemade syrup and homemade ice cream is divine, and the combinations are limitless.

Of course you know that children will adore these and will love you for making them. But try serving thick shakes or frosteds to a bunch of adults

who might not have had one in umpteen years, don't expect one, and don't even think they want one. After the first sip just sit back, watch them enjoy, and listen to the compliments.

> 1 cup strained unsweetened cocoa powder
>   (preferably Dutch process)
> 2 cups cold water (or cold black coffee)
> 2 cups granulated sugar
> ¼ teaspoon salt
> 1½ teaspoons vanilla extract

In a heavy 2-quart saucepan off the heat, stir the cocoa and water (or coffee) until smooth (a wire whisk will blend them quickly). Place over moderate heat, change to a rubber spatula, and stir, scraping the bottom constantly until the mixture comes to a low boil. Add the sugar and salt and stir until dissolved. Bring to a low boil again and let simmer slowly for 3 minutes. Remove from the heat and set aside to cool. Stir in the vanilla.

Store in airtight jars in the refrigerator.

Cold Drinks

(made with Homemade Chocolate Syrup)

The colder the better for cold drinks. If you have room, chill the glasses in the freezer (or fill them ahead of time with cracked ice or ice cubes and let them stand awhile to chill). If the drink is made in a blender, it is good to chill the blender jar in the freezer, too. Or place the prepared drink in the blender jar in the freezer for about half an hour and then blend again just before serving. Or if you have prepared the drink ahead of time in a glass or a pitcher, and if you have room enough and time, place that in the freezer for about half an hour before serving; then stir from the bottom just before serving.

COLD CHOCOLATE MILK

For a very chocolaty drink, stir ¼ cup of Homemade Chocolate Syrup into 1 cup of cold whole or skimmed milk for each serving. For a milder drink, use a bit less syrup or more milk. For a richer drink, use Half-and-Half in place of the milk, or use light or heavy cream in place of part of the milk.

CHOCOLATE FLOAT

Add a scoop of chocolate ice cream to a large glass of the above Cold Chocolate Milk. Serve with a long-handled spoon and a straw.

CHOCOLATE FROSTED

Prepare the above Cold Chocolate Milk. Place it in a blender with a scoop of chocolate ice cream for each glass of milk, blend until foamy, and serve quickly in a tall glass with a straw.

OPTIONAL: *Top with whipped cream.*

NOTE: *The amounts for a drink of this type are flexible. Use twice as much ice cream and half as much milk for an extra-thick and rich concoction. Or substitute very strong black coffee for all or part of the milk for a Coffee-Chocolate Frosted.*

GROWN-UPS CHOCOLATE FROSTED

Prepare the above Chocolate Frosted, adding about 2 tablespoons of dark or light rum, crème de cacao, or Kahlúa for each serving while blending.

A CHOCOLATE SODA

In a tall glass stir ½ cup of cold milk with 3 to 4 tablespoons of Homemade Chocolate Syrup. Add ½ cup of carbonated water, stir lightly, add a scoop of chocolate ice cream, and, if the glass is not full, add more soda. Top with a generous spoonful of whipped cream. Serve with a straw and a long-handled spoon.

VARIATION: *Use a scoop of half-chocolate and half-coffee ice cream (or use all coffee) in place of all chocolate.*

CHOCOLATE BROWN COW

In a tall glass stir 3 tablespoons of Homemade Chocolate Syrup into ½ cup of cold milk. Add 1 cup of root beer, stir slightly, and add a scoop of chocolate or vanilla ice cream. If the glass is not full, add more root beer. Serve with a straw and a long-handled spoon.

VARIATION: *For a Black Cow, substitute Coca-Cola for the root beer.*

CHOCOLATE EGG MILK

For each 1-cup (8-ounce) serving, place a raw egg in a blender or a mixer and blend or beat just to mix. Add 3 tablespoons of Homemade Chocolate Syrup and ¾ cup of cold milk. Blend or beat until foamy and serve quickly in a glass.

CHOCOLATE BANANA MILKSHAKE

For each serving, puree about half of a large ripe banana in a blender. Add 3 to 4 tablespoons of Homemade Chocolate Syrup and ½ to ¾ cup of cold milk. Blend until foamy. Serve quickly in a tall glass.

OPTIONAL: *Sprinkle a bit of nutmeg over the top.*

COLD RUM-CHOCOLATE MILK

For each 1-cup (8-ounce) serving, dissolve 1 teaspoon of instant coffee in ¼ cup of boiling water, cool, and then chill. Mix ¼ cup of cold milk with 2 tablespoons Homemade Chocolate Syrup. Stir in ¼ cup heavy cream, the cold prepared coffee, and ¼ cup light or amber rum. (This drink is best when it is especially cold. If possible, place it in the freezer for 20 or 30 minutes and stir from the bottom before serving.)

OPTIONAL: *Top with a bit of whipped cream.*

VARIATION: *For a Brandy Alexander Chocolate Milk, substitute 2 tablespoons of brandy or Cognac and 2 tablespoons of crème de cacao for the ¼ cup rum.*

GIRL SCOUT PUNCH

Depending on the number of servings, mix Homemade Chocolate Syrup and cold milk (¼ cup of syrup to each cup of milk) in a punch bowl. Add a generous number of small scoops of chocolate and/or vanilla ice cream. Top with a generous layer of softly whipped cream (it should be soft enough to spread over the top of the punch), and a sprinkling of grated or shaved chocolate. Serve immediately. Ladle into cups or glasses, including a scoop of ice cream with each portion. Serve with spoons.

Hot Drinks
(made with Homemade Chocolate Syrup)

The following (and all) hot chocolate drinks should be served in well heated cups or mugs: Fill the cups or mugs with boiling water and let stand for several minutes before using.

HOT CHOCOLATE MILK

Follow directions for Cold Chocolate Milk (see page 271). Stir occasionally over moderate heat until it just comes to a boil. Beat or whisk until foamy. Serve in a cup.

OPTIONAL: *Top with whipped cream or a marshmallow. And for a surprise and an extra-chocolaty drink, put a small piece of semisweet or milk chocolate, or a few chocolate morsels, in the heated cup before pouring in the hot chocolate milk.*

HOT MOCHA

Mix equal amounts of strong black coffee and Hot Chocolate Milk. If you wish, add additional sugar or honey to taste. Just before serving, beat or whisk until foamy. Serve very hot, with optional whipped cream or a marshmallow on top. Or top with a spoonful of candy chocolate coffee beans.

HOT CHOCOLATE CAPPUCCINO

Prepare the above Hot Mocha, using extra-strong coffee. Pour it into a heated cup, filling the cup only about three-quarters full. Add softly whipped cream to fill the cup to the top, sprinkle rather generously with unsweetened cocoa powder (through a fine strainer), and serve immediately. The heat will melt the whipped cream—O.K., it is supposed to.

CHOCOLATE HOT BUTTERED RUM

For each serving, mix 3 tablespoons of Homemade Chocolate Syrup into ¾ cup milk, Half-and-Half, or light cream. Place over moderate heat and stir occasionally until it just comes to a boil. Stir in 1 generous teaspoon of dry instant coffee. Place 1 teaspoon of butter in a large heated mug or cup, and add ¼ cup light rum (I use Bacardi silver label). Beat or whisk the hot drink until it is foamy and then pour it into the mug over the butter and rum. Serve immediately.

OPTIONAL: *Top with whipped cream.*

NOTE: *This is a cold-weather drink. I met it at a ski lodge in Colorado where the temperature was below zero. It was served at tea time in front of a roaring fireplace (hot toasted banana bread was served on the side). This will warm you all the way through in a hurry.*

VARIATION: *I have also had Chocolate Hot Buttered Brandy made with Cognac in place of rum and it was equally wonderful.*

Bonus Recipes

When I wrote the recipes for my dessert book, they were my favorite desserts and I thought that was it. I did not expect to write another book. And then there was a cookie book with my favorite cookies (in addition to those already in the first book). Now I just can't complete this collection of chocolate recipes without including a few of my chocolate favorites from the other books. Here they are.

Chocolate Mousse Torte

6 to 8 Portions

Of the many recipes that were born in my kitchen, this was one of the most exciting because it became The New York Times*'s 1972 Dessert of the Year.*

It starts with a chocolate mousse mixture. Part of it is baked in a pie plate. When it cools, it settles down in the middle, leaving a higher rim. Then, the remaining unbaked mousse is placed over the baked mousse. And it is topped with whipped cream.

> 8 ounces semisweet chocolate
> 1 tablespoon dry instant coffee
> ¼ cup boiling water
> 8 eggs (graded large or extra-large), separated
> ⅔ cup granulated sugar
> 1 teaspoon vanilla extract
> ⅛ teaspoon salt

Adjust rack to the center of the oven and preheat oven to 350 degrees. Butter a 9-inch ovenproof glass pie plate. Dust it with fine, dry bread crumbs and set aside.

Place the chocolate in the top of a small double boiler over hot water. Dissolve the coffee in the boiling water and pour it over the chocolate. Cover, place over low heat, and stir occasionally until the chocolate is melted and smooth. Remove the top of the double boiler and set aside, uncovered, to cool slightly.

In the small bowl of an electric mixer beat the egg yolks at high speed for about 5 minutes until they are pale lemon-colored and thickened. Gradually add the sugar and continue to beat at high speed for about 5 minutes more until very thick. Add the vanilla and chocolate, beating slowly, and scraping the bowl with a rubber spatula until smooth. Remove from the mixer.

Add the salt to the egg whites in the large bowl of the mixer. With clean beaters, beat until the whites hold a definite shape but not until they are stiff or dry.

Gradually, in two or three small additions, fold about half of the whites into the chocolate (do not be too thorough), and then fold the chocolate into the remaining whites. Fold only until no whites show.

Handling as little as possible, gently remove and set aside about 4 cups of the mousse.

Turn the balance into the pie plate; it will barely reach the top of the plate. Very gently spread it level and place in the oven to bake.

Cover the reserved mousse and refrigerate.

When the mousse has baked for 25 minutes, turn off the oven, but leave the torte in for 5 minutes more.

Then remove it from the oven and place it on a rack to cool. (The mousse will rise during baking and then, while cooling, it will settle in the center, leaving a high rim.)

When *completely* cool, remove the reserved mousse from the refrigerator. Handling as little as possible, place the refrigerated mousse in the center of the shell of baked mousse. Mound it slightly higher in the center. Handle it gently or it will lose the air that has been beaten into it.

Refrigerate for at least 2 to 3 hours, or all day if you wish.

TOPPING

> 1½ cups heavy cream
> 1½ teaspoons vanilla extract
> ⅓ cup confectioners sugar

In a chilled bowl with chilled beaters, whip the above ingredients until they hold a shape. Spread over the unbaked part of the mousse, excluding the rim. Refrigerate until serving time.

NOTES: *An alternate, attractive way of applying the whipped cream is to place it in a pastry bag fitted with a medium-size star-shaped tube and, as Jean Hewitt did when she prepared this torte to be photographed for* The New York Times, *form a lattice pattern of the cream over the top of the unbaked mousse, and a border around the edge.*

To serve, place the pie plate on a folded napkin (on a platter or cake plate) to hold the plate steady when serving.

Queen Mother's Cake

12 PORTIONS

Jan Smeterlin, the eminent pianist, picked up this recipe on a concert tour in Austria. He loves to cook, and when he baked this to serve at the reception following a command performance for the Queen Mother of England, she asked for the recipe. Then she served it frequently at her royal parties.

It is a single-layer, no-flour, ground-nut, chocolate torte, covered with a thin chocolate icing. It is typically European: simple, elegant, and extraordinarily delicious. The cake may be frozen before or after it is iced, but while the icing is fresh it has a beautiful shine, which becomes dull if the cake stands

overnight or if it is frozen. So to enjoy this at its very best, ice the cake during the day for that night. But I know several people who always have an uniced Queen Mother's Cake in the freezer.

> 6 ounces (1¼ cups) almonds, blanched or
>   unblanched
> 6 ounces semisweet chocolate, coarsely cut
>   or broken
> 6 ounces (1½ sticks) sweet butter
> ¾ cup granulated sugar
> 6 eggs (graded large—no larger), separated
> ⅛ teaspoon salt

Adjust rack one-third up from the bottom of the oven and preheat oven to 375 degrees. Butter a 9 x 2½- or 3-inch spring-form pan and line the bottom with a round of baking-pan liner paper or wax paper cut to fit. Butter the paper and dust all over with fine, dry bread crumbs; invert over a piece of paper and tap lightly to shake out excess crumbs. Set the prepared pan aside.

The nuts must be ground to a very fine powder; it may be done in a food processor, a blender, or a nut grinder. They must be fine, and should resemble cornmeal. (However you grind the nuts, if they are not smooth and equally fine, or if they have become lumpy from overblending, they should be strained. Place them in a large strainer set over a large bowl and, with your fingertips, press them through the strainer.) Set the ground nuts aside.

Place the chocolate in the top of a small double boiler over hot water on low heat. Cover until partially melted, then uncover and stir until completely melted and smooth. Remove the top of the double boiler and set it aside, uncovered, to cool slightly.

In the small bowl of an electric mixer cream the butter. Add the sugar and beat at moderately high speed for about 2 minutes. Add the egg yolks one at a time, beating until thoroughly incorporated after each addition.

On low speed add the chocolate and beat only to mix. Then add the almonds and beat only to mix, scraping the bowl as necessary with a rubber spatula.

Transfer the mixture to a large mixing bowl.

In the large bowl of the electric mixer add the salt to the egg whites. With clean beaters, beat only until the whites hold a definite shape but not until they are stiff or dry.

Stir a large spoonful of the beaten whites into the chocolate mixture. Then gradually (in about three additions) fold in the remaining whites.

Turn the mixture into the pan. Rotate the pan a bit briskly first in one direction, then the other, to level the top.

Bake for 20 minutes at 375 degrees. Then reduce the oven temperature to 350 degrees and bake for an additional 50 minutes. (Total baking time is 1 hour and 10 minutes.) Do not overbake; the cake should remain soft and moist in the center.

(The following direction is from Mr. Smeterlin and, although I do not understand exactly why, I always do it.) Wet and slightly wring out a folded towel and place it on a smooth surface. Remove the spring form from the oven and place it directly on the wet towel. Let stand for 20 minutes. Then release and remove the sides of the spring form. Place a rack over the cake and carefully invert. Remove the bottom of the pan and the paper lining. Cover with another rack and invert again, leaving the cake right side up to cool.

The cake will be about 1¾ inches high. If the top is uneven (if the rim is higher) wait until the cake is completely cool and then use a long, thin, sharp knife to cut the top level.

The cake will be fragile and should be handled with care. (Chilling it briefly will make it safer to transfer to a cake plate, but then it must reach room temperature again before you ice it; if the cake is cold it will make the icing dull.)

Place four strips of wax paper around the outer edges of a cake plate. Transfer the cake to the plate, placing the cake upside down.

If you have a cake-decorating turntable or a lazy Susan, place the cake plate on it.

Now prepare the icing.

ICING FOR QUEEN MOTHER'S CAKE

½ cup heavy cream
2 teaspoons dry instant coffee
**8 ounces semisweet chocolate coarsely cut or
  broken**

Scald the cream in a medium-size heavy saucepan uncovered over moderate heat until it begins to form small bubbles around the edge or a skin on top. Add the dry instant coffee and stir briskly with a small wire whisk to dissolve. Add the chocolate and stir occasionally over heat for about 1 minute. Then remove the pan from the heat and stir with the whisk until the chocolate is melted and the mixture is smooth. Transfer to a small bowl or place the bottom of the saucepan in cold water to stop the cooking.

Let the icing stand at room temperature, stirring occasionally, for about 15 minutes or more until it reaches room temperature and barely begins to thicken, but only slightly.

Then stir it to mix (do not beat) and pour it over the top of the cake. Use a long, narrow metal spatula to smooth the top and at the same time spread the icing so that a little of it runs down the sides (not too much on the sides—the icing on the top should be thicker than that on the sides). With a small, narrow metal spatula smooth the sides.

Remove the four strips of wax paper by pulling each one out toward a narrow end.

Mr. Smeterlin left the top of his Queen Mother's Cake perfectly plain, but if you wish you can place a row of twelve Chocolate Curls (see page 264) around the border, as I do.

Queen Mother's Cake may be served just as it is (which is the way we served it for all the years I made it for my husband's restaurants), or it may be served with whipped cream on the side.

Mushroom Meringues

24 RATHER LARGE OR 36 MEDIUM MUSHROOMS

About twenty years ago when I entered an international cooking Olympics, I created this version of Mushroom Meringues. And I won first prize for originality. Since 1974, when my dessert book was published, I have seen these Mushroom Meringues for sale in stores from coast to coast. And I have seen the recipe in newspapers and magazines. I am extremely proud and delighted when I see that other people's Mushroom Meringues look just like the ones I made for the Olympics.

They are meringue cookies, or petits fours, that look exactly like real mushrooms.

They call for patience, talent with a pastry bag, and dry atmosphere. (I should tell you, though, that although a dry atmosphere is always considered

essential to the success of dry meringue, I have made these innumerable times during the past twenty years in Miami Beach, where it is almost always humid. And they are always perfect.)

They may be made way ahead of time.

½ cup egg whites (about 3 to 4 whites, depending on the size of the eggs; they may be whites that have been left over from some other recipe, frozen, and then thawed), at room temperature
Scant ¼ teaspoon salt
¼ teaspoon cream of tartar
1 cup granulated sugar
1 teaspoon vanilla extract
Unsweetened cocoa powder (preferably Dutch process)
Chocolate (see Note)

Adjust two racks to divide the oven into thirds and preheat oven to 225 degrees. Cut aluminum foil to fit two 12 x 15-inch cookie sheets.

In the small bowl of an electric mixer at moderately slow speed, beat the whites just until they are foamy. Add the salt and cream of tartar. Increase the speed to moderate and beat for almost a minute more until the whites hold a soft shape. Continue to beat and start adding the sugar, one rounded tablespoonful at a time; beat for about half a minute between additions. When all of the sugar has been added, add the vanilla, increase the speed to high, and beat for 7 to 8 minutes more until the meringue is very stiff and the sugar is dissolved—test it by rubbing a bit between your fingers. (Total beating time from start to finish is about 15 to 18 minutes, but it depends on the power of your mixer.)

To hold the aluminum foil in place, put a dot of the meringue in each corner of the cookie sheet. Cover with the foil and press firmly on the corners.

Do not let the meringue stand. Fit a large pastry bag (preferably at least 15 to 16 inches long) with a plain round tube, size #8 (⅝ inch in diameter). Fold down the top of the bag to form a deep cuff on the outside. Support the bag by placing it in a tall, narrow jar or glass. Using a rubber spatula, transfer all of the meringue to the bag. Unfold the cuff and twist the top of the bag closed.

On one piece of the prepared aluminum foil shape the mushroom stems first. You will need a wet knife—rest a small sharp knife in a glass of water. Hold the bag at a right angle and close to the foil. Squeeze from the top of the bag to press out the meringue gently, while slowly raising the bag straight up. The base of the stem should be a bit wider for support. Keep the stem as straight as possible. Hold the bag upright and steady with your left hand and, with your right hand, shake—do not dry—the knife and use it to cut the meringue away from the tube, cutting flush with the tube. The stems may be about 1 to 1¾ inches high (the taller they are, the more difficult), but they may vary as real mushroom stems do. They should be placed ½ to 1 inch apart on the foil. (Some of the stems may fall over on their sides during baking, so it is a good idea to make a few extras to be sure that you wind up with a stem for each mushroom cap.)

Strain cocoa through a fine strainer lightly over the stems to imitate soil and natural mushroom coloring. The stems will bake on the higher rack.

On the other piece of foil shape the mushroom caps. Holding the bag straight up and close to the foil, press on the top of the bag to press out even rounds of the meringue. The caps should be placed about ½ inch apart. The caps may average about 1 to 1¾ inches in width and ¾ inch in height, but they may also vary as real mushroom caps do. Sharply twist. Release pressure on the pastry bag and slowly and carefully move the bag off to a side of the mushroom cap to avoid leaving a peak on the top—the tops should be as smooth as possible.

Strain cocoa lightly over the caps. These will bake on the lower rack.

The measurements I have given are approximate—don't worry about them. Smaller or larger mushrooms are equally attractive. Even Mushroom Meringues with crooked stems or with a slight point on the cap will look great when finished.

Bake for 1 hour or a bit longer depending on size, until the meringues may be easily lifted from the foil and the bottoms are firm to the touch. The longer they bake the drier they are—and the better—but they should not be allowed to color (it affects the taste). Turn the oven off, prop the oven door open a little, and let the meringues dry out even more in the turned-off oven.

When they are cool, remove the meringues from the foil. They may be placed on a clean piece of foil, on wax paper, or on a tray. If the tops of the stems are not flat, immediately, while the meringues are very crisp, use a finely serrated knife or a sharp paring knife to gently saw (cut) any points off the tops of the stems; the top of each stem should be parallel with the base.

The baked tops and stems may be kept uncovered at room temperature for weeks before they are "glued" together with chocolate.

One ounce of chocolate will be needed for every 5 mushroom caps if they measure 1¾ to 2 inches in diameter. Using this formula, figure how much chocolate you will need. Cut the chocolate coarsely and place it in the top of a small double boiler over warm water to melt slowly on low heat. When almost melted, remove from the heat and stir until completely melted and smooth.

Hold a mushroom cap upside down. With a demitasse spoon (or any other small spoon) spread a layer of chocolate over the bottom of the cap, spreading it just to the edge. It should be thin but not too thin. Place a stem upside down on the chocolate.

Now the mushroom must stand in that position, upside down, until the chocolate hardens completely. There are several ways to do this. The inverted mushrooms will rest securely in small cordial glasses, small brandy snifters, small egg cups, or in an empty egg carton—it will depend on their size.

If you have used real chocolate (see Note) carefully place the mushrooms in their cordial glasses or egg cups or whatever in the freezer or refrigerator only until the chocolate is firm. *Do not freeze mushrooms after the chocolate has hardened*—it will cause the finished mushrooms to come apart. Remove and store at room temperature.

Do not cover the mushrooms airtight. I have kept them for weeks and longer in open straw baskets in an air-conditioned room. They become drier, crisper, and better.

Serve the mushrooms either standing upright on a platter, or tumbled in a basket like real mushrooms, which these will resemble to an unbelievable degree. (Try a napkin-lined basketful as a centerpiece—at dessert time pass it around.)

The number of mushrooms this recipe yields will depend on their size—approximately 24 rather large or 36 medium. If you want more, prepare and bake one batch, and then repeat; meringue should not stand around any longer than necessary before baking.

NOTE: *Almost any chocolate may he used for this recipe. But I definitely recommend a compound ("imitation," or the kind that does not have to be tempered; see page 5 for a description and a mail-order source). It will never discolor and the mushrooms may be kept for weeks or even months. Compound chocolate will harden quickly at room temperature and it will not be necessary to chill the mushrooms in order to set the chocolate. Other chocolates, or "real" chocolates, are liable to discolor after a day or two unless the chocolate has been tempered. However, if the meringues are to be served the day the chocolate is applied, use any semisweet.*

Black Bottom Pie

8 PORTIONS

Marjorie Kinnan Rawlings, the Pulitzer Prize-winning author of The Yearling, *also wrote a delightful cookbook.* Cross Creek Cookery *(Charles Scribner's Sons, 1942), which is a mouth-watering account of the food served in her home in central Florida. In it, she says of her Black Bottom Pie, "I think this is the most delicious pie I have ever eaten . . . a pie so delicate, so luscious, that I hope to be propped up on my dying bed and fed a generous portion. Then I think that I should refuse outright to die, for life would be too good to relinquish."*

My recipe is slightly different from Mrs. Rawlings', but my sentiments are the same.

CRUST

This is traditionally made with bought gingersnaps, but since I often want to make it when I don't have gingersnaps, I do it the following way. (You could substitute gingersnap crumbs for the graham-cracker crumbs, ginger, and cinnamon.)

1¼ cups graham-cracker crumbs
1 tablespoon granulated sugar
1 teaspoon ginger
1 teaspoon cinnamon
2 ounces (½ stick) sweet butter

Adjust rack to the center of the oven and preheat oven to 375 degrees.

In a bowl mix the crumbs with the sugar, ginger, and cinnamon. Add the melted butter and stir with a rubber spatula, pressing the mixture against the sides of the bowl until well mixed. The mixture will look crumbly but it will hold together when pressed into the pie plate.

Use a 9-inch glass pie plate and follow the directions for lining it with aluminum foil and for baking it, chilling it, and removing the foil (see page 176).

FILLING

2 ounces (2 squares) **unsweetened chocolate**
1 tablespoon (1 envelope) **unflavored gelatin**
¼ cup **cold water**
1 cup **granulated sugar**
1 tablespoon **cornstarch**
Salt
4 **eggs** (graded large or extra-large), separated
1¾ cups **milk**
2 tablespoons **dark rum**
1 teaspoon **vanilla extract**
⅛ teaspoon **cream of tartar** (see Note)

Melt the chocolate in the top of a small double boiler over hot water on moderate heat. Remove the top of the double boiler and set it aside, uncovered, to cool slightly.

In a small cup sprinkle the gelatin over the cold water and set aside.

In a small bowl mix ½ cup (reserve remaining cup) of the sugar with the cornstarch and a pinch of salt. (It should be well mixed.) Set aside.

In the top of a large double boiler stir the egg yolks lightly with a small wire whisk or a fork just to mix.

Scald the milk uncovered in a small, heavy saucepan over moderate heat until you see small bub-bles or a wrinkled skin on the surface. Stir in the sugar-cornstarch mixture and pour very slowly, in a thin stream, into the yolks—stirring constantly.

Place over, but not touching, hot water in the bottom of the double boiler on moderate heat. Cook, stirring gently and scraping the pot with a rubber spatula, for about 12 to 15 minutes, until the custard thickens to the consistency of a medium cream sauce. Remove the top of the double boiler from the hot water.

Remove 1 cup of the custard and set it aside to cool for about 5 to 10 minutes. Stir it occasionally until it is tepid.

Meanwhile, to the remainder of the custard in the top of the double boiler, immediately add the softened gelatin and stir until thoroughly dissolved. Stir in the rum and set aside.

Gradually add the 1 cup of reserved, tepid custard to the chocolate, stirring constantly with a small wire whisk. Mix thoroughly until smooth. Add the vanilla, stir, and turn the mixture into the prepared crust. Spread level and refrigerate.

In the small bowl of an electric mixer at moderately high speed, beat the egg whites with a pinch of salt and the cream of tartar until the mixture increases in volume and starts to thicken. While beating, gradually add the reserved ½ cup sugar and continue to beat until the mixture holds a shape—not stiff; it should be the consistency of thick marshmallow sauce.

Gradually fold the rum custard (which may still be warm) into the beaten whites. If necessary, pour gently from one bowl to another to insure thorough blending.

Pour the rum mixture over the chocolate layer, mounding it high in the center. (If there is too much filling and it looks like it might run over, reserve some at room temperature. Chill the pie in the freezer for about 10 to 15 minutes, or in the refrigerator for a bit longer, to partially set the filling. Then pour on the reserved portion and it will not run over.)

Refrigerate the pie for 2 to 3 hours. Then prepare the following whipped cream.

WHIPPED CREAM

1 cup heavy cream
¼ cup confectioners sugar
1 scant teaspoon vanilla extract

In a chilled bowl with chilled beaters, whip the above ingredients until the cream holds a shape. (It should be firm enough for easy serving, but it tastes better if it is not really stiff.) Spread the cream evenly and smoothly over the filling. Or use a pastry bag fitted with a rather large star-shaped tube and form a heavy ruffled border of the cream.

OPTIONAL: *If the cream was spread smoothly, sprinkle it with coarsely grated or shaved chocolate; if it was put on to form a border, fill the center with the chocolate.*

NOTE: *To measure ⅛ teaspoon, fill and level ¼ teaspoon, then cut through the middle and return half to the box.*

Coffee Buttercrunch Pie

8 PORTIONS

This rich creation is the famous Coffee-Toffee Pie from Blum's in San Francisco. (When we went to Blum's in San Francisco they told me that they have stopped making this; now the only way you can get it is to make it yourself.) It has a crunchy crust, a smooth, rich chocolate-coffee filling, and is covered

with coffee-flavored whipped cream. Without the whipped cream it may be frozen.

I never know what to answer when people tell me, as they often do, that this is better than sex.

CRUST

This may be doubled. The extra crust may be frozen.

½ package pie-crust mix (measure the
   contents into a measuring cup and use half)
1 ounce (1 square) unsweetened chocolate
¼ cup light brown sugar, firmly packed
   (strained if lumpy)
2½ ounces (¾ cup) walnuts, chopped very fine
   (they must be chopped fine, not ground)
1 teaspoon vanilla extract
1 tablespoon water

Place the pie-crust mix in a mixing bowl.

Grind the chocolate in a nut grinder, or chop it coarsely and then grind it in a food processor or a blender. Stir the ground chocolate into the pie-crust mix. Stir in the sugar and nuts. Mix the vanilla and water and gradually drizzle the mixture over the pie-crust mixture—do not pour it all in one place—while using a fork to stir and toss. The mixture will be lumpy and crumbly. Stir it very briefly, but do not try to make it smooth; it will hold together when you press it into place.

Adjust rack to the center of the oven and pre-heat oven to 375 degrees.

Use a 9-inch ovenproof glass pie plate and follow the directions for lining it with aluminum foil, baking, chilling, and removing the foil (see page 176). However, for this recipe *bake the crust for 15 minutes*.

Meanwhile, prepare the following filling.

FILLING

This may be doubled if you have made two crusts. The extra crust with the filling may be frozen.

1 ounce (1 square) unsweetened chocolate
¼ pound (1 stick) sweet butter
¾ cup light brown sugar, firmly packed
(strained if lumpy)
2 teaspoons dry instant coffee
2 eggs (graded large or extra-large)

Melt the chocolate over hot water and set it aside to cool.

In the small bowl of an electric mixer cream the butter. Add the sugar and beat at moderately high speed for 2 to 3 minutes. Mix in the cooled melted chocolate and the dry instant coffee.

Add the eggs one at a time, beating for 5 (five) minutes after each addition, and scraping the bowl occasionally with a rubber spatula.

Pour the filling into the cooled baked crust. Refrigerate for 5 or 6 hours, or overnight. (The pie may be frozen now or it may be refrigerated for a day or two. If you freeze it, freeze until the filling is firm and then wrap airtight. To thaw the frozen pie, unwrap it and let stand overnight in the refrigerator.)

Either just before serving or a few hours before, prepare the following whipped cream topping.

TOPPING

2 cups heavy cream
2 tablespoons dry powdered (not granular)
instant coffee or espresso
½ cup confectioners sugar
Optional: coarsely grated or shaved chocolate
(to be sprinkled on top)

In a chilled bowl with chilled beaters, whip the cream with the instant coffee and sugar until the cream holds a definite shape. But do not overbeat; it must be firm enough to hold its shape when the pie is served, but it is more delicious if it is slightly creamy, rather than stiff.

Spread the whipped cream smoothly over the filling. Or apply it in fancy swirls, using a pastry bag fitted with a large star-shaped tube.

Sprinkle the top with the optional grated or shaved chocolate.

Refrigerate.

Chocolate Cupcakes

24 Cupcakes

These cupcakes, and Brownies, are the desserts I usually make when I am asked to make something for a cake sale.

2 cups sifted all-purpose flour
1 teaspoon baking soda
¼ teaspoon salt
½ cup unsweetened cocoa powder (preferably Dutch process)
5⅓ ounces (10⅔ tablespoons) sweet butter
1 teaspoon vanilla extract
1½ cups granulated sugar
3 eggs (graded large, extra-large, or jumbo)
1 cup milk

Adjust two racks to divide the oven into thirds and preheat oven to 350 degrees. Butter two pans of cupcake forms, each pan with twelve forms and each form measuring about 2¾ inches in diameter. Sift a bit of flour over the pans, invert, and tap to shake out excess. Or line twenty-four 2¾ inch forms with cupcake-liner papers (see Notes). Set aside.

Sift together the flour, baking soda, salt, and cocoa, and set aside. In the large bowl of an electric mixer cream the butter. Add the vanilla and sugar and beat to mix. Add the eggs one at a time, beating

until smooth after each addition, and scraping the bowl with a rubber spatula as necessary to keep the mixture smooth. On the lowest speed alternately add the sifted dry ingredients in three additions with the milk in two additions. Continue to scrape the bowl with the rubber spatula and beat only until smooth. Do not overbeat.

Spoon the batter into the prepared pans, filling the forms only two-thirds to three-quarters full. There is no need to smooth the tops—the batter will level itself.

Bake for 25 minutes or until the tops spring back when lightly pressed with a fingertip. Do not overbake.

Cool the cakes in the pans for 2 or 3 minutes; then cover each pan with a large rack and invert. Remove the pan and turn the cupcakes right side up to cool on the rack.

OPTIONAL: *Ice with the following Chocolate Cupcake Icing.*

CHOCOLATE CUPCAKE ICING

6 ounces semisweet chocolate (see Notes)
⅓ cup heavy cream
1 tablespoon granulated sugar
1½ tablespoons sweet butter

Place all the ingredients in a small, heavy saucepan over moderate heat. Cook, stirring occasionally, until the chocolate is partially melted. Remove from the heat and stir constantly until the chocolate is completely melted and the mixture is smooth. Transfer to a small, shallow bowl. Let stand, stirring occasionally, until the icing reaches room temperature.

Hold a cupcake upside down and dip the top into the icing; twirl the cake slightly, and then continue to hold it upside down for a few seconds for excess icing to drip off. Repeat with all of the cakes. Then, after dipping them all, dip each one a second time. If there is still some icing left, the cakes may be dipped a third time. When the icing gets low, transfer it to a custard cup, or a coffee or teacup, but don't try to use up the last bit—the cakes won't look as smooth.

NOTES: *1. When baking cupcakes, if you have only one pan with twelve forms, reserve the remaining batter and bake additional cakes after the first panful. If you bake only one pan at a time, bake it in the center of the oven.*

2. Lining the pans with papers is a convenience and a timesaver. The cakes take on a better shape, they rise higher, and they stay fresh longer.

3. The chocolate for the icing may be any semisweet. If you use 1-ounce squares, they should be coarsely chopped. If you use a thinner bar chocolate, it should be broken or chopped. Morsels, of course, should be used as is.

To freeze cupcakes after they have been iced, just let them stand until the icing is no longer sticky. Then place them on a pan or tray in the freezer until they are frozen firm. Then cover them with a large piece of plastic wrap, turning it down securely on the sides and under the bottom, and return the pan or tray to the freezer. To thaw, let stand at room temperature until thawed before removing the wrapping.

Santa Fe Chocolate Wafers

36 WAFERS

These dark, thin, crisp cookies are easily mixed in a saucepan. They are very fragile and not suitable for mailing. They are wonderful for a cookie jar or serve them with ice cream or mousse for dessert.

1 cup sifted all-purpose flour
½ teaspoon baking soda
⅛ teaspoon salt
¼ pound (1 stick) butter
6 ounces (1 cup) semisweet chocolate morsels
⅓ cup granulated sugar
¼ cup light corn syrup
1 teaspoon vanilla extract
1 egg (graded extra-large or jumbo)

Adjust two racks to divide the oven into thirds and preheat oven to 350 degrees. Cut aluminum foil to fit cookie sheets.

Sift together the flour, baking soda, and salt and set aside. Cut the butter into ½-inch slices and place in a heavy 2½- to 3-quart saucepan. Add the chocolate morsels, sugar, and corn syrup. Stir over low heat until melted and smooth. If the mixture is not smooth (some morsels do not melt completely) stir or beat it briefly with a small wire whisk. Remove from the heat and let cool for 5 minutes.

Then stir in the vanilla and the egg. When smooth, add the sifted dry ingredients and stir and mix vigorously until smooth. Transfer to a small bowl for ease in handling.

Use a rounded teaspoonful of dough for each

cookie. Place them at least 2 inches apart (these spread) on the cut aluminum foil (8 cookies on each piece of foil), keeping the shapes as round as possible.

Slide cookie sheets under the foil and bake for 10 to 15 minutes (see Note), reversing the position of the sheets top to bottom and front to back once to insure even baking. If you bake only one sheet at a time use the higher rack, and with only one sheet in the oven the cookies will take less time to bake. The cookies will puff up in the oven and then they will flatten—they are not done until they have flattened. These will crisp as they cool and they should be very crisp, but be careful not to overbake or the chocolate will taste burnt.

Let the cookies stand on the sheet for a minute or so to firm, and then slide the foil off the sheet and transfer the cookies with a wide metal spatula to racks to cool. Store airtight.

NOTE: *If, after the cookies have cooled, they are not crisp, you may replace them in the oven briefly to bake a bit longer.*

Chocolate and Peanut-Butter Crescents

66 COOKIES

These are small, candylike cookies that take time and patience. They have a crisp chocolate dough wrapped around a peanut-butter filling and are formed into crescent shapes.

COOKIE DOUGH

2 cups sifted all-purpose flour
⅓ cup unsweetened cocoa
¼ teaspoon salt
¼ pound (1 stick) butter
1 teaspoon vanilla extract
1 teaspoon dry powdered instant coffee or espresso
¾ cup granulated sugar
1 egg

Sift together the flour, cocoa, and salt and set aside. In the large bowl of mixer cream the butter. Beat in the vanilla and sugar. Add the egg and beat until thoroughly mixed. On low speed gradually add the sifted dry ingredients, scraping the bowl with a rubber spatula and beating until thoroughly mixed. Transfer the dough to a small bowl for ease in handling and set aside at room temperature.

Prepare the following filling.

FILLING

¾ cup smooth (not chunky) peanut butter
½ cup strained or sifted confectioners sugar

In a small bowl thoroughly mix the peanut butter and the sugar, or place them on a work surface and knead them together with your hands.

Adjust a rack to the center of the oven and preheat oven to 325 degrees.

To shape the cookies: On a large piece of wax paper or aluminum foil place the cookie dough in mounds, using a slightly rounded teaspoonful (no more) of the dough for each mound—in order not to make them too large it is best to measure with a measuring spoon. Instead of doing all at once you may prefer to measure only a fourth or a half of the dough at one time.

Then do the same with the filling, using a level ½ measuring teaspoon for each mound. Roll them between your hands into small balls. If it is too sticky to handle simply leave it in mounds and use a knife or small spatula to lift the mounds. Place these on other pieces of wax paper or foil.

Pick up one mound of the dough, roll it between your hands into a ball, and flatten it between your palms until it is very thin. Then, place one ball or mound of the filling in the center of the flattened dough. With your fingers bring the dough around the filling and pinch the edges to seal. Roll the filled dough between your hands into a cylindrical shape about 2 inches long with very slightly tapered ends. Place the cookie on an unbuttered cookie sheet and as you do, turn the ends down slightly to form a short, fat crescent.

Continue shaping the cookies and placing them ½ to 1 inch apart—these do not spread.

Bake for 13 to 15 minutes, or until the cookies are barely firm to the touch. Reverse the cookie sheet front to back once to insure even baking.

OPTIONAL TOPPING: *Confectioners sugar or vanilla sugar (see Note). While the cookies are baking spread out a large piece of wax paper or aluminum foil and sift or strain 1 to 2 cups of the sugar onto the paper or foil, forming a mound of sugar.*

As soon as the cookies are done immediately transfer them with a wide metal spatula to the mound of sugar and roll the cookies around to coat them thoroughly with the sugar.

Then place the cookies on another piece of paper or foil to cool. When the cookies are cool, roll them again in the sugar.

NOTE: *To make vanilla sugar: This must be prepared ahead but can be kept for a long time (and can be used for topping all kinds of cakes and cookies). You will need a few vanilla beans (available in specialty food stores). Place the beans on a board and with a sharp knife split them the long way. Fill a 1-quart jar that has a tight cover with confectioners sugar and bury the beans in the sugar. Cover tightly and let stand for at least several days or a week before using—the sugar will have absorbed the flavor of the beans. Sift or strain the sugar immediately before using, as it will absorb some moisture from the beans and become lumpy—it will have to be strained again even if it was done beforehand. As the sugar is used it may be replaced. If you replace the sugar often, the bean itself should be replaced after a month or two.*

Chocolate Tartlets

60-75 TINY TARTLETS

These are tiny cookie cups with a baked in chewy chocolate filling. To make these dainty French cookies it is necessary to use very small, shallow individual tartlet molds; they may be plain or fluted. Mine are French; they are assorted shapes and they vary in diameter from about 1 to 2 inches. There are Scandinavian ones, generally a little larger, made for Sandbakelser cookies—they may be used for these tartlets. Or you may use plain round, shallow French tartlet pans about 2 to 2½ inches in diameter and ½ inch deep. These little pans should be washed with only hot soapy water; anything rougher would cause the cookies to stick. Don't make these if you are in a hurry; they take time.

FILLING

4 ounces (generous ¾ cup) blanched almonds
6 ounces (1 cup) semisweet chocolate morsels
2 eggs
1 teaspoon instant coffee
¼ teaspoon almond extract
½ cup granulated sugar

In a food processor, a blender, or a nut grinder, grind together the almonds and the chocolate—these must be ground fine. (In a blender it will probably be best to do it in two batches, using half of the nuts and half of the chocolate in each batch.) Set aside.

In the small bowl of an electric mixer at high speed beat the eggs for about 5 minutes until very thick and pale in color. On low speed mix in the coffee, almond extract, and sugar, and then gradually beat in the ground almond-chocolate mixture. Transfer to a small, shallow bowl for ease in handling and set aside at room temperature.

PASTRY

6 ounces (1½ sticks) butter
Scant ¼ teaspoon salt
1 teaspoon vanilla extract
½ cup granulated sugar
2 cups sifted all-purpose flour

In the large bowl of an electric mixer (with clean beaters) cream the butter. Mix in the salt, vanilla, and sugar, and then gradually add the flour, scraping the bowl as necessary with a rubber spatula. The mixture will be crumbly. Turn it out onto a board or smooth work surface. Squeeze it between your hands until it holds together. Then, with the heel of your hand, break off small pieces of dough (about 2 tablespoonfuls at a time), pushing away from you on the work surface. Form the dough into a ball. If it is not completely smooth break it again.

Adjust a rack one-third up from the bottom of the oven and preheat oven to 350 degrees.

With your fingertips press a small amount of the dough into each tartlet mold (the molds do not have to be buttered). The pastry shell should be ¼ inch thick or a little less, and it should be level with the rim of the mold—use your fingertip to remove excess dough above the rim.

Place the molds on a cookie sheet or a jelly-roll pan. With a demitasse spoon or a small measuring spoon, place some of the filling in each shell. The filling may be mounded a bit above the edges but only a very little bit or it will run over. It is not necessary to smooth the filling, as it will run slightly and smooth itself as it bakes.

Bake for 20 minutes until the pastry is barely colored. Reverse the cookie sheet or jelly-roll pan front to back once to insure even browning. Do not overbake these or the filling will be dry instead of chewy.

Remove from the oven and let stand until just cool enough to handle. Then invert each mold into the palm of your hand and, with a fingernail of the other hand, gently release and remove the mold.

NOTE: *If you do not have enough molds to bake these all at once the remaining pastry and filling may wait at room temperature.*

INDEX

D

W

Wakefield, Ruth, 109
walnuts, 10
West Coast Brownies, 150
Wheat Germ Chocolate Chip Cookies, 115
whipped cream, 11
    folding in of, 15–16
white chocolate, 6
Whole-Wheat Brownies, 155
Whole-Wheat Chocolate Chip Cookies, 117
Whoopies, 142
Wilbur's #37 Darkcote Confectionery Coating, 5
Wolfert, Paula, 259
World's Best Hot Fudge Sauce, 258

A Note About the Author

MAIDA HEATTER is the author of seven dessert books, the latest being *Maida Heatter's Brand-New Book of Great Cookies.* Two of her previous books— *Maida Heatter's Book of Great Cookies* and the *New York Times* best-seller *Maida Heatter's Book of Great Chocolate Desserts*—were awarded the James Beard Book Award. She is the daughter of Gabriel Heatter, the radio commentator. She studied fashion at Pratt Institute and has done fashion illustrating and designing, made jewelry, and painted. But her first love has always been cooking. She taught it in classes in her home, in department stores, and at cooking schools across the country. For many years she made all the desserts for a popular Miami Beach restaurant owned by her late husband, Ralph Daniels.

She prepared the desserts for the 1983 Summit of Industrialized Nations at Colonial Williamsburg, Virginia, for President Reagan and six other heads of state.

Ms. Heatter's late daughter, Toni Evins, a painter and illustrator, did the drawings for the first six of Ms. Heatter's books.

Photographs of chocolate by Susan Mitchell.